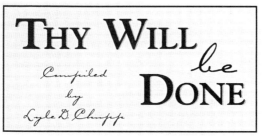

THY WILL be DONE

Compiled by Lyle D. Chupp

---

134 TOUCHING PERSONAL STORIES
OF FATALITIES AMONG PLAIN PEOPLE

Compiled By And Available From:
Lyle & JoAnn Chupp
780S Van Buren St.
Shipshewana, IN 46565

ISBN 1-890050-20-2

Dear Friends,

We would like to dedicate this book to all the good people who have taken time to write a story for this book. We realize this must have been quite a task. I'm sure that unless people have gone through a death experience in their family, they can't know of the trials and heartaches these families have gone through. As we compiled this book, we had a sense of guilt lying within us. We realize that for many, they had to relive their experience, and thought we might be intruding on their personal lives. We want to apologize to all of these people.

Our hope is that this book, now that it is compiled, will help any families that have gone through a death experience. We also hope that it will help anyone who reads this book find a stronger relationship with the "Heavenly Father."

A big hearty thank-you would like to be given to all who wrote stories for this book. We hope you will be able to overlook the mistakes in this book, for we are only human, and thus, far from perfect.

Love & Prayers,

Lyle & JoAnn Chupp & Family

Notice to all the families who have had a death experience, but weren't contacted to submit a story:

We are sorry we missed you! It was hard to know of everyone's situations. If we missed you, or if you have gone through this kind of experience since this book was put together, you are welcome to still submit your story to us.

We might consider printing a second book or adding to this one sometime in the future.

Owen Borkholder: Aug. 10, 1931 - Oct. 19, 1984

Submitted By Dorothy Borkholder; Nappanee, Indiana

We were just an ordinary family consisting of Dad, Mom, seven boys and seven girls ranging in ages from 29 to nine with three boys and three girls married and living not far from home. Thus, we were busy trying to raise our family in a home that would be pleasing to our Father above. We had lots of ups and downs, trials and errors along the way as we were very much human.

We faced some tragedies on his side of the family, but as for my side, Dad, Mom, brothers and sisters, and our children were all in good health and on the go. I had never faced the loss of a real close family member on my side.

October 19, 1984, dawned just like any other day over the years, and we went about our chores just like usual. The older ones at home went to their jobs, and the younger ones and us did the chores and milking.

After breakfast we sent the scholars on their way to school, and Dad went with the carpenter crew, which was made up of a brother-in-law, a married son, and perhaps one or so other men. He did carpenter work when the work on the farm could be handled by the boys at home. When the need arose he stayed at home and helped the boys.

The carpenters were just a few miles from home working on a small addition to a trailer home. As the day wore on it became quite windy outside.

Dinner time came and went by, then soon after someone was knocking on the door. I wondered, "Who's here now?"

I went to the door and there was a stranger to me. He said, "I'm a neighbor to Toby's and I came to tell you that Owen fell."

"What happened, is he hurt?" I asked.

"Yes, he is hurt. He fell from the rafters onto the cement and they have taken him to the hospital," he said.

"Well, is he badly hurt or how is he?" I asked.

He didn't really answer that question right out, instead he said, "I can take you over to the hospital."

"Oh," I said, "right now?"

"Yes," he said, "and you'd better take a few things along over in case you might want to stay overnight."

My mind was trying to grasp all of this as I quickly got ready and gathered a few things together to take along. I was not dreaming in the least bit what I would meet when I got there, since he had fallen only like around eight feet or so.

Of course I was anxious and worried of what I'd find when we got there, but I was not prepared for the words I received when I walked in the emergency room door. Our son who had been working with him was standing right there. He had gone along over with the ambulance with Dad.

He said, "Dad is gone."

"Oh no, this can't be true," I thought. But yes, it was ever so true; there was no awakening from a dream and thinking, "I'm glad that was just a dream."

It was too final and too true to really grasp at that moment. The tears and sobs could not be controlled. We asked if I could see him.

Pretty soon one of the hospital staff came and said to me, "I really don't think you want to see him now, as they haven't cleaned him up yet, do you? Wouldn't you rather remember him the way he looked this morning? But if you still want to you can."

So I said, "I'll just wait." I am thankful to that person now, for that advice. For now when I think of him I do not have that picture in my mind. When I saw him again he looked just as if he was in a very peaceful and happy sleep. Which with God's grace we hope was given to him. Oh, blissfully, happy, heavenly home, what a gain if we can enter in.

They told me he was standing up on the rafters and someone handed him a piece of plywood from the ground. As he pulled it up, it flipped and knocked him down, as it was very windy that afternoon. His foot slipped off the rafter and he fell about eight feet onto the cement.

God only knows what caused the fall, but we are sure it was God's planning. He had worked on many high places, which to me was very dangerous, but he gave it no second thought, for heights did not scare him. There he was only a few feet up where he would meet his end in this world. His death was caused by a skull fracture.

My mind and feelings were numb as we drove home that afternoon. I couldn't even think to let the children know. We did stop at one of our daughter's and the son went and told her.

I couldn't even think to send for the school children or anything when we got home. My world had come crashing down, all broken to pieces, lying at my feet. I could never really describe my feelings that afternoon. There just are no words to describe those first days and nights.

Soon the neighbors started coming. The school children came home not knowing what these people were doing here until they came inside and were told. The ones at work came home to be told the sad news. One of them did some other errands before coming home and it was quite late before he found out about Dad.

No one thought in the morning what we would have to face before the day was over. Only with the strength and help from above was I able to go on. How anyone without God could ever go through something like this I do not know.

I knew this was God's planning and He does not make any mistakes. But oh, the heartache and questions. Why us? To the human mind the family surely needed a Dad's guidance.

It had been a full-time task for two, now here I was left alone to go on. My first thoughts were, "No, I can't go on alone." I felt like I was in a very tight place with walls on all sides and no way to get out. So I had only one way to go and that was to look up to a much higher power than myself or I would have suffocated. That first night was a very long night. Whys, whys, and more whys, with very little sleep, came my way.

Morning finally came. That was a Saturday. Friends, neighbors, and relatives came and got everything ready for the viewing and funeral which was to be here at home in the shed on Monday. What a blessing to have such kind friends and neighbors. Everyone was so helpful and caring in our time of need. Do we really appreciate enough what we have here in our fellowship?

By evening I was so exhausted and weary that I thought maybe I could go to bed and sleep a little, to rest my mind, to forget all about my grief and problems for awhile. But I was so very wrong. Saturday night turned out much worse than the night before. I would doze off and instantly awake with the most frightful feeling of despair that I have ever had. I hardly knew what was going to happen to me till finally morning came. I don't believe I will ever forget the feeling of that long frightful night as long as I live.

Sunday came and with it came some dreary weather all day long, but lots of friends and relatives from far and near came to show their respects and that they cared and shared our sorrow and loss.

That evening I dreaded to see night come even though I hadn't slept since Thursday night. I went to bed with a prayer repeating over and over in my mind, "Lord, help me, please help me."

And finally that night I did get a little sleep.

Monday morning came. This was the day of the funeral and the last earthly glimpse of our Dad and partner. How could we ever go on? I was told, "Take only one day at a time." I have found this to be ever so helpful.

After the funeral was past, things were back in place, and we were left to be on our own. How could we cope alone?? Dad's place was empty when we sat down to eat. When we had to make a decision there was no help from Dad. When we all gathered together in the evening there was one chair empty. When it was time for family devotions there was no Dad here to lead. Never again on earth would we be able to feel that good feeling of "the day's work is all done and we are all gathered in for night," since Dad just will not be here anymore.

How would a little boy of 10, who was always by the side of his Dad whenever possible, cope with the loss of his Dad at this tender age, was a heartbreaking question. The questions could go on and on, but we knew we must stop asking questions, begin to turn these things over to our heavenly Father, and let Him lead the way.

At the funeral a friend gave some advice I have never forgotten. It was, do not give up family devotions because Dad is no longer here. And yes, I agreed we needed it then more than ever. We needed to pray and ask for guidance and strength as we struggle along on this weary road of life.

I must not look far into the future, but take one day at a time. I am sure the Blessed Lord will always be there to help me overcome if I truly seek His way. We know He makes no mistakes, so why should we question His plans for our life?

What would become of the farm? Did we want to go on farming or not? Many more decisions had to be made. I am not a born leader; I'd much rather stay in the background. Dad had usually pretty well been the planner of things around here. Now it was up to me. This was not an easy task.

But yes, I wanted the boys to do the farming and us women would also chore, if they thought we could keep everything under control. The married children thought this should work out all right and if we needed assistance, they would be willing to help us out. So that is what we did.

The son that just turned 16 took over most of the responsibility for the farm. Of course, at times he needed assistance, but with everyone willing to help we made out like this fairly well until an older one got married and the one that was farming wanted to try another job. At that point I turned it over to the married son.

Time has a way of healing our broken hearts to a certain extent over the years, but those precious memories of our loved one will always be with us. Even though Dad is gone now for 10 years, his influence is still around us and I daily think of him.

I used to wonder, does it just open the wound when we talk about a departed loved one to someone or what should we say? Now after parting with one, for me, I say, no, it does not. It may bring tears, but it still makes you feel good to know others still remember your loved one and care to share memories with you.

He will always be missed by the family, but by the grace of God we hope we can all reach that heavenly home and once again have a complete family circle.

I would like to conclude that only through the sustaining mercy and help from above were we able to rise above our grief and hope-lessness. Plus the many prayers, cards, words, and letters from our thoughtful friends from far and near helped. No one will ever know how much those encouraging letters mean until you are at the receiving end.

So let us all strive to always have peace and kindness rule our lives and be prepared to meet our maker. We never know when we walk out the door, if we will be able to walk back in. Life is so short, and death, oh, so final!

Rosemary Mishler: May 12, 1987 - Oct. 19, 1992

Submitted by The Alvin Mishler family, LaGrange, Indiana

On May 12, 1987 we were blessed with a healthy little girl. We named her Rosemary. She was a good baby till she started getting her teeth; then she was very fussy. She had black eyes and hair, and it seemed everybody noticed her when we went somewhere. She always wanted to go along when we went to church. She was the baby when her Dad was ordained minister and often went with us to church. She always had little friends to play with.

She was five years old and always talking about going to school. She loved to sing and could write her own name and the names of all her brothers and sisters as well.

School started in August and time went on. Her oldest brother was out of school that year and she enjoyed being outside with him.

On October 19, 1992 the day started out like usual; Alvin left for work. The children left for school and she was very happy that morning. She went from window to window to wave to the children as they left for school. Little did we know that an angel was watching her.

I remember she was so happy and content that morning. I started with the laundry and John was to haul some coal home from the neighbors that day. She wanted to go along, but I said she better stay at home. She said, "Okay, I will."

I went on with my laundry and I didn't know where she was so I went to the house and called her name. She answered me. I asked, "What are you doing?"

"Oh, I am just sitting here."

I said, "Okay," and went on with my work. A little later I had to get something in the house. I called her again.

She said, "I am still sitting here."

I asked, "What are you doing?"

"Oh, I am playing church."

That was something she often did, but usually she had her dolls and was singing. This time she had no books or dolls; she was waiting for her brother to come home. She gave me a sweet smile and stayed sitting where she was.

By the time I was finished with the laundry, John was coming home with a load of coal. She ran for the road to have a ride with John.

He had to use the tractor to back the wagon in place. He did that while I was gathering the eggs and she was with me at the time. All of a sudden she went for John as he was taking the tractor to put in its place. He was turning around to back up when she came up on his blind side and stumbled against the back wheel, hit her temple and fell down.

John heard a little scream and looked. She was lying on her back between the two wheels. He just picked her up and brought her to the porch. He called for me, but couldn't find me. He went to get a horse ready to go for help. I came in the other door and found her lying on the carpet with her face all bloody and I saw life was gone. Oh my.

Then John came in and we just cried. I asked him what happened. He thought he drove over her, but we later found out he didn't. That was 10:30 a.m. I went over to the neighbors and told her what had happened.

I knew we had to get Dad home, who was working with a carpenter crew, and the children home from school. People started coming. The children came, but they couldn't get hold of my husband. They tried again and finally at 1:00 p.m. he came home, but he didn't know what had happened. The children and I went out to meet him and told him what had happened.

A lot of people came for the viewing. We had the funeral at the home place on the 22nd of October with a full house. We have missed her sweet voice and her singing ever since, but she is in a place where we all want to be.

Gone But Not Forgotten

Elmer Yoder: Dec. 19, 1934 - Oct. 4, 1991

Submitted by Carolyn Yoder: Topeka, Indiana

The morning of October 4, 1991, was misty and dreary. We got up as usual and ate breakfast. At 5:20 Elmer was ready to go to work. He went to the door to leave, but then he stopped and went back to the bedroom. I thought he had probably forgotten something. Then he left on his bicycle for Redman Industries where he had worked for 17 years.

We had spent the evening before with one of our children, so I decided to read the daily paper before doing the breakfast dishes. Elmer had not been gone very long when there was a knock on the door. I thought it sounded like our neighbor Larry Hostetler's knock, so I was not surprised to see him at the door.

He said, "Carolyn, Elmer was hit and he is hurt badly. I am here with a driver that will take you to the scene if you want to go." At first I didn't know what to do, but then I decided to go.

It had happened in front of the Vera Fry and Wayne Miller residence, one and a quarter miles from home. No ambulance was there yet when we got there. He lay at the roadside, in a very serious condition. I knelt by his side and talked to him, but he couldn't answer me. He seemed to realize I was there, as when I quit talking, he would moan. As long as I talked he was quiet.

He had been riding his bicycle behind a road cart which had lights and he also had a large blinker on his bicycle. A 4-wheel drive pickup truck coming from the other direction passed a van and hit the horse head-on. The horse was killed instantly. We will never know how Elmer was hit. His left arm was broken, his left leg shattered, and he had a bad head injury.

The ambulance finally arrived and took him to the LaGrange Hospital, where a helicopter with a trauma doctor was waiting to air-lift him to Bronson Hospital at Kalamazoo, Michigan. By then it was getting foggy, so weather conditions didn't allow that to be done. A neighbor took my son-in-law, Wilbur Hochstetler, and me in a car to LaGrange. When we got there they told us about the weather and that they decided to do the surgery at LaGrange. He also had very serious internal injuries.

The children were contacted and told to come as soon as possible. Wilbur and I sat in the waiting room. Those were some very anxious moments. As soon as I had seen him at the accident scene I had gotten this feeling that our days together would soon be over. Two of our daughters had also heard the sirens and could see the flashing lights at the scene. Their thoughts had also been of their Dad.

While in the waiting room, a kind lady that was on the E.M.S. came and sat beside me. Next, Elmer's foreman arrived, then the children got there. They told us to come meet with the trauma doctor in the conference room, as he wanted to talk with me. At the door-way we met our family doctor, with a very serious look on his face. The shocking words he told us were, "Elmer didn't make it."

Oh, what shall we do? The trauma doctor still wanted to talk with us and explain all his injuries. It was hard to really grasp what he was telling us, but he was very concerned that we knew all the details. Such an empty, hopeless feeling. They allowed us to go in to see him there at the hospital.

What to do next? I didn't want to go home, but we did. The children went with me. As we walked in the door, I saw his plate and coffee cup as he had left them on the table. I realized he would never sit at the head of the table again.

Soon other people came. There were decisions to make and funeral arrangements to make. No more was Elmer by my side to help me.

At that time my 90 year old Mom was living in her house in the same yard with us. Her health was starting to fail and by May 8, 1992 she was gone. In seven months' time we laid two loved ones to rest in the cemetery not far away.

Death is so final and leaves a very empty feeling in your life. God has promised not to leave us nor forsake us. At such a time those promises help to endure and help us along the way.

I cannot put into words the feelings I had when the coffin was closed the last time and my loved one was lowered into the grave to be seen no more.

John Henry Hochstetler: Oct. 5, 1952 - Feb. 3, 1971

Submitted by Mary Ellen Mullet, a sister

January 18, 1971, was a very wintry day, cold, with snow blowing. The sun would shine, then snow again. This pattern lasted all day.

Since we were expecting our third blessing in five weeks, I had been attending monthly LeLeche League meetings for nursing mothers, in Bremen. I had some books I wanted to return, but had no way to go, and deep down I wasn't sure I wanted to venture out in this weather.

In September I had been in an accident when the brakes failed and we ran into a block building. That had given me a little fear of the road. I have since completely overcome this fear with prayer and trust.

Finally, after some prayer that day I called Leanna Schmucker. They had plans, and she couldn't go, so I felt that was my answer. Later that evening Leanna came and said their birthday party for Grandpa was canceled and she would take me after all.

On our way home, at approximately 11:00, as we were coming into Nappanee with snow flurries in the air, we had to stop for an accident. Parked behind a semi, not being able to see what was involved, Leanna and I talked about being in an accident. When we finally moved on I saw a maroon-colored car and told Leanna it looks like my brother's car.

At the police station I asked who was in the accident. The

policeman answered, "Hochstetler." Getting out the report and looking at it he said, "John Henry Hochstetler."

I asked, "Is he hurt? That's my brother." He only answered that they were taking him to the Elkhart Hospital, but I didn't like the look on his face!

I asked him if someone had told my mother. He said that a cousin at the scene said he would, but asked if I would please go, so she would be sure to find out.

When we got to my mother's house it was decided that Leanna would take us as my cousin didn't have much gas left. My Aunt Maude was staying with Mom that night and after taking her home we headed for Elkhart with heavy hearts.

All the way to the hospital I prayed that if my dear brother of 18 years would have to die, that we would have a chance to talk to him if he wasn't prepared to die.

Approaching the information desk at the hospital Mom asked for John Henry. They had not admitted anyone by that name. Calling back to the emergency room we overheard her say, "Well, do they know?" and then "I wish you would."

She hung up and told us someone will be with us in a minute. Numbly, I walked to the side of the hall and leaned against the wall, expecting to hear the worst.

The friendly nurse came around the corner, took us in her arms and told us he was gone. What a shock, this baby that was born the day after his father was buried!

The nurse went to the waiting room and sat down with us. We discovered that this nurse had worked in the hospital 18 years earlier and remembered my father's death after being sick for one week of spinal-bulbar polio.

On the way back to Nappanee, we stopped at the funeral home. The undertaker said we could view him if we wished. He looked so peaceful, as if he was just sleeping. His death was from a head injury, but his beautiful thick hair hid the injury.

Three days later on a cold January day, he was laid to rest beside the father that he never knew.

John Henry had stopped at Ozzie's Restaurant to talk to someone. The waitress wanted him to sit down to have coffee, but someone was waiting to meet him at D and D Station. So he replied, "No, I have to go meet my friend." Shortly after pulling out on the road a truck hit an icy spot and came over on his side of the road, causing the accident.

Precious memories, how they linger!

"JOHN HENRY HOCHSTETLER"

Through deepest grief our son was born,
With deepest grief we're left to mourn
Our grief-born son — The youngest one.

He never saw his father's face
Whose breath of life had ceased four days
Before he came — His breath to claim.

He was our stay through those dark days
With his defenseless, helpless ways,
His father's name — And his the same.

We shared his joys and sorrows, too,
As he from child to manhood grew-
These eighteen years —With smiles and tears.

With arrow swiftness death came by
And took our son,-no last good-bye-
No time or place — To yet embrace.

"FATHER AND SON"

Together now— their race is run,
The unseen father—unseen son,
While our hearts yearn — For their return.

Now side by side in death they sleep—
Within their graves so cold and deep,
Together now — Though cold the brow.

God have mercy, hear our prayer:
Help us all these griefs to bear;
And understand — A Father's Hand.

Help us to trust in Thee Alway,
Be Thou our strength, our hope and stay,
Until we meet — At Jesus' feet.

Father and son never saw each other. Father, John Henry Hochstetler, died Oct. 1, 1952. Son John Henry was born Oct. 5, 1952

Alan Hochstetler: May 5, 1960 - Feb. 3, 1990

Submitted by Perry and Fannie Hochstetler: Ligonier, Indiana

It was the 22nd of December 1989, a very cold day with a high wind from the west. That morning we had 18 degrees below zero. The warmest it got that day was two degrees below zero. Our son Lyle was planning to have his wife Ruth's family, the Schmuckers at their house for Christmas dinner the next day. They had also planned on having our family, the Hochstetlers, there for Christmas dinner on Christmas day.

I offered to help get ready for it, but Ruth said she thought she could manage all right with the children at home from school. Their Christmas vacation had started that day. Then she said if I wanted to take care of their three youngest ones in our home, they would be able to put things away and everything will stay put better. I told her I would do that. The next morning they brought the little ones over after breakfast.

Around 11:30 a.m. Lyle's Perry Dean came running to our house. We live a little bit north of them up the road. He said, "Grandmother, Mom said for you to come over right away, our washhouse is on fire, and bring the fire extinguisher."

I said, "I will as soon as I can."

Linda, their oldest daughter, ran to Joe Bontragers, our daughter Rosemary, living a bit further north on the opposite side of the road from us and told them. Joe gathered up their extinguishers and started across their yard for the road to go to Lyles. About that time another one of Lyle's children came running, saying, "Mom said call the fire trucks."

Joe dropped all the extinguishers right there in the yard in the snow and ran for the barn. He could have taken the bicycle, but he thought with the wind he could make more time with the horse and buggy. The roads were a little slippery from hard packed snow.

Lyle had gone back to the woods to cut, and bring up, a load of firewood and knew nothing about what was happening at home. The boys ran back to the woods and told him. They didn't have enough clothes on for as cold as it was, but couldn't get in the house for more either.

Perry Dean's feet were frostbitten a little bit. Lyle tied the horses to a tree and took off running home across the fields, probably somewhere over a half mile from the house. The snow was deep and he was wearing heavy insulated boots that slipped a little with almost every step he took.

I used our big fire extinguisher but it was all to no avail. Ruth, Rosemary, and I went around the house to the sunporch. We got a few pieces of furniture and some dishes out. Otherwise, it was so smoky we couldn't get more.

The fire trucks, friends, and neighbors soon came. Nothing was saved except what we got from the sunporch. All the clothes they had is what they were wearing. We don't know what caused the fire.

We were living in the basement of our new Daudy house at the time. The main part was far from finished. We told them they could live with us until their house was rebuilt. That is what they did. They had seven children at the time.

Kind friends and neighbors were soon coming with clothes, food, beds, bedding, and other things. I don't know what we would have done without their help. It was all so greatly appreciated, it seemed we couldn't express ourselves enough in words.

People from near and far came to help rebuild. Our two single boys, Ernest and Alan, not living at home, also helped, as well as our other children. The last week before the house was finished, Alan mentioned something several different times about having a sore leg.

The last time he came, he was here for supper. Again he said his leg hurt so bad. I asked him, "What did you do, bump it or something?"

He said, "Not that I know of, but it really hurts."

Why I didn't pay more attention or suggest he go see a doctor is more than I will ever know. There was so much going on with people coming and going to help on the new house. It seemed we were always getting ready for the next day's help. I just didn't stop to think like I should have.

It was six weeks after Lyle's house burned down that the new one was ready for them to move in. Plans were made to help them move in Saturday, February 3, 1990. During the time of rebuilding the weather had warmed up more.

At that time Joes had a three week old baby, Doretta. Joe's sister Edna was their hired girl and they had asked Alan if he would take her home Saturday morning. He had said he would. When he didn't show up at the appointed time, they waited a little longer and he still didn't come. Joe went to a phone and called him, but got no answer.

It was unusual for Alan not to come and say something if he couldn't do it, as he was dependable. When Joe got no answer he called someone else to take Edna home. He thought maybe he should go to Alan's house and see if something was the matter, but he didn't. We thought maybe he had forgotten about it. Alan lived at the north edge of Topeka.

The day went on as moving days do. By evening we all went home, glad that Lyles once more had a house of their own to live in, thinking now we would all go back to normal living again.

On Saturday night it got colder again and snowed. It was cold and cloudy all day Sunday. We went to church at John Wingards. In the afternoon we viewed Orva A. Miller then went home. On our way home we went right past Alan's house. We looked in, but saw no one. We never gave it a thought that not all was as usual at his home.

Monday, February 5th Alan didn't show up at work. It was very unusual for him not to come to work or call and say why he wouldn't be there. At 3:00 p.m. a co-worker Jerry McCoy, a good friend of Alan's, thought he would stop in at his house to see why he wasn't at work. He said he thought maybe he was sick with the flu or measles. Measles were visiting many homes at that time. They had expected him at work on Saturday, also. We don't think he had intended to go on Saturday as we feel his leg hurt too much.

Jerry knocked on the door at the house. He then tried to open it, but it was locked and nobody came to the door. He went out to the garage. He opened the door and found Alan lying right there on the floor beside his truck. He was dead, lying on the cold cement floor.

Jerry said it was such a shock he lost his senses. He went up-town and reported it to the police. Soon cops and other people were there. They searched all through his house for a clue to what could have happened, finding nothing. They had taken him to the funeral home before we knew anything had happened.

That morning I had done Lyles' and our laundry as Lyles didn't have any clothes lines yet. Around 5:00 p.m. a cop drove in the lane. I wondered what he wanted to tell me. He knocked on the door. I opened up. He said a few words, then said he came to tell me they found our son Alan, dead, lying in his garage.

I must have been dazed. I can't remember the exact words he said as it didn't seem to sink into my mind what he actually said, and yet I knew what he meant. I then asked what had happened.

He said they didn't know. They had searched everything and couldn't find a thing that could have caused it. He said they didn't think there was any foul play. Next he asked, "Is Perry at home?"

"No," I said, "Not yet, although he should be home soon."

He asked where he was working, so he could go tell him.

I said, "I can't remember for who, or where, he was working. Go ask Lyle, he knows."

Lyles happened to see the cop drive in our lane. Ruth said to Lyle, "Something must have happened; go over to your Mom right away."

He was on his way over when Red, the policeman, started to Lyles. Lyle told him where Perry was working, so off he went in search of him.

Then Lyle came on over to me. We talked a little about what could have happened, our minds blank. He then went home to do his chores. Soon Rosemary came over asking, "What did the policeman say?"

I told her what he had said. She also asked, "What happened?"

I said, "I don't know."

We sat at the table crying. Soon Perry walked in the door, looked at us and asked, "What happened?"

I said, "Didn't the policeman tell you?"

"No," he said. "What is wrong?"

Then I told him the policeman said they found Alan's dead body in his garage. Then he also asked, "What happened?"

I said, "They don't know."

Pretty soon the policeman was back; they had missed each other on the way. Red repeated the tragedy to Perry then offered to help if he could. He took son-in-law Joe to tell our son Lamars, 16 miles away.

They also stopped at Toby Troyers to see where Ernest was working. He was working for Redman helping set up trailer houses. At this time he was working close to the Indiana and Illinois state line, four hours away. Toby Ann said she would get hold of him as soon as she can, which she did.

Lamars, Lyles, Joes, and again friends and neighbors came to help and sympathize. We felt shocked and numb. Nobody had any idea what caused his death. Our minds were heavy and yet so blank. After all the people had left that Monday night, Ernest still wasn't there. Perry and

I waited up for him. He finally came. Again the first question asked was, "What happened?" We again said we didn't know.

The next day our family was sitting together trying to figure out what happened. All at once Ernest said, "Didn't he complain about having a sore leg?" We said, "Yes, he did," and just like that it came to my mind, he probably had another blood clot. He had had a blood clot eight or nine years earlier. The doctor had him off from work and on medication for a little while.

Then it all started making sense. We feel the blood clot let loose and went through his heart. By all appearances, he had started his truck to leave, then felt something was happening and quickly got out of the truck. Some articles were lying on the floor that he had in his truck. The door of his truck was open and he was lying at the back end of his truck on the floor with his right leg bent under him. He had vomited a little.

An autopsy was taken and they couldn't find anything, except it did show he had carbon monoxide in his lungs. So we know he didn't die right away. How long he lay there before he died, conscious or not, we will never know. We have many questions we will never have any answers for, as to how this all happened, but we will always wonder.

The undertaker said this must have happened Saturday, February 3rd and he was there until Monday at 3:00 p.m. when he was found. On Sunday two of his friends were at his house. Nobody had answered the door so they thought he wasn't at home and left.

Later on we found out in his last days, he had told some of his friends he had a blood clot. He had also said he didn't feel well. They said he walked with a limp. We didn't see him in his last days.

How we and all of our family felt is hard to explain. Those who have experienced such a tragedy have an idea what it's like.

The funeral was the following Friday, a day later than usual. The reason for it was they didn't bring him out to our house from the funeral home till Wednesday. They just said they couldn't have him ready any sooner. Later we found out he was frozen so hard from lying out in the cold so long they couldn't do anything with him till he was thawed out. That was the reason they kept him a day longer.

The hurt is still deep. We can't help but wonder why he had to have such a cruel death. But we trust God had a reason for it to happen this way although we don't understand why. We know what

He does is well done. We have learned to accept it and live with it and say "Thy Will Be Done." We hope Alan still had the chance to ask for forgiveness before he died. We will never know.

Jonas E. Yoder: Apr. 28, 1952 - July 17, 1995

Submitted by Emanuel and Fannie Yoder, Baltic, Ohio
Witnessed by Gideon and Anna Yoder

It was July 17, 1995, at 3:15, a warm day. We were headed to New Bedford to pick up peaches on our way home from John A. Yoder. Jonas had hitched up a new horse to get him shod at the blacksmith shop at Henry Rabers. His wife, Ada, rode along to the mailbox for mail and walked back. We met him at Sam Brenly bridge on County Road 59. The horse didn't want to cross the bridge when we met him. We talked a few words on the go.

Right then the water truck blew his horn halfway up the hill because his brakes were not holding and he was overloaded. We hurried our horse to get out of the way. The truck passed us about 70 feet from Jonas on the cart. We heard a thud, then his horse ran up the lawn with the harness on him but no cart. He ran to their lane and walked on in. Ada caught him.

I told Anna, "That hit him." Oh, my! I looked back and saw Jonas lying beyond the other end of the bridge. The truck was going up the next hill before it stopped. This all happened so quickly.

A Kaser boy was riding with the truck. He jumped out as soon as the truck stopped and ran to Wilda Mullet to call for help. I walked over to Jonas, said his name, and checked his pulse, but life had fled. Jonas lay on his right side. His head was on the grass, his hip on the blacktop edge, his legs were crossed above the shoes, and his hands were together in front of his face.

The truck backed down and back across the bridge. He called to his company by CB and she asked for more directions. I told him to tell her TR 151. He did and hung up. He stopped the motor. He was shaky.

Anna was in the buggy where we had stopped. She tied our horse at Kenny's garage and went with the Semac van to get Ada. The van had come in time to see the horse go up the hill. Ada had caught the horse before it got to the barn. Anna said, "Come, Jonas was hit."

The girls came running from the patch and came along. They picked up their son Melvin at the sawmill. Neighbor's Raymond was also there and came along.

A red car was the first to come to the scene. They asked if they could help and also asked how to get to Charm. I told them to go to Steve Rabers and tell him Jonas Yoder was in a wreck. Steve was working with a tractor and came that way, not realizing it was Em's Jonas as he was always called. Wilda came next and asked who it is. I told her, "Em's Jonas."

Oh, not Jonas! She went on her way to tell neighbors to the west. By that time Ada and the children had arrived. Ada passed me on the bridge and asked, "Is he living?"

I said, "I don't think so." Ada said, "Jonas, Jonas," and touched him and the girls called "Dad". They all put their hands on him.

The squad came, checked him, and covered him with a sheet. Soon the family was in the cool squad as it was very warm in the sun. Wilda took Anna and Henry R. Erma to get Em. Fannie and Andy living at home. They left word at Fender's Fish Hatchery. John Scherer came and offered help. We sent him to Bishop Mose Hershberger and Melvin Hershberger came along, too. More of the family was summoned.

The Sheriff Department was notified to get Emanuel at Artwood where he worked. Emanuel was brought to the wreck at about 4:20. He didn't know which of the boys it was until he got there. State Patrol did the Investigation. By the looks of the cart tracks, Jonas was off the road and for some unknown reason the horse backed in front of the truck.

The truck wheel went over the cart and smashed it to slivers. The truck had a high and flat bumper, about cart seat height, that picked him up and possibly carried him to the other end of the bridge, and then rolled him off to the side. His straw hat was about six feet from his head on the grass. He had probably rolled over a couple times as his shirt was dirty all over.

The truck had a fiberglass hood. There was a crack from the headlight up and down and the headlight was broken. About six inches up from the headlight there was some hair that looked like some of his beard.

I was questioned first, then the driver. The squad lady asked the Patrol what it takes to move him. He said, "You call the prosecutor and the coroner. It looks like an accidental death caused by injuries." The coroner said to bring him to the hospital. It was 5:15 by the time he was moved. Second Patrol came and they measured everything and took pictures. Anna went home with the family by van and I came with the buggy after we got the OK from patrol to move the cart off the road. Eli D. M. Yoder's children came with the one horse wagon, loaded the cart, and took it to Jonas's above barn.

There was a large funeral on Thursday of about 800 people.

On day at a time, sweet Jesus,
That's all I'm asking from you;
Just give me the strength to do every day,
What I have to do.

Yesterday's gone, sweet Jesus,
And tomorrow may never be mine;
Lord help me today,
Show me the way,

One day at a time.

Daniel Borkholder: June 11, 1968- Sept. 16, 1973

Submitted by Al & Ruth Ann Borkholder: Nappanee, Indiana

It was the summer of 1973. It seemed our cup was full and running over. We had in our 11 years of married life, been blessed with seven lively, healthy sons, the oldest one being 10.

I had them all gathered around me, out in the yard. They were helping snap green beans. We were expecting another child in about two months, so I decided to get them used to the idea of another family member. "Would you all like to have another baby, sometime?"

They, of course, were happy about it and I told them that maybe one of these times we would have one. I then asked them what they would name a new baby.

"Norman!"

This answer came immediately from little Daniel, age five. I wondered how he so readily had a name in his mind. "Oh," I said, "Suppose we have a girl for a change, then what would you name her?" And again, without hesitating, Daniel came up with a name. "Rachel!" he said.

In the early morning Al would walk to the far end of the pasture field to care for some calves that were penned down there. He would usually go alone, after milking and before breakfast. The younger children were still asleep. But in late summer, Daniel started waking earlier and would want to go with his Daddy. I would see them go from my kitchen window, hand in hand, Al with his man-sized strides and Daniel skipping and running to keep up with Daddy.

All these incidents passed, along with those happy summer days. Little did we realize how precious those things actually were. Just little everyday things. Had we known what the future held, we would have treasured those times to the fullest!

It was Sunday, September 16. Since the birth of our baby was already two weeks over the due date, we had asked a niece, Marietta, to stay with me, so Al could go to church. He took the four oldest and had asked Daniel if he wanted to go, too.

"No," he answered, "I want to stay home and play with the dove."

The day before Al had seen a white dove sitting on the housetop. He thought it unusual as we didn't have any white doves around our farm. He didn't say anything to anyone about it. He didn't know that anyone else had seen it, but apparently Daniel had seen it, too.

So I was home with the three youngest. That forenoon, Daniel asked me to read to him. I told him to get me some books and I would read him several stories. Then he said, "Sing to me, Mom."

I asked, "What shall I sing?"

He brought me the Kinderlieder and said "Sing 'Müde bin ich'." So I sang to him.

Al came home from church and lay down to take a nap. The one and a half year old and the three year old were also napping, so I took the chance to also relax on the rocking chair. A neighbor boy had come over and they wanted to play ball.

Since our house is on a rise and all the yard slopes down to the road, it has never been a good place to play ball. The boys came trooping in and asked if they could go across the road and play in the pasture field. I didn't know what to answer. I was thinking about it and then I glanced over and saw that three year old James was still sleeping. I thought it wouldn't be so bad if he wasn't along and all the while they kept asking and I still hadn't answered. I guess they took my silence as consent, and ran outside again. I still am not sure, why I didn't say yes or no. It's one of those things we have no answer for. I am not sure how long they were playing, when Daniel said "I'm tired and I'm going home." His brother said to wait and he would help him across the road. But Daniel started running and said "Don't worry about me!"

From the house I heard brakes screeching and soon a woman was screaming, "I hit a little boy! I hit a little boy!" While running out across the lawn I somehow became over balanced and fell headlong on the grass. I jumped to my feet and ran out to the road and found Daniel lying in the ditch. He lay there, curled up, just as he often was in his bed. There was no blood, but he was unconscious.

Other traffic that had been coming had stopped, and as I picked him up someone said to me to get in their car and they would take us to the hospital. In the meantime Al had still been sleeping.

Marietta woke him up and he ran out to the car, carrying his shoes. He got in the car and also the woman who had hit him. Her name was Adelle. All the way to the hospital, Adelle kept praying aloud to Jesus.

I tried to find a pulse on Daniel, but could not find one. I wanted to cry, "Dear Lord, let him be alive," but I knew I should pray for His will to be done. But what if it was not His will for Daniel to live? Oh, such a hard prayer to say, and say it from the heart!

The five mile ride to the hospital seemed to take forever! I think in my heart I knew he was gone, but I did not want to accept it. The doctor asked us to wait in another room while they checked him. And oh, the feeling when he told us that life had fled! I can not put such a feeling into words. Only those who have experienced it know what I mean. How could we ever give up one of our precious children?

Meanwhile back home the children and family anxiously awaited word. Somehow word arrived there before we did. I had forgotten about Adelle and after we were home awhile, someone told us that she and some other people were out beside the road. I told Al, "Why don't we go out and talk with her."

When she saw us coming, she turned her back. She just could not face us. I went to her, she turned around, and I took her in my arms and we cried together. She was so sorry and we told her over and over, that we held nothing against her.

She had seen Daniel standing beside the road and she had slowed down. She thought he was going to wait till she passed, but for some reason, at the last second he darted out in front of her.

Adelle was a 19 year old girl, going to college. This affected her so badly that she couldn't go on. She came to the viewing one evening and brought her father along. She also came to the funeral along with a friend who could understand German and who translated parts of the sermon for her.

Life was not easy the following weeks, months, and yes, even years. Even now as I write, 21 years later, the tears still come. It's like opening an old wound, when we recall these memories.

It was also a hard time for the boys. It is hard to see your children go through these hard times and there is so little we can do to take their sorrow away. It's something each had to work through for himself. We knew that Daniel was not in the grave, it was only his shell.

But being human, we also mourned for that part of him. He was always so full of life— he could smile with his eyes and when he ran it seemed as if he had springs in his feet. And when we tucked him in bed at night we would get a big hug and he would say "Ich gleich dich!" For all that and more we mourned. But if this was God's will, then Jesus, help us to take it, one day at a time!

A week later on a Sunday afternoon, our baby was born. It was a little girl. After seven boys we had a little girl. But our hearts were still so full of sorrow, life seemed so precious, that it didn't really seem important, is it a girl or boy. But life goes on and we had to decide on a name. Suddenly the scene from the summer came back and I could hear Daniel say, "Let's name the baby Rachel!" After talking it over, we decided on Rachel. It was so hard to know that he would never see the baby that he named.

While I was still in the hospital, a nurse brought in a rose in a vase and said that it was from Adelle. She had wanted to come in and give it to me herself, but she said she just couldn't face me. I thought, dear Adelle, how can we ever get across to you that we have no grudge or hate for you. So with a prayer in my heart and tears in my eyes, I wrote her a letter that same day. It would be many years later, that I would learn that she kept and cherished that letter. I feel it was God's leading that I wrote it. I have no memory of what I wrote, only to again assure her that we hold nothing against her. A month later she came to our home with a friend of hers and we had a long visit.

She told us a bit of her life. Her parents weren't Christians, and as a child she walked to church herself. I think she said there was a church near her home. During the time of trial she went through, her father admitted that she had something that he did not have. She was hoping that this would change him. We told her if one soul is saved then Daniel's death will not have been in vain.

We only saw Adelle once in the following years and could we have seen into the future, we would have seen our paths would cross again. Fourteen years later, on a Sunday evening, we were visiting a friend who was recently widowed. Her one son, who was not Amish, was also visiting her. They were good friends with Adelle and went to the same church. They told us that Adelle's daughter was hit by a car and was unconscious. It happened on September 16, the same day that Daniel had been killed. This friend of Adelle also told us that September 16, never came around that she did not think about the accident. And all these years she had a fear that one of her children would be hit.

I again wrote to her and she later answered us. She told us that her daughter was in a coma for three weeks. It took almost a year of therapy until she was her normal self again.

We now meet Adelle occasionally, as she works in our doctor's office. In 1993 she lost her husband to a heart disease. So her life has had its share of trials. She is a very remarkable person. It seems that the trials she has faced have only made her faith more sound.

As I write this, it will soon be 21 years that this took place. We have been richly blessed in all these years. We have a family of 13 children, 10 boys and three girls. We also have nine grandchildren and one is named Daniel.

It is such a comfort that when we think of Daniel, we know he is in Heaven. We would not bring him back to this world if we could. The Lord giveth and the Lord taketh away, blessed be the name of the Lord.

I would like to share a poem I wrote in his memory.

Oh sing for me, Mother, will you please?
He begged of me as he climbed on my knees.
Oh yes, I'll try; what shall I sing?
And the Kinderlieder he did bring.

Sing 'Müde bin ich, geh zur ruh
  Schliesze meine augen zu.'
How little did we think that he
  In a few short hours to that rest would be.

God was speaking loud and clear,
  But we frail humans could not hear,
Till the screech of brakes, a woman's scream
  Brought us running to the scene.

It seemed an Angel pillowed your fall,
  Curled up as if sleeping, no suffering at all;
Thy Will, not ours, Oh Lord we'd pray,
  But oh the words were hard to say.

But life goes on and we must smile
  In spite of heartache, in spite of trial,
But with God's Grace we face each day,
  And all hope to meet him in Heaven some day.

Your memory, dear Daniel, will always be
  In the hearts and mind of your family.
Little reminders are everywhere,
  Your toys, your clothes, your empty chair:

Your dark shining eyes, how innocent, how sweet.
  And when you ran, you had springs in your feet.
Your "Ich gleich dich," before you'd sleep,
  Your kiss and hug, for these we weep.

As he was loved, so is he missed.

Dean Ray Yoder: Dec. 17, 1966 - June 21, 1976

Submitted by Perry O. Yoder

This is a true story of Dean Ray, age nine, and his three brothers.

It is June again and it brings back memories of our dear son, Dean Ray, laid to rest on the 21st of June 1976.

It was on a Monday. The day started out with the boys and me in the garden pulling weeds and the girls doing the washing. When we were done, the two little boys Dean, age nine, and Ernie, age six, went to play.

They played so nicely all day; they did not fuss as they were making hay. Little did we realize the Death Angel was so close.

In the afternoon I started to cut some dresses, but I couldn't get them finished. Rosa finally made the remark, "Well Mom, why don't you get done with those dresses?"

I told her I didn't know why, I just wasn't in the right mood.

We had supper then. Dean always sat beside me at the table. He had a head full of curls. He was a boy that was always ready to go, so after supper I said I would take those chairs and the table over to Ed's. They had lived at Uncle Emanuel Zehr's little house for a while after they were married.

By the time we had everything loaded the buggy was full, so the boys stayed home. Dad went along. He said, "We don't have a battery."

I told him, "We won't be gone long." It was not even an hour until we were home again. Rosa had gone to work. The other two girls were gone. When we left, Dean had been sitting on the new wagon we had gotten them. As we left, he had waved his hand and had a big smile. I did not think of it being his last smile and his last good-bye wave with his hand.

Little did I think that they would go back to that hay field where the tractor was. After we left he ran all the way back a long lane to the culvert and walked across it. He then ran for the tractor, which had the keys left in it. He started it with the baler on it and made a circle, driving real close to the ditch. I feel God's hands were over him. What else kept him from driving into the ditch?

Our 12 year old, Wilbur, went back and told him he didn't have it in the right place, so he got on and put the tractor and baler in the row where it had been. The two boys got off and started back home. Our 15 year old and the youngest were on the bicycle heading back and the chain had come off, so they met in the lane.

Our 15 year old said he wanted to go have a ride too. So they all went back to the tractor, unhooked the baler and took off with the 15 year old driving. He thought what if something should happen with the tractor? What would Mom and Dad say?

He took another look towards home to see if we were coming home already, then he drove at a high speed to the end of the field. As he was getting ready to turn, he thought, what if this tractor would flip over and someone would get killed?

Just like that Dean put his foot on the brakes. The tractor flipped.

It was over within a wink of an eye. Dean was pinned under the fender. It got the back of his head and killed him instantly.

We believe the 15 year old was also caught somewhere as his shirt, T-shirt and pants were torn. He was close by Dean as he was all covered with what splattered from Dean's head. He did not know more than that he had rolled himself away from the tractor. We feel he was very close to being trapped under it, also.

The boys got up and looked to see where Dean was. They saw he was under the tractor and tried to pull him out, but they couldn't. They came home and waited till we came. The youngest came running out to the road and said, "Dad and Mom, Dean is back there under the tractor and he is dead."

Oh, I just screamed and told Dad we have to get back there. We drove back there faster than the horse had ever gone. We got off; we never even thought of tying up the horse. He just stood there.

Yes, it was all over. It was the longest day of the year. Dean's face was turned toward the setting of the sun. I looked, but could not see him at first. Then I did.

Dad went back home to do some calling at the neighbors and I stayed back there alone. No, I was not alone. God was talking to me. "Be thankful in everything, be thankful he isn't crying and calling for help and we could not do a thing."

Everything was quiet. I just walked the field and prayed. I had a pain in my chest for days. I was so thankful the other boys didn't have to lie in the hospital. The 15 year old had two ribs broken, but we didn't know it until the day of Dean's funeral. He had such pain so they took him to the doctor and they bound him real tight.

The boys were all in shock. We could talk to the 15 year old and he would talk about it. The 12 year old didn't say much, but he cried more. One morning he came out and lay on the couch. I heard him saying something to himself. I heard him say, "It's a long time."

I asked him if he was dreaming about Dean. He said he was. He said he dreamt Dean was here and he was just singing and singing those songs that he always wanted to sing when Dan Schwartzs came. Then he just cried and cried. I let him cry as that is healing to the heart. He said it had been a long time since Dean was there to play with him.

Oh, my heart just ached for him. It is a feeling you can't describe to someone else. You can only experience it yourself.

The seat in church, the seat at the table, and the front seat of the buggy are empty places. It also left an empty spot in school.

How little we realize how many friends we have until a time like that. I know it was really hard to give him up, but we know God makes no mistakes. The 23rd Psalm was just the way it fell in place, God wanted him now, while he could still get him out of this old sinful world. God's plans are not ours. His ways are always right.

Sometime after that I had a dream about Dean. I saw him with a group of children. I said to him, "Come here, Dean, I want to see you."

He just said, "Mom, I am all right."

Oh, it was such a relief to my aching heart. I could have a good feeling for him. Some dreams have a lot of meaning to them.

I don't know what Dean would have grown up to be, so we will leave that all in the good Lord's hands. He was very close to his sister Naomi. I just pray some day we can all meet in that beautiful heaven. God does not let us forget Dean even though he left us 18 years ago.

LaMar Diener: April 19, 1958 - March 7, 1963

Submitted by Jake Diener; LaGrange, Indiana -from an article in Family Life (1968)

On the morning of April 19, 1958 my wife and I headed for the LaGrange County Hospital. We had been looking forward to this event for some time.

Just before noon our family doctor met me in the waiting room and made the announcement I had been waiting for all morning. "You have a six lb. three oz. boy," he said. "And everything is just fine," he added quickly.

How thankful we were that everything was over and all was well with our first child. I knew my parents would be happy, too, for this was their first grandchild.

We named the baby LaMar. When he was two days old we brought Mother and baby home from the hospital. How pleased we were the first few weeks when many of our friends came to see the new baby. Yes, life seemed great, as it does to all young parents with their first child. Little did we realize the heartaches, cares, trials, and sleepless nights we were soon to experience.

LaMar was a very fussy baby, nervous and upset much of the

time. Our family doctor told us not to worry, he would grow out of it. Months went by and we began to realize not all was well with our little one. He didn't respond to love, play with toys, or do any of the things other babies his age were doing.

Our family doctor advised us to take LaMar to a baby specialist at Elkhart, Indiana. The specialist told us not to compare our baby with other babies, since all babies are different. "Your baby is just slow," he explained. "He will be all right. He's just a little behind other babies."

Since LaMar was our first child, we didn't realize how far behind he really was. Finally, when he was almost ten months old, we decided to take him to a clinic in Urbana, Illinois. The clinic was about forty miles from where my folks live near Arthur. At the Urbana clinic a child specialist examined LaMar. We didn't know that we were about to receive the greatest shock of our young lives.

The words came slowly from the elderly doctor. "Your boy is a victim of cerebral palsy. He will never be like other children." He went on to explain that LaMar had a brain injury, before, at, or soon after, birth.

"You will have a hard life caring for this child," the doctor told us. "There is no hope for help from the medical profession." He did, however, prescribe Phenobarbital for his nervous condition, which did help to calm him at times.

Before we left, the doctor told us, "Now don't criticize your family doctor for not telling you your child is retarded; this is a very hard thing to tell parents."

Only those who have had the experience can realize the struggle we had within ourselves in the days that followed. We as parents had come face to face with the fact that our first child would probably be an invalid all his life. Why did this have to happen to us? We knew, of course, that such things happened at times to other people, but to us? Why us?

Why us? We asked ourselves that question hundreds of times. What had we done that God would permit this to happen to us? As we struggled with this question, a portion of scripture became very precious to us, the first three verses in St. John 9.

"And as Jesus passed by, he saw a man which was blind from his birth. And his disciples asked him, saying, Master, who did sin, this man, or his parents, that he was born blind. Jesus answered, Neither hath this man sinned nor his parents, but that the work of God should be made manifest in him."

In these verses we found comfort for our troubled souls. We were made to realize by God's word that our child had not been affected because of our sins, which were many, but that the works of God should be made manifest in him.

Life was not the same. We began searching for help from chiropractors. We took LaMar to many different chiropractors and they always gave us faint hope that with treatments he might someday walk and talk as other children. Of course, we clung to the slightest hope these doctors offered.

Many nights LaMar cried and cried until the early hours of morning. At times we felt we were tired almost to the breaking point. We always asked God to help us through these times when we had to see our child suffer.

Not all our life was sorrow. We also had much joy and many blessings to be thankful for. On May 5, 1961, Kathryn Ann was born. She was a blue-eyed chubby girl and such a good baby we hardly knew she was around. She grew fast - so fast that we could hardly grasp the fact that she was developing normally - so strong and healthy like other children.

On March 7, 1963, almost five years after LaMar was born, another sudden shock came into our lives.

For a few days LaMar had been feverish and our family doctor had given us medicine for him. When we got up on the morning of March 7 we noticed that LaMar was worse and had a high fever. We called our family doctor but he was out of town. We then phoned a doctor from a town nearby and he came to our home almost immediately.

"You have a pretty sick boy," He said. "I think you'd better take him to the hospital." Then he added, "Don't be too optimistic."

We arrived at the hospital about 10 A.M., little realizing that we would be there only an hour. At eleven o'clock life fled from LaMar's frail little body. His soul had gone to a place where he was no longer different.

Once again life was different for us. Now we had only one child to care for and she was healthy and strong. How thankful we were for this.

On January 4, 1964 Wanda was born. She too was a normal baby, healthy and very alert. Everything was looking brighter again. We had two healthy children. We could come and go as other families with healthy children did.

Two years passed. On August 20, 1966 God gave us another little boy to love and care for. We were so happy to have another boy, for we had to part with our other one three years before. We named him Lyle.

The doctor assured us he was okay. But he was also a very fussy baby, and we soon began to realize that he was not responding and gaining as he should.

But we thought, oh no, it just can't be what we fear it might be. He just can't be retarded like LaMar was. Haven't we had more than our share of trouble already?

Lyle was seven months old when we took him to the baby specialist at Elkhart. He told us exactly what we feared we would hear. "For some unknown cause your boy has had brain damage. He will also be retarded." But the specialist told us Lyle might not be as bad as LaMar was.

As before we had a hard battle to accept this latest tragedy in our lives. Why us again? Once more we clung to the scripture that had become so precious to us some years before - "That the work of God should be made manifest in him."

As time goes on, Lyle doesn't seem to get much stronger, although he does respond more than LaMar did. He loves attention and caressing, which we are thankful for.

Lyle was two years old in August. He still doesn't sit by himself, but holds his head and back fairly well.

There are many heartaches and tears in caring for a "special child" but it keeps us humble before the Lord. We have often thought we'd much rather have our boys this way, than if they should be healthy and strong, and grow up to lose their souls in eternity. All in all we have a lot to be thankful for, even if at times the way has seemed dark.

A Memorial

LaMar Lynn Diener at five years old
Left this world to join God's fold,
He was one of God's chosen few-
Temptation to evil he never knew.

He left this earth in heaven to sing,
The rest of us closer to Jesus to bring.
Though parents and sisters miss him so-
We're glad for LaMar that he could go.

Levi R. Bontrager: Feb. 19, 1955 - Sept. 6, 1992

Submitted by Mary Lou Bontrager

June first. Another year has gone by. Many ifs and whys in life's path I don't want to dwell on. It's all for a reason and I want to accept it. God said, "I will never leave thee, nor forsake thee." God took us through dark valleys and high mountains. I still praise His Name. I love Him.

We, as a family, have a lot of good memories. Levi was never healthy so we struggled with health problems a lot. He was in and out of the hospital. We tried everything under the sun, but I guess we couldn't buy health.

I still appreciate my husband's personality. He was friendly and had a soft heart. He would never do anything to hurt anyone's feelings. He hardly ever got upset with me in our 15 years of married life.

He had a severe seizure at one o'clock, June 1, 1989. This was the third one in two weeks. We had still been waiting on the doctor's reports of the first two. I will never forget that horrible night. I am a strong woman, but the stress got to me. I could hardly walk.

Our bedroom was full of neighbors and ambulance guys. I once again got ready for the hospital. I was gone for seven weeks without going home. Oh, my poor girls! I shed tears for them, too.

This seizure lasted four solid hours and still had slight seizures the next four hours, going in and out of them. When I was finally allowed to see him, I thanked God that my husband was able to hold himself still.

He was white as a sheet and had all these machines on him. You name it, he had it on him. With all the seizure medicine they shot in him, he was knocked out for four days. The doctor told me some hard words. They had given him ten times the medicine that they usually give a person and they still had not been able to stop the seizures. I told him I sure hope I never have to see something like that again. He told me that with the seizures he's got, I probably would see more.

Four days later Levi woke up when I said his name. He couldn't talk with all the tubes and everything, but tears rolled down his cheeks. He never was the same after that. The medicine had taken its toll and we saw many seizures after that. Two weeks later he had blocked bowels. They doubled his dose of seizure medicine in order to take him off of it for surgery.

At that time they could then give him pain medicine. One of the five doctors came for his daily checkup after surgery. He looked at the bottom line listing the seizure medicine. Not realizing that the dosage listed there was a double dose, he put him back on the medication at that rate for three weeks. Talk about burning up a brain!

When the doctors realized they were giving him a double dose, they cut the dosage in half and sent us home. Levi couldn't walk, talk, or feel himself. He had no control of his kidney and at times he didn't know his home. I have seen the days, too, that he didn't know me. It was so sad.

He was home for two weeks then back to the hospital we went again. They lowered his seizure medication some more and they said they were going to put him in a nursing home for life.

I said, "I want him at home for as long as I can take care of him." We had a lot of struggles. Dad was like a child. He learned to walk, talk, and feed himself again. He regained control of his kidneys. He was finally able to do all this on his own again. I praised God and gave Him thanks. It was such a lift to me.

Neighbors, friends, and relatives would stop in and take him along to places since he wasn't able to drive a horse anymore. As time went by he was able to ride his bike. It really wasn't the safest thing, but I tried to send a lot of prayers with him asking God to protect him.

He would go to town, or to see friends, taking notes with him. They would write back. He never was able to write his own name correctly anymore or write a check out. He didn't know his coins either. I just made sure he had enough money in his billfold and trusted the people to help him.

He did write two notes during this time of disability. It looked like a first grader's writing. I did figure out what he had written, but it wasn't easy. I often shed tears and prayers to God. Levi was finally able to read advertisements in the paper. It took him around 15 minutes to figure out one small ad. When a letter came by mail he would try to read it, but would then finally give it to me, saying, "I just can't read it."

He was able to again feed his two horses. He kept his barn and buggies so clean they almost shined. I have learned accepting is the hardest thing to do in life. I often looked at my husband. I loved him dearly, but he used to be a man and now my two little girls were more advanced than my man. I often thought of the doctor's words.

If Levi could have his pick of life he would not have chosen this. We took care of him for three and a half years. During that time he often had seizures. His hardest ones lasted from a half hour to an hour and his daily slight ones 15 to 20 minutes. Medicine didn't control them completely, but it seemed to help some.

I have seen the days I was scared to see the sun go down. That was when he got his severe seizures and yet God carried me through. In those three and a half years Levi was depressed very few times. I don't know if he felt that I was able to do it all, or if his mind just didn't really see his own disability. I thanked God for his daily happy heart.

On September 6, 1992 we took the Saturday off for family time and went to Fun Spot Park with some friends. Levi was as happy as a lark, as we all were. We did not realize how our day would end. When we got there I asked Levi, "Do you think you should take rides? Maybe just a few?" I was afraid he would get a seizure.

He answered, "I want to be able to take them all or whatever I want." Once as we were walking side by side, he squeezed my hand real hard and smiled. He was so excited and enjoying himself. He also requested to go on a ride with Wanda alone and with Diane alone, too.

After we ate supper at a restaurant Levi had a slight seizure. We did what we could and thought he was all right again. Almost at our friends' house he had a severe one again. We again did what we could, but he went into a semi-coma. We at times didn't know if he was just sleeping or if it was something worse. Sometimes he had seemed to just sleep them off.

We were so used to seeing them, and since he had always got out of them before, we just didn't expect anything else. But God had other plans. Even though we miss him, we don't want to wish him back, as he suffered so much.

I saw something in his last seizure I had never seen before. A few minutes before he died, his arms were limber and he reached up. I feel he was asked to come, by angels.

Losing a loved one is hard. I hope and pray nobody else has to go through what I did. I felt my strength drain out off my body. I prayed to God telling him I absolutely could not carry this load. He has helped me. I prayed too, for God to forgive the people. They don't know what they are doing.

I also appreciated all our company, letters, prayers, and many a deed. Even little deeds of advice and encouragement for me. God's love is measureless. May God bless you all.

I want to share our poem about Levi. The girls' poem is from his three and a half years of disability until his death and mine is of his day of life.

In Loving Memory

Was a long sad year
  Since Levi died so dear;
Our family's day off on September 6,
  For a long time Levi was sick;
To Angola we went to a park,
  We all had a merry good start;
We all had been excited,
  Not realizing, we will get parted;
Levi was happy as a lark,
  Could almost see his eyes spark;
Picnicked, rides, and games to play,
  Levi enjoyed every bit of the day;
Didn't leave without eating either,
  On the way home. Levi to the Golden Shore,
Lord there's three more pleading,
  So don't forget your leading;
All the gossip, that was true,
  Lord forgive them, you love them too.
Levi we still miss you a lot.
  But you're so much better off with the gain you got.
With all the suffering that you had
  It's enough to make anyone sad.

We still love you-Mary Lou, Diane, Wanda Sue

We Miss You Dad-Levi R. Bontrager

Dad, how we miss you more than words can say,
Memories often linger when you went away.

First, the seizures came; We really couldn't tell,
Just what the problem was, but knew you were not well.

We'd call the ambulance time and time again,
To help you with your seizures; To go away again.

Once a seizure lasted four long, anxious days.
Doctors gave you medicine; Still Dad, there you lay.

You opened once your eyes, And tears began to roll.
The damage had been done; medicine took its toll.

You couldn't walk or talk Your mind was like a child.
Oh, the pain you went through All this long, long while.
We recall the day That they anointed you,
These memories are so touching As you, your vows renewed.

Mom was there to help you So you could understand.
Your brothers, sisters, parents, Gently clasped your hands.

You didn't seem to know us, we loved you just the same.
Looking forward to the day We'd take you home again.

Mom cared for you so much; Her heart would ache for you,
The tears she cried were many Not knowing what to do.

Mom did the best she could; She'd bathe, feed you and read,
While you lay there in bed Not knowing your needs.

Your strength came back again; That you could walk around,
"Family Time," was precious; Our love did so abound.

You'd feed your horses again; And help us here and there,
While Mom worked at the factory; To try and do her share.

Precious times were spent in going out to eat,
Or on a family picnic, which really was a treat.

We have so many memories of times with you, Dear Dad.
You did the best you could; This makes us very glad.

The last day of your life We went out to a park.
Then visited some friends; And didn't realize we'd part.

Suddenly a seizure came; The battle raged within,
Your soul was gently taken; You're free from cares and sin.

We tried to give you medicine, but it was all in vain,
Your end was here, life was gone. We hope to meet again.

People say what they will; They just don't understand
All about your illness; We feel it was God's plan.

The doctors said if Dad could choose the life he'd live,
You never would pick this Dad, this we do believe.

So, rest in peace, Dear Dad; God bless your weary soul,
We know you're up in Heaven; You're once again made whole.

We rejoice in knowing your life was not in vain,
You taught us many lessons; New insights we have gained.

We see the Grace of God; His understanding love,
Through trials, pain, and sorrow; God sent these from above.

It comforts us to know your health is now restored,
You're beckoning to us from Heaven's Open Door:

We'll do the best we can the things we knew we should,
And follow your example; Being patient, kind, and good.

Someday we hope to meet again with Angels in the air;
Then live with you in Heaven where all is bright and fair.

Your daughters, Diane and Wanda

Lydiann Stoltzfus: Mar. 12, 1989 - Aug. 9, 1994

Submitted by John & Elizabeth Stoltzfus, Honey Brook, Pennsylvania

It was a beautiful summer day in August, busy hay season. We had a lot of hay we hoped to bale. How little we knew what lay ahead. I washed in the morning; the girls played so nicely that I really didn't hear much from them.

They then helped me pick the first cantaloupe of the season. That was a big highlight for them, especially for Lydiann. She just loved cantaloupe and watermelon. We took a walk around the garden afterwards. Lydiann slipped her hand into mine. How precious! Little did I realize it would be the last time...

After lunch and a nap, the girls wanted to go watch the men

unload some hay. They had a great time. I went up to the barn to tell John I was going to the phone. Lydiann wanted to go along, but I told her not this time. Oh, why didn't I just take her with me!? I have to lay these thoughts aside and realize it was the Lord's will. This has been quite a battle for me.

While I was at the phone, John went back to the field to bring up another load of hay, and my 13 year old brother, Elmer, who was our hired hand, went to start the milking. The girls were jumping on the bales. With a hearty good-bye, Lydiann waved to her Daddy.

Elmer took Becca, our two year old, with him and let the other girls come along on their own.

Martha, our four year old, told us about what happened after that. Lydiann decided to climb down the ladder while Martha ran out the door and around to the lower level that way. They were racing to see which of them could get there first. We don't know why Lydiann decided to go down the ladder, she was not used to climbing the ladder.

After they were both down, Lydiann decided to climb back up. When she got to the top, she looked down to Martha and told her to come up, too. At that point she fell. She fell eight feet and landed on her head. We often think of other children that have fallen farther and were still OK.

Elmer heard some crying and came to see what was wrong. He told Martha to quickly go get her daddy. When John and I got there, Martha told us what had happened. Lydiann was crying, but we couldn't get any other response from her although we kept calling her name.

I told John to run for help and I picked her up. I don't know if I should have moved her, but it seemed so wrong to just let her lie there on the floor. She had no outward bumps or bruises. I have since been told that often makes it worse.

By the time I got to the house, she had stopped crying and her eyes were still. Oh, Lord, stay near us! We felt so helpless. Elmer was with me. It seemed like an awfully long time until help arrived. While we waited, I sponged her with a washcloth which made her gasp for breath. I felt her breathing get shallow, but I could still easily feel her heartbeat, so I had hope again.

The first fellow there said her pulse was normal. When the ambulance arrived, they soon decided that they would need to fly her to Phila. Children's Hospital. That was quite a blow. The helicopter was there in a short time. I can't describe the feeling of watching my child being put alone into a big helicopter to be flown to a hospital I had never seen.

John's mother came to stay with the girls. That made it easier for us to go, but I still felt so bad for the other girls. They just couldn't grasp it all. Elmer called my parents and asked them to meet us at the hospital. The poor boy was so scared. I'm not sure we can ever understand what he went through after we left.

A kind neighbor took us to the hospital. It was an hour's drive. On the way, we kept thinking that Lydiann would recognize us when we got there. We arrived at the hospital at 7:00.

We really appreciated our driver as he stayed at our sides so we wouldn't be alone in that big hospital.

They let us see her right away. What a shock it was to see her lying there with all those tubes and not being able to get any response from her. A doctor talked to us and told us she had moved her arms and legs when she had first arrived. He also told us she would probably never again be the same. I guess I didn't fully grasp what he was saying, so I can't say that it really bothered me.

Dads arrived about an hour later and then the tears really started to flow. It was so good to see someone we knew. When we finally got to see her again, quite a while later, we had another shock. She was on full life support. Oh, how we longed for a response, even just a little movement, but she just lay there, very still.

At midnight they told us that she was stable and we might as well go get some sleep. I kept thinking, in the morning she will wake up and everything will be OK. To say, "Thy will be done" was our wish, but it was so hard at a time like that.

At 3:00 they knocked on the door. How that tore through my heart. They told us Lydiann had taken a turn for the worse. They thought we might want to be close. It was hard to accept that this was happening. They said soon after we left she had gotten worse and they had worked for two hours to stabilize her again. That was when they came and got us.

They told us we had two choices. One was to do some more tests to be sure there was no life left in her brain, or we could have them just remove the machine. That was so hard to accept. We told them to do the extra tests and then called John's folks asking them to come down. It was a very hard forenoon, but well remembered. We talked and cried together.

At 11:00 they were able to tell us she was brain dead. Death is so final. We thought we had been prepared for this, but maybe that just isn't possible. After they removed the machines, we had some time alone to hold her. It felt so real, her body was still soft and limp.

Then they had a small prayer for us and we had to leave her at the hospital. It was so hard to leave her there, but I guess that is all part of letting go.

It was a shock to see so many people at our house when we got there. The girls came running with smiles, the innocent little ones. How could we ever explain this to them? It felt so good to hold them close.

They brought her body out at around 9:00.

We didn't get to bed very early, and my parents stayed for the night. We slept lightly until 3:00 when Martha awoke screaming. Oh, how reality hits in the dark. It was such a lift to have Dads there in the morning.

We made her clothes and dressed her. It was hard to imagine that it would be the last time. Little Becca just couldn't understand why we left Lydiann in the coffin. She came to me and said, "Mom, get her out." It is so hard to explain death to a little child.

It was a long day with many people in and out all day. It was touching to see so many friends. John's parents stayed with us overnight. At 9:00 in the morning we had a small funeral for the family and close friends. The sermon was very touching, soothing, and yet so heartbreaking. Then to see her four uncles carry the coffin out to the barn for the big funeral.

We came back to a house that was all back in order. That meant a lot. It was so hard to see our friends and family leave.

After that, the girls seemed in a daze. There were memories everywhere, sweet but touching. We had lots of company over the next few weeks. Neighbors and friends helped with the crops. Mail was a great pastime. How unworthy we felt.

After four months we were blessed with a healthy little boy, named David. What a blessing! It was joy mixed with sorrow. We felt it was soothing for the girls, how they cuddled him. Also, it was good for us to hold him in time of deep *zeitlang*.

After the baby arrived, the girls were finally willing to sleep upstairs again. Before that they were afraid to sleep upstairs. It makes one feel so helpless to watch one's children go through grief and not be able to help them more.

It has now been two years. It is hard to grasp. They say time is a healer, although we still have days of deep *zeitlang*. We hear of other happenings that make our hearts bleed again. We need the Lord's help in accepting His will as we know the Lord makes no mistakes.

Many thanks for all that was done for us. Our wish is to do likewise to others in need.

Albert Miller: Jan. 1, 1994 (date of tragedy)

Submitted by Abner Miller, Hartly, Delaware

There were six passengers in a van on their way to Kentucky, Wisconsin, and Michigan. With them were our sons Johnny, Albert, and Allen. The others were friends and cousins of theirs, Iddo Yoder, and Linda and Miriam Yoder.

At around 8:00 AM they were headed south on Interstate 81 about ten or 12 miles north of Harrisonburg, Virginia, in a van driven by Ale Schwan. They were in the right-hand lane, but were slowly drifting over into the left lane.

Johnny hollered, "Watch out!" but it was too late. He said later it was quite a feeling to see they were going to hit the guardrail and be unable to do anything about it. It just went crash, crash, crash. Everything happened so fast. He was wondering how was he going to get out of this alive.

According to the police report, the van flipped end over end, and spun around several times. This threw Albert, Allen, Iddo, Linda, and Miriam out of the van. Ale and Johnny had both been strapped in in the two front seats and so were still in the van when it came to a stop. It was on its top, about 150 feet from where it had first struck the guardrail.

Johnny remembers Ale saying something as soon as it was all over, but he can't remember what it was he said. Johnny's right hand was hurt a little, but otherwise he was OK. Ale was pinched in pretty tight. They had to cut the van to get him out.

Johnny got his seatbelt undone and found a way to crawl out of the van. The first person he saw was Miriam off to the right a little ways. He asked her if she was all right and if she knew where the others were. She started to get up, but collapsed back down again. He saw that there was something wrong with her leg.

He told her he was going to see if the others were OK. He could see a leg on the guardrail a little ways back, but couldn't see who it was from there. On his way there, he passed Linda who was walking around. Her shoulder appeared to be out of joint.

Next he saw Allen come walking up the embankment. Iddo wasn't too far from Allen, lying on the ground. It looked like he was trying to get up, but wasn't quite able.

Johnny kept on walking back along the guardrail to where Albert was lying. Albert was lying there with one leg on the guardrail and the other on the ground. He was gone. Passed away to a better land. Johnny asked Allen if he had seen Albert, and he said he had.

Soon after that, the police, fire trucks, and ambulance arrived. Everyone except Johnny and Allen were taken to Rockingham Memorial Hospital. The two of them were put in the police car to talk with the police. Allen passed out in the car, so he was taken to the hospital too. The police told Johnny to ride along in the ambulance and they would be in later to talk to all of them. Allen said later, he thought he passed out because of how warm it was in the police car.

It was several hours later when the police finally made it to the hospital to talk to them. The police told them that they should call home and let their families know what had happened. Sharing the bad news wasn't a very easy thing for them to do.

It is hard to think about Albert leaving the world in such a way, but we thank the Lord he didn't have to suffer. He no longer has to be in this sinful world, but he is sadly missed by the family.

Delmer Jay Lehman: Aug. 11, 1983 - May 6, 1991

Submitted by Ernest M. and Ellen Lehman, Middlebury, Indiana

On August 11, 1983 our sixth child was born, a son Delmer Jay. He was a very fussy baby while teething, with lots of earache problems. After he had his teeth, he was a good little boy. Over the next couple of years he was seldom sick. He was usually a happy little chap, needing very little discipline.

At age five, we had tubes put in his ears, because he was so hard of hearing, and again at age six. The second time Dr. Peers, an ear specialist, took out his adenoids too, in hopes of helping his drainage problems.

When he started having headaches we got his eyes checked. Glasses seemed to help at first and he wore them faithfully, but it didn't stop his headaches. Chiropractic treatments gave him relief from tightened shoulders and neck problems, but not for long periods of time. We noticed too, that he had poor balance and would often stumble and fall. He was very good-natured about it and usually just chuckled.

When the headaches were real bad he would throw up. We decided to take him to our family doctor who had checked him before, too. He ordered a CAT scan to be done at Goshen General Hospital. We went back to our doctor the same day to find out the results.

He said, "Your son has a cancerous brain tumor." What a blow! We had feared the worst, but it was such a shock to hear the truth. Delmer saw we were upset, so I asked him if he knew what we found out.

"You have cancer," I told him.

"Oh," he said, "I don't even know what cancer is."

It was a hard evening as we went home to tell our other children and the neighbors. Sleep did not come for a long time. We went to Fort Wayne the next morning where they had scheduled us to see a neurosurgeon. We saw Doctor Canavati and he wanted us to admit him to Lutheran Hospital right away. They put him in the Pediatric I.C.U where he got excellent care.

The next day they did surgery to put in a shunt to drain fluid from his brain. The tumor was in the back of his head, by the base of his brain, and fluid could not drain. This caused pressure and threw off his balance. Right after this surgery we noticed that his pupils dilated better. They planned to do surgery two days later to remove the tumor.

Delmer dreaded it so much, though he tried to be brave. It was a long six hours. He was in surgery as we prayed, "Thy will be done." The doctor told us later that the tumor was the size of an orange and they got all they could see. He said, "It's malignant and very aggressive, very apt to grow back."

Those were difficult words to hear! We were so afraid the surgery would affect his brain. We soon could tell his mind was clear when we went in to see him and we were so thankful.

He was so very sore for a long time. He had to relearn to sit up, hold his head, walk, and many other things. His left side was affected the most and he had to learn to control his leg and arm again.

Through all this, we had lots of help to carry on at home from family, friends, and neighbors. We also had many visitors and phone calls at the hospital. The prayers and support from our friends and loved ones could be felt. We appreciated it very much!

The physical therapists worked with Delmer to improve his coordination and balance. They did another CAT scan, a bone marrow test, a spinal tap and later an MRI to see if he might have cancer elsewhere. Everything showed negative.

We took him home after being there two weeks. He learned to walk again after two weeks at home. Doctor Canavati referred us to an oncologist to see about taking radiation and chemotherapy treatments. We went to see the doctor and were very disappointed to hear there was only a 50 to 60 percent chance of it not coming back. That was if he took all the treatments they recommended over a full year's time.

Knowing this and being aware of all the side effects he could have from the treatments, we had a very difficult decision to make. We finally decided not to give him any, after much prayer and talking with our families about it. We hated so to make him sick again, when he was now so full of energy and on the road to recovery. His headaches had disappeared completely. His eyes didn't quite work together after surgery, but it didn't seem to affect his vision much.

He felt so good and was his usual bouncing self all summer, trying to keep up with the rest. In August he had a baby brother, Wayne. Delmer was very enthused and spent lots of time with him. By fall he could ride his bike again and was ready to start school. At one time we didn't know if he would ever be able to go. He was in the first grade with seven other boys and one girl. Oh, how he loved school and his teacher! He did well in his school work and hardly missed any school.

During the first part of March he starting getting headaches again like he had before surgery, with his balance being off some, too. We had to accept it all over again as we realized it must have grown back. We called Doctor Canavati. He said he could do surgery again, but agreed with us that it would probably happen all over again. He could be paralyzed after another surgery or even brain damaged. He did prescribe medication to keep down the swelling of his brain. Delmer did not want to go back.

He had one real bad day in March. He couldn't keep anything down all day and had a bad headache. That evening his teacher brought him lots of cards from his schoolmates. She said they all prayed for him. He was treated extra special in school. The other children went out of their way to help him have fun and be a part. He got much better again and could go to school half days.

His spare time was spent writing, coloring, and playing with Karen, his tag-along. His chores were to get eggs and set the table if he felt like it. Sometimes he came in with some broken eggs after an encounter with the rooster. Every evening we had to guess how many eggs he brought in. He was usually cheerful and oftentimes singing.

This went on until the last week of school. He had been in church on Sunday. He skipped along ahead of us that morning, as always, anxious to go to church. On Monday morning he got ready to go to school, but couldn't go because of a bad headache. The pain relievers didn't help much that morning. We had asked for help from a hospice nurse, so she came out and started him on morphine for pain. He woke up several nights that week in awful pain. He would cry out if it was real bad and often said, "Oh my head!" We could control it somewhat with the medicine and he was so patient and brave.

Ernie took him to school for an hour or so one day. He was very tired, but happy, when he got home. He exclaimed so about the budding trees and the beauty of springtime. He came in once and said, "Mom, come here." He showed me a tulip just opening up. We had only one bright red tulip by the house that spring.

One night we woke up and Delmer was singing snatches of "Beautiful Home." Another time when I thought he had a headache he started singing, "Today is mine, tomorrow may not come. I may not see the rising of the sun." We realized we might soon have to part.

After this he was only up for meals and short periods of time. Noise began to bother him more, so we tried to be real quiet, talking in hushed tones. We had lots of callers through this time. Grandparents, aunts, uncles, and his little cousins and friends stopped by to see him, some about every day. Delmer was glad for everyone and we appreciated it too. He got many cards and small gifts and was always so willing to share. He liked to see little children happy so he would give them some of his candy or other goodies. When it hurt too much to be up, I fed him. He ate well and would comment on how good things tasted.

On Friday Daudy Lehmans came to see him. He missed the big dinner at school on Saturday. His teacher brought his report card over and told him he was ready for second grade. He had worried that he might not pass if his books weren't done.

Sunday was a hard day, with his pain real bad. He vomited quite often, not able to keep his medicine or anything else down. Vomiting made his headaches more intense and the pressure made his vision blurry. We prayed, "Lord take him home!" It was so hard for all of us to see him suffer so! He realized he had to go and talked some about heaven. His mind was very clear and he always knew who talked to him, though his eyes were mostly closed.

By evening the hospice nurse brought morphine suppositories for pain. At 8:30 he said he had no pain. Daudy Millers stayed until 11:30 so we could rest, then went on home. At midnight he answered me with a shake of his head. Again, he had no pain and seemed so relaxed. At 1:30 I noticed him breathing a little irregularly and with a rattle, snoring as if in a deep sleep. At 2:20 he passed away, so peacefully, without a struggle.

Praise the Lord, his pain is gone forever! One of our lambs is now where we all want to go. The Lord giveth, the Lord taketh away, blessed be the name of the Lord.

> *Jesus has taken a beautiful bud,*
> *Out of our garden of love.*
> *Borne him away to the city of love,*
> *Home of the angels above.*

> *...God can read each falling tear,*
> *He sees the heart that's needing cheer,*
> *He knows the path that's hard and drear,*
> *Don't give up for "He" is near!*

Left behind his earthly family: Parents: Ernest M. and Ellen Lehman, Brothers: Kenneth, 15; Steven, 14; Michael, 10; Wayne, nine months. Sisters: Noretta, 12; Lori, 9; Karen, 3.

The Saddest Homecoming We Ever Experienced

Freeman Lambright: Nov. 27, 1959 - June 26, 1995

Submitted by Chris J. Lambright, Shipshewana, Indiana

On June 20, 1995, we started out on a trip to Kansas. It was me and my wife, Anna Mae, and all five of her brothers and sisters and their companions. First we went to Kalona, Iowa, visiting there for a day and night with relatives and friends.

The evening before we had left, Freeman's and us, along with some of the other neighbors had been to Dale Fry's for an ice cream supper. Of course we had no idea that that might be the last time we would see each other. We would of course have wanted to make special "Good byes"; so little do we know.

The night after visiting Iowa, we went to Jamesport, Missouri, to visit old Bishop Dave Schrock and a few others well-known. From there we went to Kansas. This is the place where Anna Mae and her brothers and sisters were born. They partially grew up there with the oldest being 16 and the youngest being six when they moved to Indiana.

The reason for their move; the Government came and took all their land and buildings. The barn had only been a couple years old, and they had had time to take it down in sections and sell the lumber to other Amish families. The government wanted the land to make an Air Base for the Navy. That land is now all under deep cement and it is hard to tell just exactly where the buildings had been. Of course I and maybe a few of the others had never been there. Anyway, there's a larger area under cement now.

We looked around awhile and tried to think how we would feel if they would come and tell us we might as well quit plowing, they were going to take all our land and home, and we have to be out in a week or so.

We visited quite a few of the people living there and stayed over Sunday, planning to start home again Monday forenoon. We visited a few more people in the morning before starting home. I suppose that was about the time something serious was taking place at home. We traveled homeward until evening then stopped to sleep at a motel in Iowa.

One of the men called home to their family and received the awful news. "Oh, haven't you heard yet. Chris' Freeman was killed this forenoon."

We thought it couldn't be true! We couldn't eat, we couldn't sleep. Tears just rolled. Tears still roll as I'm writing this, a year and half later.

We tried to brace up the rest of the way home. We came home on Tuesday afternoon to a yard full of buggies, the house full of people and the bedroom full of children and grandchildren, wife and five children crying and crying. It was all so final. Yes, the circle was broken. God's ways are not our ways. I am hoping this was God's will, all to draw us closer to Him.

In Loving Memory of our dear Husband & Daddy

Five long months now are past
Since we saw your dear face last.
Oh! I'd like to hold your hand,
But trust you are in a better land.

On the 27th of November
Is your birthday, we'll all remember.
Husband, Daddy, brother, and son,
How we all miss you, "Dear One".

I'd really like to talk with you,
To ask you, "What shall I do?"
There are so many, many things,
And don't know what tomorrow brings.

Your singing voice so nice and clear
Makes me wish that you were here,
When I see your shirts and shoes,
I just think it can't be true.

There's so many things I so regret,
But think you'd say you could forget,
You were not the type of person to be,
To hold a grudge against anyone or me.

There's so many things I'd like to say,
But what else can I do but pray.
I know you'd say I am forgiven,
But oh! How my heart aches within.

And with God's help I want to try
And live better till I die,
And hope to meet you some glad day
Up in Glory Land not far away.

— Lonely wife and children

In Loving Memory of Freeman

Oh! My brother Freeman so dear,
How did we know your end was so near?
Never did I think the evening before
That I couldn't talk with you anymore.

In the morning I went to work at Jayco
When the news came down there, Oh! What a blow.
My brother Floyd called me, and said, "Home we must go,
Brother Freeman got killed." I just said, "Oh, no!"

Down in the field cultivating corn,
Then on his way home trying to beat the storm,
What were you thinking with the horses out of control?
We'll never know, God's taking care of your soul.

"Daddy! Daddy!" cried one little girl.
But already he was taken out of this world.
Now to be over on that beautiful shore
Where sorrow and pain shall be no more.

You didn't have to suffer, like some people do,
But still I ask, why did it have to be you?
But we all know, you are now from sin free,
Would I have been ready? It could have been me.

My parents were not at home at the time,
But friends and neighbors were helpful and kind.
I was looking forward when they would finally be home,
But what a sad reunion when they walked into the room.

Oh! My brother Freeman so dear,
Why didn't I help you more while you were still here?
Now to go on at home, I'll give it a try,
But sometimes, Oh! So hard, I just break down and cry.

Certain places, we miss you deeper,
Like in church, I can just see you watching the preacher,
Or singing the Lob song, such an effort you put in,
But we still all know, you're better off in Heaven.

One morning I was just walking along,
When I heard the girls sing this beautiful song,
The song they sang, my dear little Daddy-less nieces,
Was 'I Have Decided to Follow Jesus.'

Now on your birthday, five months will be gone,
Sometimes it seems it just couldn't be that long,
To me, he's talking louder than ever before.
Let's all try and be ready to meet him on that shore.

Since this happened, I think I cried almost everyday,
So 'zeitlang' and many adjustments along the way.
When I go into the house, you're not in your chair,
Or out in the field, you're just not there.

Oh! My brother Freeman so dear,
You always seemed to be in good cheer,
To help other people you went out of the way,
No matter what you already had planned for the day.

Sometimes I just stop, Oh! This can't be true,
How shall we go on without somebody like you?
If only we could even just touch your finger,
Precious Memories how they linger.

Each day I miss you more and more,
Oh! If only you'd be here like you were before,
Beautiful memories is all I have left,
Of my dear brother Freeman gone to rest.

— Sadly missed by your youngest brother, Jr.

"The Day God Called You Home"

We knew little that morning
God was going to call your name,
In life we loved you dearly
In death we do the same.
It broke our hearts to lose you,
You did not go alone.
For part of us went with you,
The day God called you home.

You left us beautiful memories,
Your love is still our guide.
And though we cannot see you,
You are always by our side.
Our family chain is broken
And nothing seems the same.
But as God calls us one by one,
The chain will link again.

— The Lonely Parents

In Memory of Brother Freeman

Two long months, Freeman, since we've seen you last.
How we still think we need you to help with our tasks.
But the good Lord could use you better than we,
So why wish you back, if you're from sin free.
The last time we saw you, we were there for supper,
Not giving it a thought, that this our last time together,
Oh! How we miss you, wherever we go,
But knowing this, it will always be so.
We can't put in words, how much we miss you,
And oh! The 'zeitlang' to talk with you too.
The hurtful look on your face, that always had a glow,
Is what makes my tears just overflow.
Lying in your coffin, looking so sound asleep,
But with your painful look, is what makes me weep.
Oh! Some days I think, it just can't be true,
Wondering why he chose someone special like you.
But we all know this, that it's all in God's hand,
So we want to give ourselves up, as this was His plan.
So let's put a period, instead of always question why?
Maybe we'll understand it all by and by.
We all hope the good Lord was in need of you,
If we small humans think it can't be true,
Our family circle is now broken and never the same,
But the Lord makes no mistakes, Praise His Name!
We all wonder, what you'd say that your wife is supposed to do,
With five little children and three going to school.
I'm sure they all wish that you'd still be here,
But they all brace them up, and are of good cheer.
There is a day coming that we all must go,
Are we ready? Or do we still have things we want to do?
Oh! Let's make ready to meet Freeman over there,
Where we all hope, he's in God's care.

— Mrs. Norman Lehman (His sister Katie)

In Memory of Brother Freeman

Dearest brother Freeman, thou hast left me,
And your face I no more see,
Empty bed and empty chair,
Oh! Brother, I miss you almost everywhere.

On June 26th, Freeman was out cultivating corn,
When up came this approaching storm,
He looked up in the sky, and said, "Well, I'd better go."
On his way home, God had something planned,
Apparently the horses took off and got out of hand.
He crashed into a tree, and he had to die,
Oh! I so often wonder Why? Oh why?
To Jayco came the sudden shocking call,
It seemed nobody could believe it at all.
However, homeward bound us three brothers did go,
Shaking our heads and telling ourselves it can't be so.
But when we got there it was plain to see,
They carried him away right in front of us three.
Oh no, what could we possibly do?
What seemed like a dream, was actually true,
We were so helpless, what were we supposed to do?
Mom and Dad were gone, and Vera was too.
So we kinda got together to comfort each other,
As we all three knew, we're really going to miss our brother,
But God makes no mistakes as we know,
Still we thought it could not be so.
But as time goes on, we might be able to understand.
Hopefully we may someday meet Freeman in that promised land.
Freeman often worked at a pretty fast pace,
But still had time for that smile on his face.
He was my brother and friend for 30 some years,
So please, forgive me when you see me in tears.
In our childhood days we were often together,
Played outside in all kinds of weather.
Many times I can picture us with one another,
So there's a reason, that I miss my brother.
The next couple lines is part of a song and rhyme,
I'm sure it was Freeman's wish as well as mine.
"Mein Gott! Ich bitt durch Christi Blut,
Machs nur mit meinem Ende gut."
Time does heal is what they say,
So let's just all Hope and Pray,
That we may someday all together be,
Up in Heaven as a happy family.

— Still Greatly Missed by a brother, Jerry

Jay Daniel Fisher: Dec. 16, 1982 - Sept. 27, 1991
Michael Fisher: August 25, 1976 - Feb. 18, 1995

Submitted by: John & Emma Fisher, Ronks, Pennsylvania

To walk away from the grave of your child is an experience you cannot easily put into words. For us, this was the second time that we had laid a child in his grave.

It's been said after a death that all partings are the same. Allow me to disagree. First of all, I feel that the parting between husband and wife are not the same as that of a parting between parents and a young child. Even that is different than the parting of a teenager.

The *finality* of death is the same, it makes no difference how death occurs. After death, the person is gone forevermore from our midst. Age makes no difference. Circumstance makes no difference.

But our thoughts, our consolation, and our acceptance of the death can depend a lot on how the death occurred. There is a big difference in our mental "peace-of-mind" of a young innocent child, versus that of a teenager or older child. This we have experienced.

We all know that a young child is innocent and need not answer or give account of his life here on earth, but where does this innocence end. Is there a certain age? Having lost a teenage son in such a circumstance as we have, has left this question heavy on my mind. That is where we must trust in the "Mercy of our Lord". Still the nagging question is not easily laid aside.

Time had a way of healing. Still that aching, longing feeling to have your child with you again is never far away. The 'zeitlang' can, and will, hit just as hard years later as at first. For me, to attend church or weddings where young teenage boys are present has been hard to cope with emotionally.

For some reason, this 'zeitlang' usually is more concerning the teenage son than our eight year old. Have we been able to accept Daniel's death better than Michael's because we believe in Daniel's innocence? Or perhaps because we did not expect Daniel to ever become "normal" again after his accident.

Perhaps I best explain our experiences. Daniel was six years old when he was struck by a semi on June 20, 1989. He was a patient in our local trauma unit for five and a half weeks. He had a severe brain injury, resulting in extensive brain damage. After leaving our local hospital, he was a patient for eight months at the A. I. DuPont Hospital for Children near Wilmington, Del. He was released on March 30, 1990.

In those eight months while at DuPont, there were only two days that no one of the family stayed with Daniel. Either I stayed at the hospital three days and Emma was at home, or she was there and I was at home. Occasionally, Mother would stay a few days so that Emma and I could both be at home at the same time. Our oldest girl at home was 11 years old at that time and so a lot of the housework became her responsibility.

At the time of Daniel's release, he remained completely handicapped. The only voluntary movements he had were with his eyes. It was in this way, by the blinking of his eyes, that we communicated. He was completely limp, couldn't hold his head, couldn't talk or smile and was fed by G-tube, a tube going directly to the stomach.

Otherwise he was healthy and outgrew three sets of clothing in the two years and three months that he lived after the accident. He showed no effects of his brain damage as far as facial or hand defects. This is very unusual for such injuries. He had his likes and dislikes and he had ways of letting us know about them! Just his facial expressions or body tone told us. He expected me to hold and rock him if I was in the house. Also, I had to hold him on my right side, the other side just would not work, nor was I to read the paper while holding him.

Around the first of August in 1991, he finally smiled for the first time. This was a major event! I found him on the morning of September 27th, not breathing, although he still had a heartbeat. It was a big shock, for we thought he was doing so well, but life had fled and nothing humans could do changed that fact.

The loss was keenly felt as we had spent many hours at his bedside or doing his daily care. My arms felt so empty and they actually hurt from 'zeitlang' to hold him again, but life went on. In all the time that he was in the hospital, I was never bothered with the thoughts of "Why us?"

There were many days in the hospital when he was so low that death did not seem far away. He survived those days and then died when we did not expect it at all. With prayers of friends and family, and with the grace of God, we were carried along day by day. Much more could be written of our days with Daniel and of his condition. As time went on, we more or less got back to a resemblance of a "normal" family. Still the vacancy of one child was deeply felt.

A little over three years had passed when we were awakened

around 4:00 early in the morning of February 17, 1995, with the message that Michael, age 18, was stricken ill and taken to the hospital with a very slim chance of survival. Only those who have ever been awakened at night with a message like that, know what a shock that is.

Michael had left home that Friday evening intending to spend the weekend at a hunting cabin in Potter Co., Penn., with his friends. The other boys thought he was sleeping as it was late at night. After six hours of driving they arrived at the cabin a little before 2:00 A.M. The others took their luggage into the cabin and then went out to awaken Michael, only to find him already cold in death. They tried CPR, but to no avail. He was pronounced dead at the hospital a short time later.

The doctor called it a diabetic seizure. We had not known Michael was a diabetic, but looking back we now see signs that should have alerted us. He had come home from his carpentry job very tired, had no appetite, was very sleepy, and drank a lot of water. On the last day of work he had left home without eating breakfast. He had had a headache, so he had taken four Tylenol, then again a second dose before lunch.

He hadn't eaten any lunch except for some chocolate candy. He hadn't eaten any supper that evening either, but ate some salted nuts later on. On top of all this, the boys were drinking a mixed drink of rum and coke. Both of these are very high in sugar. The doctor said his blood alcohol was not high enough that a healthy 18 year old would have been showing the signs of alcohol. We feel his sugar levels rose so rapidly, he never knew he was dying.

The shock, the unbelief, the heartbreak can hardly be put into words. To have your son leave home supposedly a healthy, vibrant youth and come home prepared for his grave is hard to find words to express our feelings. And there still are times when all this hits anew and is almost as hard now, as it was at first, to fully comprehend that it really did happen. Death is so final.

It was mentioned to us before the funeral that the experience we had had with Daniel would help us through this ordeal. Let me say this, experiencing a death of one of your children, or whoever it may be, is not easy. But at least the first time you won't know what to expect, nor realize how 'zeitlang' would hit so hard. The second time you know all too well what pitfalls are waiting "just around the bend". I found myself worrying needlessly about what I would do or how to deal with such and such. As I gazed at our son lying there in death, only my own shortcomings seemed to come to mind.

Another part that made Michael's death so different from Daniel's is that Michael left behind a very special friend. To see Linda suffer such heartbreak was very emotional. There was so little we could do to comfort her in her sorrow and bereavement. Also the boys who were with Michael are very special to us all. There is a bond between us that only those with a similar experience might perhaps understand. They continue to come from time to time and are much appreciated. They fill a void in our family.

We wish to express our sincere thank you to all who have been so supportive and understanding in our ordeal. We feel it is only through the grace of our Lord, and the prayers of family, friends, and strangers that helped us thus far.

Nathan Schmidt: April 1, 1985 - Oct. 26, 1994

Submitted by: Phenas & Effie Mae Schmidt, New Haven, Indiana
This part written by Effie Mae

It has now been over two years since we laid our dear Nathan in his cold grave. Little did we realize when he was born, that we would have him such a short time. He was born at 12:20 AM on April 1, 1985. It was a Monday.

He was a nice plump little baby with such a nice pink color, but his main valve was not opening and closing like it should have. At about 9:00 AM, my husband Phenas, my mom, and my aunt Effie Mae rode with the J. J. R. van to Riley Hospital in Indianapolis. There they had him checked out with x-rays, etc.,. They came home that evening around 9:00.

He was such a healthy looking baby you would have never thought there was anything wrong with him. They made another appointment about a month later to do some more x-rays, etc. Then they had us schedule to come back in December for a heart catherization test. We talked it over with both of our parents and others and they thought it would be best to wait a little to see if he might outgrow it. Such a test could be fatal. That suited us, too.

The doctors told us to watch for signs like blue lips, blue finger tips, and shortness of breath. In his nine and a half years he never showed any of these signs. He seemed just like a normal typical boy.

I often have to think, "What if he would have just showed some signs of something?," but he just never complained. There are a lot of *Why's?* I guess we shouldn't put a question mark where God puts a period. His ways are not our ways. We just have to think it was all for a reason. Not just for us, but for everyone. Often there are times I wish I could do things over when he was still with us on this earth, but what is done, is done. Now we can only learn from our mistakes, which I still often fall short. He was the oldest of five children and oh how we miss him.

This part written by Phenas:

It is hard to try and write about the death of our son since it is just a little over two years ago that it all took place, so suddenly and unexpectedly. I felt things, but really couldn't put them together.

For example, the last time Nathan went to church with us, I felt *so* heavyhearted that Sunday morning, but didn't know why. Also, during the last six to eight months of his life I had such a soft spot in my heart for him. I could hardly discipline him. If I did, I had to walk away in tears. I didn't feel good for about a week before it all happened. I told my wife that I didn't feel good, but really didn't know what was wrong. There were times that I would sit down at the table to eat with the family and it seemed like someone was missing. I would count them and we were all there. This happened different times before he died. My wife felt and had done the same thing, but we hadn't told each other.

We all started out the day like normal. Since I do carpenter work, I left for the job. I was working about five miles from school that day. During that forenoon at work I felt so heavy. I still didn't feel good. I had even told myself that I just didn't know what is wrong with me. I had decided to go home after lunch since I had things I could do to get ready for church.

Right about that time in school is when Nathan jumped up to catch the ball he and his friends were playing with and fell down. His friends thought right at the moment that he was just being silly, but soon realized that something was wrong.

The teachers were called out. They came to his aid with mouth to mouth, but no response. They called the EMS and my brother-in-law from school called my contractor. Then they called me on the job and told me one of the boys got hurt and I had to get ready to go home, he would be right out to take me.

As of then, I didn't know it was at school. It was such a shock when they called. My first thought was death, but I tried to push it aside. Then I had to think about what my father-in-law told me when their six year old son was killed. He had prayed, 'Unser Vater gebet'. I started to pace the floor with lumps in my throat. My eyes burned with tears, but I fought them back until my ride came.

When he arrived he told me, "It is Nathan, and he's probably still at school." We drove straight to school. Upon arriving at the school, it is very hard to put into words how I felt. I saw all the people and EMS' and on top of that there was a helicopter sitting in the school yard.

The first person I saw was my wife being supported by a neighbor, Ruth Schmucker. My wife came to me and told me, "It's Nathan, and they don't have any hopes for him."

It just threw me in a daze and shock. I saw I had to brace up to support my wife and two daughters that were also at school. I know I couldn't have held out if it wouldn't have been for the help from above. By that time they had him loaded in the helicopter and were leaving, so I never got to see him at school. We got a ride to the hospital and I was able to see him there. Life was gone and he looked so peaceful lying there.

This part written by Effie Mae:

The morning of Oct. 26, 1994, started out like any other morning. I was in the process of getting ready for church, which was supposed to be here the following Sunday. It dawned bright and clear with a heavy frost. We were still living in the summer house with plans to move back into the main house after church. I had things I wanted to get done before my sister Beth and Mary Schwartz, a cousin, came to help me that day. I was washing dishes when Nathan came in showing me how he plays basketball. He was going through motions. It seems I paid so little attention to him. He told me that the boys at school told him he was really good at it.

I had a dish with some table scraps I wanted emptied so I told Nathan to empty it. He took it without a complaint. I had a letter I wanted mailed so I asked him if he would put it in the mailbox for me. I thought he was going to tell me he didn't want to since they were always afraid they were going to miss the bus. But, he took it out of my hand and raced out the door and down the lane and mailed it. He then got on the bus never to come home alive again.

At about 11:45 we were just ready to sit down to eat lunch when a guy came from a nearby feed mill and told me that one of the boys had fallen at school and was unconscious. I knew it was Nathan as we had only one boy in school. Beth told me later that the guy said they had called the ambulance, but I didn't even hear him say it. I just couldn't believe that it was quite that bad. I figured he had bumped his head on the cement somehow and he would be all right again.

When I got to school and saw him lying on the gravel, I knew life had fled. The teachers, Jake and Sovilla Brandenberger, father and daughter, were out there and had him covered with a shawl. Oh! What a feeling that was to see him lie there and know there was nothing I could do.

The volunteers were working on him until the EMS came. I kneeled down by his head and ran my hands through his hair. I called his name, but got no response. The paramedics made me get back. I wish I would have just held him one last time. After all, he was my son! My youngest brother, James, who was in the eighth grade, went to call my husband.

I felt so alone! I don't know what I would have done hadn't it been for the support I got. Mom and Dad were so far away from home. They were on their way home from the Health Mines in Montana. My husband finally came and we went to the hospital where they put us in a quiet room till they brought us the word that our son had died. I can still hear those awful words.

A part of me just wanted to go with him. They then told us we could go see him before we go home. He looked so sweet and peaceful. If we could have just talked with him one last time. There is nothing more final than death!

I wanted to go home and not have to face anybody. I wanted to get on with our normal life, that was not to be. It never does get quite normal again. There is always one missing in anything you do or wherever you go. During the next three days we lived in a daze. We felt so numb. Friends, neighbors, and family took over our everyday living which we feel very thankful and unworthy for.

Phenas' folks came Thursday morning. Oh! What a relief it was to see one of the parents. That was about the first time we could both empty out and cry! It lifted our hearts to have them here. They live about 230 miles south of here in Salem, Indiana.

Grandpa Brandenbergers stayed here with us the first night. Then after that Phenas' folks and sister Wilma stayed here. We can't begin to thank everyone how we appreciated that! On Thursday afternoon, at about 4:00, they brought Nathan back. He looked so nice and peaceful in his casket, just like he was sleeping, but he didn't hear us talk with him.

My folks finally came home Friday morning at 11:00. What a sad homecoming, but I think my brothers and all were relieved to have them home. They took an autopsy of Nathan which showed he died from an enlarged heart. He didn't have that from birth, it just got that way throughout the years because of the valve not working right. They said his heart was like an old man's heart. It wore out! That just didn't seem right.

We estimated about 500 people viewed him Friday evening. The funeral was Oct. 29, at 1:00 PM. We had funeral in two places, in the house and in a 30' x 60' tent in the yard. In the house the funeral was conducted by Elmer Graber of Allen County. Ben Girod of Salem, Ind., conducted the funeral in the tent. With approximately 500 people attending, everything seemed like a dream.

On March 10, 1995, four and a half months after the funeral, we were blessed with a baby girl, Margaret. She will never have memories of her big brother. Then on April 1, 1995, our mare had her colt right on Nathan's birthday. He had really been looking forward to the colt. One of the last things Nathan helped my husband do was get the box stall ready for the colt. We had put up some kick boards.

Our graveyard adjoins the school playground where our children go to school. Sometimes it keeps the memories a little too fresh.

We had a lot of company after the funeral. We found out there are a lot of caring people in this world. Thanks to all! We now again have six children: Frances, ten; Laura, nine; Kristine, seven; Phenas Jr., six; David, four; and Margaret, one.

Martha Miller: Feb. 27, 1980 - Aug. 10, 1980

Submitted by Mr. & Mrs. Lester L. Miller, New Haven, Indiana

On February 27, 1980, we had a little girl named Martha. She weighed seven pounds and ten ounces. She looked healthy and was chubby. She had two older sisters named Rachel and Elizabeth Ann and one brother named William. Two years later she had another sister named Esther.

Martha always sweated a lot and always had a rash. She ate pretty good and she cried every time I gave her a bath. She also cried a lot when she was held. She never played with toys. She always played with her hands. She always had a smile even when she didn't feel her best.

On Tuesday, August 5, 1980, she had a doctor appointment for her six months check up. I asked the doctor different questions. He didn't seem to like it very much that I was asking all those questions, but he checked her really well and said he couldn't find anything wrong with her.

On Thursday she was very fussy and Lester held her most of the day. Every time she was sleeping, he tried to lay her down and she would start crying again. I was trying to get my work done so I could go see Rosa Nusbaum the next day. She was bedfast and I had planned to help Mom take care of her. On Thursday evening Lester had a horse to shoe yet and when we went to bed that night she was quiet, but wasn't sleeping. I woke up around 3:00 and checked on her. Again, she was lying there not sleeping. We don't know if she slept any or not. I went back to bed and when we got up in the morning I checked her again. She was breathing real hard and her face was all sunk in. We knew something was seriously wrong so I didn't give her a bath that morning.

Friday morning I started over to Rosa Nussbaum's place, but first I stopped at my oldest sister's to leave the other children there and I told her I thought something was wrong with Martha. When I got to Rosa's place I asked Mom to look at the baby. She said we should take her to the hospital.

We took her to the hospital and they put her on IV and our family doctor got a specialist. Then they put her on the sixth floor, but she wasn't there very long before they put her in an intensive care room where she could get more attention. On Saturday night the nurse sat her up to feed her and she just cried. When the nurse laid her back down again she was quiet. That was the last time we heard her cry.

On Sunday afternoon we were sitting in the waiting room and saw the nurses were getting a little uneasy. Then we saw Dr. Castor go by the waiting room real fast and throw his coat on the desk. We stepped out and saw the doctor grab the baby out of the incubator. We went back into the waiting room and waited. It wasn't long until they came and said her heart had stopped, but they got it going again.

They put her on the respirator and Dr. Castor turned her over to Dr. Lewis. He just takes care of small babies. She was bigger than his usual patients, but he still took care of her. He was very concerned.

We noticed he was on the phone a lot, calling other doctors to find out what her problem was. As long as she was up there he didn't leave the room. He questioned us closely about green beans and honey. After a while there were about six other doctors standing around the desk having a meeting.

At around 8:00 Sunday evening, Dr. Lewis came and told us they had taken different tests and found she had sugar diabetes. Her sugar was up to 1300. They gave her real strong medication and got it down to 350, but then she started having jerks from the strong medication.

Before all this they had been sticking her every hour to take blood samples for tests. They had stuck her so much they couldn't find any more veins as they kept collapsing. So on Monday they did surgery on her arm so they could put a tube in to feed her. She went into a coma then.

Her heart stopped a couple of times, but our family doctor came and told us her brain wasn't damaged yet and they wanted to do all they could. When it stopped the third time, my dad walked up there and saw what they were doing and told them to leave the machines off. Dr. Lewis came in and told us he thought it was a good idea to take the machines off.

They told us to go up to the crib. They took the machines off. She was gone right then. We could just see the color leave her. That was at 4:00 Monday afternoon. They let us hold her for quite a while. Lester didn't want to hold her and to this day he says he doesn't know why he never did. He's sorry that he didn't hold her. He wishes he would have.

We asked the Lord for His will. If it was His will to leave her with us as a sick child for her lifetime we would have been glad to care for her. But if it was His will to take her home to Him, we were glad to give her into His hands. We know she went to a happy home that will be forever.

As for us, we don't know where we will go. We know we will go to a home forever, but is it Hell or Heaven? We don't think any of us want to go to Hell, so let's do God's will and hope we can get in just a little corner of Heaven. Let's not forget God. He gives and He takes. Let's live His will, not our will.

She still had her smile when she was lying in her casket.

Noah E. Barkman: Nov. 6, 1977 - Jan. 22, 1996

Submitted by Eli A. & Ada Barkman, Fresno, Ohio

It was a nice winter morning on January 22, 1996, with the temperature in the low 20's and a light cover of snow on the ground. The boys went to work as usual: Vernon and Melvin here at our engine shop; Roy at Crawford Manufacturing; Robert and Eli Jr. at K and B Lumber; and Noah went with his employer, Daniel E. Stutzman, and another employee Ivan D. Hershberger to cut timber on the Bruce Bickel farm in the Bakersville area. That is about 15 miles from home.

Amanda helped me start the laundry, then she also went to work in our shop and I finished the laundry. Maryann cleaned the Sunday shoes and straightened up the house. Since it was such a nice day, we decided at noon that Amanda and we would go to our acreage about three miles south of here, where we built a Kootenai log house, and do some varnishing.

Maryann stayed at home to take care of the laundry. Amanda went to the phone to call in some orders just before we left. She said she had never had a time like this before to call. She didn't know at the time yet, what was wrong or why it went just so and so. We weren't at the log house very long and had just started to varnish, when a paramedic and our son Vernon came and brought us the most shocking news we had ever heard.

The paramedic said he had received a report of a logging accident that Noah was involved in and it appears it killed him instantly. Amanda and I were upstairs. I was just listening to see if I could figure out who was there. I thought I heard what he said, but to make sure, I went down the cellar steps about halfway and asked him if he said it killed him. He said, "Yes, I'm sorry, Mom."

He said Noah had already been picked up and taken to Coshocton Hospital and handed us a business card with the doctor's name and phone number and said we should call him. He also asked if there was anything that he could do for us. We can't explain the feeling to anyone that hasn't had such an experience, and couldn't think of anything for him to do except take Vernon down to his home and tell his wife what had happened.

We just stuck our brushes in a small bucket with water, closed the varnish containers, hitched up our team and went home. What a meeting to come home and meet the other family members on an occasion like this. Eli called the doctor soon after we were at home.

He said he didn't know if Noah even had any broken bones, but he wanted to take some x-rays yet that evening. He also wanted to know which funeral home we wanted. It was then stated in the Coshocton Tribune the next morning that he had died from a broken neck.

Daniel and Ivan stopped in soon after we were at home and explained to us as well as they could how they think it happened, since no one saw it happen. Daniel later wrote a story of the accident, so I will now give it.

I had the boys start cutting on a fence row of young cherry-elm and some oak trees. The location was north of the house about 200 yards with the fence row running east and west. After they got started, I went south of the house where they had piled some pine logs and started cutting them shorter for hauling.

Around 10 o'clock I was done and went back to the fence row to start skidding logs out of there. The boys came over a little bit later and we took a short break. The boys said they might try to finish cutting before they quit for lunch. I said that was all right as I will keep on skidding through lunch time because it was starting to thaw.

Everything was going good when I happened to glance back to check on my skid of logs and noticed Ivan come running over the hill from where they were. I stopped and Ivan came over and told me a tree fell on Noah. I thought, Oh no! and asked a second later, "What should we do? How bad or serious does it appear to be?"

He gave me the shock of my life when he said he didn't think he was living anymore. My first instinct was to call 911 for help. The time was approximately 1:10 - 1:15. I ran to the house and was lucky that someone was at home. Mrs. Bickel called 911 and I ran back to where the boys were cutting.

Ivan moved the dozer and the logs off the road so the squad could get in. When I got back to Noah, I was hoping for any sign of life. I checked his pulse and skin color and saw that I couldn't help him anymore. Ivan came back a little later and we tried to determine what might have happened during the longest 20 minutes we ever had while waiting on the squad. First a paramedic came in and checked him and told me there is nothing he can do for the man. The squad came soon and took a look at him too, but they couldn't help him either.

They called the coroner and we had to wait on him yet for about another 35-40 minutes. While we waited, they and we checked things out, and thought we might have figured out what had happened. After the coroner was there, he called a detective yet to check everything out before they moved him. Finally after about two hours or so, they moved him to the squad and took him to the hospital.

It appears he was cutting a small cherry tree and it fell into a nearby elm tree. As near as we can tell, he then cut the elm and as it went down, the cherry tree fell on him as he was getting out of the way. How things happened, we will never know for sure, but we all had to think it was the Lord's will. May we learn a lesson and be ready when our time comes.

We greatly miss Noah at work and the help he had provided. There will be no other like him.

— *By Noah's employer, Daniel E. Stutzman and family*

We too greatly miss him in our home, but we try to accept it as the Lord's will and hope our loss is His gain. We know what the Lord does is well done and makes no mistakes like we do. Neighbors, friends, and relatives showed much help and concern at this time which we are very thankful for.

His funeral was held here at home on January 25, with some over 400 people attending. The sermon in the house was by Levi Nisley from Iowa, Emanuel Helmuth from Wisconsin, and Bishop Aden N. Yoder. The sermon in the shop was held by minister Abe D. Miller and minister Roy A. Troyer. Pallbearers were Roman J. Mast, Neal D. Miller, Ivan J. Miller, and Owen A. Yoder. Ivan and Owen are the boys that used to sit on each side of Noah in church.

Noah was buried about a mile from home on the Alvin Barkman farm. This cemetery was started in Sept. 1951. My father, Jonas N. Stutzman, age 34, was the first one to be buried there. He fell from a ladder while picking apples and also died from a broken neck.

My mother, Lovina (Beachy) Stutzman, age 59, died in August of 1967 from pancreas trouble. Eli's father, Albert D. Barkman, age 68, died in April of 1994 from a lingering illness of Alzheimer's disease. Eli's oldest brother, Robert, age 61, died the day before Thanksgiving, also in 1994 from a blood clot. He had had hip replacement surgery a few weeks earlier. Then Noah left us so suddenly at the tender age of 18 years, 2 months, and 16 days.

He is survived by his bereaved father and mother, five brothers:

Vernon married to Ella M. Stutzman of Fresno, Ohio, Melvin, Roy, Robert, and Eli Jr. all at home; two sisters Amanda and Maryann also at home; one nephew; two nieces; and many friends and relatives.

He was our youngest son with one sister younger than he was. We have been richly blessed with visitors, sympathy cards, letters, nice poems, and food brought in since the passing and funeral of our dear son. We want to express our sincere thanks for it all.

Death is a heartache
No human can heal.
Memories are keepsakes
No human can steal.

Steven Ray Miller: May 13, 1993 - Feb. 28, 1994

Submitted by: Polly Miller, Topeka, Indiana

The day, May 13, dawned bright and clear like a summer day often does. People were going off to their jobs like usual, but David stayed home because we were going to the hospital to have a baby.

What joy, we were expecting and had prepared for our firstborn and were anxious. Also it was our first anniversary. What more could we want? We were only at the hospital a little while before they said they would have to take our baby. Surgery had been the farthest thing from my mind when leaving to go have our baby.

Upon coming out of surgery, the nurse and my husband were by my side, saying we had a son, but he weighed only 3 pounds 11 oz. and was 15 inches long. He needed to be transferred to South Bend Hospital. Why?? Why?? Dear God, what did we do wrong? But no questions to be asked. God knows best.

The phone calls started coming, but how could we explain? Many prayers were sent upward; was our son going to be okay? I called the hospital often during the day and they told me of some improvements.

The day came for me to be released from the hospital. But oh how it hurt to go home without our baby. My arms were aching to hold him. I had only been allowed to touch him before he was transferred. A week went by before I was allowed to make a trip to South Bend, not realizing what to expect.

There was our baby, oh so tiny, with tubes all over and looking to us like a long recovery to gaining and growing. We never realized some of the pain he would have to endure. He was so lovable and sweet, yet again we had to leave him there. It was comforting to know that he had good nurses caring for him and the good Lord watching over him and giving us strength to go on.

He spent three weeks in the hospital. We went to see him every other night and weekends.

The day arrived to bring him home, oh dear Lord, give us the strength to care for this child you have entrusted to our care. He was on oxygen to bring him home. He had medicines and many different doctor appointments to meet. Still only weighing three and one half pounds, he had a hard time gaining, yet he ate well.

It sure was nice to be a family all together at home. He needed special care, but I was so thankful he was with us. Days turned into weeks, and weeks into months, with monthly checkups in South Bend and Goshen.

He was still not gaining fast, yet he was the most content baby. He started playing with some toys at three months, but the older he got the less active he was. Oftentimes I asked the doctor, "Is there anything wrong with our child?" Why doesn't he gain and start being more alert and active. The only thing he would do was he'd always smile for us. He was just the size of a newborn, but was older. The doctor said he'd snap out of it and start growing one of these days. Well, you want to believe what the doctors tells you, but . . . we were beginning to wonder if they are not telling us something.

When he was seven months old, we took him to Indianapolis to Riley Children's Hospital as his kidneys were not working right anymore. The doctor checked him and scheduled him for surgery January 21, 1994. This was a month away as they weren't in over the holidays. Christmas was hard, knowing our only child had to again be hospitalized, yet we wanted to do all we could for him. I don't know if I could explain some of the feelings I had while spending time at home and caring for our loved one. People were really nice in sending cards and encouragement.

The day came when we had to leave for the hospital. They were expecting to keep him two to three days. Both of our moms went with us. We checked in at the Ronald McDonald House and got our room, spending the night before taking him to the hospital the next morning.

Never will I forget the feeling of handing our child over to the nurses to be taken into surgery, not knowing how he would survive it. He was away from us for six hours. Nurses reported every now and then on how he was taking it. He pulled through okay and was taken to recovery. Well, we thought, now everything is okay and we can take him home and our lives will be back to normal again.

Then they said they were going to run tests and keep him till they could find out why he was not growing like he should. David went home to go back to his factory job and the mothers stayed with me. Their presence helped me tremendously. Every day prayers were said.

Being only human, you sometimes wanted to question why? Why? We are too young, but again knowing He chose us for the parents and we loved Steven so. I could feel His presence, helping me along, for alone I never could have gone on. They ran tests and tests again, only to have them come back and showing nothing serious yet.

There was a small hope that maybe there was nothing wrong. He needed oxygen now most of the time and was given a feeding tube down to his stomach. He had a strong little heart, yet was so weak he slept most of the time. Through the test they found heart murmurs, hernias, and cataracts in both eyes. What else could be wrong with our son? He was slowly losing out, oh how could it be?

So they said one more test, a brain scan. I was in our room, with Steven sleeping in his crib, and the mothers were there too when the doctor came with the results. "Your son has Lissencephly. An illness of the brain, mentally retarded, and usually a life span of birth to 2 years." He said most don't survive birth, but Steven was given life and we were granted him to love, hold, and have with us. He said there was no cure. No, I can not explain what my feelings were, only again, why? Why? David would call every day to see how he was doing. Well, that evening I had to tell him the sad news. Oh how hard. Yes, we want to accept.

David again made arrangements to come down and stay till Steven could be released. The doctors said since there was no more they could do, we could take him home and care for him at home. I had learned everything anyway.

Many friends came to visit. It was so wonderful to have people who care. Caring for Steven took more special care than any other baby, but he was so content, hardly ever fussed and slept a lot. So we held, talked, sang, and read books to him a lot.

The days went on and we got back to a normal schedule, we just hardly ever went away. We only took him to church three times. We were home three weeks from the hospital and he was still with us.

Monday morning, February 28, 1994, came and my mom and three of my sisters came for the day. We made donuts and had a good day together. Steven was very restless and wanted to be held a lot. They went home, but I felt uneasy, for I felt that he might not make it through the night. At 4:00 he started breathing harder all the time, so I told David to contact both parents to come and be with us. We got company that night, but said we'd rather they wouldn't stay, except sister Ruby and her family were along so they stayed. Both parents came and he was slowly losing out. I fed him at 8:00 and I was holding him all the time now. At 8:20 he relaxed and life was gone. I was holding our baby and yet there was no life anymore.

"Our baby, our baby", was not meant to remain here with us anymore. God had called him home to the wonderful place where he need not have any more pain; but pure happiness. Neighbors came to prepare for the viewing and funeral.

Numb! Feelings to cope with. Empty crib. Empty everywhere. All his clothes and gifts. What do we do? Arms that ache to reach into his crib and hold him.

Yes, this was reality, we had to move on. God was a very present help indeed. Many friends, family, church people, and neighbors came to show their sympathy. The funeral was held with a fair attendance. After the funeral everyone went home and we were *alone*.

Friends visited, many cards were sent, yet the pain of loneliness was still there. The months went on and we still missed him every day. Now two and a half years have gone by and not a day goes by that we don't think of our dear Steven with loneliness and a longing to hold him once more. But we can say, oh how beautiful Heaven must be, for he is so happy and carefree. May we meet him on the Golden Shore.

God has since granted us a daughter to take care of for Him. Sweet, lovable, and so healthy, but never will she replace the special place Steven has in our hearts. Each child is special and unique in their own way. May we daily live for Jesus to meet our loved ones by and by.

Noah M. Troyer: Oct. 31, 1956 - March 28, 1974

Submitted by: Mahlon & Erma Troyer, Sugarcreek, Ohio

This brings back many precious memories, but with God's help we will do the best we can.

It was on March 28, a nice spring morning when Mahlon and Noah left for work as usual. They picked up Ben and Levi Yoder who also worked at the sawmill. The sawmill was a few miles from our place.

They each started their own work as usual. Each one had their own work to do. Mahlon and Ben were busy working in the lumber yard while Noah was operating the fork lift and accidentally backed too close to the edge. It tumbled off the loading dock, pinning him underneath. Nobody was there to see it happen.

A few minutes later a man in a pickup drove in to buy sawdust and saw what had happened. He went and told Levi and then Levi went to tell Mahlon, which was not easy. They don't think Noah found anything out as it happened, oh, so quick.

This happened just before dinner. In the meantime, our daughter Mary, was at home from school not feeling well in the morning. She was wanting to go by noon, so we had dinner early. She was upstairs getting ready and I was just done with the dishes, when two men came up the porch steps.

I saw right away it was the workers from the mill. I just knew something must have happened. I thought I couldn't open the door, but when I did, they just about couldn't talk. Oh, what a shock. I wasn't myself. It was a good while until I finally asked, "Is it my husband or son?"

They said "Your son. They think he is gone."

I thought it just couldn't be. "Where is my husband?"

They said he went along with the squad to the doctor. It must have been an hour and a half before he got back. That was the longest hour I ever had.

The doctor thought he died of a broken neck. There wasn't a scratch on him. The neighbors came from all directions. Oh what would we do without neighbors at a time like this.

After the men left, they stopped at the school house and told our son Willis he was supposed to go home, not telling him why. He just couldn't think why he should go home. Then when he came and saw all the neighbors there, he soon found out.

The funeral was Sunday with lots of young people. Noah and two of the neighbor boys were very close, always together. He was not with the young folks yet.

He was 17 years old. In March it will be 23 years since the accident happened. It was a day we will never forget. We feel it was the Lord's will. He had one brother and one sister both married and each have a nice family; six nieces and five nephews. God makes no mistakes.

Mahlon's brother and family lived across the road from us. About six weeks later his wife died of cancer leaving him and their three children. So again the viewing and funeral were here. He has married again and has a nice big family.

Wishing all our sorrowing friends God's blessings.

Ronald Ray Miller: Dec. 16, 1958 - Apr. 24, 1970

Submitted by Wilbur & Emma Miller, Bunker Hill, Indiana

It was a beautiful spring day, April 24, 1970. My husband, Wilbur and I were hurrying to get our work done so we could go with two other couples the next day on a weekend trip. We had been rolling the yard. Ronnie wanted to continue but my husband said, "You come with me to do some grinding."

We lived on the farm, milked cows, and had a few chickens. We have four other children, Jerry, Marcia, David, and Stanley. Ronnie was the youngest. Jerry was in the barn. David and Stanley were doing small chores, Marcia was in the house with me.

When Wilbur went to grind, he sent Ronnie up into the oats bin overhead to push the oats to the hole and down into the grinder. When Wilbur had enough oats he moved to the shelled corn bin, also overhead. Everything was going as it should and the grinder was almost full, when the corn quit coming.

Immediately Wilbur thought of Ronnie being up above. He crawled the ladder as fast as he could, the grinder still running. There was a rope over the corn bin, pulled tight down into the corn. He laid down on the corn and pushed his hand along the rope and found Ronnie's hand. Ronnie pulled on his dad's hand so it meant he hadn't been in very long. There is no way you can pull someone out of a vacuum like this.

Wilbur quickly ran to the house, calling as he came, "Mom, call for help. Ronnie is in the corn bin!" I got on the telephone and called neighbors, friends, relatives and soon the yard was full of vehicles and everyone was there to help.

Grandpa Miller said, "Get the chainsaw to saw the floor out of the bin." A neighbor grabbed the saw as Wilbur couldn't carry it and he soon had a hole sawed but oh my, where was Ronnie's body? Would the saw hit him?

The corn seem to flow so slow and then it was down where they could see him. The hole had been cut on the other side, so his body wasn't touched by the chainsaw. Thank the Lord for that.

A neighbor girl had just graduated from nursing school and she went up the ladder and jumped in the bin. She gave him CPR till her lips were sore and blistered. Others tried too, but Jesus had come and taken him to Heaven.

The ambulance came and took him to the hospital where the doctors pronounced him dead. We felt this just couldn't be happening to us. It always is someone else, but yes, our youngest child was gone.

When we got home the house was full of people. Helping hands were everywhere, we didn't have to think about chores or food. Then we did have to make funeral arrangements. Oh my, who do we call first? My father and brother were in Switzerland, but were to come home the day before the funeral. Another brother contacted them and they came to Indianapolis instead of Florida. How glad we were for family and friends again.

The viewing brought over 1,000 people. Wilbur did a lot of farm work for others in the community, so he was well-known. The next day at the funeral there were 500. Ronnie's classmates from school sat in a group at the front of the church. Then they carried the flowers. What a touching scene. Our lives have not been the same since, but we know God knows best and we rest assured Ronnie is with Jesus in Heaven. Some day we will meet him there. What a day that will be!

Aden Schlabach: April 25, 1984 - Dec. 20, 1989

Submitted by Alvin & Lucinda Schlabach, Sugarcreek, Ohio

December 20, 1989, was a very cold and snowy day, but it started out as usual. My husband went to work and the children headed off to school. I cleaned Sunday clothes and washed off the bedroom since we were to have church in a week and a half. The children colored in the forenoon, like they often did, never knowing what God had planned for us till the day was over.

A week before, while coloring, David, Aden's younger brother, had said "Aden will become an angel." A sting went through my heart since they already had a cousin Noah in eternity. I said, "You mean Noah is an angel." But he did not answer me. I guess I was not ready to accept something like that. Why do we want to push it aside when God speaks to us like that?

The day went on and the school children came home. Jonas went choring and often took Aden along. Aden was a cheerful boy and often played alone. Amos, Ivan, and David played in the snow. The girls helped me get supper ready for the children since Alvin and I had intended to go to a Christmas banquet. Alvin came home from work and went into the shop. The children came in to warm themselves. I can just hear Aden saying to David when they went out again, "Won't you go along?", and David said, "No". Little did I realize these will be the last words I would hear Aden say.

Ivan was sledding and Aden asked if he may ride with him. They went down towards the barn with Ivan lying on the sled and Aden kneeling over him. A gas truck pulled into the alley beside the barn. The boys didn't see the truck and the truck driver didn't see the boys. They hit the truck's front wheel and they flew off the sled. The truck's back wheel went over Aden's right leg. Aden hit the truck hardest because he was kneeling on top.

As Alvin was coming out of the shop to go in and get ready to go away, Grandpa called his name and said he thinks there's been an accident down by the barn. He ran down and oh what a sight to see the two boys lying there. Ivan was crying and Aden was about eight to ten feet away, not moving at all. He had a slight heartbeat yet. The boys were put on blankets in the barn. I didn't know anything was wrong until Grandpa came running up the cellar steps and said Aden was killed while sledding. I just ran for the barn without putting on more clothes in zero degree weather.

The truck driver called the squad. We lived in town and soon many neighbors were there. One offered me her coat and scarf. Two squads came and they worked on Aden awhile to get his breathing and heart going. He was put in the Baltic squad and I went along. They put Ivan in the Sugarcreek squad and Alvin went along. Both went to Millersburg Hospital. Miller Doddys living with us got a neighbor and picked up Schlabach Doddys and they came out to the hospital too.

The doctor came and asked permission to take Aden to Akron, so we gave him permission. Soon they came back and said his heart had stopped beating and there was no more hope. It was a shock, but we were thankful he didn't have to suffer. They took x-rays of Ivan's leg and sewed three stitches above his eye. After they cleaned up Aden, we went in to see him. Now we could feel how others have felt.

While we were at the hospital, Alvin's sister came walking in to see us. She was visiting her husband's dad. My first words were, now we know what you went through. Their son had died suddenly in March.

We had left home leaving the children with the neighbors. I often wonder how the children must have felt until we came home again.

This happened Wednesday evening around 5:00. The funeral was Saturday and Christmas was on Monday. Then the next Sunday, we had church. Without the neighbors and relatives and God's help, we couldn't have gone through all this.

Two weeks later, David stood on a chair and asked, "How did Aden look in the barn?" Sometimes when we had company, he crawled up on my lap and acted nervous. That showed he was lonesome and needed attention. Then it was time to help him look at a book.

One evening while one of the girls and I were washing, she said she had seen a smile on Aden's face while he lay in the casket. I had seen it too, but hadn't said anything to anybody, because I figured I had just imagined it. As I write this, it seems just like it happened yesterday.

We often think of him being in heaven with the angels and hope we can all meet him someday. We all have precious memories of him.

Frieda Yoder: Oct. 31, 1983 - February 1984

Submitted by: Jonas & Verba Yoder, Fredericksburg, Ohio

Greetings in the name of the Lord Jesus Christ. As we sit here and try to put our thoughts into words, it is hard at times to describe.

When we go back to the year 1983, we were blessed with a baby girl named Frieda. She had one sister, Rosanna, three years old and a brother Myron, one and a half years old, who also welcomed their little sister.

On October 31, she was born with her bladder on the outside and her pelvic bones weren't grown together. We had to put a clean Vaseline gauze pad on her bladder every time we changed her diaper. Doctors planned to do surgery, but then decided to wait till about one year, until her bones grew stronger. She was in Akron Children's Hospital where she stayed six days to have blood and dye tests done. Then we brought her home and what a joy and blessing to be at home as a family again.

Frieda was a healthy girl as far as we knew. She weighed eight pounds, one ounce and her appetite was good, although she kept having diarrhea all the time.

We will now write part of a poem:

Five times she went to church with us,
As health and weather would permit.
How thankful we shall always be,
As often we still think of it.

Whenever we would talk to her,
She was content and brave.
Little did we know how soon she'd be
Resting in her little grave.

Her last day of life on earth
We all went to church together,
From there we went to Doddy Yoders
For a visit and stayed for supper.

She did not seem to want her bottle,
That night when we put her to bed,
At two o'clock she would wake up,
For the last time to be fed.

Then Monday morning came along,
The ground was covered with snow,
Not suspecting things unusual,
So on our toils we'd go.

Dad had left to go to work,
Mom had her washing to do,
Rosanna was up and getting dressed,
Myron was in bed yet, too.

But first, I'd check the baby yet,
  She lay so quiet in her bed,
Oh, what shock to find it so,
  But little Frieda's life had fled.

Friends and neighbors gathered here,
  Each one with a helping hand,
To share with us in time of sorrow,
  The things we may not understand.

Three months and six days she stayed with us,
  Our hearts still often ache,
But we want to accept whatever,
  God can give and God can take.

Frieda's funeral was held on February eighth,
  The day we bade our last farewell,
And all the kindness shown to us
  Is more than tongue can tell.

She has gone to be with Jesus,
  Where the streets of gold are laid,
Where the tree of life is blooming
  And the roses never fade.

Let us prepare to meet her there,
  Where there will be no setting sun.
Let's all accept to do His will,
  And gently say, "Thy will be done."

Mark J. Miller: Jan. 5, 1969 - July 3, 1984
Vernon J. Miller: Mar. 15, 1961 - June 5, 1987
Joshua J. Miller: July 17, 1970 - Aug. 2, 1995

Submitted by Mr. & Mrs. John C. Miller, Newcomerstown, Ohio

I will try and write about our three boys. They were all so healthy and so soon gone. Sometimes it still seems like a dream. But we feel it was God's will, so we want to be in His will and accept what He has for us. Although it is hard at times, the Lord gives us grace as we need it. Pray for us.

The third time the death angel came, we thought it couldn't be. We thought we just couldn't go on anymore, but that is what Satan wants, so we had to commit it all to God. These are some verses that helped us. I Thes. 4:13-14, Isaiah 26:3-4, Isaiah 41:13, and James 4:8.

It wasn't easier the third time. God was with us every time and he was very near the third time, also. Pray for us as we want to be in God's will and it isn't easy. By the grace of God we want to accept what he has for us and go on. Praise His name! Let's all be ready when he comes. We don't know when he will come. For some it is just in a twinkle of an eye.

We still have two sons, Paul married to Emma Lou Miller and Dale married to Sue Mullet. We also have three daughters. Vera is married to Steve Yoder, Esther is married to Dave Yoder and Lois, who is in Virginia at Faith Mission Home, is not married. We have 16 grandchildren.

Mark J. Miller

I was at the sewing when the word came that our son, Mark, had an accident. I went home and my daughter-in-law took me to the hospital in Dover, where Mark lay unconscious from a concussion. This happened around 2:30. They had the breathing machine on him. We thought surely once they had him at the hospital they could help him, but his heart was crushed.

They said if he would have lived, he would have been like a vegetable. So we are glad he could go home to be with his Maker. He lived about three hours after the accident.

Dad went along with the ambulance. The accident happened on Road 102, close to our home. Mark was coming back to our place after taking something to Dad over at Paul's. Our son Paul was coming from our place with the tractor and they met at a sharp, blind curve. Paul stopped the tractor, but Mark hit the back wheel. Mark had the three wheeler. It was a wonder Joshua wasn't with Mark, since Joshua and Mark were about like twins. They were together a lot.

This happened on Tuesday and the funeral was Friday at Maranatha Church. He was buried at the church cemetery. We had the viewing at our home. Lots of people came. Oh it was so hard to bear. Mark had been so healthy, never sick and gone so soon. One of his schoolmates wrote a poem about him, that they read at the funeral. The school children sang; they also cried.

I can easily see how a non-Christian could get bitter at God, like at a time of death. But it drew us closer to God. We just thought we had to go tell people that we thought weren't living right that they have to make it right with God.

Dear Mark

Mark was a happy-go-lucky 15 year old,
With loads of energy he could not withhold.
He was lively, full of fun, and a good worker too,
With a big smile for everyone who would come into his view.

It was a sad incident that happened July 3rd of 84,
When Dear Mark was called home to God's open door.
It was a three-wheeler accident that caused his death,
And shock overwhelmed us when Mark took his last breath.

The ambulance raced to the hospital with speed,
Where doctors and nurses did their best deed.
But God saw fit to call our Dear One home,
The parting was hard, but we knew we were not alone.

Jesus was his Friend and Mark had received Him in his heart,
It's a great comfort to know we won't always be apart.
Of course we do miss him but we'd never wish him back,
'Cause he is where beauty is serene and happiness does not lack.

Homesickness fills our inside especially when we go to church,
And when we sit down at the table there's always an empty perch.
We also miss him when we have our family devotions,
For he always added a bit of spice and some extra emotions.

At times our heart aches so much for him,
And tears fill our eyes to the brim.
Our family circle has now lost a special link,
But we're looking forward to a reunion at the grand meeting rink.

"Lois, please don't cry for me,
I'm happy and I feel so free.
Joshua, my companion, I know you miss me so much,
But don't give up 'cause one day we'll be back in touch."

"I know, Esther, you'll take my place in choring,
And Vera, I always enjoyed you, 'cause with you, things were never boring.
Now Vernon, my big brother, whom tussling with was fun,
You'll take my place in milking and picking corn and do a job well done."

"To the grandchildren I love dearly, I'll see you in heaven someday,
And Dale and Sue you'll miss me, but keep looking up to God's way.
Paul and Emma Lou, please don't feel so bad,
God wanted this to happen and I'm feeling happy, not sad."

"Then Mom dear, your love and kindness were always there,
I can't wait till you join me in the heavenly place so fair.
Dad, you were the best Dad I could ever ask for,
And I know you too are looking forward to meeting me at Jesus' Door."

We all miss Mark so much and his energy-filled attitude,
But we wouldn't wish him back to a world that's so crude.
There will never be anyone who can take his <u>special</u> place,
But we are all looking forward when we meet him face to face.

— Sally Hershberger

Vernon J. Miller

Three years after Mark passed away the Lord called Vernon home. He was 26 years old and had been married one and a half years. They didn't have any children.

He was on his way to Coshocton to get a part for the combine. It had rained, and they said when it rained the road was slick as ice. The road was wet and he met a pickup at a curve. They hit head on. They life-flighted Vernon to Col. Grant Hospital. He lived four days after the accident. At one time they had given us hope.

Friends dropped in. We stayed with Sally from Monday until Friday when he passed away. Oh we thought it couldn't be. Another of our young boys so healthy and gone so soon.

People went home with us from the hospital and helped us chore. What would we do at a time of death, without friends. Everyone was so kind to us, hearts were so touched at a time of death. Oh how we ached for Sally, his lonely wife. This time it was different for us. Vernon wasn't at home anymore, but he was helping on the farm. We feel he was ready to go, so we want to go where he went. God gives us the grace as we need it, but it was such a big hole in the family now that two sons were gone.

One who has not gone through death, just doesn't know how it is. You are so helpless at a time of death. You see and feel the greatness of God.

Dear Vernon...

It's been a long two years,
Without you, my Vernon dear.
My life, it changed so much
Because I lost my one crutch.

June 1, which was on a Monday,
We got up just like any other day.
As I waved good-bye and you gave me that sweet special smile,
How little I realized your life on earth was on its last mile.

The sad news came to me when I was at work,
You were in an accident - my insides started to perk.
How bad, I really didn't know,
So to the hospital I raced and they said to Columbus you must go.

The next couple days I was in a tizzy,
My emotions were up and down and sometimes made me dizzy.
Lots of people stopped by to say "I care,"
And there were so many who kept us in their prayer.

I just couldn't wait to see you that first night you were in,
And then you squeezed my hand real tight which really made me grin.
But dear, that was the last response I got from you,
Except when I said "I love you" your heart rate went up too.

I was so proud of you because you put up a good fight to live,
You were always such a strong person and so willing to give.
Then on Wednesday I told you, "I would be strong for you,"
And that's when I felt I released you into our Lord's hand too.

Then on Friday, June 5th of '87,
The nurse and doctor came to tell me that you went to Heaven.
At first - SHOCK - then reality came rushing to me,
That our life together had ended and your smiling face I'd no longer see.

The tears they flowed and my future looked so dim,
"Can't I go to heaven where I can be with him?"
"Lord, WHY, just WHY did it have to be me?"
My child, I love you very much, but I know it's hard for you to see!

Thanks so much for the love you gave to me,
And thanks for the encouragement when I thought it just couldn't be.
Now life goes on and I need You to lead the way,
I'm looking forward to meeting Vernon in Glory someday!

— Sally (4-29-89)

Joshua J. Miller

Joshua was chopping corn for the silo and his brother Paul was hauling it in. His dad, John, was raking hay in a strip below the corn. When John saw the wagon standing still for a while, he went to look and here Joshua was under the wagon and life had fled already. Oh we just thought it couldn't be. Another son gone. The house so empty and four of our children and in-laws were in Haiti. We had the two grandchildren and had wanted to go to the airport to pick them up that day. Then the Lord had other plans for us. We sent word down to Florida about what had happened. What a meeting, coming home from Florida.

Our other son and his family had left that morning to camp for a few days. We could hardly get in touch with them. Friends and loved ones came. We could feel the hand of the Lord. But oh the parting was <u>soo</u> <u>hard</u>. <u>Another son</u>.

More about the accident: We know if Joshua had unhitched the wagon and it started to roll a little, he would have thought he could stop it. We think he would have been afraid it would hit Dad down in the other strip.

John had to come home to tell us. I thought he was having a heart attack because he was holding his chest and crying. His brother Paul came home and had to take his tractor to get the wagon off of Joshua. It is something we will never forget.

God is a healer, but the scar is always there. We trust we can go where our three boys have gone. We have so many nice memories of our three boys. All three boys died the first part of the month.

Mark - July 3, 1984
Vernon - June 5, 1987
Joshua - August 2, 1995

This verse has really helped us. Deuteronomy 33:27

Joshua and Mark were always together, like twins. Now I trust they are together again.

A Flower In Full Bloom

On August 2nd, 1995, God reached out His hand,
To pick a beautiful flower to add to His bouquet so grand.
It was the right season and the flower was in full bloom,
The time was also right, it was close to noon.

Josh loved life on the farm and a good worker was he,

Time was always spent hunting and fishing and of course a camping spree.
A friend he was to everyone and always thinking of others,
Time he gave so freely to family, friends, and brothers.

Mom, Dad, and family he always enjoyed so much,
Having fun playing games, teasing, laughing, he added his special touch.
A special Uncle he was and the children loved him so,
He played and tossed them in the air until each face was aglow.

"Wake up, Lois, I gotta tell you about my date."
"Yeah Josh, you're in love - can't it just wait?"
But Lois would always wake up and listen to what he had to say,
He was so happy the past two months - Marnita made his day!

Josh's life became complete when Marnita he met,
The many fun times you had together, I'm sure you'll never forget.
Marnita, your special touch of love, just made his face beam,
You were the love and joy of his life and the wife of his dream.

Josh, your life had many hurts but you stood brave and true,
It was great to see how your walk with God grew.
Your love for life was shown in full service for our King,
Thanks for that great example, it makes the tears sting.

Josh, your life, it speaks so loud and clear,
The memories we have will always be dear.
It's hard to imagine we won't ever talk again
Or hold your hand or see you smile - you were such a gem!

We know you are in heaven and as happy as can be,
I can picture Vernon and Mark with open arms saying "Come and see!"
We love you and we miss you and think it can't be,
But what rejoicing there will be when we all can join you three!

P.S. Tell Vernon I said "Hi!"   —A Friend, Sally (8-05-95)

Johnny Hostetler: Aug. 25, 1986 (date of tragedy)

Submitted by: Sam & Emma Hostetler, Fredericksburg, Ohio

August 25, 1986, I was going to do laundry that morning then I got word that our fourth married daughter needed me since she was going into labor with their first child. Johnny was doing chores in the upper barn. I went up and told him I had to go to Atlee's.

He asked, "What shall I do?"

I said, "Come along with me."

We were there all day. He ate dinner with us. Katie went to the Care Center that afternoon. Johnny and I went home around three o'clock. When we got home, I decided to do laundry yet. He went out to do chores early, then came in and asked me if I'd mind if he went swimming.

I hesitated to say anything at first, then asked, "Are you going alone?"

"No, Eddie is going with me, or don't you want me to go?"

"You may go," I said. "But don't stay too long."

The boys each ate a cupcake. I had told them not to eat too much before they went into the pond at Ivan Weavers'. The two boys swam for about an hour and were already on their way home when they met three of the neighbor boys and their dad. They persuaded them to go along back for another swim. The others stripped down to their swimming trunks, but Johnny just sat on the bank for a while.

Someone threw a lighter into the pond and said, "Come on, Johnny, see if you can fetch the lighter."

He went into the water without taking off his denims. The others soon detected that he was having trouble. One of the boys tried to help him when he called for help. He felt that he was being dragged under, and all of a sudden Johnny just loosened his grip and let go. The other boy surfaced, but Johnny didn't.

I had been to the phone shanty to make a phone call when I heard sirens, never even thinking something might be wrong with the boys at the pond. Someone knocked on the phone shanty door. It was one of the boys saying Johnny went under and didn't come back up.

It was only a matter of minutes till the squad went past. A neighbor lady came and asked if I wanted to go along to the hospital. I quickly got ready and we picked up Sam at Curry Lumber, where he worked. When we got to the hospital they had already put the breathing machine on him.

He looked so peaceful as he lay there. The only sound was the rhythmic sound of the breathing machine. One of the squad men told a neighbor they had gotten no response at all at the pond while doing CPR. They worked on him all the way to the hospital. By the time they got there his color had turned nice and pink again, but he didn't breathe.

The whole family came to the hospital that evening. As we stood around his bed, we all prayed, "Thy will be done, Lord." I kissed his forehead and whispered, "Johnny," but it was all in vain. They kept the machine on till the next morning. When they took it off, there was no response.

Son-in-law Levi and daughter Ella stayed with us all night. Daughter Katie was at the Care Center all night and didn't know what was going on. The next morning she had a little boy named Samuel. This was our second grandchild. She came home from the Care Center that same day and was able to be at the funeral. Atlee's and the baby stayed with us then for two weeks.

The funeral, which many attended, was at daughter Barbara's (Wayne Hochstetler). Johnny was a quiet-natured boy and was well liked among his friends. In school he was always a good pupil. He was also an obedient boy at home. He always asked permission from the parents for anything he wanted to do. We have many pleasant memories of him.

Several times that summer, he had asked me a question that I later thought maybe he had a feeling that something was going to happen. One day, just out of the blue, he asked me if he had a good white shirt, and another time he asked if he had a good suit coat. Each time I assured him that he did.

Our oldest son, Aaron, had their first child in October. A son whom they named Johnny. We now have 12 married children and 40 grandchildren. We still have three children at home. We are a very close family.

In times such as these, all one can do is bow our head and say, "Thy will be done." We trust he is now in a home, far above us, and our desire is for someday the whole family to be where he is. We received lots of mail and company which really meant a lot.

The voice is mute and stilled the heart, that loved us well and true.
Oh, bitter was the trial to part, from one so good as you.
You're not forgotten loved one, nor will you ever be.
As long as life's memory lasts, we will remember thee.

David Borkholder: May 25, 1974 - July 29, 1995
Submitted by: Monroe & Clara Borkholder, Bremen, Indiana

Friday, July 28, 1995, was a beautiful day. The factory workers had off that day, so early in the morning David left for Miller's

Buggy Shop. He was working on two buggies in his spare time. He came home around 9:30 and told me he wanted to work in the shop till two o'clock.

He had also made a Grandfather clock for his girlfriend's birthday. He had it all finished and in the meantime, he had it all set and running.

When David came home again he said that he had gotten some buggy parts for us since one of the buggies was for us, and asked if I had any cash. I said I didn't, but I could write out a check. He said that wouldn't do him any good as he needed cash. I remembered that Mark had some cash up in his room, so I gave him a $20 dollar bill and asked him how much our bill was.

He said, "Oh, that is close enough." He said he had to be at his girlfriend's place by three o'clock, so I quickly made some dinner so he could eat before he left. Of course, he said he didn't have any time to eat since he was running late already. He hurried and got cleaned up. He had just gone upstairs when the doorbell rang.

I said, "David, Earl is here. Should I tell him to come upstairs or will you come down?"

He said, "Either way."

David came down and they visited for a while. After Earl left, he quickly got his clothes and got dressed since he was running rather late. On his bike he jumped in a hurry and went out the lane and up the road. I did not know it would be my last memory of David.

Before he left, I had asked him when they would be back. His girlfriend's family was planning on biking to her uncle's place in the afternoon and spend the evening there. Then early Saturday morning, they had all planned on going on an outing. He said probably around four o'clock and that they were planning on spending the weekend here since church was to be at one of our closest neighbors.

It was very warm that Saturday afternoon; in the 90's. I kept wondering why he wasn't home yet, then I thought maybe they'll wait till it cools off a little before starting home. Between six-thirty and seven PM a car drove in and soon the doorbell rang. It was David's girlfriend's Dad. He just stood there by the door. I could see something had happened. He asked if Monroe was at home, but he had just gone to one of the neighbors. He just stood there a couple seconds as it was very hard for him to tell us the news.

He said David just drowned in their pond a couple of minutes ago. I thought, oh no! Then I had to think God makes no mistakes and we just have to give ourselves up to Him. I always have to think we are not promised more than today. He gives and He can take.

One of our neighbors came and we went to let our married children know. On our way home we found out David had been rushed to Elkhart General Hospital by the Nappanee Ambulance, and they were still working on him. So we headed for the hospital. David's girlfriend and her parents were there waiting. Our son Mark was there also.

All the way to the hospital, I was praying that we just want to give ourselves up to whatever our almighty God has for us. In the meantime, all our children came home and had planned on going to the hospital. Before they were ready to leave, the sad news came that he had passed away at 8:28 PM.

By the time we came home, our kind and loving neighbors had gathered and cleaned out the shop and had it ready for the viewing. What a blessing! All our children and partners spent the night with us except daughter Ruth, since she had left for Arthur, Illinois, early Saturday morning. We had a little problem to locate her as we didn't know of a phone number near where she was staying. All we could do was pray to our Heavenly Father to bring her home safely. It sure was a blessing to see her home again with the rest of the family. It seemed like the longest morning till her van drove in. I just could hardly thank our Heavenly Father enough for her safe journey home.

At that time of the year, the flowers were all in full bloom. I never thought about it before, but had to think there was a reason why. I really got a comfort from watching my rose buds and seeing how the petals spread out and how perfect a rose can be. I just love to go out early in the morning and take a look at the roses and other flowers. I've gotten quite a few roses and I'm still craving more.

We want to thank all our known and unknown friends for all the encouraging cards and letters we received. We all hope to meet our loved ones someday. Let's keep looking up!

David M. Borkholder: May 25, 1974 - July 29, 1995

Returning from biking on a hot summer day -
David sought a quick dip in the pond's cooling spray.
What a shock! What a grief! When the sad news was spread,
That David had drowned in the cool pond instead!

Oh, why should this fair youth, be thus taken away -
Was more than mere humans could relate that sad day.
No one could save David; God's will was much stronger;
His time on earth finished and he couldn't stay longer.

The grief was heartbreaking, a love-life was shattered;
Left behind a girlfriend and all else that had mattered.
Mark, his brother at home, had a sad broken soul;
His brother had left him, no words could console.

Shocked was the community, friends came from afar;
Relatives gathered with bike, buggy, and car.
Over two thousand viewers came Monday P.M.
The long line seemed endless, the roads in a jam.

But before the funeral, Mark dreamed in the night,
He saw into Heaven, golden streets gleaming bright.
David holding ten roses sat upon Jesus' lap -
Our Savior, Counselor, who'll broken hearts wrap.

Nine roses were yellow, one for Mom and for Dad,
The rest of the yellow roses for the family they had.
The red blooming rose with Carla's name thereon -
Showed his love for Carla that David had known.

Mark heard David singing; he was singing, "Farewell."
First to his brothers and sisters he loved here so well,
Next, to Father and Mother, his farewell he sang -
Last, to Carla, his loved one, his sweet farewell sang.

Golden streets that Mark saw led all to the chair -
Where Jesus was sitting in heaven so fair.
Many flowers were blooming and he heard a new song,
That the ransomed will sing with God's holy throng.

The next scene Mark saw, the family sat grieving;
In the shop for their son who shortly was leaving.
In a cloud, arm outstretched, David beckoned them, "Come".
But an angel said, "No," and drew back his arm.

So we'll have to make ready, meet David up there;
In that Beautiful place Jesus went to prepare.
What a comfort and joy was the dream God had given -
To console broken hearts, and a glimpse into heaven.

Though David is gone, his light still shines bright,
For he read God's word, and prayed into the night.
Prayed for his loved ones and the battles of life,
For peace and love, and the ending of strife.

God heard David's prayers and took him away,
To draw more souls to repentance that way.
Let us heed God's call and prepare us today,
For we'll never know when God calls us away.

Neighbor - Clara Lucille Burkholder

Lena Fern Esh: Mar. 7, 1995

Submitted by: Levi Jr. & Sadie Esh, Ronks, Pennsylvania

We will try and express our feelings and thoughts of what transpired in our hearts and minds from the time our daughter was diagnosed with Wilm's Tumor, a cancer of the kidney, till death did us part.

August of 1993 was a typical summer, having the sun putting the mercury into the 90's. On Wednesday evening, August 18, things were as usual with the children wishing us a 'Good night' before going to bed. Lillian, David, and Lena Fern slept upstairs and Linda downstairs in the crib.

At 2:30 we were awakened by a shrill cry from Lena Fern as though she had a rude awakening of some sort. I went upstairs to see what was wrong. She complained of a sore stomach, on her far left. Of course, as parents do, a little rub and assurance things will be fine by morning took care of it.

The next night we were again awakened by the desperate cry. She again complained of a sore stomach in the same spot. This time I really did try to see if I could notice anything out of the ordinary, and I noticed a hard spot, the size of an egg. The appendix being on the right, I didn't think it could be that, so we assured ourselves things were fine.

The next morning I had to make a trip to New Jersey and left before she got up. At 9:30 I called home and she was doing fine. Sunday afternoon she grabbed her stomach, saying it hurt. At the same time she jumped up and down, then told us, "Now it doesn't hurt anymore."

That was a little alarming to us. A doctor appointment was scheduled for Monday evening at 7:00. After the doctor examined her, he told us she probably had either a ruptured spleen or a tumor. We thought it's probably only her spleen, being optimistic about it. A 9:00 AM, Tuesday appointment was made at Lancaster Community Hospital for x-rays. While doing the ultrasound, we kept asking the nurse different questions as we tried to read her reactions while looking at the screen. She would not directly answer any of our questions, only telling us, "I only run the machine, I am not a doctor."

By 10:00 AM, we were called into a conference room and the news was broken to us. "She has a Wilm's Tumor, and yes, it is cancer."

We can still so vividly hear those words and relive our thoughts as they raced through our minds, and only now realize how our bodies went into shock.

Isn't it wonderful how the Lord has made our bodies to put them into shock when told of tragic news. Thus sparing our lives even if we can feel every artery leading to the heart about to burst. We didn't shed a tear for five minutes, until we looked into those beautiful, innocent blue eyes. That was when reality set in. An innocent three year old having cancer.

The doctor told us it is one of the most curable types of cancer, with an 80 to 90 percent chance of full recovery. The hospitality at Lancaster Community Hospital was wonderful, which was such a lift. They helped us contact our parents. I thought my emotions were under control until I heard my dad's voice on the phone. At first I could not speak and thought he might hang up. Then all I could do was cry and he still wasn't informed why we wanted to speak with them.

We were given the option of four different hospitals to perform surgery. We chose Hershey Medical Center, approximately 35 miles from home. Wednesday, August 25, at Hershey Medical was a day of more tests and a CAT scan. By this time we could see the left side of her stomach bulging outward. We were told it could double in size every few days. She also complained more because it was pressing into her other organs.

Surgery was scheduled for Thursday morning, which made Wednesday night somewhat miserable; consuming all the different liquids needed to prepare her for surgery. She asked me to massage her feet. After a few minutes I thought she had fallen asleep until she said, "Dad, I'm never going to get well again."

Those words are still clearly heard in our minds when reminiscing over that time. She left for surgery at 10:00 AM. We got a call at 7:00 PM in the waiting room that the tumor was removed without complications; they only needed to close her back up. At 8:00 PM we saw our daughter in the recovery room. Her first concern when she woke up was the rag doll that was given to her upon entering the hospital!

The surgeon took us back to the Lab, at our request, and showed us the mass. It was the size of a small cantaloupe. She had a speedy recovery, spending only three days in ICU. On Monday, I had the job of caring for Lena, because Mother wanted to get our oldest daughter, Lillian, off to her first day of school. On Thursday, Sept. 2nd, Lena Fern received her first shot of chemotherapy, part of a weekly treatment for the next 15 months.

Looking back over those 15 months, we had a lot to be thankful for. She was our sunshine. Cheerful, never complaining; often commenting on how good a life she had compared to some other children she saw. In fact, her health seemed to be so good that we wanted to discontinue her chemo treatments because those bills were adding up faster than our income and we still had six months to go.

We presented our case to her doctor at Hershey Medical Center. His theory was, why stop when she is doing so well and can so easily tolerate the treatments? Plus we have a 95% chance of a cure with this plan. We did continue with chemo as they recommended and that we will never regret. As we look back now, we would have had that burden on ourselves of trying to save financially instead of the best health care that we knew of.

Her last treatment was given on December 3, 1994, and what a joy it was for the whole family. I can still picture the family sitting around the table one Saturday evening in December. My thoughts reminisced over the past year, how blessed we were with our family.

On December 12, Lillian was home from school with a sore throat. Lena Fern cried because she pitied her so much. On December 23, I came down with a bad case of the flu, which kept me indoors for a few days. I can still picture Lena Fern come running across the living room floor, jumping onto the sofa and massaging my feet for five minutes, then assure me she would be back in about ten minutes. This was done for a few hours and is a memory I still treasure.

By 7:00 PM Christmas day, I started getting chest pains.

Thoughts raced through my mind; I'm only 29! This pain is just my imagination, but they didn't subside and I ended up in the hospital. After a bag of IV I felt great. My only problem was dehydration and that was causing muscle spasms.

We had one more appointment at HMC, to have her catheter removed, which was implanted under her skin and connected to a main artery. She had received all her treatments through this catheter. This appointment kept being delayed because of weather conditions etc. We finally had it scheduled for February 15th.

On January 16, Lena Fern complained of a sore chest in the vicinity of her catheter. We weren't alarmed, but figured it was from a bump, which usually caused some pain.

January 17, is an evening that we still cherish. My 30th birthday, which brought friends Menno and Ruth Miller and Amos and Barbie Esh for an evening of coffee and cake. What we remember most of that evening is Marianne, daughter of Menno and Ruth, and Lena Fern taking turns singing a song solo. We still recall just watching them as they both loved to sing. The tune was correct and the melody from little girls singing is precious to hear.

A week later, after grace is silence, Lena Fern asked, "Do you know what I prayed? I said, 'Thank you for this food, sorry for my sins, and may I go to Heaven sometime?' Mom, what did you pray?"

We were both somewhat taken off guard by her prayer and the question to Mom. I recall very clearly, we both just stared at each other. After a while Sadie said, "I wonder if we aren't going to have her very long."

During the next two weeks she occasionally complained of a sore chest, always at the same spot. On February 5th, Lena Fern had a wonderful day at church. She was bright-eyed and cheerful, playing doll with her cousin Katie Mae. Her blond hair had grown back enough to put it into small braids. Never did we give it a thought that this would be her last time in church.

Monday, February 6th, we made an appointment at Hershey for a checkup, to see if all was clear to take the catheter out. The standard procedure was to take x-rays again before removing the catheter, to make sure it won't be needed anymore.

February 7th was a nice, snow-covered, brisk day. I had to help man a stove booth at the Harrisburg Sports Show, so I took Sadie and Lena Fern along to Hershey Medical on my way up. Things were going along as usual, till I was called on the telephone. Sadie was on the line, calling from HMC.

My first thought was that they are already done and she's not into staying there all day. But no, her reply was "Lena Fern's cancer is back." How could it be? They had removed her kidney! But now it was in both lungs. I went into shock again, this time more than the first time knowing how serious it was if it had spread to the lungs.

For over an hour I frantically looked for my driver amongst 60,000 people. They kept paging him to no avail. We finally met and went back to the hospital, finding Lena Fern in good spirits.

She wasn't concerned. She felt fine and got a kick out of all the tests. We had an overnight stay at the hospital and were told of our options, which were few. In fact, only one, which was giving her large doses of chemo which would make her so sick that she would need to spend weeks in the hospital. Then her chance of a cure was slim.

All this time, she was running around, enjoying the toys they had. We left that day, deciding on getting a second opinion from the doctors in Mexico. The news from them was heartbreaking. They did not advise us to even come down. We found a natural program and our spirits were lifted again. This seemed to be working fine for two weeks. Then we noticed she was taking short breaths while sleeping, and complained again of chest pains. She wanted to be elevated to sleep.

On February 23rd we were going to a housewarming gathering in the evening for my sister Ruth and her husband. Lena Fern was not feeling the best, although she did pull her little sister around on the express wagon that day. When the time came to leave, she insisted she wanted to go. We had an 80 mile drive. After about 55 miles she said she wants to go to the hospital because her pain had suddenly increased. We continued our journey and left the other children with our parents.

While our plans were being made, to stop at the hospital, Lena Fern sat on the sofa taking fast, short breaths, as her lung capacity was cut down to 65% with multiple tumors in both lungs. We arrived at Hershey and she was relieved of her pain just by giving her oxygen. Her regular doctor was on vacation until the next day, so they assigned us another doctor, who we weren't too impressed with.

Our concern for that evening was to have Lena Fern comfortable.

We already knew what her chances were if we opted to give more chemo. Our biggest problem was we had not expected this, at this point, and only a few hours before she was pulling her sister in the wagon. The first thing this new doctor told us was, if we don't give chemo that night, she might die within a few days.

We were not ready for that news, in such a tone of voice. We both stayed at the hospital that night and the next morning is one we will never forget. We had to decide if we would take her home and keep her as comfortable as possible, or try the chemo route.

We prayed like never before for an answer. It just wouldn't come. The nurses kept coming in, asking if we had decided what to do. It was the hardest decision we ever had to make.

We finally called a parent whose child also had a relapsed Wilm's Tumor. After we heard his testimony, we both had peace of mind. Yes, his son was still living, with some aftereffects of his treatments, but he'd only had a wee spot on one lung, where Lena had large spots on both lungs.

We decided to take her home. When we informed the doctor of our decision, the first thing he said was, "You made the right choice." Their support was great. They cried right with us. We asked Lena Fern if she wanted to stay in the hospital or go and be with Jesus.

She said, "I want to go to Jesus."

Arrangements were made to have a supply of oxygen at our house, plus a hospital bed. Hospice was scheduled to come out every few days, to check on her condition. We asked them if this would continue for a few months.

She kindly replied, "I'm sorry, but it might go a few weeks, probably only a few days."

Watching her continuously take those deep, short breaths had us trying to increase the oxygen, which she wanted only at level two. Every time we turned it up a notch, she would notice instantly and tell us to turn it down. Once she went over to the oxygen tank to read the number on it. I asked her what it read.

She replied, "Two." Her words were spoken one at a time, in between each breath. Twice a day she would want to take a warm bath because it seemed to give her some relief, besides the morphine, which she was taking every four hours.

At 3:00 AM on March first, Lena Fern woke us up, asking if we would sing for her. We asked her what we should sing, and she requested, 'John Brown Had a Little Indian'. It was a favorite that Grandma had taught her. Singing at three o'clock in the morning was something we never tried before, but we were just pleased to be able to do something for her.

The next night we were awakened by her singing, which she didn't recall in the morning. It was such a thrill, as her singing had completely stopped. It was enough just getting her to speak during the day because every word was hard labor. Every day we could see her going backwards and her suffering increased.

Our thoughts were, "Why would a four year old need to go through such pain?" When lying on the sofa, she did not want anyone walking past because of the wind effect that it caused. Giving her a pillow had to be done very slowly, so as not to make air movement, which took her breath away.

On the evening of March second, Lena Fern requested our help with her evening prayer. To this day we have never seen someone use such energy to pray. It took everything she had. After her regular prayer, we started a conversation amongst ourselves, which upset her.

We asked her what the problem was. She said she was not finished; she was still praying silently. We asked her what she prayed. Her reply was, "I was asking if I can go to Heaven."

The next day she kept asking questions. While I was massaging her feet, she asked me if Jesus will massage her feet when she is in Heaven. In the afternoon she asked Sadie if there are any bathtubs in Heaven. While carrying her from the bedroom to the sofa, her oxygen line got caught on the furniture and pulled it off her face. She grabbed the nose piece and held it to her nose, as she fully depended on it now. She also asked us if we would pray by her bedside, since her energy was about extinct.

On Sunday night, every time I checked on her, she was awake because she couldn't get comfortable. She had to sit upright because of the fluid in her lungs. Monday, March 6, was a long day. She could not seem to rest. She did walk to the bathroom, but spent the rest of the day on Mama's lap or the sofa.

Monday evening she was so tired, but could not sleep. We cut out a cardboard box to make a bridge over her lap so that she could rest her head in a forward position. This worked for about 20 minutes. We also gave her morphine every two hours to relieve her pain. Next, I sat beside her in her bed, with her head cradled against my side. That kept her slightly comfortable for approximately two hours.

At 11:15 she asked if I would massage her feet. I was so glad I could do something to help comfort her. She also requested a pop tart and a drink of milk. Of course, being optimistic, we thought she might be improving again. A little while later she asked who was beside her. I looked and could see nothing, while still massaging her feet. I thought I heard what she said, so I asked her again what she had said.

She repeated, "Who is this beside me?"

Seeing nothing, I asked her, "Does it look like Jesus?" She turned her head 90° and looked for a moment, then looking me in the eye she said, "Yes it does."

Those were the last words she spoke to me. At 4:00 AM, Sadie was holding her and she simply said, "Medicine." She was given more morphine, which she usually drank with peach juice. About an hour later she reached up and removed the oxygen from her nose and went into a coma. We carried her to the sofa and held her for 45 minutes, until the Lord came and took her home to massage her feet.

Words will not describe how we felt. Nearly two years have passed now, since we parted with our dear one. Life goes on, though it will never be the same, nor do we wish it to be. Every day she lives on in our hearts. The Lord blesses in so many ways. Many friends we've met; others we've learned to know better. How precious is the support of family and friends through times of grief! The different stages of grief are essential in healing, although individuals vary in how they deal with each stage.

Let us all strive for the Heavenly goal, where we hope to join our loved ones and meet our Redeemer, to be parted no more. Oh to be worthy of those glorious promises!

Marcus Richard Schlabach: Aug 3, 1985 - Aug. 16, 1986

Submitted by: Richard & Mary Ellen Schlabach, Tuscola, Illinois

We started the day out as usual, on August 8, 1986, little realizing what the day would bring. We had a family reunion the following day so I wanted an early start on my laundry. Marcus was enjoying his last 15 minutes with his daddy before he had to go to work.

Marcus never did learn to crawl, but was walking. When Dad (Richard) left for work he came to the basement to tell me he was leaving, little realizing the tragedy lying ahead of us in the next 20 minutes. With the noise of the washing machine, it was difficult to hear what was going on upstairs.

It was so unexpected, when I came upstairs to find little Marcus in the bathtub with the hot water running down his back. Oh, what a pitiful site, hard for me to put it into words. As I picked him up the skin fell off from under his arms on down to his bottom. I thought, Oh please Lord, help me. This can't be real. I cried with him and took his clothes off. I thought why, oh why, didn't I take him with me to the basement.

I put Marcus in his crib and gave him his bottle. I ran to the road for help, no one was in sight. Again I thought, Oh Lord, help me. I need help. We lived on a road with not much traffic and one half mile away were the closest neighbors, which was also where Richard worked. Running back to the house, I knew something had to be done quickly.

Marcus was crying with pain, oh if I could just trade him places. I tried to quiet him, then ran to Richard for help. It was the longest one half mile I ever rode on my bicycle. We came home still finding Marcus in severe pain. The people he worked for said they would send a taxi to run us to the hospital.

Little did we know about burns and we wrapped Marcus in a blanket and headed for the car. A lesson we learned through experience is never wrap a burn victim in a towel. Always flush with cold water and then wrap in cold wet towels.

We started on our so-thought short journey to the hospital not knowing the long journey ahead of us. Marcus was a little more at ease. When we arrived at the hospital, they immediately started cleaning up his burns and giving him oxygen and IV liquids with pain medicine.

The doctor didn't work on him long till they informed us that he would be transferred by helicopter to St. John's Burn Institute in Springfield, Illinois, for better care. It was a heart sinking experience to watch them lift our dear little Marcus in a helicopter with all the tubes and bandages he was carrying. We stood and watched them disappear in the distance, not knowing what would be next.

Since there was limited amount of room in the helicopter, we had to ride to Springfield with our driver. With a two and one half hour drive to Springfield, we had some time to think about our morning and what still might be ahead of us. In our minds we were thinking a four to six week stay in the hospital with a lot of care. Never once did we think of a life or death situation.

We found Marcus in his room at the Springfield Hospital around 2:00 PM, with more machines and bandages than before. While we were still trying to accept more changes, the doctors called our attention, wanting us to sign our signature to allow them to transfer Marcus to a Shriners Rum Institute in Cincinnati, Ohio, where he could get more and better care. We felt like it was very important for us to accept this. They informed us they had already scheduled a lear jet to fly us to the next hospital, all they needed was our signature.

Richard and Marcus arrived at the Shriners Hospital Friday night at 12:00 PM. It didn't take Richard long to realize the doctors and nurses were waiting for them. The doctors took little Marcus to examine him, then came back with a full report, which brought a new picture into our minds with some more shock to absorb.

Since the jet was small, there was only room for one passenger. When my folks, Richard's folks and I arrived at 6:30 Saturday morning, the report wasn't good. The doctors said that Marcus had third degree burns over 46% of his body, with most of his burns on the back side of his body. With his young age and nearly one half of his body scalded, the doctor said he would give him a 50/50 chance of pulling through this, but he probably would not. All he thought they could do, was to try their best, but left it up to a higher power.

As we traveled on through our journey, we thought the road couldn't get any rougher, but we wanted to keep our eyes focused in the right direction. By this time they kept Marcus pretty well sedated on morphine drugs and on a breathing machine at all times. We would get some response, but very little. Mostly by a squeeze of the hand. A couple of days went by and Marcus would show some improvement which would lift our hearts. Early in the morning of the third day we were awakened by the nurses. They informed us that Marcus had noticeably fallen backwards during the night and thought our Savior was calling. But then to our surprise, he pulled through and everything started going uphill again, but not for long.

As days went by his body started to swell and fill up with lots of fluids and infection. It seemed from that time on, infection just gradually took over his body. We could see this happen, from day to day as the medication was losing out. After a long seven days of watching him suffer, we were getting to the point where we thought it would be easier to give him up than to watch him suffer. But this was still a difficult decision since he was our only child at that time.

As we were getting towards the end of the seventh day, not knowing which way to turn or how to feel, our parents gathered with us in prayer. We asked the Lord that he would carry us, that we wanted to fully surrender and give up to what he has in store for us, and be able to accept His plan. We didn't have to wait long till our prayers were answered. It was approximately 11:40 PM when the nurses came and called us to Marcus' bedside telling us that he was losing out rapidly.

We stood at his bedside watching him slowly fade away. At 11:45 PM, August 16, 1986, was the final time. Pneumonia claimed his life. Oh, how ready we thought we were to sacrifice our only child to take him away from pain and suffering, not knowing what lay ahead of us.

Facing the reality of the loss of a loved one was not as we had expected. Going home to share the viewing and tragedy with our families, friends, and neighbors, and them sharing their sympathy with us did help to ease the pain from the loss of our loved one. But there comes a time when life goes back to a regular daily pace when everybody goes about their duties of life. This left us alone to completely face reality.

We still wanted to remember that Saturday morning before his final calling when we had asked for help and said we wanted to give up and accept what He had in store for us. Thus giving us our duties, but also helping to carry the load for we knew this was God's plan. It is hard to imagine the quietness of a home when there are no children around to make those extra noises after a small child has been a part of your home for a year. Suddenly they are not here anymore. I also have some thoughts I would like to share with you from another point of view. Whenever we lose a loved one or have a tragedy in our lives, we tend to focus on the sorrows and the hardships this creates. I hope this can be taken the way it is meant.

There are also ways to gain in our life in these situations, this can bring us closer to God. We hear our ministers say: God calls home a little lamb so the sheep will follow. Since we had this happen to us, we have a much clearer view and understanding how this really does affect us. Yes, we have been separated from Marcus temporarily, but

God has promised us if we believe in Him and are willing to live in His ways, we can spend eternity with Him. Knowing this does strengthen our will to live a God-fearing life and strive to do His will. It also lets us picture in our mind of meeting Him on that Heavenly shore.

We do wonder if our concerns were too earthly and God needed our attention and maybe we were not strong enough against trials and temptations. Our plea is that while on this earth we will all strive sincerely to work together in love and harmony to do what is pleasing and acceptable to our Lord and Savior. Let's make His ways our ways. In a closing thought we can say, the Lord has given and the Lord has taken. Blessed be the Lord.

Rhoda Elaine Miller: Mar. 27, 1991 - Oct. 7, 1994

Submitted by: Raymond B. & Ruth Miller; Areola, Illinois

Memories of our dear daughter Rhoda Elaine Miller, who was born March 27, 1991, and went to be with Jesus on October 7, 1994.

Rhoda was our sixth child and was welcomed to our home by her two older sisters, followed by three brothers. After not having had a sweet baby girl in the family for almost ten years, there was indeed cause for rejoicing at her birth. The years passed and Rhoda was no longer a baby, but an energetic three year old. By this time, another little girl had joined our family, making it four girls and three boys.

When the scholars were in school, Rhoda enjoyed playing with her five year old brother Jason. They often played doll and she was often heard singing the songs 'Jesus Loves Me' and 'Meet Me There'. We realized she had a gift for singing at such a young age, but we didn't realize how soon she would be called to be an angel of God.

One day she unexpectedly said, "When I'm six, I'm going to go to school." Of course we didn't realize at the time that she would be called into eternity before reaching that age. Our second child, Christina, was born with Cerebral Palsy so we had added a bigger, wheelchair-accessible bathroom and bedroom addition to our house for her.

On Thursday night, October 6, our neighbor had stopped in to help Raymond while he was working on the platform for our deck. Since we were to have church at our house the following Sunday, the platform needed to be finished and also some concrete steps needed to be moved over to the south side of the house. Our neighbor had offered to help Raymond move the steps that night, but Raymond told him he would wait until Friday night. After he left, Raymond had a fleeting thought of moving the steps anyway, but he decided, "No, I'm going to wait until tomorrow night."

In looking back, we cannot help but think, oh if only the steps had gotten moved that night, maybe we would have been spared the agony of losing our precious daughter to death. But who are we to question God's ways?

On Friday night, after coming home from work, Raymond decided to put up some guttering on the north side of the house. While he was doing that, Rhoda told him three times, "Daddy, I like you. Do you like me?" and Raymond answered, "Yes, Rhoda, Daddy likes you, too." What precious words these were and also some of the last ones she said.

After Raymond finished that, he went out to the shop to get the skid steer. Jason and Rhoda climbed on the bucket while he took off the posthole digger, then he drove up toward the house. Raymond had thought they were both kneeling in front of him, and neither he nor Jason saw Rhoda when she climbed up on the back of the bucket. Miriam had gone outside at that time and looked over in time to see her fall off.

She yelled real loud at Raymond and he looked up in time to see her fall, but couldn't stop in time and the wheel went over her head. Miriam said Rhoda usually had a big smile on her face when getting a ride, but that time her smile was missing. It makes me wonder now, if she realized something was about to happen.

Miriam then came in all excited, saying something which I couldn't understand. But I realized by her tone of voice that something was very wrong. When I got outside Raymond was coming up the walks with Rhoda in his arms and he said, "I drove over her. She's gone."

The children then went for help, while I sat on the steps holding her in my arms. She had a bad cut in her hair and it was bleeding at the back of her head. When the first EMT got there, she asked about doing CPR, but we said no because we felt sure she was gone because of the way her head looked.

When the ambulance arrived they hooked her up to a heart

monitor and we were told she still had a heart rhythm and they wanted to take her to Sarah Bush Hospital. After the coroner told us she's still fighting for life, we finally gave our consent to have her moved. Oh, the pain I felt while we were waiting for them to put her in the ambulance, realizing that her chances for survival were so slim. It was then decided that Raymond would go with the ambulance, since only one parent was allowed to go along.

Our neighbor took Raymond's parents and me in their car. After the doctor checked Rhoda at the hospital, he told Raymond "You were right. You should have just kept her at home."

He realized that we hadn't wanted to have her moved. After Raymond's parents and I got there, two nurses came into our room to tell us that Rhoda didn't survive. How does one describe the pain and agony of being told that a beloved child has been called into eternity? Only somebody who has had a similar experience can realize in full, the heartache one feels at such a time.

We then went into the room where Rhoda was. She looked so natural, with her eyes half closed and her mouth open enough to see her teeth, but so quiet and still in death. We were glad for the time we spent with her in the hospital room, seeing her look so natural and so much like the sweet little girl we knew.

When we got home at 10:00 PM, we were overwhelmed when we saw how many of the neighbors and relatives were there, showing us they were concerned, just by being there. In the following days we realized anew how much neighbors are needed at a time like this. The preparations for the funeral were made lighter by the work of many willing hands. We could not have made it though the next trying days and even weeks if we had not felt the love and concern shown to us by our neighbors, relatives, and friends. How much we appreciated all that was done for us.

In closing we might add how this experience has helped us realize anew how fragile life really is and how suddenly God can choose to cut this fine thread of life. We felt awed to think that He chose us to give up a "rosebud" to be planted in His garden of love. It was not the path we would have chosen, nor has it been an easy path, but we want to trust that this experience was His will for us.

Neither do we dare ask why this has happened to us, but rather seek to do His will so that we might be counted as one of His unworthy servants, in that great judgment day.

Orva Lee Yoder: June 25, 1989 - Aug. 19, 1995

Submitted by: Ferman & Vera Mae Yoder, LaGrange, Indiana

On June 25th of 1989 we were blessed with our firstborn child named Orva Lee. A healthy little baby, little did we realize he was not to grow up to be an adult on this earth.

In October of 1990, one evening I was in the barn doing chores and Ferman had gone across the road to put his horses in the neighbors' barn he was using that day. All of a sudden I realized Orva was not around anymore, so I went to check on him and Ferman was coming in the lane with him. Ferman said Orva had been standing in the middle of the road and a few cars had stopped so that they wouldn't hit him. Oh we just thought there must have been a protecting hand over him. We were so thankful we still had him with us.

In September of 1991, one morning he wanted to go outside to play while Ferman was getting ready to go to the neighbors to fill silo. I let him out till Ferman was ready to go, and he was only outside maybe ten minutes. I had stepped outside and asked Ferman where Orva was because I had seen that he was ready to go.

He said, "I didn't see him, didn't know he was outside."

An old truck came roaring up the lane and said there is a little boy down in the pond. The pond is south of the house at the bottom of a hill beside the road. We all just took off and ran for the pond and got him out and he was just one muddy little boy. But again a protecting hand was watching him. The dog was with him and he was just as muddy as Orva was. But we were so thankful we still had him.

Life went on without us realizing his time to leave us and go be with Jesus was coming close. On August 19, 1995, we got up and started our day as usual, doing chores and eating breakfast before starting our day's work. We were eating breakfast when he woke up. He came out to the kitchen, but he didn't want any breakfast.

We both had a full day planned. We had invited company for supper on Sunday evening, so I had eats to fix, cleaning to do, and over three bushels of peaches that had to be canned. Mom was planning on coming to help me.

Ferman had three logs loaded on a wagon, two in front chained together with a chain binder and the other one in the back chained to the wagon. He wanted to take them to his parents' to get them cut. Well, like usual, Orva and Wayne wanted to go with Dad so we decided they could both go along. They were planning on being back for dinner. Ernest, Mary Beth, and I stood in the driveway and watched them go. We all waved good bye to each other, but not realizing we'll never get to see Orva's face again.

We went down to the basement and started with the peaches. Mom had stopped in a little before they had left, but then she had gone up to town before coming back to help. The children were playing outside. I had only done about seven quarts when I heard them saying, "Mom is in the basement."

I looked out to see who was here and I saw a police car. I just thought, "Now what?"

I saw Ferman was with him and then saw Wayne, but Orva just wasn't there. This happened around 8:20 Saturday morning.

They had been going east on 100 S a little east of 100 E, going down a long hill when the horses were spooked by something. Ferman wasn't sure of what, but then saw a motorcycle coming from ahead. He couldn't control them and they turned off on the north side of the road into a lane, made a U turn and headed west on a sloping, bumpy yard.

It was enough that the two logs shifted and started rolling. Orva Lee had been sitting on top of them. He went down first and the logs landed on top of him. Ferman got his horses stopped, but there was no fence or anything to tie them up so he just dropped the reins because he just thought he had to get to Orva to get the logs off of him. The man on the motorcycle also helped him. They got the logs off, but saw there was not much hope of life there anymore.

The other man went for help and Ferman and Wayne were by themselves until others came. After they had gotten the logs off, he went back to his horses. They still stood where he had left them, with nobody holding the reins, but they were shaking all over. There must have been an unseen hand on them. The police then brought Ferman and Wayne home. When I saw them, I went out to meet them. Wayne came over to me and said, "Mom, Orva died."

I just said, "Not Orva," but he said, "Yes Mom."

By that time Ferman was also with us and the police left to tell the neighbors. It seemed like a long time till somebody came. Mom was the first one to come and she didn't know what had happened.

It was probably 15 to 20 minutes that we were alone, then the neighbors dropped in one by one. By ten o'clock the undertaker was here and wanted information. Then he said, "You realize there will be no viewing."

Ferman had told me that we will never see his face again, but I was still hoping to. Oh, I just thought, "Why not, why can't we touch his lovely face just one more time." But again we know it is all for a reason. God makes no mistakes. When the undertaker left, he said he wasn't sure we could open the coffin at all, but when he brought Orva back on Sunday evening we were relieved to see him open the coffin.

We could view everything except his head. I often get the longing to touch his brown wavy hair. Saturday was just like a dream. By noon there were a lot of people here and by evening, they had all the cleaning done and the peaches canned, washed, and we were ready for the viewing. By eight o'clock in the evening, all our brothers and sisters and families were here, both parents, and lots of other people.

Oh, I just can't put on paper how we felt by evening. Everybody left for home for the night and we went to bed, but we slept very little. At around three o'clock that morning, the ambulance went past our place.

We just wondered, "Who now?" but we never did find out who it was. On Sunday there were a lot of people that went through and on Monday too. Oh, I just had to wonder what would we do if nobody would come! The funeral was on Tuesday with a fair attendance. A lot of people were here for dinner and some for supper. We had lots of company and mail afterwards.

Marion was 11 months old when this happened. On Monday morning he just cried and cried. I held him and then Ferman held him, but he didn't want us. Finally Wayne took him and he was quiet, but it was almost more than Wayne could handle.

Orva had often taken Marion and played with him or rocked him. Marion was really attached to him and all of a sudden he wasn't around. Again we said if only we could have taken him in to the coffin so he could see his face. Since we couldn't, he didn't seem to realize who it really was, but the other three did.

The children were all so close to each other. Orva was the oldest and it seemed like he was their leader and all of a sudden, he was gone. They didn't want to go to bed to sleep, his pillow was empty. His chair and everywhere we went, he wasn't there. It just seemed like a dream. We thought, we'll wake up and all will be normal again, but it never did get quite back to normal.

There were days we just didn't know what was wrong with us. We weren't sure how we should handle the children, they were hurt so easily. A few weeks after this happened, all four of them started with a rash. We started putting cream and other stuff on them, but nothing helped Wayne and Marion. We finally managed to get Ernest and Mary Beth cleared up. We finally took the two boys to the doctor because Wayne was just coated with it.

Doctor said it was like impetigo, but since they were under so much stress they needed an antibiotic for their blood since it was all through their body. That did help them. Wayne once had a dream that really helped him. He dreamed Orva came down and lay beside them to take care of them. After that they went to bed better. It was another protecting hand for them.

Some more of us had some good dreams of him, too. Yes, we have gotten some blessings from this already. It draws us closer to God, and He was always ready to help whenever we asked and needed Him. All things are possible with the help of the Lord.

As we loved him, so we miss him!

Jonathan E. Schmucker: Sept. 23, 1977 - Oct, 14. 1995

Submitted by: Elmer & Katie Schmucker, Garnett, Kansas

Jonathan was a vibrant teenager. He greatly enjoyed life in general, but especially the great outdoors. He loved hunting, fishing, swimming, skating, skiing, playing ball, and hunting raccoons. He was born an outdoor person. He shot his first squirrel when he was only eight. He liked outdoor jobs. He used to be disappointed if it was raining and he had to work in the shop. He wanted to be outside. But all of this came to an end so suddenly, so tragically.

He had just started a new job about a week and a half before he was gone. I was so concerned about this job. It was about a 65 mile drive one way. He made better wages than he had ever made before and probably better than he had ever hoped to make. He really enjoyed the job (laying waterlines) and the people he worked with, but it was such a long drive. He was getting up early and getting home late, plus winter was coming up with possible icy roads. Maybe this concern is what made me go through what I did that last week.

The last week he was with us, phrases of a song kept going

through my mind. It was about a young boy that had a job and every morning he'd rush off to work and his mom was so concerned about him. At night she'd wait up for him till he was safely home once again. Then one night he didn't make it home. The sheriff came to tell them he had been killed on his way home at a curve in the road. This just kept going through my mind over and over all week.

Then towards the end of the week another song started coming to mind. It was the song 'I Need the Prayers of Those I Love'. One song would come and then the other. I wondered why are these two songs coming to me so much. They were there over and over again.

The day before our dear son was killed, my mother, sister, grandmother, an uncle, our daughter, and I had gone to Kansas City. I told Mom how these two songs kept coming to me. I don't remember but I don't think I even mentioned Jonathan's name.

Mom just reached over and touched me and said, "I want you to know we are all praying for Jonathan." I started crying and said thanks, he needs it. The very next night our dear son was gone.

He came home from work that last evening and he was one happy boy! He had gotten his first check from his new job and it was a nice one. I am so glad he still had the joy of earning and receiving this check. He went to town that evening to a friend's house. He used to work with him. His little son crawled over and sat on Jonathan's lap the whole time he was there. Jonathan loved children. About 9:45 he told his friend, "I'm going home to bed. I'm tired."

He came home around ten o'clock. I was so glad our son was home safely once again, but then I knew he wasn't going to stay because he didn't park his pickup where he usually does. He had cut some wood last winter to sell. He drove out to the shop and was loading some of this onto the back of his truck.

He then came in the house and asked me, "Mom, where is my coat?"

I said, "It's on your hall tree over by your dresser."

He didn't say anything for a while and I asked, "Did you find it?" He answered, "Yes."

I had just brought his coat down from the attic the week before, thinking he would soon need it. I was sitting on a recliner in the living room, Elmer was on the couch half asleep. Our other children had already gone to bed.

Jonathan then came into the living room and I asked him,

"Wouldn't you like to just stay at home and go to bed? You could sleep better and so could I."

I don't remember what he said. I asked him where he was going and he said he was going to be with some of his friends where they usually got together. He wanted the wood he put on his truck to make a bonfire. It was a chilly evening.

He then just stood there and looked at me as if waiting to see what I would say. Faye, our daughter, and Marcus, a son, got up and were with us yet, too. I remember I went over and touched him. I don't remember what all was said.

As he left, his parting words were, "See ya." He hardly ever said 'good bye'. His parting words were almost always 'see ya' and my parting words to him were usually, "Be careful and be good."

I thank God for these last precious moments with our son. It was as though he came home to let us have these last precious moments together. I was sad because he left again after I thought he was safely home. Sometime between the time he left his friend's house and came home he must have met these other friends and decided to spend some time with them. They said he didn't say much that evening and was just kind of quiet. He had many, many friends.

About 1:30 AM I woke up and heard someone knocking on our door. I woke Elmer and told him someone was here. He quickly jumped out of bed and went to the door. This was unusual. Usually if someone came he'd have me go to the door because I could get into my housecoat faster than he could get dressed.

I stayed in bed, but heard the word Jonathan. I immediately jumped up. I then heard the words, "You've got to get your wife." Oh, Lord, no.

It was the sheriff. He had asked Elmer if we had a son Jonathan. Elmer said yes. The sheriff said he'd been in a serious accident. Elmer asked if he was in the hospital, thinking this way he would know if he was still alive. That was when he said "You've got to get your wife."

I went out to them then. He then again said, "Jonathan has been in a serious accident." I reached over and touched him and asked if he was still alive. He just stood there and said nothing for a while. Then he said those awful words we will never forget. "Jonathan is expired."

Oh no, dear God. Please no. My worst fear had actually happened. I so often thought something like this could happen and now it actually had. I had always prayed to God to keep his shield of protection and love around our precious son.

Jonathan was on his way home. We don't know how it all happened and we probably never will. He had no one else with him. This was also unusual because he almost always had one or both of his two best friends with him.

We could see by the tracks on the road that he got the truck off the side of the road, right at a curve. He got off too far and when he got back on the road, his truck rolled several times. It threw him out and landed on him. He died of massive head injuries.

We don't know why he went off the side of the road like that. Did he go to sleep? Earlier he had said that he was tired. Several people said they had gone that road just before Jonathan did and they said there were all kinds of deer on the road in this area. Was he dodging a deer? We don't know.

It is a curve that is pretty tricky after dark. A friend said she has several times almost done the same thing at this same place. An uncle just recently told me he almost did the same thing at the very same place. We don't know, but we have a God who does. If we were supposed to know, God would have made it known.

We feel Jonathan's time was here and this was God's way of calling him home. Twelve years before on the same road, not even a mile apart, I had a ten year old nephew that was killed in a car and bicycle accident.

At the time of his death, Jonathan told my dad, "David was my best friend. I wish it could have been me instead of him." Twelve short years later it was him. After the sheriff left we had the awful job of waking our dear sleeping children and telling them their big brother was gone. I asked Elmer if we couldn't just let them sleep till morning.

He said, "No, we have to tell them."

Faye was 15, Marcus 12, Leander nine, and Eugene six. It was such a long night. We also went down to tell my folks. Another hard job to be done. My parents had already lost three sons and a grandson in tragic sudden deaths. Oh God, why Mom and Dad again?

We also stopped to tell one of Jonathan's best friends. Sonny and Jonathan were together a lot, every weekend and even during the week. How it happened that Sonny was not with Jonathan this last evening we don't know, but it must have been God's plan. Sonny has a brother Melvern that was usually with them too, but he was in Minnesota helping a carpenter crew at this time.

My mom then came over to our house after we got home. I just had to ask, why if God wanted Jonathan, couldn't he take him as an innocent little boy? But I know he would not have touched as many lives as a little boy. He had friends near and far. Mom said let's pray if there is hope for God to give us hope. Jonathan was a kind hearted giving guy, but he was a young teenager and didn't always make the best choices. But I, as his mother, didn't always do the best either.

This is why God gave His ONLY Son, because he knew we were human. That we do make mistakes and that we do need forgiveness.

The first night when the trooper came to talk to us, there was one very bright star shining. I kept thinking, I hope this is Jonathan's star. Then next day when I told about this star, my dad said the night after my two brothers were killed, there were two bright stars like this.

We were so heartbroken, so sad. I asked, "Why us? Why Jonathan?" Then I said, "If it had to be someone, why not us? Why not Jonathan?" Elmer reminded me of some of Jonathan's friends. If it would have been them, their dads would have been on their own because they no longer had their partners with them to share the tragedies of life.

Right at first they told us they feel it was instant. This was not what our bleeding hearts wanted to hear. We wanted to know if he still had time with God if he needed it. We then heard he still lived ten minutes. Ten precious minutes. A cousin of mine from Indiana, who had also lost a son, told us his driver had talked to a waitress in town and she said one of the cops had talked to her after he had left the accident and he told her it looked as if Jonathan had cried.

How my heart bled to know our dear son lay there all by himself and cried. But oh, how it rejoiced to know that he still could. The mother in me wanted to be with him and comfort him, but it's like some friends told me, "You probably wouldn't have been much comfort to him."

I said, "Yes he probably would have had to comfort me."

They also told me sometimes we need time alone with God. Oh, what if I had been there and taken this precious time away from him. We must accept and know God knew best. The evening before the funeral, there were many, many people here. We had Jonathan out in our shop. The others were eating supper and I had gone to the house.

All at once Elmer came up to me and said, "Come quick, come." I thought, oh no, what happened now?

He took me to our bedroom and we looked out the window. Out on the roof of the shop where Jonathan was sat a dove. It sat there as though it was guarding the building. It would turn its head one way then the other. We had never before had a dove on our buildings like that. Thank you, Lord, was all I could say.

One of Elmer's brothers also shared with us the day of the funeral how he had noticed Jonathan's eyes so much the evening before. He said they just glowed and sparkled. He said, "I thought it must have just been the light." That night he then dreamed, "It wasn't the light. If it had been the light, it would have had to have been in a complete different direction." He said this is all he dreamed. He told us he had never had a dream that was so clear and so vivid.

After the funeral, we were trying to go on with life, but it was so hard. About a week and a half afterwards, Faye got up one morning and said, "I dreamed about Jonathan last night!" I consider her dream a gift sent directly from God, to help us and strengthen us day by day. She dreamed Jonathan was outside our house sitting on a bench we have out there. She went out to him. He had no cuts, no more bruises, everything was healed. She asked him if he'd like to come back?

He said no.

She asked, "Are you here with us and we just can't see you?"

He said, "No, but my spirit is."

"Can you see us?"

"Yes."

An airplane flew over real low and she asked him, "Is this about where you're at?" He answered, "Yes, something like that."

She also asked him, "Have you seen God yet?"

He said, "No, but I can hear Him and the angels."

Elmer and I then came out to them, too. One of us asked him if we should get our younger boys; we could hear them playing in the background.

He said, "No. It would be too hard for them when I have to leave again."

Pretty soon he said we had to go back into the house.

We could not watch him leave. She said he seemed sad that we couldn't go with him. As we were going back to the house, he again said, "See ya."

Faye said, "After a while I went out again. I guess I hoped he was still there. He wasn't, but he had left a note for us." He wrote: Dear Mr. & Mrs. Elmer Schmucker, Don't cry for me or about me. (She couldn't remember if he said for or about.)

He then wrote more but she couldn't remember what all it was. But the last line he wrote to us was, Tell the boys and guys around here to obey their parents. He then signed it. Your son and an angel of God, Jonathan Schmucker

She said his signature was exactly like his signature. She had also asked him something that he said he could not answer. She couldn't remember what she had asked him. When she woke up she could not believe she was in her bed. She thought she was outside the house, where it had all taken place in her dream.

Elmer asked her if it was Jonathan and an angel since he had signed his name Jonathan and an angel. She was very clear on this. She said, "Jonathan was the angel."

We feel our anguished prayers of that awful strife filled night when Mom and I prayed for God to give us hope, if there was hope, have been answered. We do not know that our dear Jonathan is an angel, but we prayed for hope. God has given us that hope in more ways than we ever expected. We want to accept it as that and try to help others through their trials, sorrows, and tragedies whatever they may be.

On October 14, 1996, a year after Jonathan was gone, I called the cop that was the first at the scene. We had never talked to him and I always wanted to. I just wanted to know any more information he could give of Jonathan's last moments on this earth. Where he lay? Did he say anything? If so, what did he say?

He said Jonathan tried to talk but he couldn't understand anything. The truck was laying on its side and he was underneath. Oh how I long to know what his last words were. I wonder if he wasn't talking Dutch. But I know if we were supposed to know, God would have made it known and it's like Mom said, "God knows."

One thing that helped me so much through all of this heartbreak, his death, the funeral, missing him etc., is the message God gave us. That he would come back and also I remembered how I felt when he was being born. He was our first and I just didn't know if I could handle this. This was just pretty hard. Then the thought came to me of all the women from Eve to me that had given birth and I thought, if they could do this, so can I.

Then when we were going through the horrible pain of losing him I had to remember how I felt when he was being born, and I thought of all the women from Eve to me that had lost children. I thought if they could do this, so can we, with God's help.

Then I thought of Mary watching her dear Son being abused. I thought if she could do this, so can I, with God's help. Then I thought of God giving His ONLY Son for you and me. If all of this was done for us, yes, with God's help so can we.

Jonathan means 'a gift from God'. How grateful we are for the precious gift that was given to us for 18 short years and 21 days.

Writing this has not been an easy task, but if anyone and especially our dear, precious young folks can be helped by this, then it was worth my time and effort and I want to give God the glory. I have enclosed a poem that God gave to me the night Jonathan was killed.

I did not know what I was going to write when I started, but I did know I wanted to use the letters of his name. I feel God helped me write it, because I could not have done it on my own. We are going on, one moment, one step, 'One Day At a Time'. God has been so good to us. It is so hard for me to grasp of all the people in this old world, that God cares so much for "one little mom," "one little family."

He not just cares for us, but has taken the time to show us he cares over and over again. I think that is probably what I have learned more than anything else through this tragedy, is to show others that there is someone who cares! Someone who knows that they are hurting and is willing to help ease their burden in some little way. May we all reach out to others and share their heartaches, their sorrows, help make each other's burdens a little lighter.

Hope and pray to meet our dear loved ones who have gone on before where we may all be together and to part no more.

In Memory Of Jonathan

J   *onathan left us on October 14, 1995,*
     The sheriff knocked on the door,
     Your son Jonathan is no longer alive.

O   *h, how can we bear this?*
     There must be a mistake.
     But God has called our loved one on.
     Oh Lord! Help us, and strengthen us for our sake.

N o longer will he ask, "What's for supper?"
No longer will he ask, "What came in the mail?"
No longer will he ask, "Mom, when will you wash?"
No longer do we call you to wake you each morn.
No longer will we see your bright smile,
No longer will we hear, "See ya,"
As you go out the door.

A lways we loved you deep in our hearts,
Now God has called us to part.

T here are so many good memories
We have of you here.
You loved to go fishing,
And hunting deer.

H ow we will make it, God only knows,
But we have Him to lean on,
And our love for you only grows.

A lways you had so many friends.
Strangers were friends you hadn't yet met.
At work, ball games you loved them, there was no end,
Sonny and Melvern were with you a lot,
Oh how we shall miss you when they are about.

N ow our circle is broken.
Our hearts are broken, too.
Oh Lord, strength for the day,
Is all we ask of you.

S o much is left unsaid, so much,
We'd like to sit down and chat,
To talk about work, hunting,
Your ball games, and the Lord,
And just this and that.

C ome unto me all that labor
And are heavy laden and
I will give you rest,
Oh, how precious to have
A God who knows best.

H   ere on earth you enjoyed the great outdoors.
How you loved hunting and fishing.
How well I remember that first squirrel,
You were only eight, then came your first deer,
How you longed for the time to be
Old enough for that first one.

M   any tears we have shed for you now,
Many more will be shed
But we'll make it some way — somehow.

U   ntil we meet Jesus,
We will not know,
Oh we hope and pray to meet,
At that Golden Gate by and by.

C   an we believe and be strong?
Of ourselves, the road looks so long.
But with God's hand to lead us one step at a time
We hope to go onward One Step At A Time.

K   indness was in dear Jonathan's heart,
Oh how we loved you — it is so hard to part.

E   lmer was Dad's name — you were his firstborn.
He was so pleased with you, his dear son.
He took time to talk when you needed someone.
Katie was Mom's name — she prayed so many times.
For God's protecting hand over you.
Mom almost left us when I was 3½ months old.
She was saved for a reason — to love and care for me,
18 years — such a short season.
Faye was my only sister — we loved to tease and goof off
And sit down and just chat —
I loved her homemade bread, how we will remember that.
Marcus was my brother just younger than I,
We had many a great time
Hunting, fishing, and swimming,
Now we must say good-bye.
Leander my second youngest brother was my little friend —
He'd feed my dogs for me — Sam & Jake
He'll keep feeding them for me, but no longer will I be there,

When he says we're out of dog food - "Can you get us some here?"
Eugene, my youngest brother, was special to me, too,
For I loved little children so,
I'd fix him little things like a silo and bow.
Little Clay was another brother,
How precious that last eve,
When I gave him a kiss and he wanted another.

R *ichly we were blessed to have you these short years,*
We hope and we pray to meet again
As your parting words were so often said, "See ya."
May God lead us all onward so we may meet
In heaven with uncles Larry, Joe, and Leon
And cousin Dave at dear Jesus' feet.
The sun will shine again, but for now it is dark.
But God will help, if we lean upon him!

Joris Miller: Died Jan. 4, 1985

Submitted by: Paul & Edna Miller, Sugarcreek, Ohio

"I think we should do some more tests," our concerned doctor
said after examining Joris again. "This has been going on for too
long. The antibiotics should have produced some results before now
already."

This was Tuesday afternoon. Joris had been sick now for eight
days. On Monday of the week before he started in with the symptoms
of a virus. He was lethargic and not eating well, then by the middle
of the week he started vomiting when he ate solids. At times he was
breathing very rapidly, and he was becoming more and more listless.
The doctor thought he had an ear infection and sore throat, so he was
treating him with antibiotics. Still he wasn't doing better.

So on Wednesday morning we took him to Union Hospital for
blood work and x-rays. After the test we were sitting in the waiting
room when Dr. Teague came to see us. "We weren't expecting
anything like this. Your baby has an enlarged heart. We are not
equipped to treat him here."

What a shock it was for we thought we had a healthy baby. True,
he was now 13 months old and he wasn't walking, but he was stable
on his feet. Joris had been a full term baby weighing in at seven
pounds, five ounces. Just the same weight his 12 year old brother and

six year old sister had been at birth. He gained rapidly in weight and height for the first six months, always being in the 50 - 75 percentile.

At six months he was sick and not eating well, but the nurse said, "He must have been eating sometime as chubby as he is." But after seven months old he stopped gaining rapidly, still nothing to be concerned about.

Now there *was* something to be concerned about. Without going home we went to Akron to the Children's Hospital. Dr. Ben-Shachaar immediately took an echocardiogram. He then turned to us with grave news.

"Your son is very ill. I'm going to admit him immediately into the intensive care unit. Joris' condition is called cardiomyopathy, which means that his heart muscle is not performing well. We're not 100% sure, but we think he had this condition from birth. The other possibility is the condition could have come from a viral infection. If he had this condition from birth he could respond to his medications for days, weeks, or years, but the long term prognosis is not good. But if his condition came from a viral infection (myocarditis) then the possibility exists that he could improve slowly and eventually outgrow it. The only way we can tell for sure what caused his heart condition is to do a biopsy of the heart. (A biopsy consists of taking a little tissue of the heart and testing it.) We would have to do that at the Cleveland Clinic where they have a surgical backup team available."

About an hour and a half later they allowed us into I.C.U. There he was with an oxygen mask, a mainline IV, and all hooked up with wires to keep tab of his heart rate, respiration, heart function, oxygen level in the blood and more.

When we came in he looked at us so pleadingly. Why don't you hold me? Why don't you help me? Can't you do something for me? There we were helpless, numb, hurting, but what could we do? They put him on medication to help work off the fluid that had been accumulating.

The first two days he lost a pound a day bringing his weight down to 17 pounds. They soon took the oxygen off and we were allowed to hold him. He was responding real well! After three days they moved him to a regular room.

By Sunday, the fifth day, he was pretty well his normal self. He ate seven jars of baby food. He played and stood alone in the playroom and we gave him rides on a little red wagon. The nurses enjoyed it when he told them the little lamb goes baa. We were very happy with his progress and even more so when the doctor told us we can take him home on Tuesday morning, which gave him a total stay of six days at Akron.

After we got him home he started walking and just being his normal happy self. The doctor said he shouldn't get sick. He shouldn't be exposed to other children for a while because if he gets sick, he'll get very sick. At first we didn't expose him to other children, but then we started to gradually give him some exposure. At this point he received a real dose of stomach flu, but he snapped back out.

So time went on, Joris had ups and downs. When he was feeling well we could not tell that there was anything wrong with him. But then eight weeks later he wasn't feeling well again. Again he became listless and didn't have an appetite. Finally he also stopped drinking fluids and wetting his diaper. So with heavy hearts we again took him to Union Hospital to the Emergency Room because it was 8:30 in the evening. The doctor on duty wanted to send him to Akron, but after calling an Akron cardiologist and finding out that Akron really couldn't do more than Union could, they decided to keep him and treat him for his ear and throat infection as they would any other child.

From the test they took they determined that his heart was probably functioning about the same as it had been for the last two months. By the second day in Union he was feeling pretty good and then he had another congested heart failure there at the hospital. Since his infection had cleared up the doctor said if we want to, we can take him home because they can't do anything at the hospital that we can't do at home. So we again took him home. He again had his ups and downs, but now the downs became lower and the ups not as high.

The cardiologist gave us a very negative picture concerning his condition. After several weeks he told us that Joris' time is running out and he wishes we would consider a heart transplant. Since a heart transplant lasts only about four years for a child, and heart transplant patients have low disease suppression because of the anti-rejection drugs they need to take for life, we decided not to do a heart transplant.

Other doctors and our ministry supported our decision. His eating become worse and his energy waned for another week till Saturday morning while holding him I noticed something was the matter by the way he held his head. We called the children together and within 15 minutes he died peacefully, no struggle, no gasping, or groaning. Gone to heaven, gone to be with Jesus, gone to that beautiful garden where he can smell the flowers continually. Gone to be with his baby sister who had died eight and a half years ago.

Joris loved back pack and bicycle rides. He loved going on walks. He was very disappointed if he couldn't go along to the pond to start the irrigation motor. When his sister Jerilyn took him to Grandma's house, he always had to stop and smell the flowers. He also loved birds. Red ones were cardinals and a brown one was a spatz (sparrow).

Today we still don't know for certain if Joris' condition was congenital (present at birth) or acquired. It is a little hard to believe his condition was congenital because of how healthy he was the first half year of his life. Since we did not do a biopsy, which would have added to his discomfort, we will probably not know for certain on this side of eternity.

Joris is an old Dutch (Holland) name. Our forefathers used the name extensively; read about them in the Martyrs' Mirror. Joris did not suffer for the faith as his ancestors did, but he did suffer discomfort because of his heart condition. We are thankful for the grace of God and that He had provided that innocent children are saved not of their own works, but because of grace alone. Just as we adults also can be if we respond obediently to the provision of grace the Lord extends.

This story was not an instant death story, although we also experienced that in our family.

On January 4, 1985, our one and one half month old daughter died from SIDS (Sudden Infant Death Syndrome, more commonly called crib death). She was a healthy baby with a radiant smile. The day before, she had a slight cold. The next morning at 7:30, Edna woke up and knew something was wrong. She went over to her bed and picked her up, but life was gone.

This past year we experienced a gradual decline in health and eventual death in our 16 month old son, as we wrote about in the story. Yes, a sudden death is very traumatic but the illness and death of our son was much more heartrending; When his health improved, our spirits soared only to have our hopes shattered to pieces when his health declined. So we were on an emotional roller coaster through his illness.

You see, it is not possible to prepare for death, regardless how much it is anticipated. The pain of our son's death seems to linger longer than the pain of our daughter's instant death. I'm sure it is different for different people. It is probably not wise to tell anyone "I know exactly what you're going through." because situations vary and our experiences in death are not the same.

What remains the same is the grace of God which will help us through whatever befalls us. Since this story was written, we had a baby girl Joy Jenise born May 25, 1995, and died April 8, 1996, also of cardiomyopathy. Because of having two children with the same problem, it prompts us to believe that their heart problems had a genetic origin and were present at birth. This is contrary to the conclusion we had formed when the original story was written.

Rebecca Marie Lengacher: June 7, 1974 - Aug. 11, 1991
Noah Schmucker: Sept. 3, 1971 - Aug. 11, 1991

Submitted by: Rebecca Lengacher

This is a sad tragedy of our daughter Rebecca Marie and her boyfriend, Noah Schmucker on August 11, 1991.

The year of 1991 started with our twin daughters, Rosalie and Rebecca Marie helping each other looking for jobs as most girls do in the community. On May 12, 1991 they started classes to join church. During the week days that they were home, I asked the girls to go with me grocery shopping and we went to the Belgium Association for lunch at Martin Schmuckers.

Rebecca Marie asked me if she could stay home and I told her I'd feel better if she would go along because where one of the twins was, the other would be there, too. But as it ended up, Rosalie and I went and Rebecca Marie stayed home, but I wasn't at ease. When we got home, she was studying her Articles for church.

On Monday, August 5, the girls came home from working at the South Whitley Turkey Farm and they decided one was going to help me make supper and the other one would work in the garden till supper. The menfolk finished the chores, supper was served and we were all going to the table when I heard one of the twins make a remark that they didn't want supper.

I said, "Oh girls, you left early this morning and we didn't eat lunch together." Then I added, "The family that prays together shall never part."

We all prayed at the supper table and the main conversation was how they had heard that day at work about the accident in Holmes County where a truck or car ran into a buggy and killed so many of the same family. On Tuesday morning, August 6, I was sweeping the floor and I was stooped over with the dustpan when something asked me, "Which one of your children don't you want?"

I named all seven of my children and I said I want them all. After the tragedy I thought I should have said, Thy will be done. But it was too late.

On Thursday evening, August 8, Menno and I went to visit a widow and our four teenagers stayed home and went to bed early. Timothy couldn't sleep and he heard Rebecca Marie dreaming, "I'm going, I'm going." He told the boys at work the next day.

On August 9, Friday morning, our family that was still at home with us got up as usual. We had two sons, Menno Jr. and Timothy, the twin daughters and three married children.

The menfolk went out to do the chores. The girls and I made breakfast and after breakfast Dad would pray and then they would be off to work with a kiss and a good bye. The dishes were washed and we went about the morning work as usual. The girls wanted to wash clothes, but the weather looked like it could rain, and it did. So we decided to sew their new dresses for their cousin Lavina and Joseph Schmucker's wedding. The wedding was to be August 22, 1991.

The girls did weekly work and I cut their dresses and sewed them. The sewing went well and lunch time soon came. We each had a big hamburger and Rebecca Marie put just about everything you could think of on top of hers. Rosalie and I teased her about a 'Dagwood' sandwich and she just smiled.

I went back to sewing and I told the girls to take a nap because they wanted to leave at five o'clock in the morning. They went upstairs and not long afterwards they were washing windows.

I asked, "Why didn't you take a nap?" It was hard for them to nap in the afternoon as they would always be doing something. Rebecca Marie came over to the sewing machine and I asked her,

"Why don't you relax just a few minutes." She lay down on the couch beside me and I looked at her face and eyes and had to wonder what she was thinking.

Her eyes were far beyond. Why didn't I ask her what she was thinking? I feel God didn't want me to know. She soon was up and helping her sister with the windows and everything seemed as usual. The dresses were soon finished and the girls were ready to go chore. They would bottle feed the calves before the menfolk came home. I had the girls try on their dresses before they went to do the chores. They did and I asked them what was wrong. They said they fit just right. So nice, I thought.

Our four teenagers were invited Friday evening to a birthday supper and singing about 12 miles from our place. When they left I kept looking down the road as far as I could see them. I thought, isn't it wonderful that they can all leave together. Menno left for a meeting. Some of the men from each church were picked to get a singing started on weekends.

I was home alone and there was a strange feeling in me. Soon everyone was home again, and oh, how I thought those footsteps sounded so welcoming and warmed my heart. I thanked the Lord that they could come home safely.

On August 10, Saturday morning, the sun came out so bright and everything went as usual. The girls went to wash clothes. I looked out of the bedroom window and the girls had an art on how to hang clothes on the line. Their clothes side by side and so neat. That is how they liked to do their work. It seemed they were always together.

Rebecca didn't feel real good that day. She was bothered with some headaches. Son Wilmer came home with his horse and Rebecca Marie went out to meet him. Rebecca said, "Hi, Wilmer." Wilmer looked at her and he told us on Sunday he couldn't tell anyone how her face looked. He said her face was so bright, he couldn't believe that it was his sister Rebecca Marie.

The yard needed to be mowed and our mower was a pony driven mower. Well, Rebecca Marie was having fun giving her two nieces rides while mowing. Dianna and Deborah loved to be with the twin aunts because the nieces were born and lived with us till 1989. It was hard to see them move. I thought there was nothing harder than when one of the children got married and moved away.

Soon it was Saturday afternoon. It was four o'clock and we still had a few more jobs to do, scrubbing sidewalks and getting Sunday dinner started. Our oldest daughter came to pick up the grandchildren to go home. Their plans were to go to a Middlebury church in the morning. As she drove past the horse rack, something caught her eye. Rebecca Marie's face was so bright.

She thought, "Rebecca Marie is my sister and Noah is her boyfriend." The thought left her until the next day.

The twins had planned for their special friends to come for Sunday dinner. They had planned barbecue chicken, blueberry pie, and homemade peach ice cream. Their dad went to the grocery store for them to get what the twins needed. It seemed everything went too smoothly.

At 6:30 Rebecca Marie's boyfriend, Noah Schmucker, came to pick her up with a car because he had left his horse and buggy at home. As they were leaving Noah's place, his father James, told them good bye and he said Noah and Rebecca Marie just waved and waved. They went to Dairy Queen for supper because that was a special place to go, and there they met some friends.

Rebecca Marie would always notice small children, because she was the youngest of the twins. She had more childish ways than Rosalie. Rebecca always wanted to walk behind Rosalie.

They went to a young folks' gathering. Noah's sister Emma was with Rebecca Marie and wondered why she stood by Noah because they had been so bashful to be seen together. Two of Rebecca Marie's friends talked to her and told us later that her face was so bright. At the gathering, everyone wondered why it seemed strange and quiet that night. I think God was talking to them.

Timothy and Emma came home to our home. Timothy heard the sirens and he wondered if it was Noah and Rebecca Marie because the sirens seemed awful touching to his heart. Rosalie also had a touching feeling when she heard the sirens around 11:30. I couldn't sleep. Seemed like I couldn't breathe.

Menno was snoring so I woke him up and told him how I felt. Menno said in his sleep, just pray again to the Lord. I did and dropped off to sleep. Soon I heard a knock on the door. I jumped out of bed and said to Menno, "That's a death knock." I managed to get to the door. It was a neighbor and he said there was an accident and they wanted us. I asked, "Are they dead?" He said, "Just come with us."

We could hardly get our clothes on. Rosalie was crying, saying, "I know she is dead." But we still didn't know. As we drove up to St. Rd. 37 and Graber Road, everything was so bright. Menno could hardly walk the closer we got to the lit up place. His heart was damaged from a virus in 1989. I thought my breath was going from me.

Menno said, "Look over there. There she lies covered up with a white sheet." How heartbreaking to uncover a body. She just looked like she was sleeping. I took hold of her limp hand and put her fingers in between mine, feeling a little warm, yet streaks of cool feeling also. Twin sister Rosalie knelt down beside me and she pleaded with Rebecca Marie, "Please just talk to me just one more time. Please." It was so sad. The helicopter had just left taking Noah for the hospital, but his life had also fled.

The police had gone to get Noah's parents, James and Katchen Schmucker. What sad news to hear that Noah had had heart problems since he was born and had a pig valve in his heart.

Police told us that they were crossing St. Rd. 37. They were over the center line of the road, but in the truck's path. Both had their necks broken. The horse was across the road, but later they had to shoot him. God can time everything, even the perfect timing to be in the path of the truck. God has our life planned. We still wonder why, but we will understand all by and by.

Noah had bought a new buggy just two weeks before and now it was all in pieces. I saved a piece of the new buggy. We had bought his old buggy just two weeks before and now it is my buggy. Our family was discussing before the tragedy that there was something special about Noah and Rebecca Marie.

The men that took care of the grave decided to dig one grave for the two bodies. This was the first death in both of our families. It changed our family life so much. No one knows until death hits your home. Many of the prayers are soothing to our pain because it is just an open wound to heal, but you learn to live with it. Menno and I could share our pain together.

Now it is two years and 13 days since my dear husband passed away to go meet Rebecca Marie and I'm looking forward to go meet them in Heaven some sweet day. Lord willing.

Thanks to all the people for their help with food and everything.

Susie M. Yoder: Dec. 8, 1986 - Dec. 19, 1989
Emanuel M. Yoder: Dec. 28, 1992 - Mar. 3, 1993

Submitted by: Melvin & Elizabeth Yoder, Baltic, OH

Susie M. Yoder

Saturday, November 11, 1989, was a cold winter day. I had decided to go to Mt. Hope to the monthly horse sale.

My wife did the usual Saturday cleaning and baking. Anna Mae and Susie, ages four and two, helped her with the dishes. In the afternoon they all went out to rake leaves, not dreaming that this would be one of the last times they both would help her. When I came home everything seemed fine. We weren't aware what I had picked up that day.

About 11 days later on Wednesday, November 22, I got sick with what I thought was the flu. Thursday was Thanksgiving, so we all spent the day at home. Friday was hog butchering day at my sister's place. I thought I'd try to help, but I didn't feel very good.

On Saturday I felt worse and did only what had to be done; some feed grinding and then the chores. When I came into the house after chores my wife said, "Well, don't you look funny. You must have the measles."

They had broken through that we could see them. Early the next morning, my wife went over to my parents, the next farm down the road, for help with the chores. I must have picked up the measles at the horse sale. A week later, on Sunday, I felt pretty good again so I took the girls for a sled ride. Later in the afternoon Mom came over, then she took the two girls along home for a while, not knowing this would be the last time for Susie.

The following Friday, December 8, was Susie's birthday. The two girls started with the measles. They both had them very hard and were very sick for a few days. Anna Mae got better, but Susie didn't. We worried about her getting dehydrated so I called the doctor. He told us to give her a lot of fluids.

By now Jonas, 11 months old, got them, too, but not very hard. Then on Friday we took Susie to the doctor. The doctor said she has the measles in her stomach and it just takes time. He didn't think she was dehydrated, but she had no control of her bowels anymore. It was so hard for us to see her so miserable. We tried to be patient and prayed for the good Lord to help us.

On Saturday she seemed better and she ate a little. That gave us some hope again. We did everything we knew for her and what other people told us to do. On Tuesday morning we decided to put her in the hospital because she just wasn't getting any better. I stayed with the children while my wife did the washing. Then I went across the field to the phone and called Dover Hospital and also got a driver.

By the time we left home she seemed to be getting worse. We put oxygen on her on the way to the hospital, but by the time we got to the hospital she didn't even respond anymore. The doctors worked on her and they told us to wait in the waiting room.

They soon came out and said they have to life flight her to Akron. A little later a nurse came and told us to come back to another room. Then the doctors came in and told us she didn't make it. She had died. At first we thought, not our child, but this time it was ours. They told us we could go in and see her, so we did. They told us it is the law that they have to do an autopsy. Doddy came to the hospital so we left for home.

The next couple hours and days are hard to describe because it just seemed like a dream till after the funeral. Then we really realized what an empty space one child makes.

We often think if we would have just taken her to the hospital sooner, but when she was 11 months old she was in the hospital for ten days with a virus infection. The medication reacted on her and she was very low for a while. It was hard for us to put her in again if we didn't have to. We just want to think it was the Lord's will. It seemed her time was here because when we made arrangements to take her to the hospital, she seemed to lose out very fast.

Our ways are not always God's ways. "God knows best." At first we thought everything would have to stop, but time went on. So with taking one day at a time, and with the Lord's help we kept going. Our loss is Susie's gain, but we often get 'zeitlang' for dear Susie. We often read or sang 'Ich War ein Kleines Kindlein' (I Was a Small Child), page 88 in the Leider Sammlung. That seemed to give some relief.

Later one of the relatives called the hospital and they said the autopsy showed she had been dehydrated and her body had gone into shock. That was why she had died so suddenly. The funeral was Thursday afternoon, December 21, a cold and windy day. The temperature was below zero.

Emanuel M. Yoder

Three years later on Tuesday, March 2, 1993, I went with a load to the Toledo area to look for used silos. I didn't get home till late that night. Everybody was already in bed. At 12 o'clock, Emanuel, the baby, woke up so Elizabeth fed him and put him back to bed as usual. The next morning at five o'clock, when I got up, I went to the baby bed before I went milking.

When I looked in I was shocked to see Emanuel lying with his face down. I touched his hand, it was cool. I quickly picked him up and called Elizabeth to come, but life was gone. "Oh no! Not again. Not us again," were the first thoughts, but yes it was and if it's God's will we want to try and accept it.

It was only the second night that we had laid him on his stomach. We just held him for a while because it just seemed like he was sleeping. He was still warm, all but his little hands, which were cool. I then went over to Doddy's in the other house for help. They went for the neighbors. The neighbors were soon here to do the chores and milking and whatever they could.

The coroner was called and he came out and examined him. He told us it was crib death or SIDS. Then the undertaker came and picked him up and funeral arrangements were made. Neighbors and relatives were here to help us carry the load, which helped us a lot.

The funeral was on Friday, March 5, a nice snowy day. Again we left part of us in the grave, but with the help of the Lord and prayers we made it through. It is something that the second time isn't easier than the first and there was never a time in our lives that God's presence seemed closer than at these times. I know it helps us to try to do our best since we would like to meet them some sweet day.

At the viewing, a man told us he has children that are out with the world and not going to church. How much better off they would be if they could have gone at this age. So we thought we have a lot more to be thankful for than we realized. A year after the funeral we were blessed with another baby boy. This helped with some empty feelings, but he still doesn't take Emanuel's place. We were glad he didn't sleep too long the first couple nights because it brought back some feelings.

It broke our hearts to see you go,
but you didn't go alone,
For part of us went with you,
The day God called you home.

Never to suffer again with tears,
Never to worry about childish fears;
Resting safely at Jesus' feet,
Where we hope same day to meet.

So lead us on, dear God, our Father,
Through the dark and lonely way;
Give us patience, strength, and courage,
Let us never go astray.

About two and one half years later on July 17, 1995, my oldest brother was killed in a tanker truck and road cart accident. Jonas E. Yoder, age 43, left behind his wife, one son and three daughters.

Mark E. Stutzman: Sept. 5, 1977 - May 24, 1984
Submitted by: Emery Jr. & Mary Stutzman, Peebles, Ohio

May 24, 1984, was the date set for the wedding of Andrew Schrock and Ruth Miller. Andrew is the son of Ernest Schrocks of Ouhland, Montana, and Ruth is the daughter of Robert Millers from West Union, Ohio. One of the gifts for the new couple was a day of beautiful weather. On our way to the wedding, our family had no idea of how our lives would be changed by evening.

After the wedding services, a noon feast, and several hours spent visiting, our family was heading home on St. Rd. 32, Appalachian Highway. We were headed east. All of our family was in a two-seater buggy: Karen, ten; Martha, nine; Mark, six; Ernest, five; Emery III, three; and Lewis, six months. Karen, Martha, Emery III, and Mark were in the back seat. Mary and I were in the front seat with Ernest setting between us and Mary holding Lewis. The children were starting to fall asleep. Mark was sitting in the left corner, asleep, the last I checked on them.

The next thing I remember was a very loud crash and then all was dark. I was aware of not having hold of the reins and rolling in a somersault. Then all was quiet. When I got up, the dust was still settling with buggy parts scattered along the road. I didn't realize that my ankle was broken although it was numb.

I walked over to where Mark was lying. I felt sure Mark was dead because he had very bad head injuries and thought the same of Mary since she would not respond. Then my ankle hurt so bad that I had to sit down. That is when I saw one of the children lying on the bank. To me it seemed like a long time until the emergency squads arrived.

The whole family was taken to our local West Union Hospital by three squads. From there Ernest and Lewis were transferred to Cincinnati; Karen, Martha, and Emery were transferred to Columbus, all by helicopter. Mary and I stayed at West Union until Saturday when we were transferred to Riverside Hospital in Columbus.

Mark was pronounced dead at the scene. Mark's death was instant due to brain and scalp lacerations, but he also had a broken nose and arm. The driver who hit us says he never saw us. His first recollection is of feeling a jolt and having his windshield shattered.

Karen had a dislocated hip, concussion, hairline fracture in her elbow, sprained knee, and stitches on the scalp. Martha had a concussion, deep cuts in the knee, and stitches under her chin. Ernest had his leg broken between the knee and ankle. Emery III had a concussion and an injured liver. He was listed as very critical at first. Lewis only had a tear on his stomach but his doctor said a hair's width deeper and it would have exposed the intestines.

Mary was semi-conscious until Saturday morning. First reports said her lower vertebra was fractured but later x-rays showed no fracture. The doctor explained that the bone had a similar appearance that a piece of ice would have if a knife would be stuck into it. She also had second and third degree burns on her hip and lower leg. Her most painful injury was a bruise on the left hip and back, where she probably connected with the truck. There was an abrasion on her left cornea which made it painful to open her eyes.

My injuries needed stitches in my scalp, shoulder, elbow and knee. The knee injury was the worst. Friends, neighbors, and relatives did well in making arrangements. The funeral was held at the Aden Yutzy home (Mary's sister), on May 26th.

They had their own excitement on Saturday, May 25th. A son was born to them and he was named Marcus. We'll never forget the feeling we had when word came to the hospital of what they had named him.

Plans also needed to be made for a new cemetery. This was the first death in our young community of eight years. The cemetery is located on the Aden Yutzy farm where a new fence was built, with some nice trees inside the fence. Dan Troyer, Bishop Jonas Bontrager, and Bishop Andy R. Miller shared the funeral services.

Bishop Jonas Bontrager had joined us in marriage 11 years earlier and we used to live in Bishop Andy R. Miller's district in Holmes County before moving to West Union.

The horse had to be put to sleep since he suffered a broken leg. After the accident I saw a horse standing beside the road eating grass with his left leg bone exposed. There was not much left of the buggy. It could all be cleaned up by hand because it was in small pieces. It was taken to a neighbor's house.

There were friends and relatives that stayed with the children at the hospitals all taking turns. There was also somebody staying with us at the local hospital all the time. By Saturday morning, Mary was still not doing too well.

With the employer of the driver that hit us, being concerned, he suggested transferring us to Riverside Methodist Hospital in Columbus. So our family doctor requested one wing of the local hospital to be closed for one hour on Saturday afternoon and Mark's body was brought in so Mary and I could view him yet before we left for Columbus.

Then we were transferred by helicopter. None of our family was able to be at the funeral. Someone in the community sent a guest book amongst all the people attending the funeral. This was very much appreciated. Then some of our relatives stopped at the hospital on their way home and brought this book along for us. We think Sunday, the day of the funeral, was the longest and hardest day we ever had.

Mary was still on pain killers, so she was still drowsy. We called the hospital where the other children were and tried to tell them what was taking place. The youngest ones didn't understand. After we were all at home, they kept asking when Mark would come home. We tried to explain that he went to live with Jesus in a home far better than we could provide here.

People of the community had the grass mowed and house cleaned up when we got home. Ernest and Lewis stayed in the hospital five days and then stayed with relatives until we came home. Mary and I were in the hospital nine days. Karen, Martha, and Emery III stayed ten days. We'll never forget how empty the house was when we came home.

Help was extended to us in many ways; through prayer, encouragement, visits, and help on the farm. Samuel Schmucker, son of Rudy and Mary Schmucker, had been working for us here on the farm during the summer of 1984. He did a very good job and his help was a big asset to us during our recovery. We also had two girls helping Mary in the house with all of her patients to care for.

In a period of three days, our community witnessed a wedding, a death, and a birth. Mark is greatly missed. We know he is being well taken care of and is far better off than we are. We'll just have to try and consider ourselves blessed and wait until the Lord determines that it is time for us to reunite.

Kevin Gingerich: Sept. 1992- Dec. 20, 1992

Submitted by: Melvin & Katie Gingerich, Arthur, Illinois

On December 20, 1992, we went to Melvin's parents for Christmas. His Uncle Lester from Indiana was there for the day. That afternoon we went to my parents' for supper. They had had church services at their house that day.

When we left for home we never thought that we wouldn't make it home. We were heading north on the Arthur-Atwood Road about two miles north of Arthur when a drunk woman hit us. She was driving at a high rate of speed and ran into the back of the buggy shattering and scattering the horse, buggy and its contents. The horse died at the scene of the accident. The woman had been at a Christmas party in Arthur.

Richard, five, our oldest child, was the only one able to walk around at the accident. He remembers quite a bit about the accident. The others were injured. Kevin and I were both unconscious. The whole family was taken to St. Mary's Hospital by several ambulances. Kevin died later that night.

Owen Helmuth had come to the scene of the accident. He got our parents and brought them to the hospital.

Little three and a half month old Kevin's funeral was December 24 at the Andy E. Mast home. It was cold that day. The parents and Dorothy were not able to attend the funeral. The preachers said at the funeral that they had never seen in this area where the parents weren't able to attend their small child's funeral.

Richard and Treva were the only ones able to attend. They had to sit on pillows at the funeral because of their bumps and bruises. Richard, five, and Treva, four, had only bumps and bruises from the accident. They were treated and released on December 22. After their release, they were taken to the Marvin D. Helmuth home to be taken care of.

Melvin had a fractured vertebra and a cut on the top of his head. He had to wear a back brace for some time afterward. It was several days before he got to come see me. When he was released from the hospital, he got to stay in the room with Dorothy.

After she was released he stayed with me. Dorothy, almost three years old, had a broken and cut leg. She was put in traction until the doctor was sure he could save her leg. She was then put in a body cast. She had to have her body cast on until the middle of March. After that, it was several weeks before she could walk again.

In May she broke her leg again. The doctor said her bones were still weak from being in a body cast so long. She got a walking cast then. She was very discouraged until it was all over with. When she was released on January 13, she was also taken to the Marvin Helmuth home.

She had her third birthday while in the hospital. The nurses sure gave her a lot of attention. One of the nurses made a large birthday greeting out of cardboard. They all put their names on it and gave it to her for her birthday.

They did surgery on me that night yet and took a blot clot off my brain. They had to shave all the hair off my head. I also had a cracked pelvis. I was in I.C.U. for two weeks. On December 27, I went backwards. The doctors said if the swelling is inward there is nothing they can do for me. They did some tests to see if it was and the tests showed that wasn't the problem.

The family had to come in and talk to me, to keep my mind working. The doctors said if they don't, I could very easily become a vegetable for the rest of my life. I was released on January 15. They set up a hospital bed for me at home. I had to have therapy until May. I had to use a walker for a while. They started therapy in the hospital and after I came home, two therapists came out several times a week. One came three times and the other came two times a week. One therapist was helping me learn to walk again and the other was working on my mind, trying to bring me back to being myself.

I can now do my own work, but tire easily. After we came home from the hospital, someone had to stay with us 24 hours a day until the middle of March. We had Eli Yoder's Rachel helping us, plus the families took turns helping every day and staying overnight.

Melvin's parents took us to church at Levi E. Schrocks on February 14. It was the first time after the accident. We came home right after church was over.

We had to have help with laundry and summer work that year. We are very thankful for all the help, food, and prayers received during and after our trials.

In September of 1994, we were richly blessed with a healthy and happy baby girl.

Matthew Lee Yoder: Nov. 6, 1993 - July 13, 1995

Submitted by: Ervin & Edna Sue Yoder, Topeka, Indiana

To our great joy, a healthy, chubby little baby boy weighing eight pounds, eight ounces was born to us on November 6, 1993. Little did we realize at that time that he had an illness.

He was six weeks old when he started out with a cold, cough, and rash. We took him to the family doctor and he gave him an antibiotic and said he should get better. It got somewhat better, then within a couple of weeks, it got worse again with a high fever at times.

We took him in again several different times giving him stronger antibiotics every time. About the third time we took him back he had a fever of 106°, and the doctor said he had to be put in the hospital. We were at Goshen Hospital for nine days. The doctors thought it was a cold virus of some kind and nothing serious. We brought him home again and a couple weeks later he got worse again.

Then our family doctor sent us to a children's specialist and he found that his white blood cell count was abnormal. So on March 4, 1994 we were sent to Riley's Children's Hospital in Indianapolis and by that time Matthew had pneumonia and was a very sick baby. They put him in I.C.U. for two days and ran tests.

He got better again, so they moved him to the regular children's floor in an isolated room since they didn't really know what was wrong yet. When we went into his room we had to wear masks, gloves, and gowns. After being there a week at Riley they diagnosed him, and oh, what shocking news to us!

They told us he had an immune deficiency that was called SCIDS standing for Severe Combined Immune Deficiency, and the only cure for it would be a bone marrow transplant. He was born without the white blood cells and that is why he couldn't fight infections. While at Riley they checked both of us and Matthew's two sisters to see if any of us would be a perfect match. We were all just a half match. They chose Ervin as the donor rather than me because I had the CMV virus and Ervin didn't. They didn't do transplants at Riley for children under 18, so it was decided we would go to the University of Wisconsin Children's Hospital in Madison, Wisconsin.

While at Riley we stayed at the Ronald McDonald house and we were there for three weeks. On March 29, 1994, we left Riley to go to Madison, Wisconsin. They had a room waiting for us at their Ronald McDonald house just a block from the hospital.

Matthew was admitted at the hospital and put in a unit where the cancer patients were, even though Matthew didn't have any kind of cancer. The reason he was put in that unit was to keep him isolated from others. These were very strange surroundings for us. We got to the hospital in the evening, and that evening yet we got a phone call from a couple living in Black Earth, Wisconsin.

We were so surprised that they had heard about us already. They came to the hospital the next day and said if we needed anything, they would take us places. Such nice, willing people we had already met and since then we have been friends. The doctors there in Madison told us that Matthew would have to have chemotherapy to kill all of his immune system, what little he had, before the transplant.

He had 11 days of chemotherapy, being very sick at times while getting his treatments. The day finally came for the transplant, April 19. They took 250 cc of bone marrow from Ervin's hip bones and screened it down to 13 cc. They then diluted it making it 27 cc and that is what Matthew got. They gave it through his IV central line. We couldn't thank the dear Lord enough that everything went okay that day. After his transplant, everything seemed to be going all right and he was doing real well with his blood counts going up again.

On May 14, we took Matthew back home to Indiana to be a family again, which we were so thankful for. May 15, the very next day after we were home, Matthew started with a fever so we took him to Lutheran Hospital in Fort Wayne. He had started with a touch of pneumonia and since it wasn't long after the transplant, the doctor in Fort Wayne wanted him to go back to Wisconsin.

On the 17th of May he was flown with Med Flight back to

Madison which was such a disappointment to us. We kept praying and trusting the Lord would help us. He was readmitted in Madison for a couple of days and after several different complications, he wasn't always in the hospital. We had him with us most of the time at the Ronald McDonald house, taking him over to the hospital's clinic for checkups several times a week.

For most of the summer of 1994 we were in Wisconsin. A load from Indiana came to visit almost every weekend, which helped pass the time for us. Finally the day came that they thought we could take Matthew home again since he was doing so well.

On August 20, we went home. What a rejoicing time, being home as a family again. We took him to Fort Wayne almost every week for checkups for quite a while after we came home from Wisconsin. He was admitted again in Fort Wayne the last of October and had to be in the hospital over his first birthday.

We thought it couldn't be, but we also wanted to accept the Lord's will. He was in the hospital due to an infection. He was hospitalized again two different times in March of 1995. One time was because he had the RSV virus. Also in May, he was back in with spinal meningitis and his liver had completely quit working. The color of his skin was a yellow-orange and it was so hard to see him so sick. He was very low and that time we didn't think he would survive and be with us any longer.

Through a miracle he seemed to change overnight and once again we could take Matthew home to be with us as a family. On Monday evening, July 10, 1995, I, Matthew's aunt, and his two sisters took him on a bike ride. He was so happy that evening and little did we know that the next morning we would take him to the hospital with a fever again.

His condition suddenly got worse. They took x-rays and ran tests but could not find the problem. On Wednesday it was decided they would do exploratory surgery to see if they could find the problem. The doctor warned us that he might not come out of it this time. We left it all in God's hands.

They found the problem. Part of his colon was deteriorated. They took the bad part of his colon out. After he came out of surgery he was on a breathing machine. This was very hard for us to see because this was the first time he was ever on a breathing machine. Other times when he was in the hospital, he was on oxygen at times, but had never been on a breathing machine. It was so sad to see our precious little boy hooked up to so many machines and IV lines.

After a while his kidneys also stopped working and he started filling up with fluids. Finally the doctors and nurses said they had done everything they could and were very understanding that we couldn't see our loved one suffer any longer. Everything was taken off and he died peacefully ten minutes later at two o'clock in the afternoon on Thursday, July 13.

Even though he went through pain, suffering and had hospital stays, he was such a great joy to have. Always happy when feeling good, he had a smile for everyone. We will never regret the time we spent with him, but rather praise God for the opportunity to have him as a gift from God. The support from the community was overwhelming with encouragement, prayers, cards and letters, visits and phone calls.

Matthew is still missed so much that not a day goes by that we don't think about our precious loved one. Yet it is a big comfort to know he's in pure happiness and we all hope to meet him one glad day when Jesus comes again.

"Precious Memories, how they linger."

Lester Stutzman: June 28, 1993 - June 16, 1995

Submitted by: Vernon M. & Ada Stutzman, Baltic, Ohio

In the last part of April 1995, we noticed our son Lester was leaning his head to one side. Otherwise he seemed like a healthy, active one-and-a-half year old, talking and such. The thought was in our mind that something more serious might be wrong, but we tried to push those thoughts to a side.

We tried different chiropractors, but they were not very successful. We also took Lester to our family doctor and he looked him over and said it was sore and stiff muscles. Since there were no other effects with it, no vomiting, not much swelling, etc. that gave us some relief. But as mentioned earlier, the thoughts in our mind couldn't fully rest.

On the second day of June we got up and Lester was up soon after, so I picked him up and put him out on the couch. Then he went to sleep again. I left for work, but by nine o'clock I got a phone call from our neighbor at home. He said that I was to come home right away. The thoughts in my mind were almost more than I could take.

We hurried home and Mom said Lester vomited three times. We went to Millersburg and there they took a CAT scan. The doctor came back and said they found a tumor and plans were being made to transfer him to Akron Children's Hospital.

With broken hearts, we tried to contact his grandparents before the squads came to transport us to Akron Hospital. The doctor there read the CAT scan pictures then took Lester in for an MRI which is like a CAT scan, but a closer look. He came out of the MRI and was taken into surgery to get an external tube working to relieve the pressure and also to drain the fluid off the brain. Soon the doctor came and said all was good at that time and took us to the recovery room.

Lester was partly awake and we were in there a few minutes. It was getting late so the nurses fixed us up with the Ronald McDonald House. The next morning, Saturday, we found Lester in more pain. They opened the valve-like thing in the external tube some more and that gave him relief again. The nurse explained that the little bag on the headboard of the crib was what was draining from the tube. It seemed like quite a lot for a small child. The next days he seemed pretty good, not on such strong pain relievers, just Tylenol and he didn't need that all the time.

We were to meet Dr. Maukkassa on Monday. He was to explain where the tumor was. He said the tumor was on the brain stem where all the nerves and vessels go through that control the rest of your body. The tumor was growing right in the most dangerous part of the neck to be operated on. The tumor was already the size of a golf ball and from the doctor's point of view, surgery had a small percent chance.

This made for a tough decision for us as well as for the grandparents. We also met with a chemo doctor about treatments, which was also a hard decision. Since we didn't know what kind of tumor it was, it would be a very small chance for a change. As we got help from above, the One who knows all best, we decided to put the shunt internal and try natural herbs.

After seven days in Intensive Care we moved Lester up to floor seven. By late in the afternoon on Saturday, June 10, we got a release to take him home. When we arrived at home, we were all quite relieved and happy. With Lester's sister, Marie, three and one half, and grandparents and visitors coming and going, Lester seemed pretty good. He wanted to get down on the floor and play with his sister and cousins. But after eight days in the hospital, he was rather weak for that.

The next couple days all seemed to be moving along real well as Lester played more with toys. He had been eating normal food up till he got sick, but now he was on a special diet and still doing good on eating, but maybe not drinking like usual.

We can't be thankful enough for those good days, because late Tuesday night things changed around. He vomited and was also pretty restless. Early Wednesday morning we called Hospice for a nurse that does house calls. The nurse soon came out and looked things over and said she will be back in a few hours with a stronger pain reliever and prescription from the doctor. By evening Lester seemed to be resting quite better.

The nurse would stop in once a day. The next forenoon, Mom gave Lester a bath around ten o'clock. Then he went to sleep, which was usual after his daily bath. Around 11:00 or 11:30 Mom came and said something was wrong. Lester was in a very deep sleep and it seemed he wouldn't wake up. Oh Lord, help us! A helpful sister-in-law made a call for the nurse to come as soon as possible and she arrived soon after.

She looked Lester over and said Lester was taking a big step ahead of us. If we wanted to contact the family, we should do it. By evening the family on both sides, as well as some neighbors, had gathered to help each other ease the wound in our hearts. Lester lingered on through the night. Around five o'clock the next morning, we could tell Lester's heart rate wasn't quite as strong. With Lester on my lap and Mom holding his hand, Lester took his last deep breath around 8:15, on Friday morning, June 16.

Then, in our weak little minds, we tried to get the little body, so free from sin, ready for burial. The funeral was held Sunday, June 18, 1995. Lester's namesake, his uncle, was making a new church suit for Lester's birthday, which would have been June 28. So Lester's little body was dressed in a new suit for burial.

All this brought a lot of questions from his sister, Marie. She and the whole family missed him very much, but there is also joy. No more pain and all the temptation down here in this sinful world. Lester was still so pure and clean.

Yes, the Lord takes and He also gives, because two weeks later we were blessed with another boy. The little one helped us a lot, but having joy while still in deep sorrow, brought such mixed feelings. God was always right at our side.

Wilma Miller: Apr. 25, 1954 - Jan. 6, 1973
Kathryn Miller: Oct. 11, 1955 - Jan. 8, 1973

Submitted by: Mrs. Nathaniel Miller, Topeka, Indiana

I hardly know how to begin to put in words on paper how everything went before and after. The anxiety, fear, anguish, helplessness, and total shock.

We had a married daughter, the Leander Jay Keims, living in Kansas. They were at our house for the Christmas holidays and left for home on Saturday morning, January 6, 1973. That evening Wilma, 18, and Kathryn, 17, were invited to their cousin Marianna's for the night. They wanted to attend church the next day.

They left home at dusk with our horse and buggy. We went on with our chores and were just done when a car drove in the lane. Two boys got out and asked if the girls were at home. "No they're not," we said. Then they said there had been an accident and the girls were involved. Little did we realize that one was gone and we would have to give up the other dear daughter, too.

The boys took us to the scene. Both girls were lying on the ground covered with blankets and unconscious. Wilma had already died and Kathryn was taken to a Fort Wayne Hospital. A driver took Nathaniel and me to the hospital.

In a couple days we thought we could ask Kathryn how this all came about, but it was not to be. Kathryn was in the intensive care unit with a breathing machine on her. The other children at home did the chores with lots of help from kind neighbors. All of them were anxiously waiting for our return.

Kathryn made no change on Sunday. The doctor said if she survived she would only be like a vegetable. Please, no. We love her so! Nathaniel told them to take her off the machine. She soon passed away.

In a daze we tried to think what should be done next. Our sons Lloyd and Aaron were in l-W service in Massillon, Ohio, and by this time were at the hospital. We all went home together.

There was Wilma in our bedroom already. There were many

questions in our mind. God only knows why. The girls had driven out in front of a station wagon. We will never know if they didn't see the car or if they thought they could cross before it got close.

Word was sent to Kansas to our daughter and her family. By the time they reached home, word was there. Their neighbors helped them prepare to return to Indiana right away by train. They came to our home at 10:30 the night before the funeral.

There was only one viewing for Kathryn. The funeral was January 9, 1973, at Orla Troyers. We had a double funeral, and that morning it was six below zero. Two caskets, two dear daughters gone at one time, were put in one grave.

Kathryn had just quit her job and Wilma worked at Emma Starcraft sewing. After her last evening of work she had stood beside the door where the workers all passed through to go home and had said good bye to them all. This was unusual for her to do so.

They could both sing very well and had everyone singing at home. But, after that the singing quit.

"The Lord giveth and the Lord taketh", "Thy will be done". I still feel the shock of it. Solomon says, "To everything there is a season, and a time to every purpose under the heaven; a time to be born and a time to die." Ecclesiastes 3:1&2

Nathaniel E. Miller: Nov. 14, 1917 - June 27, 1985
Submitted by: Mrs. Nathaniel E. Miller, Topeka, Indiana

Nathaniel died on the morning of our youngest son's wedding day. During his last five weeks he had a hard cold and we could not get him better. He was up and around all the time and helped some with the chores until the last morning. He said he would not help milk to save his strength for the wedding day.

I made our usual breakfast and after breakfast I did the dishes while he again rested. As I was finishing the dishes, he came walking out of the living room looking very pale. I asked him if he didn't feel good. He shook his head and walked to the summer kitchen. I gave him a chair to sit on and called Lloyd, our son, who was outside choring. Lloyd lives here and does the farming.

We wanted to take him to the hospital but he did not want to go, so I said I would stay home from the wedding with him. He got rapidly worse and did not seem to be aware of anything. Lloyd called the EMS and tried to revive him by mouth to mouth resuscitation. Nothing we could do helped. How helpless a person feels being by someone like this. By now it was time to go to the wedding. Neighbors came again and kindly showed their sympathy and helped in every way they could.

Word was taken to the wedding home. It was hard on the part of the family that was there. At mid-afternoon, LeRoy and his new wife came home to shed tears with me. The newlyweds did not open their gifts on their wedding day. After the funeral, we all went to the bride's home and they opened their gifts.

So it is. I am still struggling on in this world, waiting on my day to go be with the Lord. Living on hope. Life on this earth is so uncertain. On Nathaniel and my wedding day we were told there would be a parting day. We were privileged more years together than some are, but oh, I wasn't ready to give him up. I never realized how it would be, but the Lord has been so very good to me.

I still have three daughters living with me. They take good care of me, as do the other children. We have a large family and the grandchildren all take time to visit me. I thank the Lord for them all.

Blessed are the dead which die in the Lord from henceforth; yea, saith the spirit that they may rest from their labours, and their works do follow them. Revelation 14: 13

We feel our loss is his gain.

Allen H. Beachy: Jan. 1, 1966 - May 9, 1976

Submitted by: Henry & Ada Beachy, Millersburg, Ohio

On April 5, 1974, our son, Allen, age eight, got sick. We thought he had the flu because he had a sore throat, high fever and swollen glands. He was pretty sick so we took him to the doctor. The doctor gave him a shot and medicine and said he was a really sick boy and if he didn't get better in a couple days, to bring him back.

Allen didn't improve very much so we took him to the doctor again. He sent us to the hospital for blood tests. We had just come home when our English neighbors came and told us Allen's blood count was real low and we needed to take him to the hospital in Dover or Akron right away.

We took him to Dover, which was closer. There they took more tests and told us they thought he had leukemia. This was a real shock for us all, because until then he had been a healthy, active boy. They sent us to Akron Hospital where he stayed for the next ten days.

He got blood transfusions and started on chemotherapy treatments. When we took him home, he was a lot better. We had to bring him back to the hospital as an outpatient every week for six months so he could get his medicine, blood tests, and spinal taps.

This was nothing to look forward to, but he was very patient through it all. He always got sick to his stomach and vomited from the chemotherapy treatments, but that lasted only one day and night. After six months, they said he was in remission and this was good news.

Allen went back to school, helped work, and played, but still had to go to Akron every two weeks for tests. In the fall of 1975 the doctor said the leukemia is coming back, so we had to take him to Akron again every week where he got more chemotherapy treatments. They just didn't seem to help very much. Still, he went to school part of the time.

The day before his tenth birthday, which was January first, Allen had a reaction to his treatment and became very sick. He vomited so much that he became dehydrated and we took him to Akron with an ambulance. He was there for two days. The doctor said there was not much they could do for him anymore.

From then on, he had many sick days, but also some good days, till he passed away May ninth. It was so hard to see him suffer so, but he never complained and was so easy to take care of. I hope we can be like that if we ever need care. He left behind eight brothers and six sisters. Two brothers were born after he passed away.

We hope this was a help for us all to bring us closer to God and Jesus our Savior. We long to see him again someday. It has now been twenty years since he's gone and we have to think how lucky he was to go at that age.

Lavina Miller: Dec. 18, 1981 - Sept. 6, 1985
Submitted by: Orva E. & Wilma Miller: LaGrange, Indiana

It was on a Friday and we were getting ready to have church services in our home the following Sunday. Most of our sisters and in-laws were here to help. I don't remember much of the day except Lavina, who dearly loved cookies, kept asking for a cookie. I knew we had some for break, but I firmly told her we needed to wait because we didn't have enough for all to eat as many as we wanted.

The others had left and I got her another cookie and sat to nurse the baby. She sat on the arm of my chair on the opposite side from where the baby was nursing, and changed sides when I changed the baby. This was routine.

When we went to do chores, an implement dealer arrived, whom we were expecting, because neighbor Joe and Orva wanted to look at a corn binder he had to sell. He parked on the road and we had all crossed to take a look. Then Orva and I crossed back, Orva to get the check book and I to resume chores.

Usually the girls would play till we asked them to come, but this evening when we heard a speeding truck come from the south, we froze as we saw Lavina come running toward the road. We shouted "Wait!"

The driver of the speeding truck heard us shout and then he hit something. It seemed as if I knew it was about to happen, and yet, I clung to the hope that she would reach home safely. But no, she was killed instantly.

Our minds were no longer aware of what was happening. We were in shock. We never heard the ambulance sirens and yet we were told they were used. We never knew who did our chores. Life stopped! We had to be told our next move.

Many friends came to share our sorrow. Neighbors had the church services. The funeral was on Monday. Then as we arrived at the cemetery, a terrible wind and rain storm came through, matching the storm in our hearts. We waited in our buggies until it let up, then in the calm of the storm, we laid our precious little girl to rest. As the casket was lowered, our hearts were shattered. "But yes, we had been told children are a gift of God", even though it may be hard to let go. Coming home we were blessed with a double rainbow. His promise!

The morning after the funeral was something only those with the experience know. We had been tired, now rested. No one around and we were to do our own chores. Where were our boots? The pails and scoops weren't in their usual places. With our heavy hearts it seemed our chores wouldn't get done. Bless the thoughtful neighbor who sent his son to help us.

We finally got done, but then coming to the house, where was our Lavina who almost always met us at the door in her nightclothes. She would ask, "Mom, do you have the milk pails washed?" And yes, we had many cookies, her favorite snack all around, but no Lavina to share them with.

It was the many people who stopped to visit and to help that made it possible to get through those first days. Lavina had always been a Mama baby. At the table, as soon as suitable, she'd slip into my lap till after prayer. There were times she'd insist I hold her and tell her stories. So much so that I at times found it was hard to fully describe my feelings.

She was a sweet girl. I wanted to hold her and tell her stories, but there was work patiently waiting. Many times she'd hug me and tell me, "I love you!" She also loved swing rides and would say, "Push me hard. Push me into the clouds." Usually in church, she would sit on my lap. She was on one side and the baby on the other. Many folks told me afterwards, they missed Lavina more because of her being with me so much.

Sunday mornings as the ministers passed through shaking hands with the women, they would also shake with the little girls. She would always refuse and try to hide, until the week before she passed away. That Sunday morning she bravely held out her hand and smiled. Of course we praised her for accepting this, but it was the only time it happened. It was very hard for me to accept it at first.

In our first years of marriage, we had one stillborn baby and one that lived only three hours. After almost seven years of marriage, we were blessed with a healthy girl to love and care for. Three years later Lavina came and then we had Homer. He was only one year old when Lavina passed away. I thought I was very thankful for the little family that was shared with us and now He asked for one of our little family.

Many of our friends and neighbors had big families, why us? We were very much aware now how very little we have to say of life. Time has healed the deep wound, though it still hurts at times, but it was all for a reason. A stepping stone in our life.

Afterwards, our six year old slept with us along the foot of the bed for a long time. But she finally accepted a youth bed, set alongside our bed. Several times afterwards, we got unexpected company and all because of a rainbow. It reminded them of us. So there was a blessing and we have many friendships deeper because of this time of trial we share.

In closing, we wish God's blessing on each and everyone!

Regina Faye Mullet: Jan. 1, 1993 - Aug. 23, 1994

Submitted by: Wayne I. & Wilma Mullet, Topeka, Indiana

August 23, 1994, was a beautiful sunny summer day. I was busy at the sewing machine all day. Daddy had gone to work at a carpentry job. Sister Doris and brother Kevin were playing as usual. Regina was in the house most of the day and just wanted me to hold her.

Now I think, why didn't I just sit down and hold her all day.

After dinner she took a long nap. We feel she was already bound for her Heavenly home. It was kind of unusual for her to take such a long nap. I checked on her once, but she was sleeping so soundly that I just let her sleep. She didn't even move when I touched her. She was always such a quiet and innocent little girl.

That forenoon she was playing in the sandbox and I was at the window watching her, thinking to myself - what would we do if someone would get her? Never realizing by evening she wouldn't be here with us anymore. She stood out to all the cousins, friends and neighbors.

A week before the accident the neighbors had come together for ice cream. She walked up to one of the men and wanted to be held. So he picked her up and held her awhile. It seemed almost anyone could hold her. She liked her grandparents a lot, too. She also liked her pacifier and was starting to talk with it in her mouth.

It was the day the milk man usually comes and I didn't realize he hadn't been there till around four o'clock. Then around 4:30 we started to milk. Regina was in the cow stable with us and I was afraid she would get kicked by the cows, so I talked her into going to the sandbox to play until I got done. She finally went over to the door, turned around and looked at me with a smile I will never forget. I went and helped her outside, never thinking that it would be the very last time I'd hold her.

About five to ten minutes later the milk truck came. I went to check on her and she was playing so nicely in the sandbox. After the milk truck left we went on with the milking.

Just then Doris came and said, "Come see what's lying in the drive. Regina's head is all flat!"

Those words still hurt so much. We knew right away what had happened. To find one of your children in a terrible sight like that, we will never forget and I'd never wish anyone else to see something like that. The wheels of the truck went over her head. We could view the rest of her body, but not her head.

We're just thankful we could see that much.

A year later, on August 25, we were blessed with a healthy boy whom we named Arlin Jay. He brought much joy into our home, but he still can't take the place of our dear little Regina Faye.

A precious one from us is gone,
A voice we loved is stilled.
A place is vacant in our home,
Which never can be filled.
God in His wisdom has recalled
The bloom His love had given.
And though the body slumbers here,
The soul is safe in Heaven.

Gone but not forgotten!

Rosie Zehr: 1980 - Mar. 23, 1983
Lucy Zehr: Oct. 1982 - Apr. 10, 1983

Submitted by: Joseph & Lucy Zehr, Grabill, Indiana

I will try and write about our two children we lost in a house fire on March 23, 1983, but not without a few tears!

We felt that something was going to happen, but we just didn't know when. We had this feeling for almost two weeks. On March 20th we were all to church for the last time. We just didn't know at that time that it would be the last time.

Wednesday morning, March 23, at 8:30 is when things took place. I was just coming in from my fiberglass shop when I saw my wife, Lucy, come running out of the house screaming, "The house is on fire!"

We had four children in the house at that time. We finally got in the south door. I held onto my wife's feet while she crawled on the floor to get the baby. The rest of the family came out on their own, by age. This was really something to go through. Something we will never forget.

They took the children to Decatur Hospital first and then they were rushed to St. Joe Hospital. I went up later around 11 o'clock and oh what a sight to see. We will never forget the experience of going through this.

We lost our first one at five o'clock PM, the same day. At that time we had three children at St. Joe Hospital and two at Decatur

Hospital. Jonas was in Decatur with first degree burns and Johnny was in for a deep cut on his arm. They were both released the next day.

Rosie died first. The funeral was on March 25th in the afternoon. Rosie was three years old. Lucy died April 10th. Her funeral was on April 13th. Lucy was only six months old. Rosie had second and third degree burns. Lucy had third and fourth degree burns. Lucy was burned worse but never passed out. She knew us till the last 15 minutes. Barbara, the third one at St. Joe, was there with some second and third degree burns. She was there for five weeks. Those were some very long weeks.

As we were having funerals, rebuilding our house, and going back and forth to see our children, we were under a lot of stress. If we would not have prayed to God and asked for help, we could not have made it through. It was all in God's hands.

It seemed like we were lost for a while, like we were in a different world. What a load on our shoulders. God helped us through. Our other children stayed over at Sam and Ruth Hilty's for five weeks. We just can't thank them enough to think that they took these seven children in and took real good care of them. Again, this was in the Lord's hands.

This really makes an empty home when two are not here. This was very hard on us when we think of the empty places at the table, in bed, at church, or wherever we go. There are always two missing, but we will leave this all up to God. He does not make any mistakes. Now we have to worry about the ones that are left behind.

This has changed our lifestyle. It brought us closer to God. Once in a while, our children and we talk about what happened and why? Then again I tell them it is in God's hands. Let's worry about us. We are older and can we go to Heaven? Rosie and Lucy, we know where they are at.

Like Jesus said, "Don't cry over me. Cry over you and your children." Is this ever true. We cry every once in a while then we seem to feel better, but we can't forget them.

There is a lot more to write, but I will try to save space for others. These little girls are gone, but not forgotten!

Again we shall say thanks for all the prayers, help, and money to all the ones that helped. We had our house built back up in five weeks, thanks to all the help we had.

We now live in Allen County, Indiana. We moved on June 19, 1984. We were blessed with two more girls named Betty Ann and Ruth Ann.

Norman J. Schlabach: Nov. 5, 1976 - Nov. 6, 1995

Submitted by: Jonas L. & Fannie Schlabach

At the time of our oldest son Norman's death, we had three boys and three girls. Norman was 19 years and one day old; Linda, 17; Daniel, 16; Laura, 14; Alta, 13; and Wayne, seven.

November 6 was just like any other day. When I got up I felt more peaceful than I had for a week. Jonas, my husband, and Daniel, with the help of our neighbor Joni Miller (my brother) and his son, William, were going to haul manure. We have a 500 foot broiler house and had to clean it out to get ready for a new batch of chicks. We had done laundry in the morning and made dinner for the men.

After dinner, Laura and I decided to go to town because Wayne was sick and didn't go to school. We had plans to leave for Harrisburg, Penn., on the afternoon of the 7th to go to a horse sale for four days. I told Jonas if we don't get something for Wayne and he isn't better, I couldn't go along.

He said to go get something from the doctor in Kidron. I also wanted to get a few items at the store, because I and two other ladies were going to take lunch to school the next day.

As I was going out the door, Wayne said, "Mom could you take Norman's birthday card along and give it to him?"

I said, "I'll go past where he works and if I see him I will tell him to come over, you want to give him something."

Norman worked for Coblentz Lumber, about one and one half miles from us, and stayed with Joe Coblentz. We can easily see their place from ours when the leaves are off the trees. We could also see their kitchen light in the mornings and evenings. We thought it best that he not stay at home with his car and Joe had asked if it was okay if Norman stayed there.

A week before Norman's death I had a dream of Norman and Daniel. I dreamed Joe came to tell us they couldn't find Norman, but he said not to worry, he will look for him. Norman always told Joe where he was going if he left. Then I woke up and someone was calling Daniel three times.

I had an aching heart and couldn't go back to sleep right away. I guess it was Tuesday evening when I told Jonas about my dream. Jonas left for a horse sale in Topeka, Indiana, Wednesday morning and stayed there till Friday evening. I thought maybe it would be him.

Wednesday evening, Linda and Daniel went over to Joe's to give Norman his birthday present and cards and to tell him to come over Saturday evening for his birthday. Wayne didn't send his card along because he wanted to give it to Norman himself. Norman gave Wayne a rabbit and rabbit pen for his seventh birthday on September 30th. Norman told Wayne he would come over Saturday night.

Every morning when I got up I had an uneasy feeling. Friday we were raking leaves and Norman came home over lunch break to tell us he couldn't make it Saturday evening, but he could come Sunday or Monday evening. I said we will be going to church on Sunday at Jonas' sister's and probably stay for supper. He said he would go to church with Joe.

He just missed church one time after he left home, and I don't know why. But then we didn't even talk about Monday evening. Friday evening when we were raking leaves beside the road, Norman went past. On his way back, he stopped in a few minutes. We talked a little and I said, "Why not come over tonight?"

He said he promised Joe he'd help set benches tonight. When he left I told him to take care and he said, "Mom, I will."

He left with a big smile on his face and a wave of his hand. Oh, if only we would have known that would be the last time we would see him alive! Sunday morning we got up to go to church. I looked out the window over at Joe's and thought they were probably getting ready too. Then Wayne was sick so I stayed home with him.

All day I had this uneasy feeling. In the afternoon, Wayne asked, "Why doesn't Norman come?" I said, "He thinks we are in church and doesn't know you are sick." I told him we would watch for him and maybe he would go past and then we'll stop him and you can give him his card. But we didn't see him.

Then Monday, like I said earlier, I felt better than I had all week. Almost as if a load was lifted off of me. We had gone to town in the afternoon and went past where Norman worked, but didn't see him. He drove a tow motor and we thought he might be outside. When we came home it was getting late and they were still hauling manure. When supper was ready, Jonas told us to go ahead and eat. They would do the chores first and that there was someone coming for a load of chicken manure and he would have to load it.

We had just finished eating when someone knocked on the door. It was one of the neighbors to see which evening we wanted to go get groceries. It was dark and while I was outside, I saw someone drive in and thought it was probably someone for chicken manure. As I came in, Jonas came up the basement steps and saw we were all there except Alta. He asked, "Where's Alta?"

I told Jonas I thought someone was here for chicken manure. Then I looked at him and saw his face was as white as a sheet. He said, "No, it's a cop."

I answered, "Not Norman!"

He said, "Yes, Norman was killed."

Still the shock. I can't describe it. Yet, I had this feeling that something would happen! Why? Still, I couldn't actually believe it. I had prayed so much for Norman. Did God answer His way and not mine?

Alta was at a school friend's house to spend the night, so Sr. B.L. Dodd and Laura went to get her. We also let my brother know who lives beside us, so he could tell the others. Then the cop took Jonas and me to the hospital in Dover. Norman had gone to Strausburg after work. He got off at four o'clock, and this happened at 4:20. He went left of center and hit a semi truck. Someone said it looked like he had reached down for something.

He lived one hour and twenty minutes. We didn't find out till six o'clock. It was so hard to accept that we didn't find out earlier and we couldn't be there. He died of head injuries. He also had his left leg broken in three places and other injuries.

On the way to the hospital we had to detour because of this wreck. When we got there the doctor was ready for us and asked if we had any questions. What could we say? I still thought this can't be true. Not our son. Always shy; more the quiet type. But, yes it was our son!

I prayed, 'God, help us through this.' We touched him and he still felt soft, but life had fled.

Atlee Coblentz, Joe's brother, had called a driver and came to take us home. On the way home Atlee said he was going to go with Norman, then at the last minute when Norman was ready to leave, Atlee decided to stay and finish some paper work. On the way back, Norman would pick him up and take him home. Norman went out to his car then came back in and asked Atlee if he thinks it's okay if he goes.

Atlee said, "Yes, I think so."

When we were almost home, we saw the house all lit up. I thought nothing would ever be the same again. Neighbors and relatives had already gathered. It was hard to leave the rest at home to go to the hospital. Later I wished they would have all gone along, but in time of shock, you can't think straight.

It has been a year now and still at times it is hard to grasp. The children all had dreams of Norman. Beautiful dreams. Linda's first dream meant so much to us. She still has dreams.

The other night she thought it was actually true. She was talking with him, but then woke up. Norman had told Wayne, "Maybe I can give you another rabbit for Christmas and then maybe you'll have bunnies for Easter."

One night before Christmas, Wayne dreamed Norman came to watch them chore. I asked if they talked. He said no, Norman just smiled. Then while choring one night, he asked Dad, "Who's going to give me a rabbit now?"

The day before Christmas, Jonas bought a rabbit and put it in Wayne's pen. Wayne didn't see it when he chored because it was inside. They were both white. Everybody wanted to surprise him and didn't tell him. After supper they told him and he had to go see it yet that night. The rest said they'd rather not have any gifts. It wouldn't seem right to open them without Norman. When Norman had left home, he only took clothes and a few items. I told him we would leave his room for him whenever he comes back.

It was so hard to part. We thought he would be back those last three months before his death. It was hard to accept, but his death was so final! We still have his room just like it was.

Ever since Norman was ten years old, he had gone with Jonas to work at his timber business during the summer months. After he was out of school, he worked in the woods the rest of his life, except the last nine months. Jonas sold his timber business in the spring of 1995.

The last couple years, Norman and Paul, Jonas' nephew, had worked alone. Norman really liked to work in the woods. I had always worried that something would happen in the woods, but that was not the time God had chosen for him.

'Trust in the Lord with all thine heart and lean not unto thine own understanding. In all thy ways acknowledge him and he shall direct thy paths.' Proverbs 3:5,6.

This is what I had written in Norman's birthday card.

We never know what the future holds, but God does, and he had a purpose in this although it is so hard to understand. In Psalms 145:18, 19, it says, 'The Lord is nigh unto all them that call upon him, to all that call upon him in truth. He will fulfill the desire of them that fear him, he also will hear their cry and will serve them.'

We know it was His perfect plan although we do not understand. But some sweet day, we too shall rise if Christ dwells within our heart and meet those gone before, where we shall never part.

November sixth is a day we will never forget because it was also our 20th wedding anniversary.

Malva O. Hershberger: Nov. 5, 1978 - Oct. 4, 1994

Submitted by: Owen & Mary Hershberger, Baltic, Ohio

October 4, 1994, started out like any other day. Daughter Alma went to her job at Hiland Wood and I went to my job at the Belden Brick Company in Sugarcreek. Little did we realize what the day would bring us. Thank God we didn't.

Son Malva, 15, was working for neighbor Raymond J. Miller, on a farm, for the third year. This fall however, with work kind of caught up and corn not ready to pick yet, Raymond told Malva he could either choose to do odd jobs around the farm or see if Dan E. Yoder from Rocky Ridge Casting had work for him for a couple weeks.

Malva went to see Dan on Thursday evening and started to work Friday morning. He worked Friday, and all the next week. On October 4th, Tuesday morning, he went to work again and took his hunting gear along. He said it would be later till he got home because he was going to go deer hunting after work.

His two brothers stood in the yard and watched him leave till he was out of sight. Around 9:20 someone at the brick plant came and said there was a phone call for me in the office. I wondered who it could be. When I answered the phone, somebody said, "Malva was killed." What a shock!

He was grinding off parts, cleaning off burrs, etc., when the grinding stone flew apart. One piece weighing six pounds hit him in the head killing him instantly. The piece flew on up through a steel roof and landed about 12 feet away from the scene.

Larry Myers offered to take me home right away. When I got home it really hit me as to what had really happened. Someone took

Atlee Millers and us over to the shop where it happened, about two and one half miles away. As we came across that last hill to Dan's place, there stood the squad with lights flashing and people standing around.

Oh what a feeling to come to such a sight, with your son being the victim. The squad people came right away and said that we don't want to see our son. Was he hurt that bad? Later the undertaker told us we might not be able to view him. But he was able to fix him up and we did view him. Thank God.

We waited till the coroner was there then we went home. By that time somebody had brought the school children home and Alma was at home, too. Neighbors were starting to come. Oh, what would we do without friends and neighbors? They came and took over for a couple of days. We would ask ourselves, "Did this really happen to us?" Before it was always somebody else, but, yes, this time it was in our house.

No more can we hear him say, "Dad, let's go deer hunting," or "Dad let's go rabbit or squirrel hunting." Hunting seasons will always bring back memories, but we try to give ourselves up to God's ways and accept it as His will.   *-Father*

The fateful morning started out like any other morning. It was the first morning that it was so chilly. Owen and Alma left for their jobs and I woke our 15 year old son, Malva, with the scholars and he had his breakfast with them. I always fried him two eggs and the rest had cereal and cookies. The morning passed as usual, eating breakfast, packing buckets and doing chores.

The day before, Malva had gone deer hunting and came home at dinner time. That morning he said he would go deer hunting again after work and took all his gear along to a neighbor's place. I packed him extra food so he would have enough to eat later in the day. How little did I realize this would be the very last time I could pack his bucket!

Since it was so chilly, I went upstairs in the storeroom and got a bag of winter caps. He was ready to leave on his bike when I called him and told him I found the caps. He came running in toward the house and I tossed him a cap. Oh, what else would we have said had we known these would be the last words and the last deed for him? I remember watching him go and thinking he was leaving later than usual. Was there something that made him linger longer that morning?

He used one of his sister's bikes that morning and his two brothers, ten and 12, both stood in the lawn and talked with him as he left and watched till he was over the hill. That would be the last time they would see him. Yes, healthy and happy, he left.

After the morning work, I started sewing carpet rags. Susie, 14; Viola, four; and baby Miriam, four and one half months, were at home, too. After sewing a while I decided to write a letter to a handicapped friend who was having a birthday.

At 9:30, we heard a van drive in and we saw Robert R. Miller was along and he came up to the house. Since he worked where Malva did, I told Susie, "I hope nothing happened to Malva."

Robert's first words were, "Malva has been killed. A grinding wheel exploded and killed him instantly."

Oh, what a shock! No words can describe how one feels at a time like this. We think we went into shock or daze that wore off slowly several weeks later and reality set in. I remember thinking, no! We have to have him yet. Being the oldest boy in the family, I guess we depended on him a lot.

Robert brought Mrs. Atlee J. Miller in then and she came along to go over to the accident. Just as we were ready to leave, Owen came home and we could both go. How glad I was to see him! No words were necessary. Atlees both went over with us.

What a feeling it was to get there with the squad there and people gathering. To find out we couldn't even see our dear son was almost unbearable. They brought us chairs and there we sat an hour or so. Many thoughts were going through our minds. It was like a nightmare had begun. After they had him on the stretcher, to take him in the squad, the coroner came and said if we wanted to see our son now we could. But we decided not to. Later one lady that was with the squad said she prayed and prayed we wouldn't look at him because we couldn't have handled it.

He had been standing with his back to a grocery cart where he put parts in after he ground off the rough spots. The parts were the hardware pieces that hold the beds together. The wheel was eight inches around by two inches thick and the piece that hit him weighed six pounds. He fell backward into the cart with his feet still on the floor. One second a healthy young boy and the next second life had fled.

Dan's son and 83 year old father were standing just a few feet away when it happened. They were also hurt.

After the squad left with our dear son, what was left to do but go home to the rest of the family? They were all at home by this time. All we could do was weep with each other. A few neighbor women arrived and made us dinner. To this day I never eat macaroni without thinking about how they stuck to my throat that day.

Soon Owen's parents came and more of the relatives. We thought, "Is this really happening to us?"

We were so numb with grief, the rest of the day is just a blur. What kind neighbors we had! Soon they were cleaning, washing buggies, mowing lawn, and everything that goes with preparing for a funeral. We can never thank them enough.

Soon the undertaker came for his clothes and information. I joined a few of the neighbor women to get his clothes. Seeing his room and getting his church suit made me realize this was so final!

How glad we were we could view him, but yes, how heartbreaking to see him so cold and still. Many people came to the viewing the next days. At the first viewing 600 friends were here. Many words of encouragement were spoken. People with similar experiences meant a lot to us.

This happened on Tuesday morning and the funeral was on Friday. It was a beautiful sunny fall day with the leaves at their peak and they came floating down as we went to the graveyard. There were over 500 people at the funeral. The house and shop were full.

Many friends, relatives, and his school friends followed us up the hill to the graveyard. How hard it was to see him lowered into the deep dark grave! Again and again we try to give ourselves up. We have to think, rest in peace.

Owen's folks, Mose E. Hershbergers, had come the first day and stayed every night and also the night after the funeral, which we appreciated very much. Having them near helped a lot. Also, some of the cousins stayed every night to sleep with the children.

The next morning after the funeral, we woke up to hear Malva's dog, Patsy, crying mournfully. Yes, she knew something was wrong! Why doesn't her master come to feed and pet her? He always liked to stand and watch his pets eat after feeding them. Those lonesome howls went deep into our hearts and we couldn't help but cry with her.

Often over the next weeks, after seven o'clock when he used to feed her, she'd sit in the drive and howl like that. She would also try to look in the door and window if she saw us inside. She was very shy of people and it was a while before any of us could even pet her. Quite a while later I moved the sewing machine while she was sitting in front of the house. It rattled and she was frightened and then once again she started her crying.

I still don't know why that affected her. I finally took Malva's gloves and cap out for her to smell and had a good cry with her. We took her along to the graveyard, too.

Last week Patsy had a litter of ten puppies. How we wondered what Malva would say. We can almost see his expression. Little things keep popping up at the most unexpected times, but life goes on. We had lots of company which we appreciated very much. People with the same experiences meant so much. We have made many friends since this happened. We never knew friends meant so much. True friends are like diamonds. Precious but rare.

A friend of mine came a few mornings after the funeral and we had a nice talk. Later she told me how hard it was for her to come, but she thought we have often laughed with each other and we can now cry with each other. "A friend in need is a friend indeed."

Friends showed they cared in many different ways. A young tree was given to plant in memory of Malva. Plus bulbs, flowers, framed verses and yes, even a hog was given to us to butcher. Two years later, my sister made cards for each of us and they had a verse she made up, inside. God bless them all!

Songs and poems have much more meaning than ever before! Life will never be the same for us. There have been a lot of whys these last two years, but with God's help we want to accept it. We wonder why it happened and where it happened, but we trust God wanted it to happen just like it did.

Our family: Owen, 41, son of Mose E. and Sarah Hershberger. I am Mary, 40, daughter of the late John G. and Viola Yoder. Our children, at the time of the accident: Alma, 17; then Malva; Susie, 14; Joseph, 12; Mose, ten; Marlene, seven; Viola, four; and baby Miriam was about five months old.

Miriam helped fill many lonely hours. She was always a smiling and content baby. That first winter she must have been the only "sunshine" around here. Almost every evening when Malva came home from work, he'd go over to her in her infant seat and get her to smile. Precious memories.

She will not remember her brother, but then she was spared the grief our other children had to go through. The first year we often went up to the graveyard. Sometimes there was a beautiful sunset. I never look at nice sunrises or sunsets that I don't of Malva. I think, if it's as nice as that, or even much more beautiful in Heaven than these sunsets, how nice he has it.

We hope our loss was his gain. We often have to think he had a nice age to leave this sinful world. He was a month near his 16th birthday. He didn't have the trials and temptations the young folks have nowadays.

Although it is hard to see his close friends and cousins with the young folks, getting partners, etc., but again we must not question God's plans. His ways are not our ways.

Malva really loved to take walks in the woods and to hunt and trap. He kept record how many different birds he saw each year. Also how many rabbits, groundhogs, and squirrels he shot. We also have many nice pictures that he drew and most of them are of wildlife. How we treasure those books! He had a collection of bird eggs in a wooden box with a glass cover. There are 26 different kinds of eggs in all. How we treasure all those things he made or collected. He had a room by himself which was, oh so empty after he left us.

Many times we all went to his room to look at his belongings and talk of the times we were all together. Precious memories, how they linger. Many times when it was hard to go on and I had zeitlang, I'd go alone to his room and let the floodgates open till I found relief again. Tears bring a healing like nothing else does and are not a sign of weakness.

Sorrow like this brings a family closer together and one appreciates the closeness much more. The rest of the children are all more special to you. Probably, like others going through this, we're always afraid something will happen again. I always worry when they are out of my sight, which is most of the time. The children feel I don't trust them anymore which I don't blame them. I'm just over protective!

Oh ye of little faith! Daughter Alma shared the same birthday Malva did. They were two years apart on that day. Two years after the parting, she had a nice dream. She dreamt Malva was with us again. So she, Susie, and Joseph talked to him and asked "How is it at the place where you are?" He got a big smile and said, "It's really nice and I really like it here." It was only a dream but how comforting for us!

We have learned a lot through this experience and can deeply sympathize with all who have gone through the valley of grief. Learning to forgive, to let go, to adjust and to accept it, all has to be done again and again. God has helped us through these two years and we trust to have His help forever. Hopefully we can live a life that some day we can all be reunited again with our dear son and brother.

-*Mother*

With a heavy heart I will try to write about this shocking accident that happened October 4, 1994, which took the life of Malva O. Hershberger.

Malva was the son of Owen R. Hershberger, my wife's sister's son, 15 years old. They live about two and one half miles from us. Malva worked on the farm at Raymond J. Millers. Sometimes when they weren't real busy on the farm, Malva would work for us in our casting shop. Thus, one day Raymond told him he would just have odd jobs for him the next two weeks before corn husking. Malva could choose to do these or go to work for me a few weeks.

One evening I was working in the shop dumping molds, and looking up from my work I saw Malva standing there. I jokingly asked, "Are you going to work for us?"

He said, "Yes, if you want me to. Raymond can spare me for a few weeks."

I asked if he could start tomorrow morning and with a smile he said he would ask Raymond. He started the next day which was on Friday. Then he worked the next week and on Friday of that week, the power unit overheated to the extent that we couldn't use it anymore. On Saturday I bought another power unit which was set up Monday.

After we had it set up, I told the man we bought it from that I would set the throttle the next morning to get the correct speed for the equipment running with hydraulics. On Tuesday morning it was rather cool. I started the engine and let it run till I thought the hydraulic oil was warmed up enough, then set the throttle on the engine. Thinking that the grinder was running at the correct speed, we shut these tools off and went into another area of the shop to work.

When Malva was finished with his job, he walked up to me and asked, "What next?"

At this time there was another man there talking to me. I said, "The job that no one really likes. Grinding."

Malva just smiled and turned around, walking to the front of the shop where the grinder was. The man I was talking to said, "Well, I think I'll go."

I said I was going to check and make sure the grinder was running right. We both walked into the room where Malva had just started grinding. At this point the man said something about one of his patterns. I mentioned those were over in another building so we went out a side door of the shop to get the patterns, instead of checking on the grinder.

We were just outside the shop when we heard a strange sound. My son Harvey came running out and said, "Malva is dead!"

I thought, "No, he's just unconscious."

Hurriedly we went inside, but life had fled. My first thoughts were why must it be someone else's boy, although I wouldn't have wanted to give up any of our boys.

What happened was the grinding wheel exploded, hitting him in the head and killing him instantly. Part of the grinding wheel struck a hydraulic pipe causing it to leak. Everything was immediately shut down. I wondered if maybe the hydraulic oil wasn't warm enough when I set the throttle and then with the motor running while we were doing other things, the oil warmed up more causing the grinding wheel to run too fast. But I couldn't check this because of the broken hydraulic pipe.

The week after the funeral I repaired the hydraulic pipe and got everything running and yes, the grinding wheel was going too fast.

Oh what a turmoil and anguish I went through when this was discovered. The grinder was worn some and I had thought about replacing it within the next week, but chances are the wheel wouldn't have broken if it would have been running at the correct speed.

Oh what grief. The whys and so forth, but to go on like this is like an endless circle in a bottomless pit. I know I should have been more safety conscious. Whether it was my fault or not, God is still a merciful God and he will forgive and console.

- Dan E. Yoder, Employer

God's Flower Garden

Sometimes we can't quite understand
Our Great Creator's way.
When he takes a life so young
And leaves one withered, old, and gray.

Whose life work seems finished,
Perhaps is waiting for the call.
While that life so young and tender
Held so much here for us all.
Then sometimes I get to thinking,
Perhaps this world down here below,
Is just a flower garden
Where God's flowers live and grow.
And perhaps when God is lonely,
Like us, He loves to roam
In his garden, gathering flowers
Just to beautify His home.
Tho' He takes the full-bloom flowers,
Drooped and withered that need His care.
Still he needs a bud or blossom,
To scatter with them, here and there.
So he takes a few choice blossoms,
Just the rarest He can find,
And because God needs them up in Heaven,
Must comfort loved ones left behind.

Timothy Wittmer: 1993 - Oct. 3, 1996

Submitted by: Ben & Betty Wittmer, Woodburn, Indiana

It was a beautiful day in the fall on October 3, 1996. We never thought what was to be by the end of the day. We were picking corn with two pickers all afternoon. Timothy, almost three years old, was an active boy. He woke up from his afternoon nap and went directly back to the field with the team and hopper wagon. This was around three o'clock. Dad took break along back for his two brothers who were picking corn. Timothy said, "Dad look, two pickers, and so many horses." He was a real horse lover.

Dad started eating chips and snacks when Timothy said, "Wait Dad till Jonas and Jacob come around and we can all eat break together." I was trying to teach them that we all eat and pray together when possible. Then after break he asked his oldest brother if he couldn't just have one ride.

He had married in May and left home and was living with her folks. Timothy just couldn't accept that. Every time he came home and left again, Timothy cried. So Timothy got his last ride.

Dad took a load of corn home. By that time the school boys were home, Bennie, 11, and Jonathon, nine, so Dad let them drive the horses and said he would do the chores that night. They took the empty wagons back and Timothy rode home on top of the hopper wagon. The one wagon had an extra round on it. Six rows of corn and it was extra full. One wagon pulled up to the elevator to unload.

When his brother Jesse came home from work, Timothy begged for him to take him off the wagon. He told him he was to give him a kiss. The last one he gave. Jesse wanted to walk back to the field to see how it was going and wanted to take Timothy along. Timothy said he would just stay here.

Dad, the girls, and I were milking and of course we often did a lot of singing at that time. We had just finished singing a song about my 15 year old nephew who was killed by lightning in June of 1993. I looked up to my 15 year old daughter and thought what could happen to her?

All of a sudden our five year old, Naomi, came running into the cow stable just carrying on something terrible. She grabbed my hands and said, "Timothy is dead."

Oh my, such words! I thought it just can't be that bad. Oh my, when I came but five feet away from his body there was no question.

The first wagon was unloaded and was ready to head back to the field. Bennie was going to unload the second load when he saw Beth, 18 months old, come out of the barn. He took her back into the cow barn. Meanwhile Timothy crawled on top of the two wheeled cart.

The horses started walking with a big load behind them. It slid the cart over and threw Timothy off and under the back wheel. The wagon went right over his head. Bennie was back out the door when he had just been run over. The horses stopped right away. They were just an old trusty team. With all the commotion, the team then went over and stood by our grapevine until sometime later when someone put them away.

It was just moments and memories too unbearable to speak of. Without God's help, we thought we just couldn't go on. I had thought at the time, everything should just stop. But time goes on. Never did we realize how final death is. Never to see his dear face again on earth. I always felt he was special from day one. He was born on my birthday.

That summer my grapevine just started to wilt. The leaves dried up and all the grapes on it just wilted and in time dried up and died. It seems like I can't get another one started. I have tried two since.

In his coffin, his little hands felt so soft and alive until the third day his little fingers felt like our dried up grapes.

In August, Jonas' father-in-law died unexpectedly and our Timothy had just learned to know him really well. The day of his funeral he asked the most questions, not thinking that, only three, a little boy of that age could ask so many questions. He also went along to the graveyard. Not realizing that in six weeks we would be putting him into the cold, cold ground.

Timothy always dearly loved horses and he went to his grave with the most beautiful horse. I guess I can say it did something to our whole family. Just brought us closer together. I hope it will always stay that way.

He may be gone, but he is not forgotten. Time has a way of healing, but the scar still remains. As of now, we just couldn't wish him back into this sinful world. We know he has a good and wonderful home, more than we could ever give him. God's ways are not our ways.

Raymond I. Plank: Aug. 30, 1968 - July 4, 1993

Submitted by: Ivan & Clara Mae Plank, Arthur, Illinois

On Saturday, July third, Raymond spent most of the day helping around home, which he often did on Saturdays after working five days a week at Central Wood, a milling shop. He had been working there for five years. He had biked to town on business in the morning and stopped at a rummage sale where he bought himself some tools. One of the last things I remember him doing was seeing him hang up his tools in his corner of the shop that he had for his own. He was doing this when I came out to see if the menfolk were ready to come in for supper.

After supper his older sister, Ruth Ann, took him to a friend's house, Lonnie Kaufman, for overnight. She wanted to use his buggy the next day so Raymond was going to get a ride with his friend on Sunday evening.

Raymond talked to Ruth Ann about a new song he had heard sung the week before at a wedding. He loved to sing, which he couldn't do very well, but often did while choring. I often heard him sing in the milk house while washing milk utensils. I could hear him while in the house.

One song he often sang was 'Does Jesus Care?' The words were so fitting for us after he was gone.

Another reason for Ruth Ann taking Raymond to his friend's was because he had difficulty seeing in the dark, and often didn't go by himself. He had what they call RP (Retinitis Pigmentosa), a degenerative disease of the retina in the eyes. One of the first signs of this is night blindness.

Also as it progresses, their side vision becomes more limited. Many friends did very well helping him find his way in the dark at young folks' gatherings, which we were very thankful for. On Sunday, July fourth, Raymond spent the morning by himself because it was not our Sunday to have church in our district. The rest of his friends went to church.

In the afternoon, being a warm day, quite a few boys gathered at Lonnie's house where he was staying, to swim in their pond which was located east of their barn. Raymond was still learning how to swim so he wore a life jacket for a while.

He then said to one of the boys, "I think I'll try without my life jacket."

His goal was a small place in the middle of the pond like an island.

No one really knows what happened, but feel he got tired and maybe panicked. Someone saw him go down and they immediately called for help. One of the best swimmers dove and found him. He brought him up and put him on a boat they had there. He then took him to the middle of the pond where he was headed, but couldn't get him to respond. One of the boys ran across the road to the neighbors' telephone and called the ambulance.

We had spent Sunday morning at Sunday School at our neighbors Levi Beechy's. After having our noon meal there, we decided to go visit my aunt who was sick with cancer. We had just been home long enough to change into everyday clothes and were getting ready to go do our chores because we have a dairy herd.

Leroy, 19 years old, had also come home to help us chore after spending the Sunday with friends. The three youngest children still at home were outside ready to go to the barn when a car drove in and two boys jumped out and wondered if their parents were home. They asked several times before the children could answer. I heard this and knew right away something was wrong. I went to the door and asked, "What's wrong?"

The boys told us Raymond went under water, but they had him back out and didn't know how he was. One of the boys stayed here to help with the milking and we went with the car, which was a passerby or with the ambulance crew. By the time we got to the scene, they had Raymond loaded in the ambulance and almost ready to leave. They told us one can ride in the ambulance and one with the person who came after us right behind them.

We didn't ask any questions on Raymond's condition because I guess we were afraid to know and they didn't tell us anything. I went with the ambulance and Ivan and Lonnie Kaufman followed in the car. The paramedics worked on Raymond all the way to the hospital and after arriving, but life had fled.

They took us to a little room at the hospital to wait. We were there several minutes when our son Allen and his wife came. They had only married two months before and lived only about a half mile from the scene. After what seemed like 15 to 20 minutes, hospital personnel came and told us they didn't think they could revive him.

The feeling we cannot describe. We were numb. By this time, family and friends were calling the hospital for details, which is how the ones still at home found out.

At the time, we didn't think it was necessary for the rest of the family to come to the hospital, but often wished since that we would have told them to come. We had a lot of waiting to do there before we could go back home. This was hard on the rest of the family at home to have to wait so long before we came back home.

The coroner at the hospital thought that an autopsy should be done since a 24 year old boy doesn't just drown. He felt like something else came over him. We finally gave our consent to this, but it was against our wishes.

The men responsible for the autopsy were out of the area for the holiday and wouldn't be back till Monday noon to perform this. Therefore the body couldn't be taken to the funeral home till late Monday evening. Words cannot describe our homecoming that evening, to meet the rest of the family. Friends, neighbors, and relatives had gathered here by the time we arrived.

Neighbors had gone after Mary Fern, our 16 year old daughter, who was at a friend's house, and brought her home. Ruth Ann was also home. She was almost home with the buggy when we left with the car. She saw us go and immediately knew something was wrong. Ivan and I were both still barefooted when we came home as that is how we went.

One of our first concerns was that we had a daughter living in Kentucky and knew she wouldn't be able to come. The neighbors had already let her know by the time we got home which we were thankful for. The funeral was planned to be held on Thursday morning, July eighth.

We did keep in touch with our daughter and her husband in Kentucky. Wednesday morning they sent word that a baby girl, named Clara Mae, was born to them early that morning. They still wanted to come to the funeral, but couldn't find a way. So kind neighbors hired a van and left here Wednesday evening for Kentucky. Neighbor Levi Beachy also went with the driver of the van.

They arrived at our daughter Dorothy and Glenn Schrock's around midnight. They fixed a bed in the van for Dorothy and the baby and loaded the other three children and headed back right away. They arrived back here just in time for breakfast Thursday morning around six o'clock.

We put Dorothy right to bed to rest. We had the joy of having her here amidst our grief, but still had a great concern. Dorothy rested in my mom's house, which is a small connection to ours, in the morning while the funeral was being held. When it was time for people to file through to view the body, she came out and sat in a recliner in the tent where the main funeral was being held.

Services were also held in the house on the main floor and in the basement. Having Dorothy here for the funeral wouldn't be so precious to us now, but nine months later we traveled to Scottsville, Kentucky, for her funeral. She and her husband and family had visited us again in March of 1994 for ten days.

They had been home around three weeks when one of the neighbors came to our door at one o'clock in the morning of April 11th. They told us our son-in-law called and said Dorothy was at the Bowling Green Kentucky Hospital on life support and it would take a miracle for her to survive. Our minds could not absorb this and we felt like it could not be true. Were we dreaming?

We were at a loss as what to do, so the neighbors suggested we go let Glenn's folks know. They took us and then we, along with Glenn's folks, went to a phone and got in touch with Glenn and stayed in contact till Dorothy passed away. They also did an autopsy on her which showed she died of Acute Idiopathic Thrombolocy Purpura.

She didn't feel well the last week of her life, but had no idea she was this serious. We did not know anything was wrong till we got the call. We did get a letter from her then on the day she died, telling us that she hadn't been feeling so well. How precious that letter is. She was 29 years old and left her husband and four small children. Two boys and two girls, ranging in ages six to nine months, at the time of her death.

We did not want to question these trials, but want to accept them as God's will. We are only human so had to battle the thoughts of why? One thing I often said is right at the time you think you have accepted it as God's will, you have to battle with self all over again.

We feel loving support from family, friends, and community are very important in a time like this, to help ease the pain. Also it is important not to despair and to keep looking up to a higher hand for help. What it has done to our family, I cannot explain nor put it on paper.

I did not write this for honor or fame, just something to share with people with similar experiences. I feel in my heart the season for now as the words go, "Glory to God in the highest, and on earth peace and good will toward men."

Joseph Schwartz Jr.: May 13, 1979 - Oct. 7, 1981
Naomi G. Schwartz: Feb. 1, 1982 - May 25, 1996
Submitted by: Joseph & Emma Schwartz, Reading, Michigan

October 7, 1981, was a lovely fall day. Our family had all been together the evening before because it was my dad's birthday. Little did we realize how soon we would all be called together again. It was such a sudden parting.

In the afternoon of the seventh, my two sisters were here and we dressed some chickens to can on the following day. When sister Mary was ready to go home, little Joseph begged to go home with her, but for some unknown reason I said not this time. She told us she can still see him telling her good bye, good bye, good bye, as she drove away. They were special good byes, forever.

After they left, I put baby Emma in her crib. (She turned one on September 27, 1981.) Then Joseph and I went out to do the chores. As I walked to the barn, he walked over to where I had some chickens in a fenced-in yard.

Our last words were, "Come with me", and Joseph said, "No Mom, I'll play here." He was trying to catch the chickens.

Thinking all would be okay, I walked on to the barn leaving him there. I had only been in the barn a very short time when a strange noise made me run to see where Joseph was. Oh, what a shock when I saw him over by the corncrib. There lay the sweet little one under a 6 x 8 log. Just that morning we had tied it up on a piece of farm machinery to keep the horses away from the corn.

I walked over to pick him up and he moaned. I thought he was knocked out of breath. When I picked him up he seemed so motionless. How he got under the log is hard to understand. By the way he was lying there, it looked like he may have been trying to swing on it because it was laying across his chest. Oh, the next trying moments. I spoke his name, but no reply. Only a moan and his body was so limp.

After he was in my arms, I immediately started for the neighbors. Halfway there I started calling for help. They heard me and came running. She was so kind a person. She tried to encourage me and said he's just knocked out of breath. But my thoughts were going elsewhere. She was trying to help. She told me to take him home. I was in a daze. She said she would call the ambulance and then be over. Her mom came over right away and was only there a few minutes when he died in my arms.

No one knows such a feeling. So helpless. Why? Why? Oh where was Joe? (my husband) At work. I sent him a message with a feed salesman but it was too late. Joseph was gone before he could come home. The ambulance was there and we were so torn apart. They took him to the hospital. How I wanted them to just leave us alone with our precious little one.

On the way to the hospital they kept asking over and over, what happened because Joseph had no marks on the outside of his body. Finally, at the hospital, six doctors tried everything. They even gave him blood. We arrived around 4:15 and at eight o'clock they finally let his body rest. They came and asked for permission to open him up and a short time later they reported to us that his heart was split and he had bled to death.

Where to and what to do next?

To leave for home with empty arms, the way seemed endless. We tried to put ourselves together, and found there was help waiting. When we gave ourselves up to God's will, He helped us through. Many times I felt if only I had been a better Mom and taken him with me, but then others say something else may have happened. The many encouraging words helped us accept that this was God's will, that our little one was called home at such a tender, loving age.

Never will I forget the first words Stepmother said to me, "If you would get a glimpse and see where he is, you could not shed one more tear." Heaven is so beautiful! If it wasn't for family, friends, and neighbors, where would one go? Help came from so many at such a needy time.

Time passed and he was laid in that cool grave, but now we realize he is a great step ahead of us. In the bedroom, his crib was so empty and it was a place for shedding many tears. The days passed slowly and on February 1, 1982, we were once more blessed with a sweet bundle of love. A nine pound baby girl, which helped to heal the broken hearts. At that time we never thought that she too would only be with us a few years. At the age of 13, she, too, was called home.

Naomi

It was a rainy Thursday afternoon on Ascension Day. We had a day of fasting and we spent the morning in reading and prayer. Such a nice morning, we were all together. She had a loving touch for all and the three youngest were so close to her. I remember her kneeling with the baby on her lap and the two little boys, one on each side. Such sweet precious memories. She was so helpful all morning. She helped dress the little ones, and helped get lunch ready. It was our last meal together.

In the afternoon she was out helping Joe. He was butchering a pig for sausage. We had plans for a family get-together on Saturday the 27th. Joe's family from Indiana were all going to come, and everyone was excited and helping get ready for the big day.

At three o'clock, Naomi came in from helping Joe and asked me if it's okay if she goes and gets ice. "Dad said I could go if it's okay with you."

I said, "If it's okay with Dad, it's okay with me."

We both told her she could go, but we didn't realize where she was going. Never to return. She harnessed and hitched up all alone, a very safe pony. Three of the other children rode along. It was very normal since the ice house was about one half mile from here and she had made the trip many times.

As I was ironing, I thought they should be back by now. I looked out the window where I was ironing, but because of trees and a hill, I couldn't see down the road. I had only walked to the porch when I heard someone talking to Joe. "Your children were in an accident."

"Is anyone hurt?"

She couldn't talk about it, only said, "Oh yes."

I ran but didn't get out of the lane when the horse came home, unharmed. Oh, maybe they were okay. Joe called me and said he would hitch up the other buggy, but before we got hitched up a neighbor picked us up.

"Are they hurt?"

He couldn't talk, only silence. My heart was beating faster, 'Oh Herr, dein wille geschehe.' I was expecting the worst. Can I accept this and then the final truth, yes, our dear, loving 13 year old was lying there so still.

The three other children were standing around her, all a bloody mess of dirt and sand. Two neighbor ladies were with them. A large group had surrounded us already, but it was so final. She had left us.

Where to, what to do? Pray, try to say a prayer. It was all I could do to get myself together to say a prayer. "Oh Herr, dein wille, nicht mein, geschehe.

She still had a very low heartbeat, but she never spoke to us again. Oh why? Why? Why? But then I wanted to accept that it was God's will.

The next days were very trying ones. All three of the other children were hospitalized. Samuel, four, had a cut on his head and couldn't eat for a day or two, and had stitches. Marcus, seven, had a broken nose and gums scraped off his teeth. Joann, 12, had a cut on her chin all the way to her gums. She was semiconscious till Sunday evening.

We didn't have the funeral till Monday, hoping all could be home by then and they were all able to be there. Life was like a dream. Many friends attended. We were at the hospital and then home and we realized that without the help from above, one could never endure such heartaches. Life goes on and we miss her pleasant face and sweet smile, but are longing to lead a life so that we can be with them someday.

Marlin Miller: Sept. 15, 1987 - Dec. 17, 1992

Submitted by: William J. S. & Martha Miller, Middlefield, Ohio

Thursday, December 17, 1992, was a nice winter day of about 35°. I was at my brother Wally's working on his new shop. Martha was home alone. Marlin, five, and Laura, 14, were walking home from across the road when a car hit them at one o'clock in the afternoon. They were thrown about 30 feet. Martha went right up to Marlin and she felt something like a "streak" or "rays from Heaven" going from Marlin towards Heaven. We think this was God's way of telling us he was taking Marlin home and giving us strength to go on. Someone came for me and took me home.

Stopped traffic and ambulances with flashing lights greeted me. What a frightful sight! I went to Martha first and talked to her and tried to calm her down. Then I went to see Laura for a few minutes. She was in an ambulance. Next I went to see Marlin in another ambulance, but they are getting him ready for the Life Flight Helicopter. The EMT's and nurses were all around him and I couldn't see him at all before he left.

He was very badly hurt and unconscious. I went back to see Laura and Martha, then the helicopter left with Marlin. The sad and helpless feeling of watching our dear son leaving this way and so badly hurt cannot be described.

I got ready to go to the hospital.

Another helicopter came for Laura. There she goes! Oh, we think it can't be! Two children gone on Life Flight! We know everything is in God's hands.

Martha's mom and dad went with us to Metro Health Hospital. We arrived at 3:45. Marlin and Laura were in intensive care. The doctor told us Laura was in stable condition. Her left leg was broken in four places and she had a very bad bruise on her head, which gave her bad headaches.

Marlin had a broken neck and crushed spinal cord and brain injuries. He was in a very poor condition. Our beloved little Marlin! Must we give him up? We went in to see him and what a shock! He was unconscious and hooked up to life support machines. By now all our children and some of our sisters and brothers were there at the hospital with us. At eight o'clock, the doctor told us Marlin was brain dead. Oh no! We thought, it is not so! Our youngest child! Our dearly beloved Marlin!

They took him off the machines and we went in to see him. He had gone to be with Jesus. The truth sank in very slowly. Oh, the heartaches and pain cannot be described! We know he is safe in the arms of Jesus, but it is so hard to give him up!

Our family stayed at the hospital all night with Laura. She had a lot of pain in her broken leg and had a bad headache. She did not sleep well all night. It was then Friday morning, we were still at the hospital. At eight o'clock Laura got her first pain shot and she slept until 11 o'clock. She still did not know about Marlin.

We called Russell Funeral Home. He said he would pick up Marlin and prepare him and bring him home that evening.

At 11 o'clock, Laura woke up and wanted to know what happened and where Marlin was. How could we tell her? Oh, dear God, help us. We all gathered in her room and told her as gently as we could that Marlin was gone to be with Jesus. She cried some, but she was still in pain and could not fully grasp what had happened. Poor girl! We felt so sorry for her.

We started to plan our dear little son's funeral. We decided on Monday, December 21, hoping Laura would be well enough to come home by then. We went home for the first time at three o'clock in the afternoon, leaving Martha's mom and dad with Laura. We wanted to be home when they brought Marlin home, but it was hard to leave Laura.

Brothers, sisters, friends, and neighbors were there to meet us when we arrived at home. Russell Funeral Home brought Marlin home at eight o'clock Friday evening. We went in to see him for the first time at home. Oh, our dear little boy! Dearly loved by our whole family! Oh, how could this be? How could we go on? Such heartaches and Laura is still in the hospital. Oh, dear Lord, please grant us the strength to go on.

We are so thankful for everybody that was here to share our sorrow and help us through. On Friday night at 11 o'clock, we went back to the hospital to be with Laura. We stayed with her during the night, then spent the days and evenings at home until Monday, the day of Marlin's funeral.

Laura had bad headaches and pain all the time and we were worried about her condition. Someone stayed with her all the time. She could not come home for the funeral. That was very hard to do, but once again God granted us the strength to go on.

On Monday morning, December 21, we came home from the hospital and had breakfast with family and neighbors. The funeral was held in our shop for the family and relatives and in the house once the shop was full.

One more viewing in the house and then the morning prayer and we prepared to go out to the shop. Marlin's casket was carried out of the house ahead of us. What an empty feeling knowing it was to be the last time he would leave our house. The funeral was from 9:30 to 11 o'clock and then came the final viewing at home. Oh, the heart-break!

The undertaker motioned me to come up. I could not go! Someone helped me up to see Marlin for the last time here at home. Oh, the pain and heartache. The sadness cannot be described! The lid was closed and we prepared to go to the cemetery. Marlin's casket was on the first buggy. Then we and the others behind him.

The ride to the cemetery was much too short! Then one more final viewing. The last time to see our dearly beloved little boy. Oh, no! The lid was being closed for the last time! It seemed this could not be true. The parting was so final and it was so hard to give him up even though we knew this is all God's will and he was safely home with Jesus. Then he was carried over to his grave and lowered in.

The men started singing "Ich War ein Kleines Kindlein" and they started shoveling the soil. There again, the heartaches and empty feeling were almost more than we could bear, but God is merciful and gave us strength to go on. Soon they were done. Our dear Marlin is now buried. The days ahead looked very, very dark and bleak. The people then left the cemetery.

Leaving him there and going home again was so hard to do, but we had to go on. We went home and had lunch and visited with relatives, friends, and neighbors. Then in the evening we went to the hospital to see Laura. She was a little better. We were so very thankful for that. Someone stayed with her all night and we went home and slept in our bed for the first time since the accident.

We brought Laura home from the hospital on Wednesday, December 23. She had a full length cast on her leg and was on a wheelchair. We were so glad and thankful to God that we still had her and that she was getting better. Marlin is no longer here, but the heartache and the longing to see him and hold him remain. The heartaches heal in time to a certain extent, but there will always be a tender spot in our heart for him. We have learned to live with this.

How we hope to someday meet him on the Golden Shore! It was so hard to give up our own child, but we feel this was all part of God's plan for us. It has drawn our family closer together and closer to God. God makes no mistakes.

Kathy Bontrager: May 31, 1987 - Nov. 1, 1992

Submitted by: Marvin & Lydia Mae Bontrager, Goshen, Indiana

On Tuesday, October 20, 1992, I took Kathy to the doctor for the first time because she had swollen eyes and didn't eat much, but slept a lot. The doctor took blood tests and told us to call in the next day to find out what the results were. (We didn't know until later that he also tested for mono.)

On Wednesday afternoon I called the office and the tests showed abnormal kidneys, so he made another appointment for Thursday, October 22. He then told us to give her plenty of liquids. He again made an appointment for her on Monday, October 26. She was about the same over the weekend. On Monday they did more blood tests and told us to call back on Tuesday.

When I called in on Tuesday, I got no satisfaction from the receptionist. Then by Wednesday morning we had such a sick daughter that Marvin said he's not going to work until he knows what is wrong with Kathy. At 5:30 that morning he called the doctor at his home and as soon as the doctor heard it was Marvin, he said, "Kathy has mono. Bring her to the office to see if she is dehydrating."

By that time she didn't even want to swallow water so the doctor gave her some medicine to take the swelling down. Her eyes and throat were almost swollen shut. By Thursday morning, October 28, she could see better and her swelling was almost gone. My mom and sisters were here that day and we had such an enjoyable day. Kathy sat around instead of lying down, as she should have been doing, most of the day.

She had gotten a few get well cards, so she sat and looked them over and over again. She had a smile all day even though she couldn't talk out loud. In the evening we were all in the living room singing songs and every so often she would say, "Sing John 3:16 please."

We have such happy memories of that day. It was the farthest thing from our minds that that would be the last day we would have her at home and all be together. Thursday night she was very restless after midnight and she didn't once complain that she couldn't breathe right.

On Friday morning, October 30, she was up and about before Marvin left for work at five o'clock. So Marvin talked to her yet and nestled her on the couch. By 6:30 I told Kenneth, then ten, to go get my mom. (My folks just lived a mile across the fields from us.) I saw that she was worse.

He had just left when I saw that she was fighting for air, so I wrote a note and sent Anna Mary, then six, to the neighbors to ask for help right away. The neighbor lady came and asked if I wanted a driver or first aid and I said the first aid. So another neighbor lady called 911. It wasn't long before the neighbors came and also the fire trucks which came first.

Those men worked on her till the first aid unit came. When the ambulance was ready to leave, my sister-in-law drove in with my mom. Was I ever glad to see them and since I couldn't go along with the ambulance, they took me to the hospital. Another sister-in-law stayed with the children at home. The neighbors said that they would call Marvin at work to let him know.

When we got to the hospital, Marvin was already there and that was such a big relief to me. We were in the hospital about 15 minutes when they came and said there could be possible brain damage, but didn't know the extent of it.

Shortly after that they came and said they have to transfer us to the Memorial Hospital in South Bend. Since Marvin was still in his work clothes, he went home to change first. It was around 10 - 10:30 when we left Goshen for South Bend and thought Kathy would follow shortly. But it was 1:30 in the afternoon when the nurses in South Bend said that Kathy was now there, but they wanted to get her settled in her room before we could see her. We sat and waited till four o'clock before they let us see her.

Sometime later a specialist from Chicago came to look at the test already taken and also do some more. They had fixed a room where we could sleep and Mom also stayed with us. Around midnight, the specialist took us to a private room to talk to us.

Such shocking news! There was no hope that Kathy would make

it. She was brain dead. There was no sleep in us anymore. On Saturday morning we were in Kathy's room awhile then the doctor came in and said that by that afternoon we could probably take the machines off because she was on all kinds of life support machines.

We decided to go home and change clothes and let the rest of the family know what we were planning on doing. By the time we got back to the hospital around noon, they told us that they took a brain scan test that morning and it showed a few good brain cells and they couldn't take the machines off yet.

She had pneumonia with her mono and that is what had caused her to go into a coma.

Our bishop, Paul Hochstetler, went along to the hospital with us. We also had the two oldest children along. That morning Kathy was jerking all over, but by the afternoon she was restful. We had some visitors in the evening and it was greatly appreciated. We went to bed around ten o'clock that night, but by 3:00 AM, we were wide awake, so we got dressed and were in Kathy's room by four o'clock.

When we walked in, we could see something wasn't quite right; her eyes were sunken. The nurse explained that her kidneys had quit working, her blood pressure was way down and she was no longer breathing on her own since about two o'clock that morning. By five o'clock the doctor said to get the family together if we wanted to because there was no use in having those machines going if it wasn't helping her.

They put Kathy in a regular bed in a larger room so we could all be together. All of my family and one of Marvin's brothers and his wife were there. We talked and prayed awhile, then at ten o'clock Marvin told the doctor we were ready to shut the machines off.

Twenty minutes later they pronounced her dead. We thought we had ourselves prepared for that parting, but really we had no idea. It was so hard to part with her. It felt like the bottom of my world fell out, but with the comfort and prayers of family and friends I kind of got over that.

Our kind neighbors had taken the rest of the children to church at John Yoders. They received the death message there and they were all at our place by the time we came home. My heart ached so much for Anna Mary because they were very close. Most of the church families were here Sunday afternoon or evening.

Marvin's brother did most of the calling to get hold of his family since they all lived in other states. On Monday morning at nine o'clock, neighbors came to help get the house ready for viewing. They loaded most of the furniture on wagons to make room for tables. We had the viewing in the basement and ate on the main floor. The body was to come out at ten o'clock, but was closer to 11:30 when it came.

The next few days were some kind of a nightmare. The funeral was on Wednesday, November 4, 1992, at the Jr. Whetstone residence. It was such a cold and windy day.

Marvin's folks stayed for four weeks to help us out since we had a baby girl born on November 7th. The first year was the hardest for me. It is still hard at times, especially when family gets together. There will always be one missing. Oh, how we long to see her once more, but there is a lot of comfort in knowing that she is in heaven and doesn't have to go through trials and temptations like we do.

We once again want to say thanks to family, friends, and the church for what they did for us. Sweet memories of Kathy.

Gone but not forgotten.

Marvin Yoder: four years old
Submitted by: Mr. & Mrs. Daniel H. Yoder, Bloomfield, Iowa

A lot of plans were suddenly changed at our home on the morning of April 7, 1988. The Lord is my refuge and strength and He is nigh unto them that are of a broken heart. Before the day was much more than started, we were a heartbroken family!

All things work out for our good, we know such is God's great design. He has a way of doing things in a way that is far beyond our understanding. But we are not to question why. 'Vas Gott tut, das ist wohl gethan.' What God hath done is done right.

On this particular Thursday morning, we were all busy getting ready to have church services at our house the following Sunday. The boys, as usual, had some silage on a small runabout wagon and went to feed the heifers down the road; a daily chore. Upon coming back, the one mare spooked and started running uncontrollably. The older boys jumped off seeing they couldn't hold them, leaving the two youngest on the wagon. Here came this runaway team heading for the lane, the two boys screaming on the wagon! I looked out the window and saw them coming at a dangerous speed!

By the time I got out there our family and Grandpas had gathered at the scene. The wagon wheel had caught on the mailbox post, throwing David, eight, out on the road and Marvin, four, apparently against the mailbox. It all happened so suddenly, no one saw exactly how or where he hit. But he got up and ran toward the house, then staggered down just as his sister caught him. We saw right away he was seriously hurt. God's grace is sufficient, His promises sure.

I quickly ran to our closest neighbors to call for help, while Daniel, my husband, stayed with Marvin and did artificial respiration. Grandpas, living in the small house, and all our family were anxiously watching over him. Oh, the tense long moments! Our thoughts went to God in prayer.

Finally, the rescue squad came and gave him oxygen, followed by the ambulance. He cried occasionally on the ride to the hospital, which put a little hope in me that just maybe he would pull through yet! He still cried in the emergency room, and again we clung to our hopes, then the doctor asked us to step outside, after which Daniel heard him say, "Looks like we have a dead child."

With that we sat alone in the adjoining room until someone came in and stood with us, now words were spoken. We felt so crushed and miserable, expecting to hear the worst. My thoughts went to God asking for help at this difficult time. I've often since wondered how people who don't believe in God would cope with situations like this.

Soon the doctor came out and told us, "He didn't make it." They called it an instant death. It is hard to describe how we felt! The shock seemed to numb out hearts and minds. We desperately wanted Marvin with us yet, and still we knew it was so final! With heavy hearts we turned to God, to find relief from sorrow. We prayed for strength and courage as we faced each new tomorrow.

Later an autopsy was done and it revealed that the two main arteries were torn from the heart. One lung had collapsed and also his windpipe was torn. He bled internally, but had hardly any bruises on the outside. About one hour after the accident, he quit breathing.

Marvin, being the youngest, was like sunshine in our family! In our minds flashed memories of him, words he'd say, snatches of songs. Just that morning I can still see him and Robert, riding on the pony as they passed the kitchen window. Marvin looked back at me with a radiant smile. We wanted all those memories of dear Marvin to stay fresh in our minds and never fade away.

With heavy hearts we turned toward home. Yes, without Marvin! By then some of the neighbor ladies had gathered to help us in preparing for church. Their sympathy shared made it easier to go on. In the following days we certainly could feel the pull of love from our fellow men. It is often hard for us humans to understand why God takes such precious ones from us at times, but it can often bring us closer to Him. We can also have full confidence that innocent ones like this are now where there will be no more sorrow, and may we all strive harder to prepare to someday go and be with our loved ones again.

We felt God let this happen for a purpose, so we want to accept it as His will. We thought we were so busy, but now our work seemed like nothing. It seemed like God was trying to wake us up and remind us what our goal is in this life.

The Lord has given and the Lord has taken, blessed be the name of the Lord. These are Job's words and have much more meaning once death has visited your home. As time goes on, we can better realize what a blessing it is that Marvin could leave this world in his young, innocent years.

God has given us our children, not to keep, but only to care for as long as He sees best. He works in mysterious ways, His wonders to perform. "God's grace is sufficient, His promises are sure; His love has no end." It is in our trials that we feel His love the strongest.

John Miller: June 9, 1992 (date of tragedy)

Submitted by: Mr. & Mrs. David D. Miller, Millersburg, Ohio

We had a family of ten children. There were six boys and four girls. John was our seventh child, and he was born deaf. He was a special boy and since he couldn't hear, we learned sign language. At a tender age we could finally communicate with each other very well. I also thought I couldn't teach him about the Bible like I should, so I decided to send him to Bible School at Camp Luz, near Kidron that summer.

His deaf friends also attended there and that made him very happy and excited. This was his second day to go and he ran for the bus. As he was going up the bus steps, he looked back and smiled and waved to his brother Robert who was watching at the window, which was unusual.

It was a nice sunshiny day this Tuesday on June 9, 1992. We

were unusually busy because we had hay to make, strawberries to pick, and I had a quilting planned for the next day. The bus stopped at four o'clock in the evening and the driver said the deaf children didn't come down to the training center on time, so they would bring John home later, not knowing that John was lost.

I didn't worry because I always thought John was in good and careful hands. My thoughts were they probably had a flat tire or bus problems. Our daughter Mabel and I were raking the driveway for the quilting, after the evening chores and David was still baling hay. Around seven o'clock Mabel said, "Mom, look here comes the sheriff and a car in front."

My first thoughts were something happened to John, but maybe he's just hurt or in the hospital. But when Veronica Starner, also having a deaf son, and Phyllis Debnar stepped out of the car and were both pale white, I knew something serious was wrong. I asked what happened and where is John?

They asked where David was.

I said just across the field baling hay.

The sheriff was standing a little way from us. I asked again and they finally said that John had drowned at Bible School. Oh, what sad words to hear! My heart beat fast and I thought, could this really be true?

The children ran over to tell my husband who was baling hay and also our recently married daughter Rosie and her husband who were picking strawberries in our patch. They were all crying and we just all cried together in great grief. I said this must have been God's plan.

Our son Robert was working late at the sawmill so he was brought home by the sheriff. He had a hard time getting out of the car and once he did, he sat on the ground shaking all over. We gathered around him and such a shock we never felt before. Soon partners, neighbors, and relatives were here.

We asked what or how it all happened and to this day we truly don't know how it all happened. They had ponds at their Bible School to wade in and there was a lifeguard on duty, but no one noticed that John was missing till they were in the room getting dressed and ready for class.

One of his friends said that John is missing. It was around two o'clock in the afternoon. The lifeguard said he is not in the water, so a great search was made in the woods and in all the many buildings. They swept the highways with airplanes and neighbors helped. They called to the training center to Veronica to say that John was missing. She told me she just yelled in the phone, "Which John? My John or David's?"

They answered not yours, theirs.

So she headed for Camp Luz to help look too. She told me when she saw John's shoes and hat on the bank, she thought oh no.

John's Berlin School teacher was contacted and she came up and they concluded to get the fire department and do water diving. They finally found our dear son in water eight feet deep. They said the life guard stood in the hallway building, hiding and hoping they wouldn't find him in there. The lifeguard could not talk to us, but wrote that she heard the screams, the most inhumane sounds she ever heard. She said even the trees had voices and the whole woods nearby shrieked in agony when they pulled out the body of John. I am still thankful that we were not there to see this awful sight.

It was not till four o'clock when they found him. The lifeguard wrote that we couldn't understand why this happened and she can't understand it either. John was such a good boy, but it was God's decision to call him home that day in the pool of Camp Luz. Panicking, clawing the water, trying to get air for his screaming lungs, but sucked down into this murky water where no one could see him.

Death was so final. No more signing to John and we went through a dark valley of sorrow and grief. Many groups of English, deaf, and even some native people came from Camp Luz to show their sympathy. It was still like a dream, but the next day when they brought his body, we had to believe. How peaceful he lay there. His shiny dark hair, our special boy. He even had a little smile on his face. Many people said how they will miss his smiling face and big wave as we passed by. John was a shy boy, but loved by all. He was very gifted in art. One deaf school girl said it isn't worth having school if John wasn't there since John was the oldest and they all looked up to him.

It was a nice sunshiny day on Friday and we had the funeral here in our barn. Around 800 people attended with interpreter, Harry Miller, for the deaf. The sermon was preached by our bishop Henry Stutzman and minister John Miller, with great sympathy and many tears shed. Lots of friends and people followed us to the graveyard.

Such a feeling we never had before. John was laid to rest in a new cemetery where our closest neighbor's father and husband of Amanda and her five children was buried in February.

At first I avoided looking up to the graveyard because it hurt so much, but after a few weeks I looked up there often and we can see his grave stone. The first one half year it made us so sad to go up there, but went better later on. Our 11 year old Susan looked up there every evening before going to bed for a long time. David had hay for the next day after the funeral, but he was too weak to do it so neighbors and our boys did it. John's teacher also came the next day and she tried to explain how they think it happened. But only God knows. That was one of our many questions from people through the following weeks and years.

One of my cousins said she was so glad to be at the funeral and to see the deaf under the shade trees quietly signing and the birds were singing in the trees above. One of the bus drivers said, "Just think, John can hear and talk now." We both cried. I said I hadn't even thought of that, but it helped me a lot.

John had a dog named Beaver and we always heard when John came out of the house in the morning to milk. John made a howling noise and so did the dog. But now, Beaver lay near the house days and nights and cried and cried for John. Such a shivering cry so we usually cried with him.

A lot of food was brought over during the time of the funeral. It was appreciated, but our hunger was little. Often when I wanted to eat, it just stuck in my throat but I had to eat so I wouldn't get sick. Days went by and finally a week. We were still in shock and it felt like we had to crawl all day. We got lots of mail which we were glad because we didn't feel like working so a few hours were spent on looking and reading letters and encouraging words which helped so much.

We knew there were plans again for a wedding for our second daughter Mabel and Ray Yoder. How could we with such saddened hearts? But with the help of our children, we said we would try and go on. It was hard to get things sewn for the wedding with the many visitors, but we were glad for everyone.

My sister Barbara had a dream soon after the funeral that a golden crown came down on John's head and slowly disappeared toward heaven. This helped me a lot. Later I had a dream that I saw John and my husband had a dream, too.

Four weeks before the wedding, our third daughter, Edna, took sick and we took her to the hospital. She had an appendicitis operation and while waiting my husband asked, haven't we had enough? We both cried, but I finally said maybe God wants us to think about something else besides the death of dear John.

We missed Edna's help in getting ready for the wedding. We had the wedding here September 10th. It was a hard day. We tried to be happy, but John was always the most excited about our weddings. Life was different and the wedding was different without John.

But life went on and Mabel and Ray moved. We had three leave the table in five months' time. The married ones come home, but John doesn't. One day my husband said, "I think John must be looking down from the sky and knows about the wedding." It is all is God's hands.

Time went on and in October we had church. On the Friday before we had church we were making pies in the morning when Junior came in and said Dad fell off the corn crib roof and broke his leg badly. Oh, my heart sank. Why us again? We took him to the hospital and surgery was needed, but they put it off till Saturday to operate because they were too busy. I went home and helped get ready for church.

On Saturday surgery was done. It took four screws and a pin in his leg. We had church without David and without John. I wondered what would happen next. This loaded a mother up again with a lot of responsibilities. We got many visitors again which helped. David said he often wept about John while he was alone and just sitting day after day. He attended church two weeks later.

We thought our life was such a struggle but tried to look out to the others who had it worse. We got so lonesome for John at times and our life looked dark. We often looked at his pictures and held his clothes and tears dropped, but it always helped to think that John is up in heaven where we all want to go and be someday.

Christmas was a hard time because we couldn't see John's happy face. We did not feel like going shopping. David was a minister and so another hard day was the first time he had to preach after this tragedy and loss. It was very hard and many tears were shed since most of the sermon was about John's death.

It was six months after the accident before we finally gathered ourselves together and John's teacher took us up to see where it happened at Camp Luz, near Kidron. It was a sad day. Some days my heart started to hurt and I thought something must be wrong, but it was just hurting so much from our parting of our beloved one.

These parting thoughts were our last thought before we went to sleep and our first thoughts in the morning, but always thought, "His will," too, for over two years or more. Our thoughts were this is a loud call from the one above and a great warning to be ready. So we want to live a better life, yet we fail and make mistakes. After four years we still think of John almost every day but we can say we don't wish him back to this sinful world and that time does heal.

We will never forget our year of 1992. I felt humbled to publish this in my own words in time of trial, but I hope it can be a help to others in sorrow.

Danny Miller: Nov. 25, 1995 (date of tragedy)
Submitted by: Melvin & Irene Miller, Middlebury, Indiana

The morning of November 25, 1995, was a chilly and cold morning. Two of our sons, Marlin, 17, and Danny, 15, went deer hunting. We had fixed a breakfast of pancakes and cereal that morning. Danny was in a teasing mood that morning like he was lots of times. I had hid his watch and when he found it he said, "Mom, you can't tease me." Those were his final words to us as he left the house.

Our oldest son had just married six weeks earlier and he, William, and his wife Elsie lived here with us in the small house. He came over in the morning to see if his brother Samuel, six, wanted to go to Middlebury with him. So he went with him. Mary, 13, our oldest daughter and I went to a benefit auction at Lester Lehmans. Melvin needed to go to the hay auction to buy hay so we dropped him off there.

This left Rachel, 11, and Marlene, eight, at home with William's wife, Elsie. I am thinking it was around 10:00 when an English lady I didn't know came to me and asked me if my husband Melvin Miller was at the hay auction. I said he was. She then said there had been an accident. I got so weak all over and felt real shaky. I thought something had happened to Melvin. Then as we were walking to her car, she said there was a hunting accident.

She took Mary and me home. All the way home I was thinking now, which one of the boys is it? This same lady had taken Melvin home earlier. Her dad has the hay auction. When we came home William and Elsie were right inside the door. I asked them right away, "Which one is it?"

They said, "Danny."

I thought I don't want it to be Marlin, but it can't be Danny either. He helped me so much with my work and he did so much for us all. How could we ever manage without Danny? I did not know.

Everybody was crying, but in some ways I felt kind of calm. I asked William if there was any hope and he said he didn't think so. I really felt sorry for Marlin. He was sitting with his head in his hands crying. Then pretty soon he stood up and went into our bedroom and flopped on our bed. Poor Marlin. He had lost a brother in marriage and another one in death so soon. He and Danny had been so close.

We will never know for sure how the accident happened. The boys had gone back together, but had then taken separate areas to hunt. They had not been in the woods long until Marlin heard a shot and he thought Danny had probably shot a deer. Later Marlin decided to come back home. When he came home Danny wasn't home yet, and then when William came home from town, Marlin said something to him. They both got the feeling they should go look for him.

They found him lying under a tree with a gun shot wound to his chest. We think he probably was climbing the tree and slipped. He had always been so careful. Marlin said he always had his gun on safety.

This is something we will never know. It helps to think it was all in God's hands. One of the neighbors called the ambulance, but it was too late.

It seems like each of the children dealt with Danny's death differently. The two youngest had problems with sleeping at night. I needed to talk with them for awhile until they could go to sleep. So far none of them can talk too much about it. I guess it still hurts too much. As for me, it helps me so much to talk to people about it. Marlin seems to deal with it by working, working, and working.

About one and one half weeks before Danny's accident, he had shot a deer with his bow and arrow. He had been so happy about that. We had put the meat in our freezer about one half mile from home. Three days before this happened, he asked me if it would be all right if he goes to the freezer and gets some of that meat for two of our English neighbors. I told him he could.

That same day he went with Samuel and me to school with the hot lunch and played soccer with the children. That evening he was hauling manure with the wheelbarrow. One of our neighbors saw him and he said it was around dusk, and sometimes it looked like two persons and other times it looked like a silhouette.

He said it looked so strange to him that he said out loud to himself, "Now what does that mean?" He said he didn't have long to wait to see what it meant.

Samuel Dean Whetstone: Age 6 - died June 15, 1995

Submitted by: Mervin & Laura Whetstone, LaGrange, Indiana and Joshua Murphy

It was a warm hazy day. In the morning Samuel and I had gone back to the fields to rake the hay for the men to put up in the afternoon. The other boys were down at my folks. Samuel had caught one of our wild kitties and was tenderly talking to it and cuddling it while I was busy. After a while I saw that he'd gone up, so I called him. Through the woods came his cheery whistle. He said he'd gone to get milk for his kitty. Then we were done and the other boys were brought up and we had lunch.

After lunch, the other three boys were napping and Samuel and I were hulling strawberries. As usual he was asking questions like, "Mom, when will Jesus come? I wish he would come today." Along with a lot of other questions, he'd ask some that don't have answers.

Around 2:30 the men, Mervin, and a friend, Joshua Murphy, came home from work and made preparations to get the hay in. Samuel was all excited and running around and helping. I often wonder why I encouraged him to go along. Didn't I see the danger? Or did I think accidents only happen to other people, the men will take good care. But nevertheless he went along. He was so happy.

I finished up my strawberries and started doing dishes. Pretty soon I heard a rumbling noise, like a wagon going fast with a full load. I thought, here they come already with a load. My brothers, Milton and David were also helping. All of a sudden, David burst in the door, his face ashen and gasped, "You'd better get the ambulance. Samuel's been hurt. The wagon went over him!"

I didn't ask any questions other than, "911?"

David said, "Yes, quickly go!"

I ran across the field to where the phone was, about one third mile from our house. Often before I'd think, wonder where I'd go for emergency help if we needed it quickly. Try the neighbors first or go for the phone. I didn't even think of trying the neighbors since I had no idea if anybody was at home. All the way to the phone I was praying, 'Please Lord let him be okay. Not my will but thine.'

I dialed 911 and gasped "Our son has been hurt badly!"

I gave them our address and said I would meet them at the end of our long lane. This all happened out behind the barn in the lane that goes through the woods, so you couldn't see anything till you got right to it. I was not sure where they were, so when the eerie, but welcome wail of the ambulance came, I was wondering how they would know where to go. I didn't know where David was. Was anybody up there to open and close the gates for them?

I sent the EMS on back and hopped into the last police car. They didn't know who I was, a neighbor or the mother, and I didn't think to tell them. Once we got there I stumbled out of the car and walked up to Mervin who was kneeling at Samuel's side. One of the police tried to stop me, but I pushed on through. Then the medics asked, "Are you the mother?"

I nodded numbly, couldn't think at all. They said, "There's no use taking him in. We're sorry, but he's gone."

Mervin's hat was off, his face dirty and smudged. More dirt on his shirt and I saw Samuel's boots lying here and there. His straw hat was lying close to him and you could see that a wagon wheel had gone over it.

As I surveyed the scene, I asked what happened. Oh, what happened? The men couldn't answer right then. The police were also asking Josh and Mervin questions and everybody was in such a daze. I couldn't even cry. I was saying to myself over and over, this isn't real. It can't be real.

I looked at Samuel, his lips gray and slightly parted. Such a nice peaceful look on his face. His eyes staring up toward Heaven, almost as if he was saying, "Is that you Jesus?"

They covered him with a tarp and Mervin and I started up toward the buildings. On the way up we met my mother with our other little boys. We took them aside and told them we don't have Samuel anymore. He's gone to Heaven. You could see they couldn't understand it.

"But where is he?" they asked.

We were reluctant to take them back there, so we didn't. I've wished since we would have gone back there since he was lying there so peacefully. Maybe they could have understood better what had happened then. My dad came soon after and he was out there when the undertaker came to pick Samuel up. Dad took the boys over and they uncovered Samuel so the boys could see him. They touched him yet and he was still warm. Our youngest often said of Samuel after he was brought back from the funeral home, "He's so cold, so cold." I think that will always stay with him.

The "if onlys" started crowding in. I thought if only I'd run faster to call for help. But afterwards I was glad they weren't there sooner. They might have taken him only to prolong his death. His heart was crushed, also his lungs.

If only I hadn't let him go along. But it seems that it is the boys' greatest desire to go along to the field with Daddy. The neighbors started coming and the hay was put in yet. Somebody helped with chores. I was in here, trying to put some things away. Joshua and sister Esther went to notify our families about Samuel. She couldn't give many details, but just the message.

My brother Henry and his wife were in the hospital. They just had a little girl that day. She couldn't come to the funeral. I felt bad for her, but it couldn't be helped.

We had a rosebush that had had buds for a while already. Samuel was always asking, "Mom, when will that flower open? I just can't wait."

He'd guard that rose, the other boys were not to touch it. The day after he was killed, I saw the bud slowly open. On the day of the funeral, it was fully open! I thought it was a miracle. What better way had God of showing us that he cared about us?

We miss Samuel a lot. He was the oldest grandson on my side. When our families gather together, it always gives me a lump in my throat to see the other children laughing and playing and knowing how much he would have enjoyed it.

I have beautiful memories of that fateful day. He willingly got up at four o'clock and helped us chore that morning, volunteered to feed the calves out in the hutch in the predawn darkness. After the chores, he helped me work in the garden all the while chattering cheerfully. He wasn't always like this. He had his moody days too.

The day went fast and before we knew it, the funeral was over and everybody was gone. Now it was time to readjust. No longer setting the table for six, only five unless Joshua stayed for supper which he often did and I think it helped us a lot to ward off the loneliness.

This was so sharp in the boys' minds for a long time I didn't hear them say his name accidentally. It was so real to them. They knew he was in the box and the box was in the ground. Our youngest suggested a few times that we go and dig it up again because he thinks Samuel wants to get out. You could tell they had it on their minds a lot.

When company came they didn't know what to play. Samuel had always been the leader, deciding what and how to play, etc. Now, all of a sudden, the responsibility was thrust on Lonnie's shoulders. He didn't know how to act and therefore we had quite a time with him. Sometimes he would cry uncontrollably for hardly any reason. I'm sure it was grief as much as the incident that started it.

The third of the boys started chewing his fingernails down so much that they bled sometimes. That has cleared up now, but at the time I just didn't realize how much those little ones have to cope with and how hard it is for them to explain themselves; so it comes out in other ways.

Our youngest is fully convinced that Samuel is up with Jesus. He often talks in his play about Samuel, Jesus, and Heaven. Just recently he said, "Mom, Samuel is calling me and I would really like to see him again." Then he asked, "How does he look again?"

I think he's starting to forget how he looked, but I had to pray, "Oh Lord, do we also have to part with him?" This is how Samuel talked before he died. "Not our will, but thine." I think a lot of children talk about Jesus and Heaven. It's just natural. So if we can just strive to meet Him there, that is our goal.

The following is by Joshua Murphy, who was a witness and a part of the accident. He was like a big brother to our boys and often helped with the farm work. He and Samuel had just started to communicate with each other since one spoke Dutch and the other English. They had lots of fun times together and this was really an ordeal for Joshua. I am grateful to him for submitting his part and may God bless all his future endeavors.

On June 15, 1995, the afternoon heat was very noticeable already, causing sweat to drip from our foreheads. Knowing we would feel warmer yet after starting to work, Mervin Whetstone sent his oldest son Samuel in to get a water jug for us.

Not much time passed until Samuel returned with a full water jug in hand. He thumped loudly and awkwardly with every step because he had his rubber boots on. Mervin told him it was too hot to have those boots on, but the young boy was determined to use them.

Giving up on reason, Mervin helped Samuel crawl up onto the wagon and away we went! As I walked along next to the wagon to help open and close gates my thoughts started to wander. I thought about the heat of the sun, about the hard work ahead of us, and how neat it was to see Mervin and his boys working together in the field. Where were the other boys? Usually there were at least two out here with us. "Must be the others are still napping," I thought to myself.

When we arrived at the field behind the woods, we could see that Milton, Laura's brother, had started to bale. I started to toss bales onto the wagon while Mervin tried to drive and stack at the same time. Realizing he couldn't keep up, Mervin asked Samuel to drive.

The six year old's face beamed with satisfaction. Samuel took the reins in hand with a smile that covered his shining face. He was helping Daddy. Since he was so short, he couldn't really see over the horses, so occasionally he guided the horses to walk over bales, but… he was still helping Daddy.

One bale at a time, the wagon finally became full. It was time to head up to the barn to unload. The lane we had to take went down a hill, through some woods, curved around a bit, then up another hill just before the barnyard. We all climbed up the tall square pile of hay and sat on the top. My legs dangled in front, Mervin stood on the standard and carefully put Samuel behind us to help protect him from falling.

I glanced at Mervin and light heartedly said, "Let's go for the ride of our lives." Little did I know that soon those words would become reality. Mervin made a clicking sound with his mouth and the horses started to pull. The load was full. The horses put their heads down and pulled even harder as we made the tight turnaround. As the ground became sloped downward in front of us, the horses had to work harder to hold the weight of the hay back.

I started to feel uneasy and quietly said, "Mervin." The wagon creaked forward. Again, "Mervin." This time slightly louder. The hay was starting to shift! Finally again almost panicked I cried, "Mervin!"

I couldn't duck under the low hanging limbs and keep my

balance on top. I must jump! Not hesitating, I jumped to the side out of danger. The sounds and sights that followed still cause my stomach to knot up.

I heard steel wheels slamming against rocks, Mervin shouting whoa, chains in the tugs clattering, Mervin shouting whoa, whoa, work horses' hooves beating the ground, and Mervin shouting whoa. I spun around just as Mervin landed on the back of a horse and flopped to the ground between the horses and the wagon. He was in front of the wheel! Without thinking, I stuck my hands under Mervin's arms and pulled. The wheel went over his foot.

"Where is Samuel? I must help him . . ."

At that very moment I turned and saw Samuel on his knees under the wagon. Then... the hind wheel had run over the small, fragile boy's chest.

"Oh heavenly Father," I uttered not knowing what else to say or do. David, Mervin's brother-in-law, ran to call for help. A few minutes had now passed. Samuel now lay motionless except for the widely spaced raising and lowering of his chest. His lungs were starting to fill with fluids. Mervin leaned over his son hoping to still feel warm air come out of his mouth.

Mervin whispered, "Samuel" tenderly "Samuel". Over and over Mervin breathed the word "Samuel" into Samuel's ear. Was Mervin the only one whispering Samuel's name that afternoon?

Samuel's heavenly Father was also calling for this young rose by name. "Samuel."

Paul Enos Yoder: Apr. 18, 1952 - Oct. 13, 1973

Submitted by: Amos & Freda Yoder, Goshen, Indiana

On Saturday evening a few of the children's friends were here for the evening. They were upstairs enjoying themselves. Amos and I were sitting at the kitchen table sipping a cup of coffee. Around eight o'clock a rescue squad went north. You always wonder now who needs help. Soon after that we saw a car coming and just like that, zoom, it was past. We both said, "My, what a speed!"

Just then the children came running down the stairs and out the door. There is an accident or fire down at the corner. Oh, our hearts felt heavy! Wonder now what? The children ran down to investigate.

Our son Paul was visiting at Perry Yutzy's, Paul's sister Rosie.

Perrys lived right on the corner. Paul was driving out the lane. We feel he might have seen the car coming, but thought he could make it. It was almost dark and he didn't realize the car was coming so fast. He pulled out on Highway 49 and just like that the car hit him in the rear.

The car burst into fire. We feel the impact killed Paul instantly. Soon help was summoned and the fire put out. By the time the ambulance came it was dark. Amos stood close by when Paul was rescued from the car. He was so charred. Oh, the ache in our hearts was so heavy. But then there was the Lord to help carry the load if we ask. God makes no mistakes.

The driver of the other car was lying in the ditch, not hurt at all. His car was also totaled. We were glad that he wasn't hurt, but we always wondered, "Why Paul?"

Maybe someday we will understand. Soon friends and neighbors came to share the grief. Calls had to be made far and near. Not much sleep that night for all of us. When Paul was brought out to the house it was so hard to bear, since it was a sealed casket. He was burned so badly. It was so touching and hard to grasp that we could no more see Paul. It was now all in God's hands. We had the funeral at our house. His wife, son, mother-in-law, and some friends came to the funeral.

About two weeks later Amos had a dream. In this dream he was repeating the accident. The car was on fire and Amos was trying to go up and open the door to get Paul out. He tried three times and the third time he tried, Amos told Paul he couldn't get him out and he asked Paul, "Do you believe Jesus was the son of God?"

Paul answered, "Yes, Dad, you know I do."

"Well ask Him to forgive you."

Then Amos woke up. He realized one spirit was telling him there was no hope and another spirit saying there was hope. Upon meditating, Amos decided to give it to the Lord and let him judge it and then he got relief. So often we try to judge and that is not for us human people.

Paul was married and had a son Kevin. He was about one and one half to two years old at the time of the accident. Rosie took care of him a while after the accident and kept him till his mother got married again. Debbie, his wife, remarried to Danny Cook. She then took Kevin and they moved away. We then lost track of them.

Amos and I often talked about how we could go about to locate Kevin again. But time went on and this kept running through our minds. One day daughter Nettie, Devon, happened to talk with a friend of ours, Crist Schwartz Betty. Nettie came back and told us about it.

Betty said her sister Joan's husband, Paul Yoder, had a ball team and one day they had a game. There was a Kevin Yoder on the opposing team. Paul decided to find out who he was. He asked him and Kevin told him. I don't remember what all Kevin told him, but Paul knew right away who he was.

He asked him if he knew his grandfather. Yes, he thinks his name is Amos Yoder. Paul told him that he now lives in Goshen, Indiana. Kevin was overwhelmed and thought maybe soon he could meet up with kinsfolk. Paul asked him where he had kept himself all these years.

Kevin replied that he had moved with his mom out west as far as Washington. As he grew up, he had a desire to come back to Indiana. He completed high school in Washington and then decided to come back to Purdue University and joined the football team. Later he got interested in becoming a salesman and got started selling sweepers for Good Housekeeping.

The company decided to run an ad for business people to send in their names and they would draw a name for one person to win a free sweeper. Well Edna Hochstetler's name was drawn and Kevin delivered the sweeper to her door. He then asked if she knew of someone who might be interested in a sweeper.

She mentioned her brother Willie Christner. He got directions and went over to his store. Kevin introduced himself and said, "You probably know some of my relatives. My dad was Paul Yoder and my grandfather is Amos Yoder and he lives somewhere up here in Indiana."

After thinking a little, Willie said, "If you are who I think you are, you have an aunt living just down the road." Kevin remembered an aunt taking care of him. "Well, she lives down the road in that white house." He was so shocked he just went home to think it over. I believe he called his mom. She was surprised and told him to go meet everybody.

So the next morning he came to Perry's door. Rosie answered. The evening before, Willie came and informed Rosie who his sales-man was. She too was shocked. Now here was Kevin. They greeted each other and finally decided to have a get-together.

The rest of us were informed. We all were overwhelmed with

touched hearts and mixed feelings. We met at Perry and Rosie's for supper. We were all there when he came in. It was an indescribable feeling. We couldn't help but cry.

He said, "Hello everybody," and started shaking hands. "Well, Grandpa," and greeted each other with hellos. It was so touching. It was joy, love, sorrow, and gladness to meet him. Thank the Lord.

He was around three years old when we had last seen him and had now grown to six feet and more. He was gone 19 years. He had lots of Paul's ways. We enjoyed the evening. He still remembered coming out to Grandpa's and playing with two boys. He decided it was Vernon and LaVern. We try and stay in touch with him.

Our hearts go out to children that had to part with parents as a child, never knowing what their parents looked like. It's a feeling nobody knows without the experience. It is a humble feeling. Only God knows the true meaning. I want to thank the Lord for helping me write this. I enjoyed it. God Bless you all.

Steven Schmucker: Nov. 27, 1964 - May 3, 1969
Submitted by: Vernon & Edna Schmucker, Goshen, Indiana

May 3, 1969, was a beautiful Saturday with the sun shining all day and it was in the sixties. I was plowing in the field south of the house and Steven was out in the field with me. As I plowed he would run along behind the plow. One minute he would be laughing and the next minute he would be crying. We did not know why.

That afternoon I went down to my dad's to get the spike tooth harrow to harrow what I had plowed that morning. My wife was going to her mom's with the pony buggy and Steven said he wanted to go along. After I was about halfway to my dad's I heard something behind me and looking around saw Steven coming down the road, running after me.

We went to Doddys and got the spike tooth harrow and went up the road toward home. About halfway down the hill by the field beside our house I heard a car coming. Steven was barefoot. I turned around to see where Steven was and he was sitting on the edge of the road picking little stones off his feet. I said, "Steven, you can't sit on the road." He got up and followed me.

Then the car came across the top of the hill, driving too fast for the hill she was on. It was a neighbor lady on her way home from

Goshen. When she saw us she braked and her car went into a skid. I thought she would run off on the other side of the road. When she saw she was headed for the ditch she turned the wheels the other way and all at once the car came toward us. She hit Steven and me and went into the ditch on the west side of the road.

The first one to come along was a veterinarian from Middlebury. He went down into the ditch and felt Steven's chest then shook his head. He then got water from his truck to wash my face. I had mud all over. When the ambulance came they took us to the Goshen Hospital and that was the last I saw Steven.

When Steven was still with us, he would sing a lot. One of the songs he sang a lot was 'Heaven Will Surely Be Worth It All'. The first verse was, 'Worth all the sorrows that here befall, after this life with all its strife, Heaven will surely be worth it all.'

"The Lord hath given and the Lord hath taken away. Blessed be the name of the Lord."

We were thinking today of our loved one
Whom the Lord has taken away,
His life on this earth seemed so short,
But he could no longer stay.

Because the Lord needed an angel
To brighten His home in the sky.
But why did He take little Steven
In the twinkling of an eye?

We do not need to know,
God's ways are beyond control.
We know Steven is safely with Jesus,
And the angels are guarding his soul.

The songs that he sang on this earth
Were heard by the angels above,
So let us thank God for His mercy
By taking the one that we loved.

Friends may think we have forgotten
When at times they see us smile,
But they little know the heartache,
The smile hides all the while.

Barbara Ellen Slabaugh: 1 year, 10 months, 25 days

Submitted by: Dan T. & Katie Slabaugh, Nappanee, Indiana

Our first child was a daughter named Barbara Ellen. She seemed to be a normal healthy child until she was about one and one half years old. She was out in the yard playing and Grandpa was watching her. He told us there is something wrong with her. She dropped down on the ground as if she had been shot. We took her to the doctor several times but he couldn't find anything wrong.

We feel we made a mistake and should have taken her to a specialist. Time went on and she started having convulsions. That scared us, so we called the doctor and he came out and he soon had her out of that. He told us that is a common thing for babies to have convulsions.

The second time she got convulsions, she went into a coma. We took her to the hospital and she died two days later. We never found out what the problem was, but we think she had spinal meningitis. They did an autopsy, but they never told us what they found. The death certificate said she had pneumonia.

We feel this was God's will. The Lord has given, the Lord has taken. Blessed be the name of the Lord. Barbara died about six or seven weeks before Vernon was born.

> *A silent thought — A secret tear*
> *Brings these memories ever near;*
> *Time slowly takes the edge of grief,*
> *But memories turn back every leaf.*

Vernon Dale Slabaugh: July 24, 1949 - July 23, 1964

Submitted by: Dan T. & Katie Slabaugh, Nappanee, Indiana

It was July 23, 1964, and another nice hot day. Not thinking what the day might bring forth, my two oldest boys, Vernon and Leon, and I went threshing that day. It was the last day of wheat threshing at Jancy Schmuckers. The boys took the bundle wagon and I ran the machine. Everybody worked hard that day to finish the wheat threshing.

I remember well that I pitched off the last load for Vernon so he could eat his sandwich before he went home. I didn't know this would be the last time I could talk with him. I think all the boys on the crew that day planned to go swimming that evening up at the Haney gravel pit, about three-fourth mile from our home. When I got home the boys were all at the gravel pit. I didn't like it a bit.

I had just cleaned up and sat down to rest when a car drove in. The first thought that went through my mind was the boys up at the gravel pit. Sure enough, it was Will Yoder (Kansas Will), and his boy Clarence. They told us Vernon was missing.

We all went up to the pit. They were dragging the pit but couldn't find the body. They got two scuba divers from Plymouth and they soon found him in about ten feet of water. I had to go to the shore to identify him. It is almost impossible to say how I felt at that time.

Bishop Simon Schmucker from the Goshen area was one of the boys that came swimming across the pit and saw Vernon's hands at the edge of the water. He told the rest of the boys that were there that somebody was out in the water. There were about 25 boys there and they checked with each other and found Vernon missing. We feel this was God's plan and God makes no mistakes. We know how other people feel that have a tragedy in the home. Vernon died one day before his 15th birthday.

The best way to cope with something like this is first think that it is God's will. Just hope our loss is the child's gain.

Edith Hochstetler: August 30, 1988 (date of tragedy)
Submitted by: Ammon Hochstetler, Nappanee, Indiana

I was asked to write a few lines about the accident of my wife, Edith Hochstetler, on August 30, 1988.

In the afternoon the sun was shining brightly, and late in the afternoon Edith went to the country store about two and a half miles away, on the bicycle. I was cutting small trees away from the fence. As time went on I got done with my work, not realizing what the rest of the day would bring.

When I got done, I went to the house. A little later a police car drove in. Right away some things went through my mind. In grade school we were taught that when there is an accident on the road and someone is killed, the police go to the family and tell them, but I put that in the back of my mind. When I came to the door, he said there was an accident and Edith had lost her life.

It was so sudden and what was there to think except the Lord has given and the Lord has taken. Blessed be the name of the Lord.

The police took me to the accident and I saw her when she was still in the ditch. A car had hit her from behind. There can be a bright side to an accident. It was her time to go and there was no suffering or being a cripple. Edith was always encouraging everyone to have lights on their bikes, but it must have taken longer to take care of things than she had planned. It happened at 8:20 PM.

The same day of the accident, Wayne Burkholder, my brother-in-law had gone to the store and gotten ten bushels of apples for applesauce for different members of the family. Something had to be done, so Walter Schwartz asked the neighbors to come and help. They did a wonderful job.

One of the ministers of the church and I were visiting and he said we were given together at marriage, but there was no time given for how long. How would we have made it if we had known which day that we would have to part? I do feel she did achieve that which she lived for. She had a great concern for the children and the future of the church.

Marcus Duane Schwartz: June 29, 1974 - Sept. 7, 1984

Submitted by: John & Fannie Schwartz, Topeka, Indiana

Marcus Duane Schwartz, ten, son of John and Fannie Irene Schwartz, had four brothers, Cletus, 22; Wilbur, 21; Michael, 18; and Myron, 13. Two sisters, Mary, 15; and Carolyn, five. Marcus was killed instantly in a car/bicycle accident on September 7, 1984.

September 7, 1984, was a warm sultry day with thundershowers in the forenoon. One of those hectic days of my life with so many things to do. Which should be done first? There were two weddings on our minds. My niece's on the 20th of September and our son's on the 27th, and my mother sick in bed with age and Alzheimer's.

Many times we wondered if she would leave us before the weddings, and many times when I jumbled this around in my mind, the thought that the healthy one can go too came to my mind. But God will help us however, I tried to console myself again and again.

All summer we were extra busy since our son was also building a new house. But on this Friday, I had a bushel of tomatoes and three bushels of peaches to do, plus we wanted to fill silo in the afternoon if the weather permitted. The men were all at their jobs and Myron and Marcus were in school. Mary and I were doing our canning in the basement and when the showers were over, I'd run over and see how the weather looked since we were to have the horses in the barn and fed. That way when John came home, the horses would be ready to go.

The sun came out at 11:00 and we went to get the horses in. Sure enough the horses didn't cooperate. Two of them ran back to the field again, and the bull jumped the fence three or four times that day. We had quite a time getting the horses in. All day was run, run, run. The wind was strong from the northeast and blew all the corn stalks over into the yard. We had visitors and I had to run to town for snacks plus try to get my canning done.

All the little things that get on your nerves plus the overloaded and burdened mind that mothers sometimes get. With prayers in mind pleading for God's help to do it all, we trudged on. Finally with chores done and supper about ready, I happened to think about our neighbor with a sick baby. She had been here in the afternoon while I was gone and asked if I could come and see what was wrong with her sick baby. I got cleaned up and jumped on my bike and went to see what I could do.

When I got there, there was nobody home, so I went home again. As I was going home, I passed the box where we pick up our daily papers, about 500 ft. from our home. I had this eerie feeling of getting hit. (It was close to the spot where our son would lie after he was hit.)

I hurried home and took extra precautions to avoid getting hit. As I turned in our lane, I happened to think of our paper. The men were all ready to go in for supper. I stopped and said, "Oh, I forgot the paper."

John knew I was tired and said, "Marcus can go. He can use my bike."

Marcus always liked to ride John's bike. He willingly got on it and went to get it. As he got on the road, I looked back and said, "Now be careful!" and he said, "Ya." I turned to walk into the house and I thought, what if he'd get hit? The chills ran down my back.

John finished up in the barn. He heard a car coming from the north and came out of the barn and walked out to the road to see if he could see Marcus yet. I had gone to the house to finish supper and get it on the table. John couldn't see Marcus, so he ran up the road. Myron was on the trampoline and saw John run, so he got on his bike and went too.

He came back and told us, "Marcus has been hit and we can't find him."

We all ran out of the house and ran up the road. I soon heard when they found him. Pitiful screaming and crying. My feet didn't want to carry me. I was praying, "God, you must help us."

When I got there, he was lying by the fence, all quiet, like he was sleeping. I knelt down beside him and rubbed him and cried with a terrible pain in my chest. Then a voice, as of many waters, said, "You now have an angel, dear," and the pain in my chest just rolled out and I could just feel him go up and I felt so at peace. Something that was too wonderful to describe, that God cared enough to talk to me. I've thanked Him many times for this. It is something I will never forget and has helped me through many trials.

Soon there were lots of people, but my first concern were his two brothers that weren't at home. Someone called them and soon cops and EMS came. I was still kneeling down beside the still form. The EMS tried to do artificial respiration and when they rolled him around, I saw how terrible his head looked, but when they did mouth to mouth, Marcus kind of gasped. I thought, oh, maybe there is still a chance. But when they did the second time, what came up was all broken up. I thought again of what the voice had said and told them to let him go. I had to think of some that were never normal and Marcus had been such an active boy and that would have been hard too.

I pictured him in Heaven and it was easy to let go, for I had teenagers that were heavy on my mind. Many people came to console us that evening yet, but one of the hardest things to accept was when the undertaker said we couldn't view him. I had consoled myself that he'd fix him up and that we'd have a nice memory. For I knew what that meant since I had lost my father when I was 20. I knew the comfort of a peaceful look in the casket.

He said, "Part of his forehead is missing and I have nothing to work with. I could put a bandage on." I just couldn't give up. I felt the children could grasp it better if they could see him again. I finally submitted and said, "Do what you can." All night long I tossed and prayed that he could fix him. In the morning I asked the neighbor to call and tell him to put a bandage on. Anything so we could see him. Then the undertaker said he used plastic and we could view him. A great relief! He didn't really look natural, but we could see it was him. The kind deeds and many consoling friends are the greatest gifts God gave to men, other than dying for us. These deeds and cards and letters helped us all to heal.

I thanked God many times for taking him in his innocence. He is so lucky! The school children said everyone waved and yelled at him when he got off the bus that evening, and he waved and waved until they were out of sight. Marcus was a very sweet child. He had many friends we found out later. He was very nervous and hyper. He walked at seven and one half months old.

We have some very good memories. As years go on, we know God meant it well. It is a comfort to know you have one "safe" in Heaven. No one can deceive him or hurt him. Praise God!

Amos Chupp: Oct. 30, 1915 - October 7, 1996

Submitted by: Dennis & Ruth Yoder, Etna Green, Indiana

This day started out just like many others. I fixed Dennis' lunch and got him off to work. Then I did my laundry before getting Lyle, 12, and Gary, nine, off to school. It was a beautiful day. When I got the children up, I looked over to the trailer to see if Grandpa was up. I did this every morning.

I remember thinking when I got up that I have got more than I can do this week. (I guess my work didn't matter as much as I thought.) I was going to can apple pie filling today. I got one batch started before the boys went to school. After the boys left, Kathy, six; Kevin, three; and I went over to give Grandpa his medicine. I did this every day. Grandpa was eating his breakfast. I sat down and talked with him for a while. He said his horse was lame and he wanted to go see what was wrong.

I remember saying, "Wait until Dennis gets home. He'll check it out for you."

He said, "I'll see."

My sister Mary came around 9:30 to help me with my apples. The children all went outside to play. At noon, sister Rose brought her children for us to baby-sit while she cleaned a house for a lady. We made a quick lunch for us and the children.

I saw Grandpa's lunch come. He got 'meals on wheels' five days a week and they always just took it over to him. Around one o'clock I went out to bring my clothes in. Then I took Grandpa's clothes over to put them away. There was his lunch on the table untouched.

I can't explain the fear and panic that went through me. I went out and questioned the children. Rose's children said they saw him head out to the barn when they came. He had given each of the children a piece of candy before he went out.

I yelled at Mary to come help me look for him. We went out to the barn and on out to the field. I yelled his name over and over. There was no answer. I didn't know what to think. We came back to the house. Mary took all the children except Kevin and went on home. After she left, Kevin and I went back out to look. We looked all over. I went out to the field again. Again I yelled, still no answer. We went back to the house to get ready since I was going to go to Warsaw to Aldi. We changed clothes, then went and looked all over again.

I had this uneasy feeling. I came back in and was finishing my dishes when I saw him come out of the barn. He didn't use his left arm. He had a hammer in the other hand and closed the barn door with the hammer. I ran as fast as I could. I tried to talk to him, but he was so weak he could hardly walk. I told him that he was supposed to go to Aldi with me. He went with me every month.

He said, "I won't go to Aldi again."

It shocked me, but I ignored it. I helped him partway to the house then he had to stop to rest. Then he told me that he fell and his left shoulder and arm hurt real bad. I helped him into his trailer. He sat on the couch and I sat with him and rubbed his shoulder for him. I looked at his shoulder but couldn't see anything. Then he told me what happened. He went out to the field to check his horse. He grabbed the horse and then his other horse came up so he grabbed her too. He told me the horse jerked and that is why he fell.

We know now that was not what happened.

He lay in the field for a couple of hours. This is the thing that still haunts me. I just can't forget it. It made me feel so bad, but I know it was supposed to be that way. I looked in the field, but he was farther back. Queen, his horse, came up to him just so he could almost touch her, then she left again. After a while she came back again. She nudged him and then she put her nose right in his hand. He grabbed hold of her halter and she helped him up to the barn.

I knew I had to go get the doctor. At first Grandpa didn't think it was necessary, but then he said he thinks he needs help. I was trying to decide what to do when Dennis came home. He went and called the doctor and asked the neighbor lady to take them. When Dennis came back, he went to change clothes. I told him I would go with Grandpa. Dennis said he'd go and I could go on to Aldi.

Jean, the neighbor lady, drove in the same time as the Aldi driver did. I was over with Grandpa. JoEllen and Sharon came in to talk with Grandpa. Grandpa asked Sharon to pick up some dirt and put it in the wastebasket, which was unusual. I helped Dennis get him in the car. I remember watching until the car was out of sight.

I left a note for Gary, nine, and Lyle, 12, since they weren't home from school yet. I felt uneasy about it so we drove down and asked Lyle and Mary to go meet the boys when they came home. They just took them home with them. We headed to Warsaw and stopped at Big Lots.

As we left there the car phone rang. It was Mom. She told me they took Grandpa on to the hospital. They thought maybe he had a stroke. We headed for home right away. We went to Mom and Dad's so I could go along to the hospital. All the time I was thinking, poor Dennis and Grandpa.

When I got to Dad's, a driver was there to take us. Before we left, the neighbor lady was there and said that Dennis called. He said they wanted to put machines on him and that the family was to come right away. We stopped to pick up Elis yet. I just thought we would never get there. I finally asked the driver to go faster. Of course we were going fast, but it didn't seem like it. That was one of the longest trips I ever took to South Bend.

I remember getting out of the car and running. Dennis was there to meet us and one look at Dennis' face and I knew it was over. The doctor came and talked to us as a family, then we went in to Grandpa. One of the hardest things I ever did.

This is Dennis' story.

As soon as I came home from work, Ruth yelled and I went over to the trailer right away. I saw right away that we needed help. I asked a couple of questions, then jumped on my bike and headed for the neighbors. On the way down I kept thinking I've got so much to do, I just don't have time to go. I called the doctor and he said to bring him in. Then I asked Jean to take us. She said she would be right down.

For some reason on the way home, I decided to take Grandpa so Ruth could go to Warsaw. I know now it was supposed to be that way. Ruth and I loaded him into the car. Then Grandpa and I headed for Nappanee. On the way up Grandpa told me everything that happened.

When we were on the outskirts of town, all at once he threw his head back. I thought it was a spasm, then I heard a sound. It sounded like a lonesome train whistle. I knew people had death rattles, but my mind didn't want to accept that fact. I kept thinking he'll be all right. He had always been all right other times.

I talked to him, but he didn't respond right away. I said, "Grandpa, Grandpa."

Then he jerked his head and said, "What?" acting as if he had just been sleeping. When we got to Dr. Anglemyrer's office, I went in and got a nurse and a wheelchair. When I came back outside, he was in a daze. His eyes weren't clear. I didn't know how I was going to get him out of the car. I looked around and there was Lonnie Borkholder.

He asked, "Do you need help?" Then he helped me. I wheeled him in and the nurse started checking him right away. They took his blood pressure. They couldn't get any reading, so they put it on the sore arm. He was really responding then. He kept saying his arm hurts. I put his sore arm down, then he relaxed right away.

The doctor came in and they went over his records. Grandpa answered some questions and I answered the rest. The doctor then told me he has to go on to the hospital. They asked me if he wanted to go by car or ambulance. That kind of shocked me, but I still kept thinking he would be all right.

We pushed him out to the ambulance. They helped him out of the wheelchair and put him on a stretcher. There was a guy on the ambulance crew that could talk Dutch. That seemed to help Grandpa. They told me to get his billfold out of his pocket. I asked if I could ride along.

"Yes, get in the front seat."

We had a flying trip up there, but it seemed endless. When we got there, the driver was soaked with sweat. He told me to go in right behind Grandpa. When they were unloading him, he said, "Boy, it's chilly up here."

They put him in bed and started working on him. I started feeling sick so I left the room. I still kept thinking he would be all right. He was still responding to me. I didn't even get to the waiting room before a nurse was there and wanted to know if we wanted him put on life machines. They had them all ready and in a matter of seconds they could have them hooked up.

I told them Grandpa didn't want them because he wanted to go be with Grandma. I didn't want to make the decision alone. Before long the nurse was out again, asking about the machines. I said, "I'm sure Grandpa doesn't want them, but I sure wish the boys were here to make that decision."

The nurse came out and said, "If there is any family, call them right away."

Reality hit and I went numb. At that time, the hospital chaplain came and she didn't leave me alone. She was always with me and that helped! The doctor came out and explained everything to me. She said, "If you put him on life machines, he'll be a vegetable. If you know what Grandpa wants and you are taking care of him, then you do what Grandpa would want."

I then told the doctor no machines, but keep him alive if possible until Dans, Elis, and Ruth got there. The doctor then told me he has an aneurysm in his stomach. My heart fell and I thought they would never get there. The doctor then told me I could go in to Grandpa. I started to go into the room and there were six people working on him. I turned around and left.

Then I met Larry and Nancy Schwartz and Joe Chupp Sarah. That really helped a lot. They really supported my decision. They all stayed with me until my family came. Minutes seemed like hours. I called at five and it was 6:30 when they finally got there. The first thing I did was ask the boys if I did the right thing. They said definitely. All I could think was Thank God.

The doctor came and talked to the family. We then went back to see Grandpa. When we talked to him, he moved his mouth, but he couldn't talk. We think he could still hear us. That was one of the hardest things we have ever done. We talked to him, but we knew he was going to die. His heart just beat less and less. He died at 7:45. He didn't struggle at all. We were all with him when he died.

The chaplain then read a couple of verses from the Bible. We then had a prayer. Before Grandpa died, we all prayed aloud for him. Brother Andrew and Ruby came just after he died, so they went to let the rest of the family know. We can't describe how we all felt, going home without Grandpa. Looking back we think Grandpa knew he'd never come home again.

It wasn't quite six months that Grandma had died and every day he would say something about going and being with her. Now he is where they both wanted to be, together. If you are taking care of somebody, make sure you know their wishes about life machines.

Precious memories are all we have left.

Joan Miller: Oct. 9, 1936 - May 5, 1995

Submitted by: Ura & Miriam Hochstetler, Nappanee, Indiana

Thursday, May 4, 1995, was the wedding day of our son Ura Lee and Lora Mae Whetstone, daughter of Dave and Alma. It was a good day of fellowship and singing in the evening. Plans were to have church at our home Sunday, May seventh, and the last day of school was Saturday, May sixth. Our youngest son was in the eighth grade, so it was a special time. Everyone that could, wanted to go.

Our daughter Ruth and her four children had a chance to go home with us and stay till Sunday when her husband Daniel Yoder had plans to come back with a load from Charlotte, Michigan. They live about 50 miles from there in Ovid, Michigan.

We spent Friday getting ready for church and Ruth baked pies in PM. Usually we just have popcorn, but thought that day it would be nice to have pie since she had lots of practice because they have a bakery in Michigan. Joan came out in the evening to help. She came on her bicycle as she did many times before.

We got supper ready and I remember thinking I want to get it ready quickly enough so she could go home before it gets so late. But she never expressed fear of going home after dark because she had lights that showed up and felt safe. People who passed her that evening said they were bright.

The three boys at home yet were all there for supper too, along with Ruth and her children. Joan stayed longer than usual, just visiting. Guess it was all in God's hands since it seemed everyone was so happy and jolly that evening.

When it was nine o'clock, my husband, Ura, came in and mentioned the fact it is so late already. Joan had left around 8:30. Son David and I heard a police car going north on St. Rd. 19, one quarter mile west of us soon after nine o'clock. I remember thinking, "Oh, surely she is home by now!" We live about four miles south of Nappanee.

Sister Ada and Eldon Yoder live just south of Nappanee, about one and a half miles on 19. As Joan was going past there a man from Nappanee who had been at Warsaw 20 miles south, went home in a drunken condition. He hit her so that she must have been thrown against an electric pole. The undertaker said she was killed instantly.

The sad part was that the man drove on and as he entered Nappanee, someone reported his driving to the police. They followed him to his home and by that time the report came in of Joan's death. It was not hard for them to put it together since some of her bike baskets were still on his van.

Ada and Eldon with their daughter Lois and husband Clell Kandel came to tell us the news that evening around 10:30. The others were all in bed except son Lavern, who had heard them come, so he joined us in our grief. At first it didn't soak in as I wondered how badly she was hurt.

She is gone, they said.

But, I thought, she was just here. It can't be true! God does grant a person strength at a time like this if we can only say, "Thy will be done."

The undertaker came in the morning and we made plans for the time of the funeral and viewing before going to school for the program. Then in the afternoon kind neighbors and friends and of her church people came to help. We didn't know what else to do except go on with church services here. The church women took over there too, which we appreciated so much. In the afternoon they brought her out for viewing. In the next days, many people came to express their sympathy. The funeral was Tuesday and laid her to rest beside Dad and Mom Miller at the Graber Cemetery.

She had an independent spirit and we sometimes wondered what we could or would do for her as her health was not so good anymore. She was still able to work every day at Veada, a factory in New Paris, Indiana. We all knew it would be hard for her to depend on others.

God in His wisdom knows when our time is here. We all miss her, but our hope is that our loss was her gain. The state prosecuted the driver and he is spending three years in prison. Our hope and wish for him is that alcohol will be an abomination to him when he gets out.

It has been a struggle to write about this because it brings back memories, but we know it is good therapy to be able to share with others. We hope this can be a help to others who have gone through the same kind of thing. An understanding heart does a lot of good to the soul.

Marlin Hochstetler: Mar. 2, 1956 - Nov. 7, 1969

Submitted by: Mr. & Mrs. Lewis Hochstetler, Shipshewana, Indiana

It was a cloudy and damp day on November 6, 1969. We were cleaning Casper Hochstetler's chicken house. Marlin was driving one team with the manure spreader and everything went well. We got done cleaning a little late, not thinking about what was in store for us. After chores I washed the manure spreader and took it home, since we had borrowed it from one of the neighbors. I came back home and left the hose fastened to the hydrant on the outside of the house. We ate a late supper, can't remember what time it was, but Mom and the girls washed the dishes after we were done.

Marlin made himself comfortable on the rocking chair with his twin brothers, one on each side since they were only 24 months old. Marlin was reading from the Bible and also showing them the pictures. He said here is the story that John Troyer had preached at our church the Sunday before about Jezebel, Ahab, and Naboth. I Kings 31 - II Kings

Marlin was one of those that took an interest in reading and, of course, the Bible also. But we didn't give it a thought at the time. Marlin was a young boy of 13 years and in his blooming years. God was talking to us, but were we too busy to stay and listen?

In June of 1969 we started to build a new house and had moved into the new house the fifth of November, but it was not finished at that time. Marlin had made a remark that he is so glad and so over-joyed that he will have a better place to stay this winter, because the old house was very cold. We still didn't realize the real meaning of what he was saying. That evening we decided to put the rest of the glaze on the kitchen floor. Around ten o'clock we sent the children to bed. They all slept in one room upstairs since the other rooms weren't finished yet.

While we were doing the floor and were almost finished, all of a sudden, Mom's paint brush caught fire. It was just like a grass fire, as close as I can describe it. Our first thoughts were we have to get the children down from upstairs, after we came to our senses.

We told the children that there is fire in the house and need to get out. I took Marlin by the hand and the other three boys. Mom took the three girls. By the time we came down the stairs, I was overtaken by smoke since the stairway was in the kitchen where the fire was. As we turned the corner that led to the hallway, I passed out. My last memory was that we would all go together, but not so.

Mom went over to a door that went over to the old house and was covered with plastic. After the plastic was tore down, we got enough air that I regained consciousness again. Marlin was in his first sleep so he was in a daze. He wanted to get out of the house, but turned toward the fire. He slipped and fell into the fire.

We gathered up the other children but we couldn't find Marlin right away. We finally found him in the dining room with his clothes burned off. I picked him up and carried him over to the neighbors, not realizing how badly he was burned. I went back to the house and took the hose to douse the fire.

I have no idea how often I said, 'Gott sei mir sinder gnadig', but here I sit 27 years later with so much water in my eyes that I can hardly write this story. We can hardly realize what we had gone through. But God had this all planned before Marlin was born. A neighbor boy passing by had seen the fire so he called the fire trucks, but by the time they arrived, I had the fire out.

By that time a doctor had come out and taken Marlin to the hospital. Mom was also admitted. The doctor said that there is a very slim chance for Marlin. We just thought it couldn't be true! Oh, it must just be a dream! Oh, I just thought it was a miracle that the rest of the family was still here. God had other plans for us, so we wanted to make the best of it.

God grant me the serenity to accept the things I cannot change, the courage to change the things I can, and the wisdom to know the difference.

Bishop John Troyer came out to the hospital to share some comforting words with us and Marlin. Marlin couldn't talk, he just murmured. He had second and third degree burns over 90% of his body.

Oh, we were so thankful that he didn't have any pain. We had asked him if he had any pain and he said no, but in the back of our minds he was still suffering. We just can't put this into words how we felt at that time.

When I came to the hospital and saw Marlin, I thought I couldn't endure seeing Marlin in that condition, but am glad the good Lord gave me the strength to sit with him till he took his last breath. He was always an animal lover. In his subconsciousness he talked about them. The last words he said just before he died, he was humming, 'Glory, Glory, Hallelujah'. That was the next morning on November seventh. He lived six hours.

Oh, deep down in our hearts a hurt and crying heart, but our almighty God has helped us through our grief. It had also affected the children and we all have missed him so much. Kind friends and relatives came and helped us redo the house so we could move back in again.

Four years later when I went to bed, I just couldn't go to sleep and when I finally did I had a dream that I was talking with Marlin. I had to weep when I saw him again! Then Marlin said, "Don't weep for me, but weep for yourself, and for your other children you may weep."

There is so much truth in that verse. We don't have to worry about Marlin, but we are concerned about our other children, and also about our own souls as well. When burdens come so hard to bear, that no earthly man can share, tears drive away the smile and leave my heart in pain. Then my Lord from heaven above, speaks to me in tones of love, and drives away the tears and makes me smile again.

In Memory of Marlin

Let not your heart be troubled
Or burdened down with sorrow.
For Marlin, now in a land of bliss
Has met a fair tomorrow.

He rests in peace, in silent slumber,
In a land where we haven't been.
In a land of joyful meetings,
Free from worry, care, or sin.

It wasn't long after that,
He took his last earthly breath.
The family, friends, and neighbors,
Were saddened by his death.

But even so it cheers the heart,
With somewhat inner joy,
To know a special place in heaven
Was reserved for this young boy.

We loved him much and it was hard
To part with him we know,
But God does call in many ways,
This time He chose him to go.

He left this world so suddenly,
His place will empty be.
His smiling face upon the earth
We never more will see.

On March 2, the year 1956,
This young boy's life began.
Thirteen short years later,
He on his deathbed sang.

He probably greets a lot of friends,
And relatives passed away.
We hope all of us left here,
Will do the same someday.

We know that he was badly burned,
But suffered little pain.
So do not grieve and weep for him.
Our loss was heaven's gain.

— This poem was written by a niece.

Norma Kaye Miller: Apr. 5, 1963 - Nov. 12, 1984

Submitted by: Perry & Laura Miller, Middlebury, Indiana

The afternoon of August third, 1980, was partly cloudy and not so warm, so our five children and we decided to play ball. We had an enjoyable time till the ball hit Norma on her left arm just below the elbow. It hurt so much that we quit playing. It hurt for some time, though we didn't think too much about it till it started swelling and kept getting bigger.

We took her to our family doctor. He said it could be lymphoma.

He made an appointment to see a specialist in South Bend. A few days later she had surgery as an outpatient. After surgery, the doctor said it wasn't what he thought and the pathologist would check it out. He did not know what it was so it was sent to Chicago and from there to Mayo Clinic.

It came back as a very rare type of cancer called Hemangoperycytoma. There were only six cases of that kind in the United States at that time. By the time the report came back, the cancer had grown much bigger at the same spot. The specialist said she might lose her arm and next it would go to her lungs, then to her bones. He said she would only live about six weeks.

What a shock! We were numb and speechless. How could we tell the rest of the family. Only with the good Lord's help. Norma said if she is supposed to live, she will. She lived four years instead of six weeks. The doctor gave us a choice of where to take her for another surgery. To Sloan Kettering in New York City, to Chicago,or to the Methodist Hospital in Indianapolis.

We chose the Methodist Hospital in Indianapolis. We took her for tests and x-rays. They put a dye in her veins so the surgeon could see where the cancer had spread. This was a very dangerous procedure, and she had to lay flat on her back. If she would have lifted her head or moved her arms and legs, it could have been fatal. We did not know this at the time.

Perry and I sat by her bed all night. The next morning she had surgery. The surgeon took the muscle out from her elbow to her wrist on top of her arm. After that she didn't have full use of her hand. A few days later we went home, then took her back for a number of checkups. On December first, she started with radiation treatments.

On Monday mornings she always remarked that she saw someone in the doctor's office or in the hospital in worse shape than she was. She and I went to Indianapolis for her treatments and stayed till Fridays. We left for home right after her treatments.

She had 30 treatments. We stayed with friends during this time. Her sister Naomi went along one week and I stayed at home. We took her back for checkups once a month, then not for six months. The cancer did not show up on her arm after the radiation treatments.

In August of 1981 we took her back for a checkup. Naomi went along. She had a sad look and didn't say much on the way down. I dreaded that trip so much. I knew something was going to happen.

Her doctor took a chest x-ray, she did this every time, but she didn't come into our room for a long time. When she came, a lady doctor, she said, "We have some problems."

She showed us the x-ray and there were spots on her left lung. She gave her a chemotherapy treatment before we went home. Norma had chemo and checkups for six more months. She had surgery on her left lung and more chemo when the spots showed up again. The only time she had any pain was after surgery and then only one or two days.

We were so thankful she didn't have to suffer pain. Later she had surgery on her right lung and a few weeks later again on her left lung. She had lots of chemo, and different medicines. A few helped for a while, then another medicine was tried. Some medicines made her really sick. She lost her hair a number of times.

In November of 1983 we took her to the National Institute of Health in Bethesda, Maryland. They gave her chemo medicines that had just come out. They helped for a while. We took her to Maryland three times and then back to Indianapolis. It seemed nothing helped anymore. In April of 1984, her doctor told us that they can't help her anymore. She had checkups and chemo to keep her comfortable until September when she was unable to go anymore.

She worked at Fork's County Line Store when she was well enough, till April of 1984. She was so patient and accepted it all so well, much better than the rest of her family. She was willing to try anything her doctor suggested. She said it may not help her, but maybe they could help some other patients. The doctors, nurses and all the people we learned to know at the hospital were so kind to us. Some of them still come to visit us.

The neighbors, friends, and relatives helped us too. We could feel the love and prayers of them all and are so thankful to the Lord for the love and strength He gave us. We always prayed, 'Thy will be done.'

She had a weak spell on October 23rd. We called all the children home and neighbors came. She asked to be anointed, which was done that evening. After this she had oxygen. Three weeks later on November 12, 1984, she seemed better in the morning and ate a little breakfast. At noon I saw she was worse again and called all our family home from work and neighbors came.

She asked for her covering. She was wearing a handkerchief on her head, and she requested prayer. After that she said, "Now I'm ready to die." She looked around the room at us all, closed her eyes and peacefully passed away at 2:50 in the afternoon of November 12, 1984. I stood by her bed and held her hand till life had fled. Oh, the pain of parting.

Her funeral was largely attended at home and at the neighbors. She left behind, father, mother, her twin sister Naomi, sister Suvilla, and brothers Glen and Gerald; many friends and relatives.

She was - - a Jewel on earth,
a Jewel in Heaven,
She'll brighten the Kingdom around God's great throne.
May the angels have peace, God bless her in Heaven.
Someday we will meet her in Heaven above.
She is still missed by her family.

Melvin Borkholder: Nov. 30, 1912 - Nov. 9, 1956

Submitted by: Mr. & Mrs. Oba Borkholder, Centreville, Michigan

Melvin and Amanda (Miller) were married on November 30, 1939. God blessed them with 13 children including three sets of twins. Melvin made his living sawing logs for whoever needed, or wanted, their logs cut. His sons remember going with him in the summer months to help him carry the saw, oil, and gas or whatever else needed doing. Because they didn't live on a farm, sometimes the children were put into other homes to help out and were fed and clothed and sent to school in exchange for the work they could do.

In March of 1955 the family moved from the north part of the Nappanee, Ind., community to the southern part near Etna Green, Ind. Melvin continued his custom log sawing, sometimes even going to Michigan to fell trees and trim them, getting them ready for the log trucks. This meant that he was often away from the family the whole week and sometimes for only a few days, leaving Mom to cope with the children as best she could.

In November of 1956, Melvin left for another couple days of sawing logs. The children remember he seemed different somehow. He told the oldest ones very earnestly to listen to and obey Mom. Those were the last words of admonishment he gave because when they stepped off the school bus in the afternoon of November ninth, they saw a neighbor lady, Mahala Schwartz, hanging up their laundry. She called the children to her and gently broke the news to them that their father had been killed by a tree limb.

Who can describe the feelings of loss and desolation as experienced by those children? Why did God let this happen when surely He knew they needed their daddy.

Later they found out more details. Joe Stutzman had been working with Melvin that day and was near enough to hear his saw, but far enough away that he couldn't see him. Melvin sawed and felled a tree, but then didn't start up his saw again so Joe thought he would investigate. He found him and as close as he could figure a limb from the tree crushed the side of his head and also made a hole in the back of his head.

Joe contacted Jack Bean, sheriff, friend, and fellow worker of Melvin's and he went and told Amanda. On his way he picked up Mahala to help out and be a comforter.

The days before the funeral are hazy in the children's memories, and afterward they were parcelled out to others in the community. Three of the boys, Perry, Oba, and Melvin Jr. were placed in the Ora and Edna Mast home. They were a childless couple and had a farm. The boys were very well treated and taught to milk cows and clean their bedrooms.

Jake went to the Pete Graber home and was treated like one of their own. Anna and Katie Mae stayed home to help care for the baby twins Mary and Larry, while four year old Clara went to live with Menno Schwartz's. The oldest twins were old enough to work out and earn money for Mom.

Many times the children were homesick and cried, but there wasn't much else to do, but accept things as they were and make the best of it. Since they were treated so well it made it easier to bear.

Amanda was a widow for two years when her uncle by marriage, David Yoder, asked her to marry him. He was 18 years her senior and lived in Wayne County, Ohio, in the Abe Troyer church district. The contrast between the south of Nappanee standard of living to the standard in Wayne County caused such confusion in the children's hearts and minds that it is impossible to describe without actually living that life.

Which is the right way?! Why is bed courtship and smoking tolerated and even demanded when the conscience says "NO!"? These children lived there in their most impressionable years and also had to farm. As one of the boys commented, "We didn't know much about farming their way and often went about it backwards."

For ten years they lived there and then David had problems with his legs. Poor circulation and eventually gangrene set in so the doctors had to cut part of it off. That didn't heal right so they cut more of the leg off, but he died on the operating table. So once again Amanda was a widow.

By this time the four oldest surviving children had married and settled into homes of their own. Oba and Anna went to live in an apartment in Nappanee. They had jobs and helped support their mom what they could; also saving toward buying a place of their own. When David died they helped buy a place for Mom in Michigan, with the advice and help of Uncle Henry. In the spring of 1968 they moved to Michigan.

The ones that weren't married all once again lived together, and all found partners over the years except Mary, one of the youngest twins, who remains single. From all these experiences, of which much more could be written, we can learn the importance of appreciating parents who care. Children now may often resent when parents want to set guidelines, but stop and think, what if they would send you to other folks to raise and didn't care enough to set guidelines?

So do appreciate the parents you have and the fact that you are all wanted together. And parents, when giving guidelines to your children, do take time to explain why it is done this way and if they have questions, then explain how and why and where so their conscience will stay awake and tender.

Oliver J. Miller: Oct. 3, 1922 - Sept. 3, 1967
Submitted by: Mrs. Edna J. Miller, Bremen, Indiana

Oliver was the son of John A. and Anna (Miller) Miller. He married Edna J. Borkholder, daughter of John J. and Fannie (Yoder) Borkholder, on December 24, 1950. We were blessed with six children, five sons and one daughter. The children's ages at the time of Oliver's death were, Robert Allen, 15; Devon LaMar, 13; Lyle Ray, 11; Ronald Dean, seven; Charlene Ann, five; and Ernest Jay, four months.

Oliver worked for Borkholder Buildings, putting metal and vinyl siding on houses and shops and he always enjoyed his work. His cousin John H. Miller and Lester Hochstetler, a Mennonite man, who was their truck driver, all worked together.

On August 17, 1967, they went to work as usual about five miles east of Nappanee on CR 52. They were putting siding on a house when his ladder slipped and he fell and broke his arm. It was a compound fracture so we went to South Bend Memorial Hospital for x-rays and to have a cast put on his arm since our family doctor, Dr. Otis R. Bowen, had surgery and was not back in his office yet. They gave Oliver a booster Tetanus shot and pain medication and we were able to go home right away. He had pain in his arm, but we didn't think anything else could be expected from a fracture like he had. He went to the doctor again the sixth day and they gave him some different medication.

On the morning of the seventh day, he couldn't swallow his pills anymore and by the evening his jaws felt funny and he couldn't eat, so we went to the Memorial Hospital right away. At first the doctors thought maybe it was a reaction of the medication he was taking, but they did more tests and finally said it was lockjaw.

The second day he had started with fever and painful muscle spasms. They also gave him tetanus antitoxin injections because his booster tetanus that he had gotten at the hospital when they put his cast on wasn't a large enough dose. He should have had a full dose of tetanus but we thought his D.P.T. vaccination was okay and he only needed a booster. We didn't have our family records along and didn't know that his D.P.T. series he had were no longer good and would have to have more tetanus.

The doctors explained that muscle spasms would continue for eight to ten days, sometimes longer. His room was kept as dark as possible and also kept as quiet as they could because any noise would start another muscle spasm again. When cars would honk their horns on the street outside the hospital, his muscle spasms would start again.

His special duty nurse said that 20 years before Oliver's case of lockjaw, she also took care of another patient with lockjaw and all the symptoms were the same. After the third day his jaws were completely locked and they gave him Cortisone shots and also medication through his I.V.

He did not respond much after the third day and I couldn't talk to him anymore. He wasn't allowed many visitors at all, but I was thankful for the kind neighbors, friends, and relatives that came to the hospital every day. I stayed at the hospital all the time, except when I would go to Lee and Millie Fry's apartment to nurse our baby who was four months old, and Millie would baby-sit him.

Lee was in 1W service at the hospital at that time and their apartment wasn't far from the hospital, so I couldn't thank them enough for their kindness and will never forget them. Also all the help that was being done for my children at home and for my foster mother for helping make our children comfortable at home, too.

His condition was the same for eight days, then on the ninth day his spasms were not quite as often anymore and his jaws weren't locked tight like before. The doctors said his condition was improving a little and that I could probably go home for the night. Mary Ellen Hochstetler, our Mennonite neighbor girl, also an RN who had stayed with Oliver and helped care for him different times, took me and the baby home for the first time on the evening of September second.

How thankful to be at home with my other children and my foster mother also. But we were all shocked when a call came from the hospital to Mary Ellen's after midnight that we should come to the hospital as soon as possible, because Oliver had started to hemorrhage. Mary Ellen and I went back to the hospital right away. The doctor explained to me that he had an inactive ulcer but with all the medication they were giving him it caused his ulcer to hemorrhage, which was a complication from his lockjaw.

He lived about 12 hours, but no response at all. We could never talk to him after the third day. I think one of the hardest things was going home and telling the children that their daddy had passed away. But knowing God's will is always right, I knew he would help us carry our burdens in the days to come; also thankful he didn't have to suffer any more.

A person feels so helpless at a time like this, but through prayers all things are possible to accept. Our kind neighbors, friends, and relatives came and helped with food and many acts of kindness till after the viewing and funeral which we all felt so unworthy of. The funeral was at Henry J. Yoders and he was buried at the Welty Cemetery.

It was a nice sunny day and many relatives came from Ohio, Pennsylvania, Wisconsin, and Michigan and many neighbors and friends from far and near came to pay their respect to our loved one. This was a sad day in our lives. As time kept moving on there were many more days of sadness, but my children needed me now more than ever before without a daddy.

I tried hard to keep my spirits up for their sake because I knew they missed their daddy too and without them my life would have been so lonely. Together we tried to go on from day to day with strength from above to meet each new tomorrow. One day at a time was always the best advice I got from others who had the same experience.

When at times as the years went on, the future was so uncertain, and I often felt I couldn't lead my family like we could have if we still had daddy here to help. Again I knew God made no mistakes. This always helped to keep leading on and not faint by the way for through prayer all things are possible.

My children are all married and I always missed each one as they got married and left home, because all of them always helped to support our family along the way. So now I have 12 granddaughters and 11 grandsons. I love them all and enjoy it when they come home for a meal and a time of fellowship with each other.

Our daughter Charlene was married about three and one half years when her husband died of cancer in 1992. They had one daughter and this brought back many memories of our loved one again. Our Lord will help us along each and every day through our prayers.

John Yoder: March 24, 1990 (date of tragedy)

Submitted by: Dennis & Judith Yoder, Kalona, Iowa

The dawning of the sun was the beginning of an extra beautiful cool early spring day on Saturday, March 24, 1990. While Dad and the children were choring and milking the cows they noticed a young dove sitting on a cow under the overhang of the barn, which was an unfamiliar sight.

Their thoughts were focused on the appointment of the corn sheller coming at nine o'clock. The rest of the chores went as usual and at 7:30 the family was gathered around the table for morning devotions and while eating breakfast, they talked of what all the day's activities were.

The soil in the fields was also in perfect shape to be worked up so a crop of oats may be planted. Plans were to shell corn in the morning and disc the field in the afternoon, and Mom wanted to do sewing. It was decided that eight and one half year old John would help Dad by watching the cob wagon while they were shelling. He just loved being outdoors. Omer, almost five, would help his only sister, 12 year old Susan, with the dishes, start the sourdough bread, and prepare the noon meal.

After a lengthy shelling job was done, the men came in to rest. John helped Susan make a "picture recipe" cake from the 'Family Life'. He then set the table and was singing the chorus of "On Jordan's Stormy Banks I Stand", 'sing the song of Moses and the Lamb by and by.' He had finally accomplished holding a tune after a long time of efforts.

Mom helped finish the dinner, then with Dawdy, who lived in the little Grandpa house, came over and joined the family to eat a hearty noon meal. Little did they realize it would be their last time together. Again, work activities were discussed among other topics and their grinding to be done. Someone mentioned that no one needed to go into the corn bin this time to scoop some down, as sometimes needed to be done.

Mom asked, half listening, "Why not?"

Someone said, "Well, Mom, the bin is clear full." (600 Bushel)

After dinner Mom thought it was John's turn to help with the dishes, but asked Dad if he needed him outside, and he said, "Yes, he could clean out the cribs where the ear corn was." So Susan and Omer washed the dishes again. Mom went back to sewing. Then John asked if he could wear his tennis shoes this time, since Mom didn't allow him in the morning. After giving him permission, he gayly ran upstairs and was so thrilled to wear them. Out the door he went as a 'happy farmer boy'.

He came back in later into the kitchen to get the mittens which lay behind the stove for his 14 year old brother Karl. Mom, who was sewing in the dining room asked, "What did you come in for?"

He answered, "I came in to get Karl's mittens."

Mom had an urge to keep on singing as she continued with her sewing, which was going so well that day. After the other children did the dishes and put the bread in pans, they went out to get the hose organized to wash off the big surrey buggy with water from the milk house with the intentions that Mom would come to wash it off while Susan put the milkers together.

Meanwhile, after dinner John went down to the corn crib to sweep out the east crib that they had shelled empty that morning and put the leftovers in a bucket to put in the west crib. He couldn't get it open so he came to the machine shed where Dad was and said, "I can't put the corn into the west bin because it is nailed shut."

Dad said, "Have Karl help you, then you can help him." "Okay", said John, turned around and ran eagerly for the corn crib with his tennis shoes on and asked his brother Karl to help him open the west crib. Karl then proceeded with the grinding for the gilts and asked John to help unload which he did. When finished they started another batch for the cows and they needed oats with corn, etc. After opening the spout for oats, it stopped coming and he asked John to go up into the oats bin and scoop it in which he had done many times before.

John crawled up along the east side shelled corn bin, took his shoes off and jumped into the oats bin, but couldn't shovel any oats down because there was something over the hole. After noticing that nothing was coming Karl went up and talked with John. He was on his knees and digging to find the broken shovel handle which was the item across the hole. Karl asked if he could get it and John replied that he couldn't. Then he also jumped into the oats bin and tried but with no success.

He said, "I'll just get oats from the big oats bin. Karl went back down the ladder, not realizing that John didn't follow, and took a wheelbarrow and filled it six times with oats from the big bin. He poured it into the grinder hopper and ground the oats. He then opened the spout about two inches from the 600 bushels of shelled corn bin to grind corn with the oats. About 55 bushels had come down when all of a sudden the corn quit coming.

A thought flashed through his mind, "Is John in that corn bin?" and he quickly crawled up the ladder and looked around. He saw John's shoes still beside the oats bin. He went back down and quickly ran over to the milk house and asked Susan if John was with her. She said no and ran along back with Karl to the crib with a flashlight and they opened the spout as wide as they could and flashed up to see but it was too dim.

He told Susan, "Quick, go tell Dad."

He was discing corn stalks in the field west of the crib and barn, getting the soil ready to sow oats. Susan told Omer to go to the house and tell Mom. Meanwhile Karl took a rod and poked up the spout to see if he was there and he was. His feet were exactly over the square hole of the spout with his toes toward the east. As Omer entered the house, he met Mom putting her chore apron on to go wash the buggy.

He told her, "Mom, come quick. Something happened to John Sylvan; we can't find him. I think he's dead." (in German)

Oh, such piercing words which stabbed his mother's heart. She quickly ran down, hoping this would not be true. She met Dad who came running from the field, and both ran into the corn crib. Dad crawled up the ladder while Mom waited below and heard Dad say, "Oh God, how can you let this happen to us?"

Mom asked if she should come up and help and Dad replied, "We are going to need more help. Go call the First Responders."

Mom went to the nearest neighbors as fast as she could go, with a dry lump in her throat with Omer's words in mind and thinking it was probably about too late. It almost tore her heart as she absorbed the beautiful blue sky with a heavenly hue. God seemed so close and yet so far away. How could a loving God be taking a loved one away from our midst without any warning? It was almost more than she could handle.

Dad's words, "We are going to need more help," urged her to go on and hope and pray for a miracle. Our kind neighbor Ellis Miller happened to be working outside the house and helped Mom call the Fire Department first and then the First Responders. His daughter and her friend were also there.

He then brought Mom home and quickly crawled up the ladder to the bin where Dad and Karl were working to get John out. They had made a hole in the east wall of the shelled corn bin, about two feet up from the floor of the bin, and let a lot of the shelled corn into the empty ear corn bin. The one they had just emptied that morning.

Of course it rolled out farther and they kept shoveling it into the hole which got rid of more corn faster. When Ellis came he was still about two feet under sight. He took a turn shoveling until John's shoulders came into view. Karl quickly cleaned the corn away from John's mouth and nose. They went along his arms and pulled them out.

Ellis kept shoveling till below his armpits then Dad and Karl took hold of his arm and chest and pulled him up. The corn started going out of the spout and was sucking Dad and Karl down. They asked Ellis to quickly go shut the spout. He started down the ladder, but Mom, Susan, and Omer were standing below in much anxiety, very close to the lever and quickly closed it.

After pulling John out they laid him on the corn and Dad started CPR until the first fireman jumped into the bin. Dad asked, "Shall we get him out?" He replied, "The quicker the better." Dad and fireman, Bud Bender, handed John up to Steve Yotly, who was standing on the catwalk, and he handed him to Ed Yoder who handed him Greg Haren who then put him on his shoulders and carried him down the ladder.

The unnatural limp body didn't look like John at all as the rest of us gazed at him while being carried down. First Responders had just arrived and they met Greg about 15 feet south of the corn crib. They laid him down and started working on him with CPR and IV into his right arm and injected medication for his heart.

By that time he still hadn't responded and we had to believe what we were seeing. Struggling with our own feelings and trying to commit to God and yet longing to keep him here with us. After about 20 minutes Air Care arrived and worked on him another one half hour or more. By that time our prayer of hope for life was not being answered and now wished they would let him be at peace. They really wanted to take him on into the hospital and under more machines and had moved him into the Air Care, but we were told he would never be the same because he had brain damage and would probably be more like a vegetable if he survived.

We did not give our consent to that. To our rescue came our family doctor, Dr. D. G. Sattler and his nurse Louise. After examining him they came over to us and said, "I'm sorry, but your son is gone. You certainly have our sympathy."

What an ugly feeling! To have to think of a funeral. What a change of atmosphere our family experienced! The first commotion had died down. The beautiful sun started to set, a red ball, a peaceful moment yet painstaking indeed! They moved him from Air Care to an ambulance. After the undertaker came, he was so kind and understanding and let us view him before taking him to prepare his body. He looked so natural and peaceful as if he had fallen asleep. But oh, how our hearts ached!

Neighbors and relatives were here to help and give us support.

Viewing started the next day in the afternoon. A 'wake service' from the young folks who sang such touching songs as "Kommet, Liebe Kinder, Kommit Herbei", "On Jordon's Stormy Banks", "Himmel ist Naher, John Sylvan ist da". Funeral services were held in the morning of the next day in a large tent in our lawn, with over 600 people attending. Burial was made at the North Gingerich Cemetery about two and one half miles east.

The next day kind neighbors and some relatives came back to help put furniture, etc., back in place. Mom was so exhausted, she thought she could not live another day! How she longed to be with John! Who had the strength to continue with daily work? It was quite a challenge for the family. To pray 'Thy will be done', and yet to think of the eternal bliss he would be enjoying and to know he is safe in the arms of Jesus, free from all sin and temptations, puts us on a test. With feelings of letting go, then again clinging to the thought of, "Why couldn't he stay here with us?"

We dealt with these feelings a long time. We needed to talk about this to help sort our feelings, from anger towards God to let this happen, to the feeling of a loving and merciful God to spare our son from this wicked world, which draws us closer to Him.

For a long time afterward the sight of the corn crib and even corn as a grain would deeply remind us of the sadness. Along with the many sounds of a tractor grinding, an ambulance, a fire truck, and the Air Care helicopter. Beautiful days are very touchy and we find it hard to sing. We found comfort in nature, especially flowers, plants, and a tree which was given in memory of John. Fluffy white clouds, going to the grave often and standing around it as a family holding hands and saying the evening prayer.

War in the Middle East also caused us to be more thankful to God that he is safely in His care.

* Reading of the scriptures.

* Psalm 23 has a special meaning for us which is so fitting at times like these.

As we have loved and lost,
    We'll try to bear the cost
Of missing you everywhere.

God in His almighty hand,
    Took you to His promised land
For His own glories to share.

Where there is Love, Joy, and Bliss,
    We do not want to miss,
Rest on, dear son, until we meet you there.

John also gave his mother a little note a few days before the incident, when he came home from school which reads as follows. On the outside it said, "Hi Mom". On the inside it said, "My cup runneth over with" - then it had a picture of a cup with the words, "Joy?, Love?, Truth?, Faith?" written in it, followed by, "From: John".

Dennis Lee Mast: Nov. 7, 1964 - Jan. 15, 1986
Lester Mast: died June 18, 1988

Submitted by: Mr. & Mrs. Marvin J. Mast, Etna Green, Indiana

Our son Dennis Lee was born November 7, 1964, which is also my birthday, and was seemingly a healthy baby and grew like most babies do. Then close to his second birthday he fell one day and by the next day he started vomiting and soon went into a coma. We took him to the hospital and he was there two weeks, but the doctor couldn't really find what caused his illness. After that he easily caught a cold or flu and croup and almost always had to be taken to the doctor for medicine.

When he got the measles, he had them very hard. Even the soles of his feet were covered! He finally outgrew getting sick easily and grew up to be in good health, or so we thought. Then in January of 1983, at age 18, he started with a cough and cold again and it seemed he couldn't get rid of it.

He was to the doctor a couple of times, but still it kept getting worse. On February 23, he was to the doctor twice that day. The doctor finally gave him some sleeping pills since he had been having trouble sleeping, because as soon as he lay down to sleep he would have to cough. So finally he just slept sitting on the couch or chair with his head down on his arms on his knees. That evening he took his medicine and went upstairs to bed, but soon came down again and said he is just so miserable and can't sleep. He also had a grayish color in his face which really scared us and we made arrangements right away to take him to the doctor.

When the doctor checked him over he couldn't get any blood pressure in his one arm and very little in the other. The doctor said he would feel a lot better if he would be in the hospital, so late that night we took him. The doctor said the next day he would run some tests and at noon we were to call him to find out what they found.

When Marvin came home from calling the doctor the next day, I was not prepared for the terrific jolt I was to get. He said his heart is three times larger than normal, his liver therefore also was enlarged and he had fluid around his heart and in his lungs!

Later that afternoon our neighbors came and said they had moved him to ICU. So we quickly got ready and went up to the hospital where the doctor was waiting for permission to insert a catheter directly into a vein to give medicine directly to the heart. This procedure was to take 20 minutes, but took one and a half hours. They kept telling us they are having some difficulty, but didn't really say what.

They were finally done and we were allowed to go up and see him and he seemed better already. With medicine he seemed to gain fairly well. The doctor then made us an appointment to take him to a hospital in Chicago to find out really how bad his heart was. On March second, we took him to Chicago where they were going to do a biopsy, a catherization, and many other tests. When the time came for the catherization, we were told where to wait. They said it would take around an hour and a half, but again it took much longer.

Three hours we waited and again we were not prepared for the shock we were to get! When they were done the doctor came and very bluntly told us he had a condition known as cardiomyopathy, a disease of the heart muscle and there is nothing that can be done for it.

We were just speechless, shocked, and numb! Oh Lord, how are we to cope with this? Oh, what are we to do now? They didn't let us take him home that day because his heart was working too poorly. He had lost a lot of weight up to that time and one day after taking a shower he looked in the mirror and saw how thin he was. He then came and asked me if that skeleton was really him!

In the meantime, our family doctor had read in the paper where they had started doing transplants in Indianapolis at the Methodist Hospital. He got us an appointment with a Dr. Hall and asked us to take him down for an evaluation. Around the middle of April, I think, we left for Indianapolis on a Monday morning and we were to stay all week or till they were done taking tests, etc.

I think it was on Tuesday sometime when the doctor came into Dennis' room and again very bluntly said, "You can't live unless you have a heart transplant and if you don't want that you may as well go home as there is no need for the rest of the tests." Again such a terrible shock for which we were not prepared. Words just do not describe it!

The doctor said he could have till the next morning to decide.

Needless to say, none of us slept much that night! Dennis' main concern was the big expense for us if he had the transplant. Finally he said, "I really have no choice if I want to live, because if I don't I'll die before the year is out."

I told him we, ourselves, wouldn't be able to pay for such a surgery, but I'm sure there are lots of people who would be willing to help. We also felt he is 18 and is old enough to decide for himself. But oh, how we prayed for the wisdom to do the right thing! He finally decided to have the transplant and after the tests were done, we were sent home to wait.

On June third we got the call through our doctor that they have a donor for him and we are to come as soon as possible. Around five o'clock that evening we left for Indianapolis under escort of the Nappanee police. It took us 90 minutes! Around nine o'clock they took him to surgery and we didn't get to see him again till 3:30 the next morning and by then he was looking better already.

His cheeks were pink again, something that he hadn't had for a long time. He was on a respirator, so when we said something to him he would squeeze our hand. He was in the hospital seven weeks and did real well. He had small episodes of rejection infection, but with medicine he always came through well. Around the first of September, he complained of not feeling well and went to our doctor. He said he thinks it is appendicitis and again sent him to Indianapolis to check for sure and yes, that it what it was.

September third he had surgery for that and was again in the hospital for three weeks. He wanted so very much to be home for his oldest brother's wedding on September 24. He was to be an attendant. He was able to come home for the wedding and enjoyed it very much again being a part of the activities around him. He was often sick and had to go back to the hospital for treatment because after transplants, the immune system is suppressed by the medicine to prevent rejection. But he would usually pull through again.

In April of 1985, they started him on a new medicine which did not have as many side effects as the one he was taking up till then. He disliked the new kind very much since it was liquid and had to be taken in orange juice, whereas the old kind was in the pill form. In June he was to Indianapolis for a biopsy and catherization, something he had to do once a year, and everything showed real good.

He started working for his uncle Dan in Kentucky on a construction crew. He liked the work and he wanted very much to be useful again. He would come home every two weeks or so. On Monday, January 13, 1986, he wasn't feeling well and unknown to us, he went to the hospital in Indianapolis to see his doctor.

They couldn't find anything wrong, so he went to his uncle Leroy's there in Indianapolis to stay till Friday. We also often stayed there when we had to stay overnight for some reason. The doctor said if he didn't feel better by Friday he was to come back and they would do another biopsy, etc. Early Wednesday morning around six o'clock, he got up to go to the bathroom and fell over and died in a couple minutes of a massive heart attack.

Leroy called our son Lester and he came right away and told us. Again such a shock and no words to describe it! Oh Lord, be with us in this trying sorrowful time, we pray! Oh Lord, how can we go on? But we had other children to think about, so we felt we must go on for their sakes. We felt like our family had been split in half and truly a part of us went to the grave with him. We were so heartbroken, but with the help of a merciful God, we tried to pick up the shattered pieces and humbly carried on.

Two and one half years later on May 12, 1988, we had a wedding at our house and the next two days a reunion since all my brothers and sisters except two, Mom and Step-dad were all going to be here. Also a lot of the nieces and nephews. It was a very happy joyous occasion. How little did we dream that in a few short weeks we would all be together again, but in a very different way!

June 18, 1988, was a beautiful summer day, not a cloud in sight. In the forenoon we had butchered some fryers and Marvin was cultivating corn. After lunch we rested a while then about 2:30 a car drove in, in a big hurry. Oh no, what now?

A friend came to the door and said Lester had fallen and cut his throat with a utility knife. It was very bad and he might not make it! At first I just couldn't comprehend what he was saying. When it finally soaked in, oh no, no, no! Oh Lord, have mercy on us. Not again! But there was no time to lose. I quickly went upstairs and told the girls what had happened and to get ready to go the hospital right away. I went back down and quickly knelt by the bed for a quick prayer. "Oh Lord, please be with Lester and also the rest of us. Help us through this trying time. Help us to accept what is to come and please let it be possible to talk to him one more time! But thy will be done!"

I later asked myself if I truly wanted His will to be done, when I so desperately wanted to talk to him yet! We quickly changed clothes, no time for showers, and some friend came and picked up Marvin and me and we left for the hospital. The rest of the family came as soon as possible. It seemed to take an awful long time to get there. When we got there, we waited a while then finally someone came and said they did all they could, but he was gone.

Again, how can one describe the feeling at such a time. Words just do not describe it! After a while they let his wife, her parents, and us go in to see him. He was a picture of health and only looked like he was sleeping. He was still warm and still had on his work clothes. The only sign that anything had happened was a small cut on the side of his neck.

He had been working on the roof of a garage at some friends' home in their church. He was putting on insulation board when he accidentally stepped on a place where there wasn't any and went down through the rafters. In going down, he hit his elbow on a rafter and the utility knife he was using jabbed into his throat and completely severed the jugular vein and his windpipe. He very quickly bled to death in just three or four minutes.

We asked again and again, "Why Lord, why? We just don't understand it." To our way of thinking, he was much needed in the home, family, church, etc. But we must be strong and brave for the sake of his wife and children!

One evening at the viewing, a brother came to us and said on Saturday as he was working in the cemetery not far from where the accident happened, he looked up and saw a small cloud. It was no ordinary cloud, very different looking. He didn't think too much about it and went on with his work. He then looked again and it was still there. In a little bit he looked again and it was gone. Unknown to him it was close to where Lester lay dying!

Again my brothers and sisters and mom all came for the funeral, but it was such a sad, sorrowful time instead of the happy, joyous occasion we had in May. We were so heartbroken and just did not see how we could go on, but God was with us through all those trying times and we thank him as we, ourselves, wouldn't have been able to cope alone. We have been humbled and made aware how small we are in the eyes of an almighty God! But go on we must, so again we tried to pick up the shattered pieces and carry on!

On September 16, a little girl was born to them which again brought much joy and happiness, but she would grow up without ever seeing her daddy. They also had a two and one half year old son. I have not written nearly everything that transpired during Dennis' sickness, but time and space does not permit it so hopefully I have written enough to give an idea of how it was.

We have two other children that aren't living anymore. A little girl died at the age of three in 1960 and a little boy at the age of 15 months in 1975. Our thoughts often go to the graveyard where they lie so still. We know they will never come back to us so we want to prepare ourselves and go to where they are. This small poem expresses our feeling very well.

"Death is a heartache no one can heal.
Memories are treasures no one can steal."

Benjamin Miller: Aug. 5, 1978 - Dec. 17, 1996

Submitted by: Mose & Katie Miller, Shipshewana, Indiana

Our day started in as any other day with never a thought that this day we would experience something that we never had before.

I went to Shipshewana with our daughter Arlene, Mrs. LeWayne Miller, and was going to take care of her children when she had a dentist appointment at one o'clock. I think we had about an hour to shop around till her appointment time. So first we decided to go to the drug store and just as we passed the stop light, we saw the First Aid and Fire Truck go.

As we went into the drugstore, Menno Lambright was sitting there and I remember asking him if he knew what was going on and he said he didn't. As always, my first thoughts were where are my children? I thought Benny would be at work and I knew Kenny was at home helping Mose, my husband, hauling manure.

Then next we went to E & S and when we got there, we could see all the blinkers through the trees. I would say they were probably half a mile from us. We still didn't know if there was an accident or a fire. We went inside the store and asked if they knew what happened. They knew that there was a bad accident and that they took the victim by helicopter, but didn't know who it was.

When we got done shopping in there, we figured the dentist would be open by then, but when we got there, the door was still locked. So we decided to go to the hardware. I had a few small items in my hand that I was going to buy when we looked up and saw Susan, my daughter-in-law, coming. She said we were talking and smiling, but we saw something was wrong right away. Then the shock!

She said that Benny had been in a bad accident and they took him to the Kalamazoo Hospital with a helicopter. She said she was there with a driver to take me over to the accident. I felt so sorry for Arlene, leaving her all alone with our horse and buggy since she had left her horse and buggy at our place. Arlene told the dentist to cancel her appointment and went home.

By the time we got to the accident, all I got to see was Benny's badly wrecked car. They had already taken Ben to the hospital. Mose came to the accident when Benny was still there, but sadly they wouldn't let him see Ben. How hard that would have been. They told Mose it looked bad. They had to cut a hole in his throat to put in a tube to give him oxygen. His head was bleeding so badly that they turned him over and drained blood out of him.

Doris Berky took us to the Kalamazoo Hospital. Bless her kind heart. What a long, hard, sad, ride not knowing what we would find once we got there. When we got there, they told us he was in the trauma emergency room. Next we had a long, sad heartbreaking talk with the doctor and social worker. They told us that Benny had a very severe head injury and that his brain was damaged and he was in a deep coma. They had already given him seven units of blood.

They said we could go see him as soon as they got him cleaned up, but warned us again and again that Ben wouldn't look like our Ben. Oh, how right they were! Please Lord, help us through this, was all we could think. They had him on a life machine and had a tube in his head to measure the brain pressure, a wire here and there for his heart and blood pressure.

I can't remember for sure how everything was. It just seemed he had wires all over him. His face was all swollen, his eyes black and blue, and blood draining out of his eyes all the time. The doctor said most of the bones in his face were broken. They said they don't like to see the brain pressure go over ten and Benny's was up to 40 already.

They told us to talk to Benny because sometimes the hearing is the last to go. We talked to Benny the best we could. At times like these, words don't come easily with tears running down your cheeks all the time. Mose asked Ben to blink his eyelids if he could hear us and he said he was pretty sure he blinked a little. But we were still not sure if he could hear us or not.

The children all came to the hospital as soon as they could. What a sad evening. Kenny stayed with us then after the other children went home. We stayed at the Kalamazoo Hospitality House for the night. We wanted to stay at the hospital, but there was no room beside Benny because he was in the emergency room with curtains on both sides of him. They didn't really want us to stay in the emergency waiting room, because there were people coming and going all night.

We took their advice, but sleep would not come that night. At least we had beds to rest on. The next morning they told us Benny was worse. His brain pressure was up to 70. They x-rayed again and the doctor said his brain was damaged very badly and that Ben would never wake up and would always be in a coma. They said we should start thinking about taking the life machine off. The doctor said he still had a little activity in his brain stem, and they couldn't take the life machine off without our permission.

We told him we wanted some time to talk this over with the family. All we could do was pray and pray to God to help us make the right decision. Before the children all came to the hospital, the doctor said he thinks that God is making our decision because Ben's blood pressure is going down. We are sure this is when Benny died, but the doctor didn't just come out and say so. We felt so helpless and all we could do was hold Benny's hand.

After the children were at the hospital, they tested Ben again to see if he was brain dead. The doctor and chaplain had a talk with us all and said that Ben is no longer with us. The test showed he was brain dead. The doctor and chaplain were very supportive, kind, and caring and cried with us. May God bless them.

They told us when we are ready, they would turn off the machine. Without God's help I don't know how people can handle anything like this. After we all had been with Benny and said our good byes, we told the doctor we were ready. We all said the Lord's Prayer together as they turned off the machine.

Nothing to do anymore, but go home. It was around 10:00 PM when we got home. Our kind neighbors and bishop and his wife were here to greet us. Our married children all stayed here for a while before going on home.

Benny worked at Redman Homes and the factory let out early that day for some reason. The last man to talk to Ben before he went home said Benny was very happy. Ben lost control of his car on the way home from work at 11:37 AM. He was going too fast at a curve and lost control, hitting posts and a telephone pole.

Benny was the kind of boy who gave his mom flowers on Sweetest Day, and took her out to eat when Dad wasn't here. One day last summer he said, "Mom, you want to go fishing with me?" I thought if my son asks me to go fishing, I'll go along. Ben and I had a great day. What precious memories.

Three different people had dreams that Benny died, before he actually died. Our neighbor saw a strange bright light above our place, that she watched for a while. The next time she looked, it was gone. That happened about one week before he died.

After the funeral our grandson was sick with the flu. When he awoke during the night, he said it was so bright. They asked him what was so bright because they didn't have any lights on. He said, "Up there by Benny. It is so bright."

Our daughter-in-law said she kept thinking about Benny one day when we had all that snow. Ben had always wanted to see a lot of snow, like the snow stories we talked about in 1978, the year he was born. Benny always liked winter and had so many plans for this winter. Then that night she had a dream that they were trying to wake up Benny. They finally got him to move and make some sounds, and then Benny got very upset and was making motions with his arms to get back and leave him alone. Then she woke up and felt better with the thought that Benny is satisfied with where he is and doesn't want to come back.

Our son-in-law was doing his chores and also thinking about Ben, when he felt a calm feeling come over him. Then he said it was just like somebody told him these words, "The gift of God is eternal life." All these signs helped us all and we hope that Benny is in the hands of our almighty God.

We had two days of viewing and heard many kind words of Benny. The funeral was at Jerry Schwartz's. The pallbearers were Benny's best friends; Jerry Wingard, Matthew Schlabach, Larry Miller, and Benny Yoder.

Benjamin Miller, born August 15, 1978, to Mose and Katie (Bontrager) Miller, died December 17, 1996. Age 18 years, four

months, and two days. He leaves to mourn:
Mother and Father, four sisters, Edna Fern
(Mrs. Daniel) Yoder, Arlene (Mrs. LaWayne)
Miller, and Susan Kay (Mrs. Joe Dean) Mast,
all of Shipshewana; and Marilou (Mrs. LaVern)
Yoder, LaGrange; four brothers, LaVern (Katie
Knepp), Nelson (Susan Hostetler), Raymond
(Marlene Miller), and Kenny at home. Two
grandmothers, Saloma Bontrager, Goshen and
Verba Mae Miller, Shipshewana.

Quick and sudden came the call;
Your sudden going shocked us all,
But we all know it was God's plan,
And hope that Benny's now in your Precious Hands.

Benny was a kind and caring boy,
To the family and many neighbors he gave great joy.
Benny loved the young and old,
He touched so many lives we were told.

Benny tried so hard to please everyone,
But his hard work on earth now is done.
We all love you so much, Benny,
And you'll be missed so by brother Kenny.

—Good-bye, Benny, The Family

B *Benny, your smile we long to see,*
E *Every time we think of thee,*
N *Needing comfort every day,*
J *Jesus, please lead the way.*
A *Always so tenderhearted,*
M *Makes it so hard to be parted.*
I *I know this is God's will,*
N *Need your loving hand, to lead us over the hill.*

M *Mom and Benny went fishing one day,*
I *Is one good memory that will always stay.*
L *Lonesome with a heart that's broken,*
L *Lots of thoughts beyond words spoken.*
E *Eternally forever how can we bear,*
R *Really only one answer, turn to God in prayer.*

— Your Loving Parents and Ken

Irene Horst: Aug. 22, 1994 (date of tragedy)

Submitted by: Mr. & Mrs. Aaron Horst, Listowel, Ontario

It was August 22, 1994, and the day wore on as the threshing machine hummed its steady song. As I lifted the bales of barley onto the elevator, I watched them drop down into the machine. The grain could be heard trickling through the pipes into the granary. The west wind kept pushing the dust gently back into the barn den. Just a perfect day for threshing, I thought as I glanced out into the field nearby. The sun shone brightly in the clear skies. A couple more hours and they should have that field baled up, I reasoned to myself.

It was always a feeling of satisfaction to see the bare fields after a crop is harvested. Since I had heart surgery done almost a year ago, I was happy to have gained enough health to be involved in the work. Two of our children, Edward, age six, and Irene, age five, realizing my condition, were on the wagon with me, eagerly helping where they could. As I observed their eagerness I thought maybe sometime in the future we would have more help.

Inside, Mother and the hired girl, Miriam, were making supper. The three youngest children were also inside, Erla, four; Alice, two; and baby Mary, four months old. This setting finds five brothers, each farming within a two mile area, so we are frequently doing our farm work together. Today, brother Amsey and his son David were helping here with the first day of threshing, while brothers Cleason, Oscar, and our hired boy were at Peter's helping with the last of the second cutting hay.

David was driving the tractor down the side of the barn bank to bring in the next load of grain. I was standing by the barn doors glancing at the running machine. All was going fine when suddenly David shouted in a terrified voice. I spun around just in time to see the tractor skid several feet downhill. Edward and Irene were directly in the path.

Edward jumped to the side and quickly tried to get Irene's attention. She whirled around and I shall never forget the frightened look on her face when she sensed the danger. There was no time to flee. The front wheel caught her foot and threw her down, driving over her entire body from toe to head.

I hurried to her side, thinking the front wheel of a small tractor might not do much damage. I soon changed my mind when I saw her lying between the front and hind tractor wheels. I picked her up off the gravel and moved her to a grassy spot. Blood began to pour out of her nose. I pushed gently on her chest and she began to breathe and kept on for several minutes.

Amsey noticed something unusual and hurried in from the field. "Shall I call the ambulance?" he asked.

"I don't think she'll make it, but likely you should," I replied.

Edward ran to the house to tell the sad news. Mother hurried out and kneeled by her side. "Does it hurt very much?" Mother asked her. "Soon the pain will go away and you can be with Jesus," she assured her, although there was no response.

By then the breathing had stopped and there was only a weak pulse. We later learned that she had died instantly of a brain stem injury.

"There come Minerva and Sarah," announced Mother. I glanced out the lane. Sarah was leisurely pushing Minerva in her wheelchair. Our two oldest daughters, Minerva, eight and Sarah, seven, had been at the neighbors playing.

"Maybe you should run out and tell them Irene is badly hurt and we don't think she will live," Mother said to Amen, Cleason's son who was also here to help. They hurried in to us and gazed on the now still body, speechless.

Soon they began questioning, "Will there be a funeral here? Will she be buried in the graveyard at church?" These were things we hadn't even thought of yet.

A neighbor policeman arrived, whom Amsey had called. An ambulance was heard in the distance. What a relief to hear that experienced help was on its way. After the ambulance had left, the police wanted a bit more information from us, then he offered us a ride to the hospital. He also explained to the children that at the hospital they would pump oxygen into her lungs and hope to get her breathing again.

We did not know what to think for we had told the children that Irene had died. Upon arriving at the hospital we were soon asked to come in and meet Dr. Conners. "Mr. and Mrs. Horst?" he asked.

"Yes, we are."

Then came those final words, "I believe she is gone."

We were then led to a room where she lay on a stretcher, still in the dress she had put on in the morning. We saw what we had expected, yet it was almost shocking as the truth pressed deeper into our numbed minds. I laid my hand on her body and noticed that she was turning cold. Yes, she had truly left us. Her Master had called and she meekly followed with no time to say good bye.

The friendly policeman offered us a ride home. Upon coming in the lane we noticed David still sitting in the other police car. Poor boy! Oh, that he may be granted strength!

In the house, the children were curious, "Has she died?" We answered yes and that is how they took it for then, although many questions came later. Soon Mommy Martin came and later Doddy Horsts. More relatives came drifting in that lived close by.

Quietly we discussed the events of the evening and also tried to think ahead what would be needed in the next few days. It is such a precious time to think back to, with parents and relatives to support us at this much needed time.

Soon came the time for our friends to go home. Later Mother went upstairs to see if the children were asleep. Irene's place in bed was empty and her smiling face would never more be seen on this earth.

In the meantime, I ventured out to the corner of the barn. The full moon was shining brightly in the still night. The tractor was still sitting there to mark the spot where the accident had happened. We had been told not to move it until we had official permission. My mind seemed to be in a turmoil as I tried to rehearse the whole evening.

A song came to my mind which I sang there in the stillness. "Jesus has taken a beautiful bud," I pondered over the words a while, "Out of our garden of love." Yes I had known this song for a long time, but it now had a deeper meaning. "Borne it away to the city of God, Home of the angels above." God seemed so very near as I gazed up into the bright moonlight. All was so peaceful and quiet. Chorus: "Gathering buds, gathering buds. Wonderful care will be given. Jesus is gathering, day after day, Buds for the palace of heaven." I pondered a while longer for it seemed to express my thoughts so well. Later we found the rest of the song very comforting too.

Mother joined me there by the barn and we brooded over the events for a while. God seemed so near. The moonbeams freely illuminated the area where, in the activity of a busy threshing day, our Master had reached down and chosen our daughter to come home to Him. Now it became clearer than ever before, how His all-seeing eyes watch over us at all times and if it is His will, He can change things instantly. It was a great comfort that she was not asked to suffer.

We thought back to the past weeks. Frequently while I was out at work or wherever, Irene would find her way to me and quietly search my face until I acknowledged her, then she would smile back and be on her way again. I remember several times when really no words were exchanged. Mother and I had discussed this and wondered what she was craving for, that we were failing to give. Also at times she would crawl onto my lap after meals.

Mother remembers one time when she was writing at the desk when Irene came and slid onto her lap. Mother found this inconvenient and gently pushed her off thinking she was getting too big to be wanting to be held so much. Later our arms were aching to hold her again. Miriam remembers her crawling onto her lap the last day she was with us, which she treasures very much.

The day before, while I was working in the barnyard, the children were swinging in the hammocks under the big maple trees in the lawn. Suddenly they jumped to their feet and headed for the orchard except for Minerva who was stranded on the hammock needing help to transfer into her walker. Minerva called after the others, but they kept their pace, all but Irene who stopped and looked back. She paused a bit then walked back and stayed with her, swaying the hammock for her.

I had stopped in my tracks and watched a moment, not knowing as a father, what I should do. Should I go over and help Minerva follow the rest? I felt very busy that morning while getting things in order for threshing the next day. Maybe I should have admonished the older children for not caring, but I decided we cannot expect them to be at her side at all times, so I left matters as they were and continued with my work.

After Irene's death I yearned for that opportunity to walk up to her with a word of praise. Sometimes at night we would wake up and she would be standing by our bedside. I guess she was hesitant to wake us up because she knew we did not appreciate her coming down so often for no real cause. Later when sleep would not come at night, we would long to see her standing there again.

Sometimes we wonder what really did wake her up although we realize more children go through such streaks. We do not think that she was more special than any other child, for she needed admonishing, too. But after giving her up, her character becomes more precious to us as we realize each is an individual and can never be replaced by another.

We decided to leave the spot and try to get a night's rest as the following days would surely be wearisome. The next morning dawned bright and clear. Mother washed the kerchief Irene had on just last evening. The blood could be washed out but the holes remained, where the gravel had pierced through. We later decided to store it away as a remembrance.

People came to help prepare for the funeral. Many faces were seen and it touched our hearts that at such a busy time, so many people left their work to help us. Thursday was the day of the funeral. A light rain was falling in the early morning, but it turned out to be a nice day after all. By night we were rather relieved that the funeral ceremony was past and although her body was laid in the grave, we were assured that her soul could rest in heaven.

On Friday some neighbors came to help with the sweet corn that had been neglected for a few days now. After they had gone home, I joined the others under the shade trees, cleaning up the last bits of corn before dinner. "Oh I wish we could be alone again and settle back to everyday living," Miriam stated.

We all agreed, although we knew we needed our friends at this time and appreciated their presence. Little did we realize that the following weeks would be filled with people coming and going daily. Saturday was the first day we were alone since the change had taken place. We wandered out to that precious spot during the day with the family. No, she was not there, but something seemed to lure us there. Another song we learned to treasure was "Gone to Bloom Above"

Gone to Bloom Above

A gentle hand unseen by us
Has plucked our tender bud;
By this alone our grief is blest,
It was the hand of God.

Chorus:
Oh gentle one, we miss thee here,
Sweet form we loved so well;
But in our Father's better care,
We know the child is well.

Sometimes while working about the barn or in the barnyard, I would cross this spot. At times thinking I will walk on past this time, but always when I got there, something would halt me. I would stand there pondering, trying to let the truth sink in. Reality seemed just a handbreadth away, not quite able to get a firm grip on it. I guess God's ways are too deep for our earthly minds to quite understand.

Sunday morning came and we got ready for church. Yes, there was one less girl to comb and that same girl was missing on the carriage. At times we would wonder if we did not feel it enough that one was taken out of our midst and wondered if someday reality would strike full force. But God has wondrous ways. We were still protected by shock and later the reality of it all came gradually as we could see she would not return and she was gone forever.

Monday morning dawned bright and clear. Another perfect day for threshing. Monday evening was almost identical to last Monday evening, weather wise, and we were also threshing. Mother set the table again for the hungry threshing crew. A week before she had also set the table and had supper waiting, but we never did gather for supper. What took place on Tuesday evening and the funeral stays linked together in our minds, and I believe also for the surrounding community.

Soon after 9:00 PM we shut down the threshing machine. "Now that job is done," I sighed with relief. The barn was full and the fields were all bare. Exhausted from the day's work, I walked to the house to ask about the chores. They had a busy day and apologized that the sows had not been fed. Out in the barn, while waiting for a pail of water to fill for the sows, I subconsciously opened the door to the barn den to review our day's work.

I stopped short! Quite taken by surprise! Within three feet of my face stood the threshing machine with small flames burning all along the top of the machine. Quickly I stepped out into the barn den. Small flames were seen all along the straw that hung over the beam along the side of the straw mow. Then I saw red embers becoming visible in the straw mow where the straw blowers had blown. Next large, hungry flames sprang up and swept over all the mow.

I ran out of the barn doors and down the barn bank yelling, "Fire! Fire! Fire!" as I went. As I ran through the barnyard, flames were already shooting out of the open hole in the side of the barn. I was granted the strength to calm down some. As I ran to the house, Mother came to the door and eyed the barn in dismay.

"It's gone!" I said, and it was gone indeed.

Again we needed our neighbors. Yes, it was another loss, but a barn could be rebuilt. Friends from far and near eagerly pitched in and the project progressed, to which we feel unable to show our appreciation enough. We cannot put into words the gratitude we have felt at that time and in the years since, for all that was done to restore what could be restored.

Never in all our lives will we be able to return all the deeds of kindness that were bestowed upon us for which we feel very unworthy. We feel God was in it all and we were miraculously strengthened through Him. We wish to thank one and all for their prayers and their helping hands during this time. The Lord gave and the Lord hath taken away. Blessed be the name of the Lord. Job 1:21

Song No. 624 in Christian Hymnal

Gathering Buds

Verse 2
Full blooming flowers alone will not do,
*   Some must be young and ungrown;*
So the frail buds He is gathering, too,
*   Beautiful gems of His throne.*

Verse 3
Fathers and mothers, weep not or be sad,
*   Still on the Savior rely;*
You shall behold them again and be glad,
*   Beautiful flowers on high.*

Verse 4
Blooming in beauty in heaven are they,
*   Blooming for you and for me;*
Follow the Lord, though the city be far,
*   Till our bright blossoms we see.*

Song No. 626 in Christian Hymnal

Gone to Bloom Above

Verse 2
In all our hearts he planted deep
*   This precious little one;*
As forth He takes His own, we weep,
*   But say, "Thy will be done."*

Verse 3
No care was lavished here in vain
   Upon this plant of love;
Tho' soon removed, 'twill bloom again
   In sweeter form above.

Verse 4
Would not our grief forever flow
   Upon thy silent tomb,
Did not our hearts this comfort know,
   We soon to thee shall come.

Verse 5
Dear Jesus, Thou hast died for us,
   And for our darling, too;
We trust Thee in each providence,
   Thy love is ever true.

Ervin L. Hochstetler: Feb. 20, 1962 - June 23, 1980

Submitted by: Mr & Mrs. Lester C. Hochstetler, Wolcottville, Indiana

It was a beautiful morning, June 23, 1980, a perfect June day.

In the early hour a slight knock on the door made my heart skip a beat as I hadn't heard anyone drive in. I had just gotten up and was getting ready to sort my laundry before chores. Since it was during the strawberry season, I had thought I would do my laundry before picking strawberries.

I didn't know what to expect when I went to answer the door, but there stood some of Ervin's friends with sorrowful faces. I knew right away something was wrong. They informed me that Ervin had been in a car accident on their way home at about 4:00 that morning. The police had asked the boys to come notify us instead of them doing it.

I asked them how bad it was and how was he hurt. After hesitating a little they said he was bleeding out of his ears, mouth, and nose. I immediately knew that it could be fatal. They said the EMS took him to LaGrange Hospital, so we called the hospital to learn more.

They had already sent him on down to Fort Wayne by then and couldn't tell us more. So with heavy hearts, we got the other children started on the chores and milking while Lester went to call for a driver to take us to Fort Wayne.

By the time our driver came and we got in to go, a police car was coming from the south. It slowed down as it came nearer. I still get goose pimples when I think about that feeling I got. A feeling *nobody knows without experience!*

I thought, I know what he is going to say. He got out of the car, and came over to tell us our son had just passed on to eternity. Oh, how terrible the news. What a shock. So final. No hope of getting better.

Since our minds were in such a turmoil, it is hard to get on paper how things went then. The policeman asked if there was anything he could do. All we could think of was to have him tell the neighbors. The kind neighbors started coming in. Never before had we felt so unworthy. Some of the neighbors then went with the driver to take the sad news to our parents, sisters, and brothers.

We didn't realize we had to call an undertaker at a funeral home of our choice since we had not had any experience with things like that. It was almost mid-morning when one of the neighbors thought about it. So then someone went and called an undertaker and made arrangements for a funeral home and also funeral arrangements.

Then we had another shock! They couldn't bring the body out for viewing for that evening. Many people came that first evening for the viewing not knowing he wasn't there yet. We had to add another day before the funeral because of the delay. The funeral ended up being on Thursday, June 26. There were two or three more funerals that day as well as two weddings, some of them related.

After the long wait before they brought the body, we were so tense and afraid we might not be able to view him. To our surprise, he looked so natural and even had a slight smile.

He left precious memories. Even though many were invited to a wedding, many came to the funeral instead. That's what a friend is! Someone who is there when we need them the most.

A week before this happened we had church in our home and he seemed so different in a way. Every time I looked at him, he was looking my way and just seemed to stare. It had given me a feeling I couldn't express to anyone. Not until afterwards. Now I have to wonder on and on, "What was on his mind?"

Soon after the funeral some of his boy friends came to spend the evening with us. It was so touching, I wanted to go to the back room and just cry it out. One of the boys caught my eyes so many times that evening, but I didn't know why. Then about a year later, he had to leave his friends too, also because of an accident. We had the funeral in the same shed.

What we do not know is when our time to go comes — Be prepared to meet our Savior.

Freda A. Hershberger: Nov. 26, 1965 - Apr. 28, 1970

Submitted by: Adam Hershbergers, Baltic, Ohio

It was 26 years in April and we miss her yet. I guess it is like the saying goes, "As you loved them, so you miss them."

It was on Tuesday, April 28, when we went to my mother's place to clean her house. It was a nice, sunshiny day. A few of my sisters were also there. It was after 4 o'clock when we were finished and started for home. Little did we know what God had planned for us.

The five children and I had taken our two-seater buggy with the three oldest in the back seat. Martha, ten; Katie, eight; Lester, six; Freda, four; and Nelson, three. Freda and Nelson were in the front seat beside me. We wanted to go through a lane that went through a pasture. It was a shortcut and the way we usually went.

There was a hog pen beside the lane and our horse didn't fancy hogs. When we came to a small creek, the horse acted kind of peculiar and stopped. I got off the buggy and told the oldest children to get off, too. I got Nelson off and took hold of Freda's foot to pull her over so I could get her off. The horse took off leaving only Freda's shoe in my hand.

There was a temporary woven wire fence gate across the lane which wasn't fastened very well. When the horse came up against the fence it opened. He went on out the lane and onto the road. We don't think he realized that he was running away because he walked part of the time.

My uncle's wife saw the horse coming and seeing that there was only a child on the buggy, waved her arms to stop the horse. He just dodged around her and went up an embankment, upsetting the buggy. Freda fell onto the road, and she and the buggy were dragged along several hundred feet.

I cannot express the thoughts that went through my mind when we ran through the pasture in hopes of stopping the horse, or when I heard that the buggy had upset. My brother-in-law told me life had fled. I thought surely they were wrong. My uncle's wife carried Freda a short distance to my sister's house. Oh, what a shock when I saw it really was true. My husband wasn't at home from his job yet, so it was a shock for him, too.

The next few days were just like a dream. It was hard to give ourselves up. After we gave ourselves up to the thought that everything was timed just so and that it was God's will, it was easier even when it did seem unbearable at times.

The coroner ruled her death as instantly killed and she didn't suffer any, for which we are thankful. She had a broken neck, jaw, arm, and other bruises. After the undertaker was there and left, we went to our home. The neighbors and friends were there and had done our chores and were there to help us endure the tragedy.

Oh, how hard it was to meet with the neighbors. But, I wasn't in the house very long until a neighbor told me she knew exactly how we felt. They too had lost a little girl. She had died in a house fire. She assured me that God never makes mistakes even though it had taken them a long time to really understand it. Yes, we miss her, but she has gone on at a tender age and was free from the temptations of the world. We were more aware of these temptations later as our family grew than we were right at that time.

In May of 1971 we were blessed with a daughter. We named her Barbara. She looked very much like Freda had. We later had two more children: Eli in 1973 and Anna in 1977.

May we all accept the words, "Thy will be done."

Kevin Bontrager: Mar. 28, 1985 - July 18, 1991

Submitted by: Mr. & Mrs. Calvin Bontrager, Nappanee, Indiana

The day started out like any other day, a busy summer day on the farm. It was two weeks before we were to have church at our house. Little did we know that by evening our little family circle would be broken. We feel it was God's will and we want to accept it that way in our weakness.

I clearly recall the noon meal. I had bought fresh homemade doughnuts just that morning and served them with the noon meal. Before going outside again, Kevin quickly got another doughnut and gave me a smug look. Of course, I didn't care, he could gladly have it.

Calvin had bought two loads of hay from a neighbor. It was around 7:00 PM. so they planned to put it in the bank barn and unload it the next day. The first load was pulled in with the team of horses. The second load also partway, but to get it all the way inside, Calvin wanted to push it in with the tractor.

Matthew, age seven, guided the wagon tongue and Kevin placed a plank between the back of the wagon and the nose of the tractor. Calvin then said to Kevin, "Now stand off to the side." Which he did.

So quickly Kevin jumped back in between the wagon and tractor for an unknown reason. At the same time, the plank slipped off the wagon. The wagon rolled back and crushed the boy against the tractor. Calvin quickly rolled the tractor backward to release the boy and laid him on the ground. We think he never realized what happened as he was killed instantly.

Matthew quickly came to the house to tell me. I ran outside, not wanting to believe what had just happened.

We thought, "Oh no! It can't be true. If only we had done this or that differently, it might not have happened!" Only a parent that experiences giving up a child can know the feelings. I told myself over and over, he is in Heaven now, what a blessing and how lucky!

His injuries included a skull fracture, a broken neck and internal injuries. Also a chunk was torn out of his upper right arm which the undertaker said he would sew just as a doctor would. How thankful we could feel that God in His great mercy called the child home so he would not have to suffer.

My mother, Lydia Miller, went down the road to tell my sister, Barbara, the Roman Miller, Jr. family of the tragedy and also a neighbor she met on the road. Jr. went to a nearby phone and called the police. The neighbor, Ralph Bontrager spread the word to more neighbors. The police were soon here as well as many neighbors, friends, and relatives.

How thankful we are that we are blessed with the support of our church at such times. The undertaker came and arrangements were made. Needless to say there was very little sleep for us.

The next few days we had lots of kind help which we appreciated so much. We had two days of viewings during which many small children, friends, and relatives came. So many comforting words were spoken and sympathy was shown towards us. He looked very natural. The largely attended funeral was held on Sunday, July 21, 1991.

Now there was so much adjusting to do. The empty chair at the table, his clothes, his brother choring, sleeping, and playing alone. Seeing the pumpkins he wanted to plant that year waiting to change to their orange color. Also all the things that hold a special place in the heart. After almost four years we still miss Kevin dearly.

But Jesus said, "Suffer little children, and forbid them not, to come unto me; for of such is the Kingdom of Heaven." Matthew 19:14

A precious one from us has gone,
A voice we loved is stilled;
A place is vacant in our home
Which never can be filled.

He bloomed a little blossom here
And did our hearts quite often cheer.
His pleasant ways, his winsome smile,
Was precious through his life's short while.

God needed one more angel child,
Amidst His shining band;
And so He bent His loving smile
And clasped our darling's hand.

No one knows the silent heartaches,
Only those who have lost can tell;
Of the grief that is borne in silence,
For the one we loved so well.

To parents, brother, sisters, all,
This came a loud and sudden call.
But sweet the knowledge we can keep,
That he in Jesus fell asleep.

Of his short life and purity,
How could it any sweeter be,
Than that of such a little child?
He was so gentle, meek, and mild.

And oft our lonely hearts will break,
In tears for little Kevin's sake,
But Jesus knows our every sigh,
And wipes the tears from every eye.

And we long to cross that river,
Long to rest upon that shore;
There to see and know and love him,
With the Saviour evermore.

—by his family: Calvin, Jane, Loretta, Matthew, Sue Ann & Elaine

— 248 —

Paul B. Weaver: Jan. 27, 1982 - Mar. 12, 1982
Wayne B. Weaver: Feb. 10, 1983 - May 29, 1984
Barbara B. Weaver: May 31, 1989 - July 12, 1989

Submitted by: Elvin & Elva Weaver; Leonardtown, Maryland

Paul

On a cold snowy winter day we were blessed with a tiny baby boy, our third child. He weighed 6 lb. 15 oz. He was only 18 inches long. Shortly after birth the doctor told us Paul had many fractures: arms, legs, collarbone and ribs. He had a birth defect called Osteogenesis Imperfecta, or brittle bone disease. Since he had breathing problems he was taken by ambulance to Children's Hospital in Washington D.C. How hard it was to part with my baby! I didn't expect to see him again.

The doctor said he had only a very short time to live. Elvin went with the baby to talk to the doctors at Children's. There he was told that baby Paul could live to adulthood What joy! Paul was kept in an isolette on a water bed. He was fed by a stomach tube because his breathing was three times faster than normal and so could not suck.

We stayed at my mother's while Paul was in the hospital. This way the baby-sitting problem for the two older ones was easily taken care of. The five year old being retarded and the two and a half year old having severe asthma made getting a sitter hard.

I went to see Paul on Jan. 30. I could not hold him, but could touch and talk to him. On Feb. 1 we finally got to talk to the right doctors and were allowed to hold Paul. I held and rocked him for an hour.

Feb. 3 we were finally allowed to bring him home! Paul's breathing had improved. He no longer lay panting with his mouth open. It often took two hours to get two ounces into him and then the feeding needed to be finished by dropper. He gained slowly and cried much. Baby Paul was a joy when he felt well. He responded as well as any newborn.

That last evening on March 11 he cried a lot. That night he was as usual, but he always fussed between 4 and 6 A.M. I woke at 5 and was surprised that he was quiet. So I checked on him and noticed he had changed position, something he wasn't strong enough to do. Then I touched him and knew.

Oh! The nightmare those next minutes were. Our precious baby

Paul gone! Gone where? To be with Him who loves us all. No more pain from his poor broken bones. Oh, how we missed our baby, but we could not wish him back.

The other children, Lena, 5, and Elvin Jr., 2½, could not understand. Lena, in her retarded innocence, just enjoyed the people coming. Elvin Jr. was so sick with an asthma attack that he had to be hospitalized that day and stayed until after the funeral so to both of them the baby just disappeared.

They were both very clingy all summer. It took a while to adjust to the emptiness of my arms and cradle. We got a lot of mail and company which helped a lot. I always pictured baby Paul in Jesus' arms, reaching out to us, waiting until we can all be reunited.

Paul was six weeks and two days old when he died.

Wayne

About a year later on a cold snowy day we once again had a baby boy with O.I. How hard that was! Wayne was somewhat stronger than Paul had been and could suck better. He had only the one fresh fracture of the arm. He needed some dropper feedings for a few weeks, but could suck well most times.

Wayne was a bright little boy. At ten months he started using some words. He stayed very weak, weaker than a newborn. That is what made it so touching when he responded so well and talked a bit, even loved a joke! He would often lie on his side on the table watching us at work or in his infant seat.

During the last year of his life, he had a fever all the time, often spiking up to 104-105°. He was very miserable most of the time because of it. He took up a lot of our time. We held him a lot. He never slept well and drank a lot of water from his bottle at night.

He lived to 15 months. In December 1983 he was in the hospital twice with pneumonia. He was better when we fixed a cool mist humidifier for him at home. I can still see him on his father's lap eating popcorn that last Friday evening. He always loved popcorn and called it "poppa". We broke off the soft puff part for him to eat.

On Saturday we had church services. It was a very warm day and Wayne was miserable, so I stayed home on Sunday. He seemed to be getting sick, but with nothing we could be sure of. On Monday night he vomited some and slept very poorly.

When I got up Tuesday morning, I knew I wanted a doctor to see him that day. Half an hour after getting up I checked him again and life had already fled. It was so hard to give him up, but a relief to know he was at peace with no more suffering.

Now there were two sweet angel babies waiting for us! After caring for Wayne so long it made such a difference in our lives. Being four and a half years old, Elvin Jr. could better understand this time, but it was still very hard on him and Lena. Lena has ever since had a hard time accepting new babies.

Barbara

We knew ahead of time that Barbara had O.I. so it was no shock when she was born. She could suck fairly well, but was more deformed than her brothers had been. She was very frail. At three weeks she had pneumonia and was in the hospital overnight. The doctor said it wouldn't be fair to keep her in the hospital, so we brought her home, too weak to eat much. She was losing weight.

Then two doctors came from Children's Hospital to see her. They said to make the formula stronger and make the nipple holes large so sucking is easier. She started gaining right away and was taking 16 ounces of formula a day instead of six.

On July 12 she was sick again. She had a high fever and slept more than normal that day and night. By the next morning she had a graying look and didn't suck after the first few hours. At about noon she stopped breathing so long I thought her heart had stopped, then she threw back her head, gasped, and started breathing again. She did this over and over. More frequently as the day and night wore on. After doing this she would sleep deeply for a time, maybe just 15 minutes.

Elvin and I took turns holding Barbara. She didn't seem conscious anymore. On July 12, a few minutes to nine she stopped breathing. A peaceful ending. The poor baby had struggled so long. After watching her struggle so long it was such a relief to know she was at peace.

Such a short life, but such a lot of good she did in our lives. We missed the dear sweet little girl. The children talked about her a lot. She was special to them all. She also lived to six weeks and two days. The children all took it as well as one could expect them to at their age. Now there are three sweet angel babies waiting for us.

As the family grows, we have three more healthy boys and another retarded girl, we can more and more see God's great wisdom in taking three innocent babies home out of this sinful world.

John Andrew (Jay) Yoder: Nov. 9, 1987 - Jan. 26, 1993

Submitted by: John A. & Ruth Yoder, Topeka, Indiana

> *There's no problem too big*
> *And no question too small,*
> *Just ask God in faith and*
> *He'll answer them all.*
>
> *Not always at once*
> *So be patient and wait;*
> *For God never comes*
> *Too soon or too late.*
>
> *So trust in His wisdom*
> *And believe in His word,*
> *For no prayer goes unanswered*
> *And no prayer unheard.*

This is just a poem, but full of meaning especially in time of bereavement. We had often prayed that the Lord rather take our children when they are young and yet so innocent than to have them grow up and be tempted and troubled and not be able to enter those pearly gates of heaven. So now we want to take this experience as an answer to our prayers. But sometimes it is a little bit harder to pray those same words as we now know how much it hurts. Yet we have told the Lord that is still what we want for all of our children.

John Andrew (Jay) was our fifth child, born to us on Monday morning, Nov. 9, 1987. He was just like all little ones, a cute wonderful little blessing. But he was a little different from any of our other children, he had golden reddish hair. As he grew older he didn't like that at all, mostly because it was different. He didn't want to be noticed. He often asked us, "Why do I have red hair?"

I would tell him that Jesus gave him his hair and therefore it was nice hair. His short five years of life weren't all trouble free. When he was little he was bothered with colic cramps and some digestive problems that caused him to throw up a lot.

After he had almost outgrown that at three months old, he was in the hospital for three days with pneumonia. He was on some different medicines. One was to keep him from sleeping too soundly, but it made him hyper so we didn't give him too much of that.

He got his health back and all seemed fine. Soon the time came that he wanted to start eating by himself and he wanted to use his left hand. He was a left-handed little guy, but that too bothered him because it was different from the rest of us. Sometimes he tried his best to use his right hand and just let the left one go limp at his side, but it just didn't work. We encouraged him to just use his left hand and that it was OK to be left-handed.

Now and then we had to punish him and quite often he'd soon come and say, "I'm sorry, I don't want to be naughty." He'd give us a big hug that meant a lot. They mean even more to us now.

He was an active little boy, a true little helper, full of life the whole time he was with us. Now we have to wonder, did he have to do all this so he could be ready when Jesus came to get him? One thing he did was he almost trained himself for the bathroom. His second birthday was on Sunday and on Monday morning he said he had to go potty. I was a little doubtful, but I took him and he did a good job. After about the fourth time he went that day, he said he wanted to wear shorts like his brothers and Dad.

As a reward, I let him, never thinking that he would keep wearing them, but he did. He was trained just like that! He had some accidents yet, but he did well. At the age of two years and three months, along came another little brother, which he dearly loved.

He held and rocked him and sang songs to him. His favorite songs were: Jesus Never Fails, Jesus Loves Me, and in later years he also sang the Peter, James, & John song a lot. I don't remember his age when he first started to ride his bike, but he really enjoyed that. When he was four and a half years old he rode his little bike beside his Dad's all the way to town, two miles. He came home all steamed up and red in the face, but very happy!

Little did we think he'd have only such a short time here with us yet.

His fifth birthday came and he got only a few cards. He was kind of hurt, but I told him that he usually got a lot and this once people just happened to forget. I too often forget things like that, but it means so much to the little ones.

Then came Christmas, and he explained that he wanted a fire truck like so and so. Well, it so happened that the cousins had exchanged names and he got a little fire truck, one with a siren that blew when you press down on it. He was delighted.

About that time, or maybe a little earlier, around Thanksgiving, he had asked me a serious question that kind of alarmed me. He asked, "Mom, when will be the end of the world?"

I tried to think that it was just another one of his many questions, and went ahead to try to explain a little about the end. After that, he would ask me the same question every so often, and also, "When is Easter?" He came to both of us, Mom and Dad, with these same questions one Sunday after church. We again explained and he went on with his play, seemingly satisfied.

At the time I told his dad that sometimes his remarks make me wonder if maybe he wouldn't grow old. He would also ask us how often we would have to sleep yet until Easter. With a little figuring, I told him about 90 times. He smiled so happily!

Then the day was here. Little did we realize that morning, what this day would bring. It was like any other day as far as we knew. That forenoon, he was playing and singing, "Jesus never fails, never, never fails, I'm glad, so glad Jesus never fails." He showed his Dad how he could now tie his shoe. His cousin Timmy had showed him how the day before. After showing his dad, he came to the sewing room to show me, too. Then he asked his questions again. This time I asked him what he knew about Easter.

His answer was, "That is when Jesus was put on the cross." So I explained to him about when Jesus would come and about the nail marks in his hands and about the crucifixion. Now we wonder, did he get to see the nail marks and did he ask Jesus what happened? Later that day, just before noon, he came to me and said he doesn't want his room painted red like he had said before. He wanted it all white. I asked, "Don't you even want red (wine) curtains?"

He replied, "No, I want it white all over," motioning with his arms all around. Now we have to think he got just that... big white room! It is a comfort to us he got his last and most important wish. Then it was lunchtime and we had noodles, one of his favorites. He also loved hot dogs and always made a smiley face on his bread with ketchup.

Now his sister does that, we can always see that she thinks of Jay. After lunch was nap time, but he couldn't sleep, so his Dad tickled him a little then we let him go. He played a while, then I asked, "Jay, would you like to get the mail today?"

I wonder over and over why, why?! I just can't quit, but I just have to think that for some reason, this was what God wanted. He was such a willing little helper, he would do anything he could do, I think he went that extra mile. So, he got his coat and cap and ran for the road.

I had told him again how to watch and wait and he did what I told him. He crossed the road and looked for mail, but there wasn't any mail there. He turned around, looked, and waited for a few cars to pass. We were watching from our porch window. I even opened the window. He saw me and said, "I'll wait, Mom."

He did, but the pick-up coming from the south was at a blind spot for Jay, behind the car going south. He thought it was OK and came running at full speed. At about his last step he looked up with a big smile on his face.

Oh! What a travail, those next few seconds, minutes, hours! Why? Why?! We just questioned and wondered. Most of the traffic just kept right on going. Martha, from across the road, brought a blanket. We wrapped Jay in it and brought him into the house. There was no question that life was gone. Oh, so traumatic!

Soon the police and an ambulance arrived and left again. Also, Jay's brothers and sister were brought home from school. Such a shock! We all took turns holding him one last time. He loved to be held. Almost every morning when he came down from bed he would ask, "Mom, can you hold me?" Then he would give me a hug and say, "I love you." Precious Memories!

Of course, I would hug him, too, and tell him how much I loved him, too. I usually read a Bible story to him too. His favorite book was #9, the one about the crucifixion of Jesus. We miss those moments so very much.

A lot of good people helped us out. The church, friends, neighbors, and also unknown people, brought things and prayed for us. God bless them all!

That night when we went to bed, I was wishing I could have a dream and see Jay all happy and alive, or something to reassure us that Jay was with Jesus. Nothing came though. I was a little disappointed. The next morning people came from every direction. That meant so much. My sisters were all here.

One sister said that her little boy, six weeks older than Jay, had a dream during the night. He said that just before the truck hit Jay, an angel was there. It took Jay and went up and up until he was real little. Then, there was Jesus and he took Jay in. It was such a comfort, and an answer to my prayer and wishes.

After the funeral came the many visitors, cards, letters, poems, and flowers. This all happened January 26, 1993. He was five years, two months, and 17 days old.

We all miss him greatly, but we do trust the Lord knows best. So we feel this is somehow the way it should be. We love him so much it is sometimes hard not to wish him back, yet we know we wouldn't want him to leave his wonderful home in heaven. We talk about him every day. A year and a half later his younger brother still misses him a lot and talks about him. We all do.

We have another little boy now. He was born on Jay's birth date and he has red hair and brown eyes just like Jay had. We can truly see the Lord works in mysterious ways, and it is hard to understand, but we love Him just the same. We now again have six children living, but not one could take the place of any other. They are all special in their own way. We love them all.

A year has passed since you have gone, and none will ever know
The love you created within our home, that secret inner glow.
There's an empty spot among us when we gather around to sing,
A special place is missing, from our little family ring.
But there is hope for another meeting, in a land we cannot see,
Where we'll be with Jesus forever, in all eternity.

Our niece that worked for us when Jay was born had a little boy the same day Jay left us. Another sister had a boy the same day as the funeral. Then later on we found out that the driver of the truck also had a baby boy that next summer and named him Jay Christopher.

Norma Yoder: Mar. 11, 1974 - Dec. 18, 1988

Submitted by: Joe & Lydia Ann Yoder, Fredericksburg, Ohio

Snow fell most of the forenoon on this Sunday which was Dec. 18, 1988. It was a beautiful sight with large flakes coming down. We did not have church services so our family of four children were at home. Little did we know that this would the last day on this earth that we would all be together.

After brunch, they all decided to go sledding and I sat inside the kitchen window watching them. After a while they all came in and started to get ready to go away. Karen (16) worked at Das Dutch Essenhaus in Shreve and this afternoon was their annual Christmas banquet. About a month earlier, Norma (14) had worked there too, just one day. Therefore she was invited too. I thought it was thoughtful of them to invite her too so Karen would not have to go by herself.

Norma was usually happiest to stay home with Dad and Mom, but she seemed excited about going this time. She was a bit shy, but had a smile for everyone.

My husband and I, along with the two youngest: Mary Ellen (13) and Mark (10), had planned on visiting the Andy Troyer family. Their daughter Susan was sick with mono at the time. We had been friends for years and the children also knew each other well.

We were ready to leave as Norma headed for the bathroom with her new dress hanging over her arm. That is where we said our last good-byes. What would we have said if only we would have known? I regretted not seeing her with the only new dress she ever asked for. It seemed so strange to me that she asked if she could have a new dress for this occasion. I made sure she got one, too.

Mark took his little pony and cart and took her to Country Dry Goods the week before. Even though it was only approximately two and a half miles, they were chilled that winter day by the time they got back. Mark didn't seem to mind the cold at all and Norma had picked out a dress in her favorite color. The material was nice and soft in spring green.

We bundled up and headed for our destination with the horse and buggy. Little did we realize what lay ahead. We had a good visit and it seemed like Susan was getting along all right. The boys played outside for quite a while.

Around 4 o'clock we decided to get ready to head home. I was standing in the kitchen ready to go when a pick-up pulled in the driveway. Looking out, I saw Karen leap out of the truck, over a snow drift and come bolting for the house. She said, "Come home right away, something is wrong with Norma."

My first thoughts were that she probably fainted for some reason. That was the beginning of what seemed to be a nightmare. Mary Ellen and Mark were left at Andy's and Joe, Karen, and I got into that truck with a complete stranger driving. His wife was with him, too. We had never seen them before and where did they come from?

The road was slick with the fresh snow and the driving was hard. Couldn't he go any faster? Didn't he realize we were in a hurry? Nothing seemed to make sense on the way home.

Definitely expecting Norma to be up and about by the time we got home, we were in no way prepared for what lay ahead. Coming from the east towards our house we saw the restaurant van that had come to pick the girls up, parked in front. We also heard the siren now. Just as we stopped in our driveway, the squad car sped up over the hill from the west.

We ran for the house ahead of the squadmen. There are no words to describe our feelings when we reached the house. Norma was gone! Joe and I knelt down on either side of her. We tried to talk to her and Joe took her pulse, but it was too late. Too late! We were numb and unbelieving. This simply could not be! Just a few hours before she had seemed fine.

Moments later the squadmen asked us to move so they could work on her. I sat down on my rocker and the pickup driver's wife helped me pray. Apparently she had followed us in.

Finally she said, "Norma is turning pink again."

I had hopes again, not realizing it was from the oxygen they were getting into her body. I was so numb that I was only partly aware of the people around. Next thing we knew, they had Norma on the stretcher and were headed out the door to the squad. We watched as her arm slid down from the cot and hung limply on the side. "Can we ride along?"

They told us no, that we would have to follow in another vehicle. Bill Nelson from the restaurant, who had come to pick the girls up said he'd take us.

Looking around, we saw this lady from the pickup standing in our living room by herself. She asked, "Don't you want to lock the door?" Joe then decided to lock up when she came out as we still had no idea who she was.

Some neighbors had gathered in the yard, but we really didn't see anyone as we left. They could tell it was serious by our solemn expressions, but had no idea what had happened.

On the way to the hospital with Bill driving, Joe, Karen, and I tried to piece these events together. Nothing made sense to our numb minds, but surely the Lord would spare her. We couldn't get along without Norma with her willing hands and cheerful smile (With God all things are possible.) We did not want to give her up in our present state of mind. Bill kept assuring us that her color had come back. Surely she'd be all right when we got to the hospital.

Karen and Bill tried to explain to us how this all happened. We tried to get our minds to listen. When the restaurant van pulled up in front of the house, the two girls got ready to go out the front door.

Norma noticed a pile of Christmas cards on the china cupboard that Karen had ready to give to friends that day. Picking them up, Norma said, "Here, Karen, don't forget these."

She handed them to Karen, who had turned around and was facing her. Norma's eyes closed and she fell backwards. Running out on the porch, Karen frantically motioned for Bill to come. He hurried in and tried CPR, but got no response. Looking up at Karen, he asked, "Where are your Mom and Dad?

"At Andy's," she replied.

We presume Bill thought we were right next door at neighbor Andy Miller's. After he told her to go get us, she ran out the door and here was this pickup in the drive. Everything was timed perfectly as they had just pulled in to ask directions. We found this out later.

Karen jumped into their truck and asked them to take her to her parents as something was wrong with her sister.

Bill couldn't figure out what had happened to Karen when she didn't return shortly. He was by himself and realized he needed help. He ran outside and right then a car was coming down the road. He stopped them and asked them to call the squad. Perfect timing again!

After what seemed like ages, we finally got to Wooster Community Hospital. We raced inside where we met Gary Wagers from the squad coming our way. Since we know him we thought we would ask some questions. One look at his face told us that he had no good news. To his relief we didn't even bother to talk to him.

Nurses came and talked to us, telling us they were working on her. They also said they don't give up as quickly on a young person as on someone older. Slowly they were preparing us for what they had to say. Bill called the restaurant informing them why he didn't arrive with his load of girls.

Dr. Gatz from Shreve (Karen knew him) and also a young Dr. Cebul were on duty. After talking to us several times, they took us to the chaplain's office. We felt sure we knew what they'd tell us next as we sat in that small room. I could see two nurses and a doctor trying to get control of themselves. Oh no! Now I was certain what they had to tell us.

Norma was gone and they had no idea what caused her death. Why!? Why did this happen to us? What had we done to bring this about? The chaplain was very helpful contacting people for us, but how could we think straight to plan a funeral? In the meantime, Bill had called one of the neighbors to bring Mary Ellen and Mark to the hospital. Thinking that it must be serious that we wanted our family there, Joe's brother Eli and his wife decided to come along, too. They picked the children up at Andy Troyers and brought them to the hospital.

The first person they saw was Karen. Eli asked, "How is Norma?" She replied, "Norma passed away."

They took us in to see Norma and I couldn't believe how beautiful she looked. Her face was so radiant that it reminded us of an angel. She had her covering on her head. It amazed me after what they had put her through. Her covering had always meant a lot to her and here they had thought to put it back on. That was really touching to us.

The chaplain prayed the Lord's Prayer with us and we felt the Lord's presence like never before. The next step was the very hardest part for me. How could a mother go home and leave her knowing what would happen next? Oh! We just couldn't do this! Feeling like we were up against a block wall, there was only one thing to do. All that was left to do was give up and turn around and go home.

That was the most heartrending experience in our lives. My heart felt like someone had stabbed it and that pain stayed with me for nearly six weeks. Finally we started on that long, dismal ride home.

We dreaded the thought of coming home to a dark house as we remembered locking the door. As we neared home we were surprised to see the whole house lighted up. How thankful we were for family and neighbors that had managed to get in and be there for us. Walking into that house is another instance where words fail to describe our feelings. Bishop Jacob Troyer came and the first words he said were, "Now don't think this is just for you. This is for all of us."

He will never know how much those words meant to us. We appreciated his kind help planning the funeral.

There was no sleep for us that night and very little the next. Each morning I wished it was all a dream. God in His mercy helped us through the next few days. The verse that came to my mind a lot was, "God is our refuge and strength, a very present help in trouble." Psalms 46:1

A friend wrote to us and said that first shock is what she feels is God's way of helping you through. If you could fully grasp it right away, you would hardly be able to bear it.

The day of the funeral was cold and rainy. As I sat and watched the raindrops hit and run down over the window pane, I thought it matched our feelings exactly.

Norma was the first one laid to rest in the new cemetery that was being started on our bishop's place. The previous summer some of the men from church had met there to discuss plans for it. When Joe got home that time, Norma had asked, "Dad, what do you think of it?"

He told her that place would be OK for him to be buried at. She was satisfied with that answer and never said more. The rest of the children were not interested in hearing about it.

Our bodies were tired and numb afterwards. Food had lost its taste and everything seemed dull and colorless for the longest time. The week afterward was Christmas. How we ached when everyone else was happy and excited, or so it seemed. I still have the present that Norma bought and wrapped for me, still neatly wrapped. I did open it, but put it back in.

Finally in the summer of '91, I was amazed at how beautiful our flower beds were, and the trees were so bright and green. After the rain, the sun does shine again. May all honor and glory be to God.

The doctors said they are humbled not to have specific answers as to the cause of death. They said it must have been related to the heart, although her heart looked perfectly normal.

Reuben A. Yutzy: Oct. 24, 1971 - June 19, 1990

Submitted by: Aden L. & Katie Yutzy, West Union, Ohio

Our family will not soon forget the year of 1990. It was in June that I made the remark to some of the boys that this is as nice as we'll ever have it here on earth and that we want to be thankful for it. Unknown to us, this was soon to tragically change.

Our pallet shop had burned down in January of this same year. With the help of many kind friends and neighbors it was soon built back and going again. By June we had our routine family life again with some of the boys farming and the others working in the shop.

For several years we had talked about damming off a long narrow ravine at the back place and this became a reality in the spring of '90. With surface water and springs leading into it we soon had a small lake. We then stocked it with fish and sent for some assorted water plants which were meant to provide cover for small fish. The plants arrived on June 19, on a Tuesday.

That evening, Eddie, 23 and Reuben came home late from the shop as they had some maintenance work to do. We had already eaten supper when they came home. After they had eaten their supper it was undecided who would ride with our neighbor in his pickup to set the plants in the lake. It was decided that Leon, 21; Reuben, 18; Steven, 14; Marcus, six; and I would go.

We rode in the truck along with spades and plants, and since I try to be a safety-minded person, I threw a coil of nylon rope on just in case. The neighbor unloaded us and then left again.

Leon and Reuben took their shirts and shoes off. We went down the one side of the lake along the woods with me tossing the plants to them and they took their spades and squeezed the plants in place about a foot under water. I left the rope lying on the bank where we started. By the time we got about halfway down the one side, we had half of the plants set.

I suggested we plant the rest on the other side. I started into the woods towards the head of the lake assuming the boys would follow me out around. Steven was at the upper end playing with a life jacket in shallow water. Before I got to the upper end Leon yelled at me and I at once sensed that something was terribly wrong. I first turned around and ran towards the boys, but then I remembered the rope and turned around again to get it.

Reuben had asked Leon if he was going to swim across to the other side since that was a much shorter distance than walking all the way around. Leon told him that he wasn't going to. While Leon had his back turned setting his last plants, Reuben started to swim across. Marcus was on the bank watching. When Leon looked around , he saw Reuben halfway across and looking exhausted. He knew right away that he wasn't going to make it.

Reuben hollered to Steven, who just minutes before was close by, asking for his life jacket, but Steven was too far away to make it in time. Leon told Reuben not to panic, but just then he went under. It was then that Leon hollered for help. I was soon there with my rope, which wouldn't have helped anyway, wondering what was wrong.

Oh, the sad words I was told then! Reuben had gone under and hadn't come back up. Leon ran for help and I tried to make myself believe that if help arrived soon enough, Reuben could still be rescued and revived, but that was not to be. He went under at 8:45

PM and he wasn't found until 5:00 the next morning.

Shock and grief, these were the things we had heard about, but had not experienced. At that time it came home to visit us.

Several months later my father-in-law passed away. He was up in years and not in good health. Yes, it was sad to part with him, but we could cope with that. It comes naturally to us that our parents will become old and pass away. It is to be expected, but the sudden snatching away of a healthy teenager who we all dearly loved was something else that can not be put into words. Also, several months after Reuben drowned, one of our granddaughters was badly injured in a pony cart accident. She was life-flighted 70 miles away to a Cincinnati hospital.

We accompanied the parents to the hospital and when we got there two social workers, a young woman and a man were waiting on us and ushered us into a small room. It was their job to comfort or counsel us. After being in there a while I told them about what had happened just months before to our son. The woman gasped and asked how we were coping with something like that. I told her that I was looking forward to some day meeting our son again. She acted very surprised that I believed something like that.

That taught us a lesson. We who are brought up as Christians and believe the gospel and have assurance of life after death have something that professionally trained counselors and therapists can not improve upon. However, we are just human and I will keep it no secret that in the summer of 1990 I many times desperately wished for the world to come to an end.

In looking back, we would much rather have had Reuben for 18 years than not have had him at all . He had started to join our church, we have many fond memories of him. His death affected others too. Suddenly there were more who decided to join church. As a family we were made much more aware that the foremost part of us, that which we can not see, continues to live even though the physical body is no longer here.

The best therapy I can think of is what another father with a similar experience told me. "Just think ahead to that wonderful day when we will meet each other again. Won't that be a joyful day?" He sincerely meant it and I believe it, too.

Kevin Miller: Apr. 13, 1992 (date of tragedy)

Submitted by: Dennis & Fern Miller, Middlebury, Indiana

It was a beautiful spring morning, April 13, 1992. John Graber was here from Berne with his carpenter gang working on the duck barn. Dennis had taken the day off from Starcraft to do some odds and ends, trying to get the duck barn finished. He took the horse to the neighbor to get him shod so he could go to town to do errands and also take treats to school for Nelson's birthday.

I was busy washing. I didn't get a very early start, so in my hurry I didn't fill the engine with gas, thinking it would last if I hurried. But that wasn't to be. I wasn't quite finished when the motor stopped, so I filled the tank and set the can back in the corner instead of on the shelf.

Just then Billy Mary came for a coffee break. We had a nice chat. Kevin and Karl were playing so nice this forenoon. Thinking back I remember they were extra sweet that morning. Mary left and I went back to washing. I was ready to hang out the last load and thought of making the twins come upstairs with me, but they were having fun walking in the warm wash water so I left them there.

I came into the kitchen, glad to be finished at last. I turned on the hot water to wash my dishes. I remember hearing the hot water heater pop on. All of a sudden there was a terrible hissing and blowing noise and I heard the twins scream.

I looked behind me and the dining room was all lit up. It was shining up through the register. I ran to the basement and the sight I saw I'll never forget as long as I live. Karl was standing there screaming. His face and arms were burned, his pant legs were melted off and his feet were burned too. The back of his shirt was all gone except for his collar. His suspenders were still there.

Looking around I saw Kevin. He was still on fire. All his clothes were gone except his diaper and part of his rubber pants. Most of his hair was gone and his skin was a tannish brown all over. I grabbed him and ran for the stairs. When I held him against me the flames went out. I ran upstairs and Karl followed me outside.

I stood outside the door holding Kevin yelling "HELP!" The carpenters didn't hear me right away as they had motors and tools going. They all came running for the house. John and his driver went to the phone to call for the ambulance and then to get Dennis at the neighbors. Billy Mary was at Mom's house and they came running too. Karl was crying and in a lot of pain, but Kevin almost couldn't cry anymore.

I wonder if he even felt his burns as they were very deep. He was swelling up fast and his skin was like leather. There was still fire in the basement, but it was so smoky the carpenters couldn't see it. Finally Jonas Graber took a pail of water and went into the smoke to put it out. He took a risk as we didn't know how much fire there was. Thank you, Jonas!

Finally the ambulance came. Dennis had Karl and I took Kevin. They let both of us go along. When we finally got to the hospital they took the boys to one room and Dennis and me to another. I had third degree burns on my arm and my hands were covered with blisters. Kevin's skin was so hot when I lifted him that it had blistered my hands.

When we went to see the twins we couldn't believe those were our little twins. They were then air lifted to St. Joseph Medical Center burn unit in Fort Wayne. Dennis and I followed with Vernon Cross. It was a long ride to Fort Wayne!

When we next saw the boys, they were bandaged from head to foot. They had tubes down their noses and throats, plus other machines and beepers hooked up to them.

Every hour the first few days their stomachs were suctioned out. The liquid that came out was black. Kevin's was a lot worse than Karl's. Twice a day the bandages had to be changed and the wounds washed. There was only one time that Kevin responded to us. We sang and talked to him anyway.

Karl had third degree burns on 35 percent of his body and Kevin had third degree burns on 90 percent.

The only things showing on Kevin were his eyes and ears and these too were covered later on. His ears and fingers were black. His head swelled up so that his eyelids turned inside out. The skin on the trunk of his body was so tight that long slits were made down the sides. Everything was done to give him a chance to live, but he died exactly one week later.

Kevin and Karl were in separate rooms, but every time Kevin really struggled to stay alive, Karl did too. After Kevin died, Karl settled down.

It was hard to leave Karl there and go home for the funeral. Kind friends came to stay with him. We now realize how hard it must have been for Howard and Lillian Miller to come and relive all they had gone through years earlier with their twins who both died of burns from a gas fire.

Karl had to stay at the hospital for five weeks. I stayed all except three nights. The rest of the family came when they could. Marlin, Kenny, and Nelson had to go back to school and Dennis and Mike went back to work. Life must go on. We had many visitors during those long weeks and all were greatly appreciated!

When Karl was finally released he still had a long way to go. He still had large raw spots on his back and also on his feet and elbows. They had to be washed twice a day till the edges bled. Many times we both cried before we were done. Then came the itching. He cried a lot because of itching, but that is past now. He wore a JOBST suit for two years, but is completely healed with no defects.

Later we found out we almost lost Karl before we even got to the emergency room. His airway was so swollen from the heat he had inhaled that they almost couldn't get a ventilator tube down.

We have much to be thankful for. We can read in the Bible that little children are promised to go to Heaven. That is a very comforting thought when loneliness starts in again.

Karl had a hard time accepting that Kevin wasn't here at home with the other boys when he got home from the hospital, but sometimes little children adjust better than grown-ups.

Just a kind warning to everyone. Never leave the gas can where little ones can get it.

Ervin Bontrager, Jr.: May 28, 1974 - Oct. 24, 1993

Submitted by: Mr. & Mrs. Ervin A. Bontrager, Topeka, Indiana

I had a feeling life was going to be different before the baby was born. Things were so different during the nine months. I don't know why, but I felt this wasn't going to be a healthy baby. There was just something there that told me.

On May 28th, we had a son born to us. We named him Ervin Jr. Many days I just cried and prayed. He was always slow in everything. We had him to a chiropractor many times. They always said he had a bad headache.

He was always fussy and took a lot of care. He was over a year old and still didn't walk alone. One day when he was in his walker, he fell down a step and landed on his head. That night he didn't sleep very much and by the next morning he just threw himself from side to side. We could see he was in pain, he just cried and cried.

We took him to the LaGrange hospital emergency room. They took some tests and finally tapped his spine. They came and told us that he had spinal meningitis. They sent us on to Lutheran Hospital in Fort Wayne.

They kept him there for ten days. He was one and a half years old at that time. When he came home from the hospital, he started to walk by himself, but we could see there was still something wrong.

We took him to Bluffton Clinic. They took some more tests. They told us he had a muscle disease and sent us to Indianapolis to Riley's Children's Hospital. They told us he had M.D. (Muscular Dystrophy)

We never saw him run, or climb stairs without crawling, but he was able to walk until he was eight years old. When he stopped walking, we took him down to Fort Wayne M.D. clinic. There they told us what kind of M.D. he had.

When he was old enough to go to school we had the School of Opportunity out to test him. They told us they couldn't take him because he was too smart. So he went to a regular school. Oh, how hard it was to send him to school knowing that he would never run with the other children.

He really liked school and never wanted to miss a day. He always had good grades. When he wasn't in school it was easy to see him slip backwards.

We had so many unanswered whys. Then we were told of a doctor in Ashton, Indiana, that might be able to help. We took him down to the doctor and he told us during that first visit that he thought he could get him to walk again. We took him back down, twice a month, for a whole year, but the walking never came back for him. Finally he said he didn't want to go anymore. I guess he felt that it wasn't helping much.

He liked to read, and read many books, some three or four times. He was given many books for his birthdays as well as lots of other things. Some days seemed short, then others so very long. He always looked forward to getting company. He often asked why we couldn't have company more often.

We had many tiring days, as some days it was very hard to please him. Many people with healthy children that can take care of themselves just don't know how it is. Yes, my days are different now. I don't have him to feed or bathe anymore. People gave us much advice, which we were glad for.

We gave him many different things, but it seemed nothing helped. Finally he just said he didn't want to take anything anymore even though we tried to talk him into it. One day he asked if he could go to gros gmay. I told him he could, or we could have gmay at home in the evening. He said he would rather go, that way he could see the church people.

That next week one evening after we had him in bed he called me over. He asked a couple of questions and I tried to answer them as well as I knew how. He also said he wanted to be forgiven for some of the things he had said that he shouldn't have.

Nobody can know the feeling that went through me then. I could see him slipping back but I didn't want to tell him. We knew it would come someday, but hadn't thought it would be so soon. We saw he wasn't feeling the best, and he asked for Orva P. Miller one evening. So we went and brought him over.

He advised us to see a doctor. We then called the doctor and he came out. He told us he had an infection and probably pneumonia and the doctor gave him some medicine. He said he was so tired.

This was the first time he had ever said he was tired. It was a shock to see him gone, but how lucky he was that he didn't have to suffer longer.

There are lots of things to remember. Yes, it was always hard to go to get-togethers and see all the other children running and playing, but he wasn't sick very often. He always enjoyed having the grandchildren over. They were one of his favorite pastimes.

Gone, but not forgotten; when people see us smile,
They don't know of the heartache all the while.

Nora Ann Schlabach: Aug. 15, 1978 (date of tragedy)
Submitted by: Omer & Ann Schlabach, Middlebury, Indiana

It was August 15, 1978, the saddest day we ever experienced. The doctor had just told us our bright, energetic little three year old Nora Ann had just passed away. I can almost hear him still, "We worked on her for over an hour, but..."

The rest of his sentence was a blur, for what did it matter? Our Nora was gone! We felt so desolate, so empty. Only yesterday she had been running and playing with the rest. Only yesterday I had rocked her to sleep for the LAST TIME.

It was 6:20, the chores were done and I had just started supper when squealing brakes and a loud thud nearly froze me. Quickly running for the door, I just got a glimpse of a child rolling around underneath the still moving car. When I got outside there was our Nora; lying on the road, so still, so silent! I gathered her in my arms not knowing if her little heart was still beating or not for I just couldn't bear to know yet. The rest of the family and neighbor Marvins were soon gathered around and Daddy also held her while waiting on the ambulance.

Just before we heard the siren she gave a feeble cry. Oh, how relieved we all were; she was alive and would soon be her sunny little self. The only injuries we could see were some superficial scrapes on her temples and wrists.

I held her and talked to her all the way to Goshen Hospital. She was semiconscious and would answer at times, but was a little mixed up. At the hospital there was the usual round of tests and x-rays and they discovered her injuries were worse than first suspected.

With lights flashing and siren screaming, she was rushed to South Bend Hospital where we were met by Omer and my parents, Joe and Ida Bontrager. Once there, we had to leave our precious one for what seemed a long time while they examined her more thoroughly.

Finally the doctor came out and told us our Nora was in a very serious condition with head and internal injuries. They would need to operate. We were allowed to see her briefly before they took her to surgery at midnight to repair a torn stomach and bladder. All through that long, sleepless night we kept hoping and praying, "Thy will be done."

Always when I tried to pray there seemed to be a group of white-clad little angels between my prayers and God. Surely this didn't mean our Nora would soon be among them, did it? For how could we ever go through life without her?

At 5:00 we were finally allowed in her room in the ICU, but what a shock! We couldn't even touch her for she was under an oxygen tent with many tubes and wires connected to her poor little body. Her bright blue eyes were wide open, but there was no sign of recognition.

At 8:00 her punctured lungs started to fill up and the beeper went off. Her heart had stopped!

We were ushered out of the room as doctors and nurses came rushing in. Oh, surely they could get her heart started again with all those machines and professional help there. But it was not to be; God had a better plan.

Dad, Mom, and brother David came to take us home where we were met by our grieving children: Carolyn, Darla, Lamar, Joe, Merlin, and Mary Jane. Kind neighbors were also there and soon our brothers and sisters came to share our sorrow. Grandmother, Nora Schlabach, also came.

We had a long hard battle to fully accept our loss, but now we can truthfully thank the Lord for taking Nora home to be with Him.

Katie Marie Miller: Jan. 5, 1974 - Jan. 15, 1994

Submitted by: Andrew S. & Barbara Miller, Goshen, Indiana

Saturday, January 15, 1994, started out as any cold winter Saturday morning, but ended as it never had before and never will again. Our only daughter, Katie Marie (Kate) and her boyfriend Carl Hochstetler were involved in an auto accident which claimed her life.

They had left in the evening to pick up their friends, Devon Bontrager and Amy Miller, to go out for supper for her birthday which was January 5. They were gone a little while when a van drove in our lane and a boy came to the door.

He said, "Your daughter and her boyfriend were in an accident a mile down the road."

I asked, "Is it bad?"

He replied, "She doesn't respond anymore."

Such a shock! We hurried to the accident site. The night was so cold. There was deep snow and the road was plowed two lanes wide most of the way. Right where the accident was, the road was only one and half lanes wide.

There had been a car coming over the hill and her boyfriend had turned to the side to avoid the other car. He couldn't see the snowbank with his lights on dim. When his car hit the snowbank, it was whirled around. The other car hit it in the front on the passenger side. Kate was thrown into his arms. At that time she wouldn't respond to him, but was still breathing.

They were just putting her into the ambulance when we got there. Carl was also taken along to the hospital. He stayed in the hospital overnight with some bruises and cuts.

They used life support on her, but got no response. We went on out to the hospital, but a nurse told us, "We lost her."

All the while, an unexplainable calm was over us. God seemed so very near and was helping us with our shock and grief.

Neither car had been going very fast. Both Kate's and Carl's glasses were on the back seat, unbroken and folded as if somebody had laid them there.

Earlier in the evening, after she had taken her bath, she had said, "I've had the most relaxing bath I've ever had. I'm just so relaxed. I've never felt like this before. Mom, I left the bath water in the bathtub. I wasn't very dirty, why don't you go and take a bath in it. Maybe you could feel so relaxed, too."

But, right at the time I was doing something else and it seemed something held me from going. Then, some of the others wanted to bathe and the water was cold, so I told them to let the water out.

Since then I have felt I wasn't supposed to bathe in it as it was her cleansing water and hers alone. I'm sure she didn't put anything else in it but what she usually did. We feel the Lord was preparing her for her death.

She was the youngest in the family, the only daughter after eight sons, so she is greatly missed by all. We can see God's ways are not our ways. We can only say, "Thy will be done." I wrote the following poem to express my feelings at that time and after.

Our Darkest Night

On a cold Saturday night, January 15, 1994,
A car drove in, then a knock on the door.
A boy said there has been an accident a little while before,
Carl and Katie Marie were hit; she doesn't respond anymore.

We got ready to go, not knowing what we'd meet at the scene,
We were told it looks bad, could see what they did mean.
They were loading her in the ambulance when we got there.
Carl was put in beside her, he also needed care.

We hurried to the hospital not knowing what we'd meet at the door,
We had an unexplainable calm as never before.
We knew that it could only come from the Lord above,
And what the outcome would be, He'd show comfort and love.

When we got there everything was so quiet,
We were met in the hall by a nurse in white.
She said, "Let's go to the chapel at the end of the hall,
We lost her, nothing could be done by the doctor on call."

It was a shock to hear our only dear daughter was gone,
We tried to give everything to God, we couldn't handle it alone.
Her brothers all came and more of the family, too.
We stood around her silent body, there was nothing we could do.

Our hearts were broken, so helpless and blue,
We prayed God would help us in what we had to go through.
We lost a dear treasure, our daughter so young and so sweet.
We hope to live a life so we can someday in Heaven meet.

We went home to a house so empty and drear,
Neighbors, relatives, and friends came, they wanted to be near.
The weather was so cold it took more effort to go,
But they came and helped their sympathy to show.

Oh, the sleepless night we were numb with grief,
Turning to God was our only relief.
People came, who lost loved ones, knew what we were going through,
Friends and co-workers came, her silent body to view.

The day was so cold, when we laid her to rest,
Lots of people came and wished us the best.
Our home is never the same, always an empty place,
We need God to be with us, as each new day we face.

Ida Fern Hochstetler: Mar. 17, 1978 - Feb. 13, 1986

Submitted by: Ervin Ray & Lillie Hochstetler, Shipshewana, Indiana

Ida Fern Hochstetler was born March 17, 1978 to Ervin Ray and Lillie Hochstetler. She had one sister Ruby and five brothers: Floyd, Ferman, Richard, Leroy, and Vernon.

Ida Fern was a first grader at Northside School. Her teacher was

Delbert Farmwald and Martha Eicher was his helper for the term of 1985-86. Her classmates were Susan Lehman and Ida Mae Bontrager. Ida Fern had an interest in singing. She and her sister often sang "Jesus Never Fails" while doing dishes. During the month of January, the scholars were learning the song "Thank-You, Lord" and she almost knew this one by heart.

On February 9, 1986, Doddy Hochstetlers had church services at their place. Earlier that morning, at 6:00, a daughter Miriam joined our family. How excited Ruby and Ida Fern were to have another sister, but our joy was not for long.

Thursday morning dawned as any other day, cold with a couple inches of snow on the ground. At the breakfast table, Ida Fern had a faraway look. I have often thought since then, why didn't we ask her what her thoughts were. Aunt Erma and her family had spent the evening before at our house visiting; we thought she is probably still sleepy.

Then off to school the four scholars went. At 3:00 PM school was dismissed. Ferman and Ida Fern were the first ones out of the school yard and were running home. The school is just a few yards west of us. In their excitement to get home to hold their baby sister again, they were running. As Ida Fern started to cross the busy highway, Ferman called her name and she turned and smiled at him. At the same instant, an eastbound semi hit her and life was instantly gone.

The funeral was Sunday, February 16, 1986. Ida Fern had made a greeting card for baby Miriam, but had not brought it home. It was found in her desk at school. The verse on it said, "What I say unto you, I say unto all, 'Watch,'" and "Abstain from all appearance of evil." The last verse the scholars were learning for a Bible verse and the other verse God must have given her.

The Lord giveth and the Lord taketh away, and we experienced both in one week's time. Eight years later, after two more boys: Ervin Junior and Marvin, another daughter Nettie joined our family. "God works mysteriously, His wonders to perform."

Submitted by: Delbert Farmwald, Shipshewana, Indiana

As far as we could tell, the morning of February 13, 1986, was just like any other morning. The pupils of Northside School arrived and classes took up as usual. Nothing of major significance turned up during the course of the school day and little did we realize what was in store for us that afternoon.

The four Hochstetler children were still very excited about their baby sister Miriam, which had been born four days earlier. The rest of us shared the excitement, but of course, we could not feel it as keenly as they could, especially sixth grade Ruby and Ida Fern, who was in the first grade. To them, being in a family with five boys, it was especially exciting to have another sister in the family to even up the sides a bit.

Earlier in the week we had our usual monthly parent-teacher meeting. Although no major problems had surfaced at the meeting, there was one point discussed that I would now need to bring to the attention of the first and second graders. Lately, in their spare time they had been busy making cards, paper toys, and gifts of all kinds for their classmates, family members, and teachers.

While this looked harmless enough at first, it was coming to be a bit of a problem. Their creations were beginning to take first place, crowding out lessons at times. Also the idea of passing cards and gifts to each other at every recess and sometimes during school time was leaving a rather cluttered atmosphere in an attempt for a quiet and orderly classroom.

No doubt this was partly my fault as obviously several of them were having too much idle time. Of course everyone, the idle as well as the others, wanted to get in on making things. It seemed each new invention served to inspire the rest to come up with something else.

When I brought this up at the meeting, the parents in their usual supportive fashion, all agreed it was probably going too far. They pledged to mention this to their children at home. I should see that there would be an improvement in the situation.

All along I was a bit hesitant to work on this because I didn't want these little children to completely stop making such stuff (at least not those unique little homemade gifts for the teacher!). Already my boxes of school souvenirs contained many crude little gifts that my dear little students had created over the years. I cherished these dearly. But the fact remained it was getting out of hand a bit.

On Thursday afternoon, several days after the meeting, I knew I had to mention this now. Without a doubt they were all wondering when I'd bring it up as I'm sure by now each of the parents had discussed it with their children at home.

So just a bit before dismissal time, I asked the first and second graders to go to the basement with me. I tried to explain the situation to them as gently as I could. As usual, they nodded knowingly. Yes, they had been informed of the matter at home and knew what I was talking about and yes, they all wanted to do better from now on. Nevertheless, the fact that the teacher had to reprimand them in the least seemed to be just a bit hard on these little children. Oh how sorry they all were to displease their teacher in any little way.

Seeing their faces all so sorry and repentant, I decided we'd sing a song before returning to the classroom. Maybe that would reassure them that all will be okay.

They had recently learned to sing "Six Little Ducks" and they all enjoyed that so we decided to sing that. With the lively motions and the words they could easily understand, it was a favorite to them all. The song took only a few minutes and it seemed to lift the spirits of these little children. Then we all trooped happily upstairs, the children reassured they had been forgiven. Indeed they would all try to do as they had been asked.

But, it made us late. By the time we returned to the classroom it was several minutes past the 3:00 dismissal time. Quickly books and lessons were cleared away in preparation for dismissing.

Had we been able to know what the next five minutes would bring, we would certainly have cherished those last few minutes together. We would have been more meaningful with our good-byes and probably we would have remembered things we wanted to ask forgiveness for.

But— we didn't know. We didn't know God had sent an angel to our school with a special mission and was even now hovering near. We did not know that a certain semi was coming down the highway at the exact right spot and what part he would play in just a few minutes. No, we couldn't know.

Barely had the last of the students left the classroom when a cry was heard above the hub-bub and hustle-bustle of thirty children putting on boots and wraps in the cloakroom. "Ida Fern was nearly hit!" someone called out.

"Oh, no," I thought. A stab of terror struck me as I went for the door to investigate. Our school house is situated beside State Road 120 and there was often a lot of traffic, especially so around dismissal time. Many of the factory workers were going home at that time also.

Barely had that first alarm registered when it was followed by another, even more urgent one, "Ida Fern was hit!"

Indeed, that first alarm had struck terror into my heart. But words fail to describe the feelings when the second cry came. Already a dozen or more students were rushing for the road, anxious to see what had happened. I knew I dare not let the panic surface that was pushing inside of me. I had to restore order and do so fast lest more of the pupils dash onto the road into the traffic that was whizzing by, obviously unaware of what had just happened. At the same time, I knew I had to get over to see about Ida Fern, to see if she was hurt, and to get help if she was.

Quickly, I ordered all the students back into the schoolhouse and tried to impress upon them that it is of utmost importance that they stay right there until they are given permission to leave. I then turned to cross the road to where Ida Fern was lying beside the highway, a short distance from the school house driveway.

Apparently she and her brother Ferman, just older than she, were racing home together. Without warning, she turned to dash across the road, totally unaware of the semi that was coming. She must have had one thing on her mind -- that of being the first one home to hold her baby sister.

Ferman yelled at her to stop and come back, but to no avail. It appeared she thought he was merely calling her back so he could gain on her. She only looked back, flashed him a smile, then turned and ran directly into the path of the semi which hit her just before she reached the other side.

Seconds later as I reached the scene, Ferman was desperately trying to find an opening in the traffic to cross the highway to get to Ida. But the traffic was extra heavy just then and he could not cross. I barely managed to persuade him not to dash through the passing traffic to the other side. Finally, he seemed to go into a slight shock and returned to the schoolhouse as I asked him to.

I instructed my co-teacher to keep the students inside if at all possible. The two oldest of the Hochstetler children Ruby and Floyd, were allowed to come out. Floyd was sent home (a very short distance from the schoolhouse) to get their mom. Ruby came over to where her sister lay. Of course, her first question was if Ida was hurt and if she was still living. All I could say was that I could not be sure how badly she was hurt.

By now cars were stopping and emergency help was called via radio. Again and again, Ruby would ask me if Ida was still living. I could not force myself to tell her what I thought. Actually, I could not force myself to believe it myself, so I repeated that I could not tell for sure how badly she was hurt. I tried to comfort her with the fact that help was on the way. But in that situation that was of little comfort. What mattered was if Ida was still living or not.

Somehow, even after teaching the emergency chapter in our health books for six years, I just could not think of the right thing to do. Thankfully my co-teacher remembered to send out my coat and several others to cover Ida with.

One of the first cars to stop was a man who identified himself as being a medical doctor from South Bend. He handed me his identification so I could trust him and then he knelt beside us to take a look at Ida. I was very glad to see him, thinking if there is anything to be done at this point, he would know what to do.

Several policemen were soon there and all we could do was wait for the ambulance to arrive. When Lillie, Ida's mom came, she asked if anyone had called Ervin at the factory. I felt so bad that I had not remembered to do that. I quickly ran to the neighbor's house and called him. He was soon there.

When the ambulance arrived, they didn't do much until the head attendant shook his head and covered Ida back up. To us, this quenched the last spark of hope that there might still be life there. According to the official accident report later, it was assumed she had died instantly and hardly as much as realized what was happening. It was ruled she died of a broken neck and massive head injuries.

Thinking back, I realize there was really not much doubt right from the start. When I first checked for a pulse and tried to decide if artificial respiration should be attempted, I saw one little wisp of breath in the frosty air and then—no more.

The rest of the afternoon and the next few days are rather foggy in my memory. After it was obvious that we could do nothing for Ida Fern and that she had died, reality wanted to soak in, but somehow, we tried to resist it. Surely this is just a dream. How could all this happen so fast and be so final? Why did we sing that song before dismissing? If we had dismissed on time, it would not have happened.

I wrestled with these thoughts for awhile. But kind friends tried to comfort us, reminding us that no, the timing was not off. Instead, it had been perfect timing, because surely God had permitted this to happen.

I am also sure the grief and remorse that I felt was nothing compared to that which Ida's immediate family experienced. Like in school, Ida had been a ray of sunshine in their home— always cheerful and everybody's friend. And now, she was gone so suddenly, without warning or farewell.

On Friday, we tried to have school. Why we attempted it, I'm not sure as things naturally did not go very well. We didn't do many lessons but our church district's song leader, Noah Miller, came and helped us practice a song we were to sing at the funeral. We appreciated that very much.

Wie Sommers schön die Blumen blühn,
Und wie die Rosen prachtvoll stehn,
So blühte hier, o lieber Christ,
Ein Blümchen, das verwelket ist.
Wie himmlisch schön und zierlich stand
Es hier, geschmückt von Gottes Hand,
In diesem Garten in der Zeit,
Und blühte für die Ewigkeit.
Nun nahm's der Herr in's sel'ge Land,
Dort blüht es schön in Jesu Hand
Geschmückt mit Seligkeit und Licht,
Blüht ewig und verwelket nicht.
Darum, ihr Eltern, tröstet euch
Und schauet hin nach Jesu Reich,
Und hört, when Jesus liebreich spricht:
Seid nur getrost und weinet nicht!

Also at the viewing Friday evening, the family requested that the school children sing a few songs. Among others, we sang, "Beautiful Home" and Ida Fern's favorite, "Jesus Never Fails."

On Saturday, after being at Ervin Rays awhile I walked to the schoolhouse. It was report card time but I knew I could not concentrate on averaging report card grades. For some reason, I went to Ida Fern's desk and opened it. There on top of her books lay a small card she had made for her new baby sister Miriam.

On this card, she had written, "Abstain from all appearance of evil. 1 Thess. 5:22." This was part of a memory assignment the older children had memorized earlier. Possibly she copied it from the board at the time.

Inside the card she had written, "What I say unto you, I say unto all, Watch." (Mark 13:37) That verse she must have copied directly from the Bible as I don't remember seeing it anywhere else.

Also in her desk was a gift she had made for me which I will always cherish dearly. How it must have saddened her when she discovered they were no longer allowed to spend as much time making gifts. Possibly she might have wondered if she should go ahead and give me the gift she had made or not.

The funeral was held on Sunday afternoon, February 16, at the Mose Yoder home, by Gilbert Lee Miller of Nappanee and Leonard Miller of the home church. Pallbearers were Ida's teacher and three of the oldest school boys, Jonas Wingard, Elmer Miller, and Maynard Beechy.

While walking past the accident site on the way to the funeral, I found several pieces of Ida's shattered lunch box. I picked them up and put them in my vest pocket where they still are. Even now, I cannot wear that vest without thinking of Ida's cheerful face which was such a bright spot for us in those few months she came to school.

I hope I can always have these memories and remember the final warning she left for us all, "Abstain from all appearance of evil. What I say unto you, I say unto all, Watch."

Crist H. Miller: Jan. 24, 1959 - April 19, 1977

Submitted by: Harold & Elizabeth (Beechy) Miller, Topeka, Indiana

Tuesday, April 19, 1977, was a nice spring day. The girls and I left for my folks, John Beechy's, to spend the day. Harold and Crist, age 18, went to the field to finish sowing oats. They were done by early noon so they had dinner together then Crist got ready to bike to the Topeka Sale Barn where he had just started working four weeks earlier.

He worked from noon until late at night. Since it was so nice he had said, "I think I'll bike to work today." Dad told him to take the buggy since it would be dark by the time he got off work. Crist assured him that he would be OK, he had good lights on his bike. He took his bicycle and left for work. For an unknown reason, Dad watched him go as far as he could be seen, not realizing it was for the last time.

Dad went on with daily work and the girls and I returned home around chore time. We did our chores. Dad remarked how glad he was that he and Crist had been able to get all the oats sown before Crist had left for work. We ate supper, finished our evening things, and I sat and quilted for a while little realizing what the evening would yet bring.

Bedtime came and we retired for the night, falling into a peaceful sleep. Around 11:00 PM I woke up wondering if Crist was home yet. He usually made it home about 10 or 11:00. Just a few minutes later there was a knock on the door.

Our first thoughts were, "Oh, Crist!"

Dad got to the door and saw a policewoman standing outside. She had a flashlight shining on herself so we could see who she was. She, JoAnn Waldron, asked, "Do you have a son Crist who isn't home yet?"

"Yes we do."

She then told us he had been in an accident about a half mile down the road. When we asked where he was now, she said, "Well folks, your son is gone."

Oh, what a shock! My mind just went into a daze. Without this kind of experience, the feeling is unknown.

She and one of Crist's cousins that had come with her, then came inside and offered some kind words.

She told us this was what they call a hit-and-run accident. A car had driven by and the driver had noticed the wrecked bike at the edge of the road. As they turned around to go back, the lights of their car shone right on Crist's body, lying a few feet into the field. They went for help.

The policewoman told us they didn't know yet who had hit him, but they did have some clues. They had found a mirror off a pick-up truck, a headlight and there was some maroon paint on the bike.

They arrested the people involved the next forenoon. It was a man from LaGrange, Indiana, and a woman from Rome City, Indiana. They had both been drinking and were traveling at high rates of speed.

Crist's cousin asked what he could do to help. Our minds were so dazed and we didn't know where to start, but we asked him to tell the neighbors and to let our eight married sons know.

Neighbors and family soon arrived. How could one go on without God, family, friends, and neighbors at such a sorrowful time? Funeral arrangements were made for Saturday, April 23 with viewing on Thursday and Friday. He had been killed instantly from a broken neck and internal injuries.

Lots of friends and relatives from out of state arrived and shared our sorrow, but the ache in our hearts is hard to describe.

The funeral was in the neighbor's barn. It was a very large funeral. Hundreds of young folks attended. God was talking to us all, a reminder to be ready to meet our end since we don't know what tomorrow will bring.

Six of his best friends laid him to rest. It was so hard to part... without a farewell. But God is here to help us through tomorrow if we ask for his help.

Crist had been the youngest son and the only son at home anymore. He helped with the farming. We wondered how we were going to go on without him. We tried our best by ourselves, and by fall we started building another house for one of the other boys to move home.

In March of 1978 we moved into the new house and had a farm sale. There were so many adjustments to make and accept. The house had such an empty spot and he is greatly missed by all. He had had a special touch with the oldest grandchildren, always playing with them and they had always looked forward to seeing their Uncle Crist.

Since the accident happened so close to home, we pass the place often. It is a constant reminder of that sorrowful night.

It is almost 18 years later and still he is not forgotten and never will be, but we would not wish him back into this world of sin and temptations. We hope to all meet again on the Golden Shore where parting and pain are no more.

Naomi Miller: July 30, 1978 - Jan. 20, 1994

Submitted by: David & Linda Miller, Bremen, Indiana

In July of 1989 our second daughter, Naomi, turned 11. She was small for her age which she inherited from her Dad. Until then, she had been a healthy strong girl. We noticed a swelling on the right side of her neck at about this time. We weren't overly concerned since she didn't seem to be sick otherwise and it wasn't really painful.

One of her cousins had an abscess drained several months earlier so we suspected this to be the same. After a week or so we took her to the doctor and he confirmed our theory. He put her on antibiotics for six weeks. When we couldn't see any change after a month, we took her back in. Seeming a little more concerned, the doctor gave her a stronger medicine. He also set up an appointment with an ear, nose, and throat specialist.

This specialist again changed the medication and set up an outpatient appointment to drain the abscess. He assured us he wasn't expecting anything serious, that it was just a matter of not having found the right medication for this kind of infection.

Right before the surgery, they had an older, more experienced doctor examine her, but we still suspected nothing serious. The stronger medicine still hadn't done anything to retard the steadily enlarging swelling. The surgery, expected to last 45 minutes, dragged out to several hours and we started getting concerned.

The anesthesiologist passed through the waiting room and told us they were closing her up and that she had stood the surgery well. He gave us no assurances that all was well, the way others waiting with us had been assured.

Finally our family doctor and the specialist asked us to step into the hall for some privacy. With leaden feet we followed them out to hear the verdict. The specialist told us, "It's something serious, but we don't know what yet," and walked away. Our family doctor was a little more cooperative and explained further. The tumor had stretched from her cheekbone all the way to her collarbone. They had removed all they could and it was being sent out for further testing. They had put in a drainage tube and she was going to have to stay at least overnight.

What a nightmare! We decided to wait until we got back home to break the news to Naomi and the rest of the family. In fact, we waited until a couple of days later when the drainage tube was removed. At that time the specialist confirmed that it was cancer, but still wasn't sure what type.

We then explained it to Naomi in as simple and easy to understand terms as we knew how. We all shed some tears. She then seemed to set her hand to the plow and not look back.

The specialist had done all he could and sent us on to an ontologist in South Bend. He in turn directed us to Riley's Hospital in Indianapolis since she was a child and her cancer was very rare. They diagnosed it as Schwaxnoma, a cancer that works on the nerve coatings.

Based on CAT scans and another examination by their ontologist, it was decided to do follow-up surgery to remove the remaining tumor that had showed up on the CAT scan. They told us that they had gotten everything in that surgery, but we found out later through our family doctor that all they found were enlarged lymph nodes which weren't malignant. This second surgery took place, October 31, 1989.

In January of 1990 we took her back for a checkup. They discovered it was already growing back, this time it was growing inward and already closing off part of the airway We had suspected nothing since there had been no swelling on the outside this time.

They contacted the Mayo clinic and started chemotherapy treatments that very evening. These lasted for five days.

Needless to say these were a long five days for everyone. They had to change IVs several times as the veins collapsed, plus all the blood tests, etc.

They had school classes in the forenoon which Naomi attended whenever possible. She received a notice every time she attended and didn't have to be counted absent for that day in her home school. We found out later she could even have taken her own books and work in there. This all meant a lot to her.

In the afternoons they also had little workshops to do crafts, etc., which were really a highlight for her.

After being home for a week or two, all her hair fell out in big handfuls. This was very hard for her to accept, but luckily we were somewhat prepared for it. We had gone out and bought a wig beforehand.

Three weeks later we again went to Indianapolis for chemo which lasted 24 hours. We were always gone three days with CAT scans, travelling, etc. This time she stayed for five days. She again went in for surgery to put in a central line directly into a main vein in the chest so all her blood work and chemo could be done through this line instead of making a pin cushion out of her.

Coming home after several days in the hospital was always a big event. The doctors and nurses couldn't understand why there was such a fuss over going home, but if they could have seen the welcome she got, they would have understood. Feeling weak and sick after her treatments and the long ride home, she usually ended up on the couch or recliner with the younger children all around seeking out those little treasures from the craft classes, etc.

Many times it was several days before she could enjoy food again. It always seemed as if she was just back in full swing again when the three weeks were up. Then it was down to the bottom again and work her way slowly back up.

We had to clean and change dressings three times a week on her central line and also once a week we drew blood out and took it to the local hospital to do blood work.

After six chemo treatments in Indy we went to South Bend Memorial Hospital for 32 radiation treatments. At first there seemed to not be as serious side effects with this treatment, but towards the last she could not eat as her throat was burned so hard and swollen almost shut. For three days she hardly ate anything and drank only ice water. She was a very sick girl.

In January of 1991, she had her last chemo treatment and all her tests showed clear! What a relief. In April all showed clear again so they removed the central line. Words cannot describe how we all dreaded those checkups and the strain we were under until we had done the tests and seen the doctor.

In February of 1993 we again noticed some swelling in her neck. Making some quick decisions, we decided to go to Mexico for treatments as our medical doctors told us they had no other treatments left to try on her. None of us was anxious to go through chemo again anyway.

We spent a month away from home with traveling time, etc. David traveled out with us then returned home. He came back to bring us home again.

Naomi received an IV six days a week and was put on a special diet. Some friends that we met in Mexico, also patients at the clinic, asked us to go to church with them which we did. Never in my life have I felt such power in prayer. It was almost like having physical contact with friends at home. Knowing that our home church also had services that day I felt certain it was the prayers of friends and family upholding and strengthening us. Later David mentioned how one of the home ministers had requested prayer for us in his message that day. Although we were 2000 miles apart I feel those prayers were certainly answered.

It was soon evident that the tumor was still growing. We tried several other herbs, etc., but nothing seemed to make much difference. In the fall Naomi started taking instruction classes with three of her classmates. By December we could see that she was slowly losing out. She had a bad cough and it was hard for her to lie down and really relax as breathing was so hard.

On January 10, David went to the doctor to get medication for her cough and pain. It seemed to give relief somewhat, but that Sunday in church she had a very rough day. She could hardly breathe with all the people around. In the afternoon she played games with the cousins. That evening after all the children were in bed, Naomi came down from upstairs and was crying. She was very miserable and couldn't lie down because of her cough. She asked, "When will this ever go away?" We tried to comfort her and rubbed her back a while until she was able to relax and get some sleep.

On Tuesday we took her to the doctor, seeking relief for her pain. He gave her a back adjustment and medication for her phlegm and also pills for pain. Most of her pain was in her upper back due to muscle spasms, which were caused by the tumor putting her body into a twist. The treatment seemed to give relief.

Tuesday evening after all the others were in bed Naomi again asked questions about her condition, etc., She said she would rather die than keep on in this misery. We tried to encourage her that death was no dreadful thing if we were ready to die. She expressed her concern about her friends and cousins who were not prepared to die. She then asked David and me for forgiveness for any wrongdoings, etc.

She planned to spend the night on the chair since she couldn't lie down. After instructing her to wake me if she couldn't sleep or needed something I went to bed. At midnight I woke up. She was kneeling in front of the stove trying to sleep. She had been cold sitting on the chair. After returning to bed I heard her praying then I dozed off. At 1 o'clock she called me and wanted her back rubbed. Her voice was just a hoarse whisper and her breathing was very labored. David woke up, too.

At 1:45 we got the other children up as it looked like the end was very near. After all joining hands in prayer, she admonished us all to follow Jesus so we could meet again some day. She told the other children to obey us as parents and do what was right.

Three year old Leann was on my lap, and Naomi took her on her lap and gave her a big hug and kiss and said, "Oh, Leann, I love you!" This was a special thought and comfort for Leann many times in the days and months after Naomi passed away.

David went to the Doddy house to get his Mom and the first thing she said when Mommy came over was, "Mommy, please come to Jesus too." She mentioned some of the cousins and friends and asked us tell them good-bye and thank them for being her friends.

At one time she asked what time it was, then she asked, "How long must I wait yet?" She raised her hands heavenward and said, "Please come." She also asked David to go with her so she wouldn't have to go alone.

During this time we often thought her last breath was sure to be any time. Such gasping and struggling was hard to endure for her and for us. We discussed the thought of having her baptized, not realizing she understood what we had said. We were surprised when she said, "Oh, but I'd like to be baptized yet if possible."

At about 7:00 in the morning Bishop John Helmuth, both grandmothers, Uncle Elis and several others were here and Naomi was baptized. Bishop John and Uncle Eli performed the baptism. Naomi was unable to speak aloud, but seemed to understand all that was going on and answered all the questions in the right way without any earlier instructions. After baptism, we were all amazed to see her get up from the chair and go eat breakfast. What a strengthening she must have received from the baptismal.

Naomi was up and about most of the day. She seemed fairly well except for a while in the afternoon she had problems breathing when quite a few people were here. Some of the family was here for supper and she ate well. After supper, she requested a bath, then played games with the other children.

David took the first shift to be up with her that night. At one time she said something about a hospital and he asked if she wanted to go to the hospital. She said, "No." Later on he heard her say, "Lord, please open that book and read." Had she had a vision?

At 12:00 midnight I was awakened very suddenly as if someone had awakened me, but David said all had been quiet. I believe the Lord woke me up. I had rubbed Naomi's back and helped her to the bathroom twice. Sitting in the recliner, her head just kept drooping forward as she could not sit back and put her feet up.

As I supported her head with my hands, she let out a slow deep sigh and then all was quiet. Life had fled with no struggle, no gasping for breath. It came unexpectedly as she had not struggled and gasped for breath like she had the night before. It was almost exactly

24 hours after getting the children up the night before that we got them up again and all was over.

To some it may sound cruel and unkind, but truly we could say, "What a blessing!" Yes, the parting was just as hard, but never could we wish her back.

It was a blessing to see her resting and relaxed. The undertaker was able to remove most of the tumor with no visible cuts or other signs. He removed a three to four pound tumor from the side of her neck, which also made her look more peaceful and relaxed.

Many times the questions come and we wonder why, but we don't want to question the Lord's way. Our goal is to strive to go where we have a good *hoffnung* that our daughter has gone.

Rosanna Miller: Sept. 19, 1947 - Oct. 23, 1956
Edna Miller: June 19, 1950 - June 10, 1986
Freeman Miller: June 28, 1951 - Mar. 10, 1972
Lloyd Miller: June 25, 1954 - May 23, 1992

Submitted by Ervin C. & Sarah Miller

Rosanna

Ervin and I were married November 12, 1946. We were blessed with 5 children. Rosanna was born September 19, 1947. She was a dwarf, but was healthy until August 1952 when she became sick with polio and was very helpless, but it did not affect her mind. She was in the hospital in South Bend for nine weeks. She was in the iron lung part of the time, so we were not allowed into her room for the first few weeks. They fitted her with a body brace and long leg braces. She gained enough strength in her forearm that she could eat by herself and do school work with a homebound teacher. She also went to the Rehab Center in Elkhart.

She became very sick with chicken-pox and pneumonia and died October 23, 1956.

Edna

Edna was born June 19, 1950, also a dwarf. She became sick the same night as Rosanna with polio. She went to the Rehab Center and learned to walk with crutches, being in a body brace and long leg braces. We needed to give both girls exercises twice a day and also some hot baths.

In January 1962 she had a spinal fusion on half of her back. She was to have the rest done two weeks later. When they took her for surgery, they discovered a staph infection. What a let-down.

She was put in isolation for nine weeks and had to wait until September to have the surgery. When she was about ready to come home they changed her cast to straighten her more and again she had a staph infection and another long stay in isolation. They had to remove some of the bone that was used to fuse. She was in a body cast for one and a half years.

At one time she had an office job and also made bonnets and coverings for other people. She was hospitalized a number of times and had several more surgeries, one for a pinched nerve in 1982. This made her back completely stiff.

After this her health seemed to decline. She had a hard cough and lost a lot of weight. She went to the Cleveland Clinic and was diagnosed as having bronchitis. Antibiotics did not seem to help. She was on oxygen from February to June 10 when she peacefully passed away. We would advise everyone to have their children vaccinated for polio.

Freeman

Freeman was born June 28, 1951, a healthy baby. On March 9, 1972, our son Freeman went to work as usual at Jayco. He came home for dinner and back to work. Before quitting time he came home and informed us they wanted him to go with Jayco's president, Lloyd Bontrager to their other plant at Harper, Kansas.

In the early evening they left with a single engine plane loaded with supplies. He had had a local plane ride once, after which he had said he didn't want to go up in one again, but he gave in and went. We feel he did a lot of praying on the trip.

They stopped in Missouri to refuel and they failed to fill the one tank. Before reaching their destination they ran out of fuel and crashed into a sludge pond near an oil well near Conway Springs, Kansas. Oh, the agony they must have gone through. The wreckage was not found until the next morning.

On the morning of March 10, two men from Jayco came to tell us the plane had crashed and they will soon be back to take us to

Lloyd's home as they will call to give details. When the call came we received the shocking news that Freeman was gone and Lloyd was seriously injured.

Freeman's body arrived at our home on Sunday, March 12. Many friends showed their last respects by coming to the viewing. The funeral was held March 14 with coworkers as pallbearers. We could feel that many prayers were being sent heavenward for our family.

Joe was born January 17, 1953, grew up and married Ida Ellen Borntrager November 8, 1973. He lives on the farm near us. They have three children.

Lloyd

Lloyd was born June 25, 1954. He married Ruth Lambright on May 10, 1973, and was killed May 23, 1992, as he was riding his bike to work at Jayco. He was hit by a van. Their two girls were 13 and six years old at the time of his death. We are so thankful for family that God has spared and for the support and prayers in our afflictions. We hope to meet our loved ones on yonder shore. Precious memories how they linger.

Ida Mae Miller: Jan. 25, 1988 - Mar. 16, 1994

Submitted by Mose and Katie Miller

On March 16, I went to help get ready for church at our neighbors, Sam Masts. The children went to school through March and on Wednesday the kindergarten class met so Ida Mae went to school. When I came home it was chore time and Mose had gone to a feed meeting so we hurried and chored.

Mose's sister which lived in the trailer had made supper for us so we ate and were done for the evening. She lived in the same lawn, just ten feet from our house in a house trailer. The oil lamp was empty so I filled it. Mose didn't have a flashlight along so I lit the oil lamp when we came up. We had it lit for at least an hour before I went to bed.

I was in bed for about half an hour when all of a sudden I heard him come in the door and say, "Oh! No!" I came out of the bedroom and saw the dresser outside our bedroom was all in flames. I had put the lamp on that dresser.

He got a fire extinguisher to try to put it out, but it didn't help any. I went upstairs to get the children. I just took them out of their beds and when we came down the stairs, the front of the house was all in flames. Mose had tried to just put the oil lamp out and had dropped it on the floor. The couch started to burn so he went to put the couch outside, but it got stuck in the doorway. It was a windy evening so the burning sofa was like a torch.

When I came down with the children I told them to get out through the basement and go to Anna's. It wasn't far from our basement door to her trailer. When I came out Anna asked where Ida Mae was.

I asked, "Isn't she out?"

She said, "No!!"

So I went back to the basement, but couldn't get in. When I was coming down from upstairs I had heard her say, "Mom." I had told her go down through the basement and never again did I hear her. Oh! What a feeling.

I ran onto the back porch thinking I could maybe get in the back door, but flames were coming from the windows already then. Mose ran down the lane and stopped the van that had dropped off the neighbor man. So he went back and got the neighbor to call the fire department.

The van came back. The lady got out and told us we would have to go out to another building since it was too dangerous to stay in the trailer. One of the neighbors went up onto the roof to try and get in the upstairs window, but was too hot. He had to come back down.

After what seemed like forever, it was actually probably 45-60 minutes, the fire trucks got there. Our house was mostly down and on Doddy's house the siding was burned on the outside. About five minutes later the fire was going all the way through it.

They had carried everything out of the trailer down to some of the dressing clothes as smoke was coming in through the wall and the insulation in the door was melting out.

Mose's parents were in Florida so we had to call them. They started for home yet that night. The children were taken to the neighbors after the squad crew had checked them out at around 11:30-12:00. At 1:00 in the morning they took me to the hospital to treat me for smoke inhalation. I came back home that night yet around 2:30.

They had started looking for her body before I left for the

hospital and found it at 3:00. According to the reports she was found with a toy angel at her side. We did not have a toy angel, but did have a glass angel that was on the other side of the house in the bathroom.

We will leave that up to God as God's ways are far above ours. A mile or two cross-country they had heard an angel singing in the night.

After they found her body, my mother, Mose, and I went to neighbors for the rest of the night. We stayed at neighbor Henry M. Troyer's until after the funeral. We all moved into the trailer then until the house were rebuilt.

The funeral was on Friday. On Saturday morning a carpenter came and wanted us to go see the house he was building and if we would take that pattern he would already have a blue print ready.

On Sunday we went to church and came home to a yard full of people. There were people coming and going all afternoon and evening until dark. On Monday it rained all day and in the afternoon they cleaned up and dug out for a new house. By Saturday there was a roof on our house. A month later we moved into the house. What a change.

We just took it a day at a time. That is the only way you can get through. We just felt so unworthy for all the help, but that was the only way we would have a house. Just thinking about it still makes me feel weak.

Rachel Stoltzfoos: Aug. 27, 1989 - Mar. 14, 1994

Submitted by: Ammon & Lavina Stoltzfoos, Clarksville, Tennessee

This is our story of Rachel, our oldest daughter who was given to us to care for, for four and a half years.

In May of 1993 she was run over by two horses. First one knocked her down and then the second one stepped on her chest, giving her a collapsed lung. She quit breathing but her daddy was right there. He worked on her then grabbed her up and ran for the house slapping her back and finally got her going again with short gasps for lack of oxygen.

We did not know if she would make it until the ambulance came, but the thought of losing our lively and happy little girl was almost unbearable then. She seemed to be conscious all the time. They put her on oxygen and a breathing machine and sent her to a hospital fifty miles away. She stayed on the breathing machine for five days and recovered fast after that. She was home again within two weeks and was soon as healthy as before.

That time God spared her for us, which we were quite thankful for. Then close to a year later the death angel came to our home and took her away suddenly without a chance for us to say farewell.

It was a nice and sunny spring day, she was wearing a short sleeved dress and boots over her shoes even though it was nice and dry. The daffodils were in full bloom. She wrapped her doll in a white blanket and held it tight and came over toward me with a big smile. She said no words that I remember, then left the house. That last smile has been so precious to me already! I have often wondered what she had in her mind.

About fifteen minutes later I missed her and wanted to go look for her but it slipped my mind. That was about the time we believe an angel came for her when nobody was around. Maybe that was a message for me. She was used to playing for hours outside without me missing her much.

Around 2:50 she was found by our neighbor boy under a cattle gate that was only tied at the bottom. It had fallen over on her, breaking her neck. He removed the gate and ran for the ambulance, even though he realized she might be gone.

In the meantime our youngest son came upon her on his way home from school. He saw Daniel remove the gate so he realized something serious was wrong for she did not answer when he spoke to her. He ran to the house and told me something happened with Rachel. I jumped up and ran as fast as I could with my crutches.

I expected this to be her death, but why?? For Ammon it was the opposite, he figured he could get her going, just like he had a year earlier. So he worked on her, but all in vain.

I was ready to let her go rather than see her suffer again. But oh, how final it felt when someone said she is partly cold already. Could this actually be true. It was hard to think properly. Did this actually happen to one of our own children? It usually happened to others and now it seemed that if it happened once, it could easily happen again.

We took her to the house. The ambulance came and they said, "There's nothing we can do."

On the way to the house I thought of what she had said only about a week earlier. She had come to me and said, "Mom, I can't wait to go to heaven."

She had said it so eagerly it gave me an uneasy feeling, but I tried to pass it off by thinking nothing would happen to her so soon after her hospital stay. I told nobody about this because I felt so uneasy, but could not pass it off after that day. She said more such things that we now wonder why we didn't expect her to leave us before it happened with such a shock.

I guess we just tried to wipe it out. I like to think it was heaven's gate she saw there. She used to be so fond of flowers, that day Reuben had a bouquet in his hand for her when he came to her on his way home from school. The day before she had really begged to go along to church while I had to stay with sick Linda. This was unusual. She usually stayed home if I didn't go.

She had said things to her friends like, "I wonder how heaven looks."

One of her friends said, "When I go I'm going to take my toys along."

To this Rachel had replied, "It's so nice we need no toys."

Did she have a vision of heaven? Now our part is to be thankful the Lord took her to that beautiful home where she longed to go and prepare ourselves to meet her some sweet day. Could we really be so lucky? Let us be thankful even at times when homesickness is really taking its course. Our Lord knows what's best, so let us say, "Thy will be done."

I know some days it was hard to do, and God's ways were hard to understand, but he has healed many broken hearts already. We never realized a cattle gate could be so dangerous. Close by was a big set of stairs that went up to some oil tanks and also a water trough close by that the men had moved elsewhere because of children. God moves in mysterious ways, His wonders to perform.

"Keep on believing God answers prayers. Keep on believing He's still up there. Trials and sorrows will soon disappear. Nothing can harm you when Jesus is near. Keep on believing the storm will pass. Look for the rainbow, 'twill come at last; trust in His promise, 'Twas written for you. Keep on believing and pray your way through."

This is being written over two years after she passed from our sight and we still miss her a lot, of course some days more than others, depending what we have going. Time does heal. God healed things we usually thought would always remain without Rachel.

Nobody will ever take the place of her. A little girl was added to our family in December after Rachel's death. She did bring much joy to our life, but we have a special place in our hearts for each one of our children and that one spot is still empty. We have many precious memories and we treasure them all.

She had made some greeting cards that day and they were still on the table when we came back into the house with her. Two were marked for her friends. I had broken my leg in January and was still in a cast. Now I feel it was a blessing since I had lots of time with Rachel in her last days on earth. She spent a lot of time on my lap, especially when we had company. My arms have ached to hold her many times since.

God has helped us through it all, and we do not regret to have had such an experience. Here is our story. It was not an easy task to give it out to be published. We did it in hopes others will do the same.

Barbara Yoder: Mar. 18, 1976 - Jan. 22, 1981

Submitted by: Willis & Lizzie Yoder, Dundee, Ohio

Barbara was one of our healthiest children, we thought! She walked at nine months and ate well, but in the summer of 1980 in July, her tan seemed to fade and she started turning pale. She had always had a dark complexion. Her nose bled off and on. Sometimes during the night she would come and wake me and say her nose was going to bleed. Then it would.

In September I took her to one of our friends, someone who knows herbs, etc. He took hold of her hand and said, "Please don't act like one woman, but this little girl has leukemia."

My heart almost fell apart, but with God's strength I went home and told the rest about Barbara. No, it wasn't easy.

I gave her the medicine he gave me for one week and she started to have a high fever of 105° - 106°. This was good because the body was starting to fight it off. During the first two evenings I gave her eldaflower and peppermint tea and the fever eased a little. The third evening I gave her baby aspirin, which was the wrong thing to give her. I didn't know it at the time but it made her blood so thin. At four o'clock in the morning her nose bled for one hour. How I wished I hadn't given her aspirin. I sponged her off with cool water and the blood stopped for a little while. All of a sudden she coughed and big clots came from her mouth. She went limp and slipped into a coma. I took her out on the porch. I was almost numb. I called her name and very weakly she said, "Yes."

We took her to the hospital and they could hardly find any blood. They tried the third place and finally they got some. Her blood count was down to three. She was very weak. They gave her several units of blood.

This was on a Saturday morning and it took until noon before they found the right type of blood that she needed. Sunday morning came and the doctors said to take her to Akron Children's Hospital. It was a very dreary and rainy day, especially for the rest of the family; two boys Maynard, ten; Wayne, two; and four girls, Linda, nine; Esther, eight; Laura, six; and Ina, three. Sister Anna and her husband took us up.

Now Barbara could walk again. The children just couldn't understand why we couldn't just take her home with us. Monday morning came and a spinal tap was taken which wasn't easy. The first time I wasn't allowed to go along, but the next few times I was. Barbara didn't even move, and I told her Jesus will help you so it won't hurt so bad. She didn't even cry and held so still that Dr. Krill said if you count to ten I'll try and be done. She quickly started to count and the doctor said slower, slower. Oh, if we only had faith like a child.

On Monday afternoon Dr. Krill told us it is leukemia. He asked if we were giving her something because it looked like the bad cells were started to fall off. That was the only time he mentioned it. He then started chemo. He was a very special doctor and very easy to get along with. We were in the hospital for two weeks, but chemo didn't seem to take hold and send it into remission.

We asked if we could take her home over Sunday. Dr. Krill said we could take her home and bring her back Wednesday. On Wednesday we asked him if we could try and take care of her at home. He said we could. Our family doctor said he would help us if she needed blood transfusions.

We gave her a lot of vitamins and minerals. Lots of fruits and vegetables, fish, and chicken. Reflexology was given twice a week. Barbara had lost some of her hair in the back, but it was growing back and was about one and one half inches long again.

We took her to Columbus to a clinic where they gave us things to give her. My sister Esther (thanks to the good Lord for sisters) came down every day to help us with the work in the house because I had a lot of things to do with Barbara. She was never hard to take care of. She was just weak and wished we would leave her alone.

One day as I was working with her I asked her, "Do you want to go be with Jesus where all the children are well again?" She looked at me and said, "Yes, I want to go."

Oh, it was so hard to ask her but I could see she was getting weaker and weaker. "Thy will be done and not mine. God's ways are always best."

The last time we took her to the hospital I was sitting by her bedside waiting for blood. A doctor came in and checked her a little. He took off his coat and checked her again, then started running down the hall. I quickly went after him and he said your daughter could go into convulsions any moment. I was so scared and I didn't want to stay by myself. I called home and asked someone to come up and stay with me. Barbara didn't have any convulsions then and I was so glad. By evening we took her home. There was blood slowly seeping from one of her nostrils.

On Saturday, January 17th she again slipped into a coma. Then on Sunday evening around 12 o'clock, she was lying right beside me in bed and she called out "Mom."

I said, "Barbara, you can talk."

She said, "Yes."

I couldn't believe it. It was so nice to hear her voice again.

On January 21, sister Esther insisted she should stay overnight, so I let her stay. At two o'clock in the morning Esther asked if she could hold Barbara for a while. All of a sudden Barbara sat up straight, held out her hand and said there is something on my hand. She said it three times in less than five minutes. I think an angel must have touched her.

At four o'clock she asked to go to the bathroom and wanted water to drink. She took three swallows and it sounded like it just fell when she swallowed. Then I carried her into the living room and put her on her bed. As I put her down, her little hands fell back and she had sort of a smile on her sweet little face.

Life had fled so easily, but oh, so, so final. I can still see the children come out of bed to Barbara's side while I held her for a half hour after she passed away.

We will never forget that morning. Yes, safe in the arms of Jesus, where we all long to meet her some sweet day.

Emma Sue Bontrager: Apr. 22, 1989 - Sept. 30, 1995

Submitted by: Amos E. & Nora Bontrager, Shipshewana, Indiana

It was Saturday, September 30. Nothing unusual that morning. We were busy as usual with Saturday cleaning and I decided to can grape juice that day. The younger children were busy at play. Amos had gone to town in the morning, and when he came home he decided to do some grinding yet before dinner. Our dinner was late, but we were all at home that day. The two oldest girls often worked, at least one of them, on Saturday. But we were all at home to enjoy our last meal together!

After dinner Amos wanted to go load up a load of firewood and take it to our school. The weather was perfect to do it. Of course, when Daddy went somewhere the children wanted to go along too. Our only son Levi Ray, then 15, always got to go along and help, even if he didn't want to! Three of the younger girls also went along. Lovina, age nine; Emma, age six; and Irene, age four.

They loaded up the wagon with what they needed, then started down the road to a neighbor's woods where they were getting it since we didn't have woods of our own. The older girls saw them leave and decided to wave good bye and they waved back. Finally they were waving with their two little hands. Our oldest daughter, Rachel, decided to just watch and wave a little longer and Emma Sue was the only one waving back by then. The wind had caught her white handkerchief on her head which stood on end and Rachel had a "precious" last picture of her on her way to meet the Lord on high.

They drove back the lane and the woodpile was right there so they just circled the pile. Amos, Lovina, and Emma started loading up. Emma was right there doing her part of picking up. They hadn't been there very long when all of a sudden the one horse was spooked and started to go and the other older horse went with him. They had heard the bump, bump, of the neighbor's wagon as they drove from one side of the field to the other while husking corn.

Amos' first thought was to get those horses stopped before they ran away. He ran up the woodpile, jumped into the wagon and got hold of the reins when suddenly he had this "sinking feeling" that one of the children might be under the wagon. He remembered passing one of the girls on his way up to the wagon and the youngest, Irene, he had helped get dirt out of her eyes just minutes before and had set her on a chair. Levi Ray had been on the other side of the wagon splitting wood, and when the wagon went he walked over to the wood pile not knowing what was going on. All of a sudden he came upon Emma Sue and he just yelled, "Oh Dad!" which Amos heard while he was getting the horses under control.

Oh, my! Such a sight to behold! Our darling little Emma. This can't be happening to us, but it was and it was real, no dream that we could wake up from. She was bleeding, so-o-o-o fast, out of her nose, mouth, and ears. Without realizing what he was doing, Levi picked her up and laid her on the ground because she was kind of lying across a big chunk of wood on her side. Amos came and picked her up, she still had a faint heartbeat and was breathing some, which gave him some hope until he noticed her eyes. Oh my! They looked so lifeless.

The neighbors ran for help right away and they also came and got me. Such a shock! Just an hour or so before we had all been together and everything was all right. How fast things can change.

The ambulance got there just a little bit before we did and already life had fled. She was finished. We believe it was instant since she didn't move or respond in any way and her eyes had that lifeless look right away. The ambulance people asked us if they should take her along and try some more, but we wondered what her chances were. They said there's a good chance that she is brain dead. We didn't want them to try anymore because we knew it was pretty well useless.

She looked so peaceful, except for the blood. She looked almost like she was okay until you noticed the eyes. We were so thankful that the wagon wheel hadn't gone over her head. She had died of a broken neck, crushed chest, and also had a broken leg where the wagon wheel had gone over her. She looked like an angel in her coffin. So pure, so innocent.

But oh, the heartache. The pain of losing one so dear! Now what? Things like this happened to other people. Wishing it could have been a dream, but no, this was real. Our darling Emma Sue had gone to be with Jesus. Jesus needed another rosebud to fill His bouquet. Oh yes, we miss her. How we miss her!

She was so full of life. A healthy, very husky little girl and she was Daddy's girl when he was at home. She usually sat with him in church whenever she could. She had a birthmark on her nose and between her eyebrows, so she was a little different from our other children right at birth. It seemed people noticed her more, for some reason people remember Emma Sue. Maybe this was the Lord's way, since Emma's mission here on earth was to be so short.

Yes, when we think of all she might have had to go through on this earth with trials and temptations, we certainly wouldn't want to wish her back and it is a joy to think she is *safe in the arms of Jesus.* Yes, we feel she made it *safely home.* Our hopes and prayers are to meet her some day in that *beautiful home* and gather at *Jesus' feet.* What joy that will be!

This is something to go through and know we couldn't have if the good Lord would not have been there to help us.

> *The call was sudden, the shock severe.*
> *Little did we know her end was so near,*
> *Only those who have lost, can tell,*
> *The sadness of parting without a farewell.*

Paul Burkholder: June 26, 1983 (Date of tragedy)

Submitted by: Aaron Burkholder, Fleetwood, Pennsylvania

June 25, 1983, had such a beautiful sunrise. It was clear and cool for June. My wife and I had just traveled home from my wife's parents, 40 miles from our home. They are John O. Weavers from Lancaster Co., Penn., and we live in Berks County, Penn. We as children were taking turns to care for them. Grandma was bedfast and worn out, although she had no pain known to us.

Some friends had traveled with us and on the way home a remark was made that we could expect Grandma to pass on to eternity any time. Yes we could, but I said, so often you hear of a sudden death of someone to go so suddenly in his youth and the older ones are left. How true. Less than 24 hours later, it happened in our family.

Our son, Paul, had spent four weeks in Ohio helping with farm work and had just come home for the funeral of Esther Nolt (Aaron), our minister's wife, on May 30. Four weeks later on June 30, was his own funeral.

When we came home from Grandpa Weavers, Paul was getting ready for the young folks' singing and was combing his hair in front of the mirror. He had to stoop to look in and Mother asked Paul, "Where are you growing?" Paul was the tallest of our nine sons.

Before going to Ohio, he was working in the barn with his older brothers and they were talking about our plans of building a retirement house in the near future. Paul casually answered, "Oh, they will probably change their plans yet."

Very little did we realize just what he meant or what his thoughts were at the time. Yes, to the comment made on the way home about how sometimes God calls a youth suddenly. God called in our home.

Sunday morning dawned bright and clear although a bit cool for June 26. We all got ready for church and on the way to church, Paul, with a few neighbor boys, passed us and we later found out Paul had a great desire to go swimming in the afternoon. Later in church when the door opened and the grown boys entered, Paul was the first one to come in, which seemed unusual.

After church we had dinner at a friend's home and started home early since we had to do the chores alone because our sons all had plans for supper. When we were ready to start the chores the phone rang. After answering the phone, someone asked if we knew where Paul was this afternoon.

"Yes, he had been with a cousin for dinner."

Next I heard my wife say, "Not Paul. What happened?"

"He was swimming and is still in the water."

Our bodies were never prepared for such a crushing blow. Stormy tears and upset stomachs followed. What should we do next? How thankful to know God and feel him close at such times. Our prayers were 'Thy will be done' and again our human thoughts, 'It can't be true.'

A kind neighbor offered to take me seven miles to the deep waters of a quarry. When we arrived the rescue squad and firemen were already there. Paul's body was still 15 feet below water. One fireman swam out and dove down but came up without Paul. He swam back in and said he needed a boat to go out to the spot and then dive again. He was in the water about an hour until they finally got his body out. A very long waiting time.

Next, they asked if anyone could identify him.

I said, "Yes, I'm sure it is my son Paul."

Oh, what a difference from him walking into church that morning to this lifeless body with his discolored face. His lips were blue and looked so cold.

Neighbors and friends gathered at the home in the evening to do chores and plan for the funeral. What a great change in a short time. Grandpa, age 89, and Grandma, age 86, Burkholder (Ezra) came. Grandpa remarked, "If only I could have taken his place."

"Yes," I said, "but it was not God's plan."

We had a very restless night with no sleep. All I had on my mind was the scene of the cold, lifeless, blue body and the thoughts he must have had when he called for help and no one came to help. Then another thought entered my mind, when God called, Paul had a view of a better home prepared in that mansion beyond the blue. That was a peace which passes all understanding.

Neighbors brought meals, but our appetite was not so great. They also furnished the meal the day of the funeral. Many thanks to all who helped in this and in prayers.

When the undertaker brought his body a few days later, he looked so natural, just as if he were sleeping. So different from the day he was taken from the still water. A visiting minister said it took the deep still water to fulfill God's plan.

June 30, the day of the funeral, was the most beautiful day with a large crowd attending from Virginia, Indiana, Ohio, Canada, New York, and different counties in Pennsylvania.

Grandma Weaver lingered on. When told of Paul she, in a low tone, asked if he drowned. She died in December 1983. Grandpa Weaver died in August 1984. Grandpa (Ezra) Burkholder died in 1987. Grandma Burkholder is still with us at the age of 98. If the Lord permits she will be 99 on November 17, 1996, and still patiently waiting.

We stood by the grave four times in four and a half years. We have been reminded that the old must die and the young can die, too. Grief needs time to heal the wound. Tears are for healing in a language God understands. Accepting is a battle that must be fought in our hearts many times. The experience of this happening we would not give up for anything and many thanks for prayers, cards, and letters from known and unknown friends in Christ. Life had to go on, but there were days that were not as easy as others to get started on our daily routine because of the missing link in the family chain.

God calls His own and this time Paul answered.

Jesus, while our hearts are bleeding,
O'er the spoils that death has won,
We would at this solemn meeting,
Calmly say, "Thy will be done."

Though cast down, we're not forsaken,
Though afflicted, not alone.
Thou didst give and thou has taken,
Blessed Lord, "Thy will be done."

By Thy hands the loom was given.
Thou has taken but thine own.
Lord of earth and God of heaven,
Evermore, "Thy will be done."

Dennis Ray Lambright: Mar. 3, 1964 - Mar. 19, 1973

Submitted by: Luetta Lambright, Shipshewana, Indiana (A sister)

It was a cold, but sunny afternoon on March 19, 1973. It was a Monday morning that started out as any normal day, except it was a very calm day after the winter snowstorm we had over the weekend. The roads were still closed and no one was moving about except a few who wanted to brave the drifts and see what our winter wonderland looked like.

Dad had gone to work on foot, while Mom, Dennis, Norm, and I were at home, kept inside by the snow. Around noon cheers were heard as big payloaders came through opening the roads. We were free. No longer held captive by the drifts. For two boys, Norm, age six, and Dennis, age nine, with lots of energy, this meant it was time to go outdoors and get rid of some of their never ending energy. They decided to go over to their neighbor friend, Eugene Yoder, across the fields a little ways, with Mom's consent, to play for a few hours.

Mom and I were just about the house doing this and that when our neighbor lady came speeding into the driveway. Fear clutched our hearts as she came running in, saying, "Dennis fell into the pond. Come quick."

We rushed around to go with her. When we got there, Dad was already there. Dennis had fallen into the tiny little pond, but it was too late. He had already gone home to be with Jesus.

Dennis, Norman, and Eugene had walked back to this little pond, which wasn't frozen over because of the little spring in it. There was a hard crust of snow blown over it part ways. The boys were standing on it, throwing snowballs into the pond watching them melt without a care in the world. Norm turned and walked away. He heard something crash and looked around. The crust had broken off where Dennis was standing and he fell in. Norm and Eugene panicked, they wanted to help but didn't know what to do. Dennis said, "Grab my hand."

Norm knelt down and reached as far as he could, but they only touched fingers and then he floated away. Then Norm decided to run up for help. He looked back once more and saw Dennis, his hands lifted up to the sky, head bowed, as if meeting Jesus.

The next few days were sad and seemed so unreal. Our hearts all aching with the thought of what lies ahead. It was hard to grasp that yesterday we were all together as a family and today one has gone, the circle now incomplete. Such heartache, but we knew God knows best and that hopefully someday we may all be together again.

Joseph M. Wickey: 1976 - Dec. 10, 1982

Submitted by: Mr. & Mrs. David Wickey, New Haven, Indiana

It was December 9, 1982, and all were settled in bed for the night. Joseph, the second youngest of ten children, was saying his nighttime prayers and when he finished he asked, "Mom, is this enough?" Then he said another short prayer. 'Aller augen varten auf dich, O Herr, und du giebst ihnen ihre Speise zu seiner zeit und du tuest deine milde hand auf und sättigtst alles vas du liebst mit wohlgefallen. Amen', and fell asleep.

Around midnight he woke up and stood at our bedside and said he can't sleep and he's scared. So Dad slid over and he finished the night with Dad and Mom. Next morning, December 10, everyone was up and about and nothing was unusual except a severe ice storm during the night and everything was a glare of ice.

After breakfast they all left for work and I wanted to finish my morning work so I could take our youngest, baby James, two and a half years old, to the doctor. I was going to leave Joseph at my sister-in-law's till I got back, but he didn't want to go. I don't know why, because I always left them there when I went to the doctor or elsewhere and they never said anything. Did he feel something we didn't know about or what? Then he wanted to play a game of Carom with me. I said I can't right now because I have to get my work done first. Our oldest daughter, who was waiting for her driver to go towork, took time out and played two games with him.

Elmer, Wilma, William, and Michael went out to wait for the bus. Joseph put on his coat and straw hat and boots and went out with the rest to watch for the bus. He didn't go to school yet, but they were all excited about the ice. All at once Joseph darted out onto the road to slide on the ice and didn't see the scout jeep coming. He fell on the ice and tried to get up and away, but it was too late and the jeep couldn't stop and dragged him 75 to 100 feet.

Life fled so suddenly.

The school children came running to the house just a screaming and trying to open the door and it seemed they just couldn't open that door. I quickly went to see what was wrong and when I opened up the door they said that Joseph got hit by a car. Then I saw him lying on the road.

When I got to him he was bleeding from his nose and ears and I could see there was no life. I picked him up and carried him to the porch. I took off his boots and hat and covered him up with a blanket till the ambulance arrived. They worked on him for quite a while and said he's got a strong heartbeat. Dad was notified at work that one of his boys was hit by a car and to come to the hospital at once.

I went with the ambulance. We went about five miles and then they called for another ambulance and they transferred Joseph to the other ambulance. I got to the hospital before Joseph did. It seemed like a long time till he came in.

When I arrived at the hospital we were both taken into a prayer room by the nurses until the ambulance arrived with Joseph. They didn't travel fast because of the ice, but soon after they arrived, three doctors came into our room with tears and said they did all they could for him, but life had fled. They said we could go to his room if we wished.

He was lying there so peaceful and he went on to a better land where we all hope to go someday. We received many encouraging letters after the accident. In one letter it was stated, "I just think you now have a family started in heaven."

This is a poem that has been encouraging for us.

On the wings of death and sorrow,
God sends us new hope for tomorrow,
And in His mercy and His grace,
He gives us strength to bravely face
The lonely days that stretch ahead,
And to know our loved one is not dead,

But only sleeping and out of sight,
And we'll meet in that land where there is no night.

Reuben A. Yoder: Aug. 1, 1983 - June 13, 1994

Submitted by: Amos Yoder, Sugarcreek, Ohio

June 13, 1994, is a day that is imprinted in our memory forever. The day started as usual with the morning chores. Reuben took a bucket of milk to the milk house, then came running back all excited. "Dad, there are two little owls sitting on the garden fence. When I got close they flew up in the tree. Now they are making sounds like the tree limb is breaking."

I walked out with him and sure enough, there on the garden fence sat two little owls. When we got close they flew back up in the tree again.

I didn't make the connection at the time, but we refer to the owl as the wise old owl. Also we have a plaque on the wall that gives the definition for Reuben. 'Behold a Son'. The father of the righteous shall greatly rejoice; and he that begets wise children shall have joy in them. Proverbs 23:24.

After breakfast Aden, age 19, went to his job at Balco Machine. The rest of the family went strawberry picking. It was a beautiful day and there were lots of berries to pick. At approximately 10:30 we were running out of boxes, so I sent Reuben to the house to bring more boxes. I can still see him like it was yesterday, "Dad, where do you want these boxes?"

I looked up and there he was coming with a large stack of boxes high above his head, pretending he was an airplane. He had a big smile on his face, which was so natural for him. After we gathered the berries and went back to the house there were customers to wait on and berries to deliver. I had a driver to deliver some berries. When I came back, the boys were all taking a nap. I also flopped down and took a short nap. When I awoke, the boys were out in the yard playing.

We had a steel gate that was bent from a colt jumping over it. So we took the gate up to the shop and straightened it out. I held hands with Reuben and Wayne as we jumped around on one end while Adam tried to stay on the other end. We were all laughing as we tried to keep our balance. Afterwards I told Adam to take Reuben and Wayne along with him and go down across the road from the barn and put up a battery fence so we could let the horses out. The fence had been down for road repair.

I walked back to our kennel and started to feed the dogs when all of a sudden the door flew open and Adam said, "Reuben was killed!"

I asked "What happened?"

"A van ran over him."

As we ran down to the accident site, I had in mind to check for a pulse, but when I walked up to him I saw that he was way beyond that. As the family gathered, I told someone to go get a sheet to cover him. I didn't want the children to see his face, because it was pretty bad.

Reuben and Wayne had always been very close. I cannot remember them ever having a fight or disagreement. Wayne cried very hard until I took him in my arms and explained to him that Reuben is no longer in that body but is safe in heaven with Jesus.

His response was, "I want to go there, too!"

"Yes," I said, "We all want to, but we have to wait until Jesus comes for us."

I'm convinced when we get to heaven we will know Reuben as it tells us in I Corinthians 15:49.

The boys were putting up the fence when Adam told Wayne to go ask Dad where to fasten the fence at the bottom end. Adam came up to the shop for more tools, and Reuben waited by the roadside until they came back. A van came down the hill, lost control, hit Reuben, went through a fence, and came to a stop against a tree.

The driver said Reuben was standing with his back against a fence post. He was concentrating on getting his van under control and did not see Reuben until he was almost upon him. He hit Reuben, flipped him head over heels and dragged him 17 feet. Reuben was lying on his belly with his head slightly turned sideways.

When I came down the driver was walking around shaking his head and saying, "No! No! No!" While we waited for somebody to bring a sheet, I noticed a jagged piece of board under Reuben's face. I lifted his head and the driver pulled it out. After Susie brought a sheet we covered him up and also folded it up like a cushion and put it under his face.

We talked to the driver and asked his name. We talked to him a little bit, but then he stood by the fence with his head in his hands. After the emergency squad arrived, they treated him for shock.

We waited two hours for the coroner, but could not locate him.

Finally an attorney came to give them permission to move Reuben. I told the ladies on the squad if Reuben's face looks better on the other side we want to view him before they go. After they loaded him on the stretcher one lady came over to us and said, "You can come look at him if you want, but it's not much better."

She then asked Lydian, "Are you the mother?"

Lydian said, "Yes."

The lady said, "Please, do not go."

My parents and I went over and took a look, but it was not good. One of the cops came by and said they needed us over in his car to answer some questions. After we were done, we talked with the driver again and told him that we held no bad feelings against him.

We then went up to the house. One of the hardest parts was when the undertaker brought Reuben back in a sealed casket. He said, "Do not open it. I treated him with strong chemicals and wrapped him in plastic." He said practically every bone in his body was broken.

That first night I did not sleep at all. Lydian slept a little bit. The next morning I got up, dressed, and walked out the door. I was thinking I could get some relief if I could take a walk. But as I crossed the yard, there on the garden fence, sat the two little owls. Memories from the day before came flooding back.

I realized then and there that there was no escape. I walked back to the porch swing and prayed, "God grant me the serenity to accept the things I cannot change, courage to change the things I can, and the wisdom to know the difference."

When the casket came back sealed, my dad had a hard time to accept it. He asked, "Can't we open it and look in there?" The next morning he came down and he said, "Now I'm satisfied to leave the casket closed for last night Reuben came and stood by my bedside so I could see him."

Lydian also had a very hard time to accept the fact that there was no viewing. So the Lord sent her a beautiful dream where she saw Reuben with his face shining like never before. This helped her a lot.

On December 6, 1985, Grandpa Beachy died. Two weeks later I had a dream. In this dream I saw him come back and lay his hand on Reuben's head. He tousled his hair, then turned and walked away. All of a sudden he vanished in the air, then I heard some beautiful singing which I will never forget. The only word I understood was 'Belonet' (Rewarded).

Again, I had not realized what the Lord was trying to show me, until the day of Reuben's death, and then it all came back very clearly. Through this experience the Lord has taught us that we do not need to know why, but to accept His will for us.

This was written with tears and with love upon your request so that it might move the heart of the reader and bring him closer to our Creator.

- Amos

Reuben

His hair was blonde,
Like the sunbeams.
His eyes blue as the sky.
Freckles on his nose and cheeks,
Like the stars in the Heavens.

Yes, had we looked
A little closer at his smile,
We could have seen
That he planned to stay
Only for a little while.

<u>Amos and Lydian Yoder family</u>
David - Nov. 5, 1973
  - married June 2, 1994, eleven days before Reuben's accident.
Aden - Dec. 8, 1974
  - married ten months after Reuben's accident.
Adam- Sept. 25, 1976
Susie- Nov. 16, 1977
Ida - July 21, 1979
Miriam- Sept. 3, 1981
Reuben - Aug. 1, 1983; died June 13, 1994
Wayne- April 24, 1985

Since then we have been blessed with two grandsons. A blessing and joy we sure do enjoy even though nobody can take Reuben's place. Each child has their own personal way in life.

In ten months' time we had changes and adjustments to make. Three less plates to set. Many a time when I was ready to cook a meal, I first had to stop and think now how many plates do I place on the table. So it is always a joy when David and Aden would stop by for a meal.

We long to tell Reuben the daily life happenings and then hear his remarks. Will it always hurt so deeply? But when we think of him with the Lord, he would tell us he has it so much better. Why do those earthly thoughts keep coming? So, it is always good to remember every day, 'Help me to remember Lord, that nothing will happen today that you and I can't handle together.' May we always look to Jesus to carry us through.

Now going back to the day of June, 13, 1994. This day started out as usual on our farm, strawberries ripe and ready to pick. We never gave it a thought our lives would be changed before the day was over. Coming in from the patch, it was time for lunch and since Amos had one delivery to make and I was taking care of customers, I can so plainly remember Reuben helping me. There was one more order to be picked up when he said, "Mother, when will we get to eat?"

The rest of the children were eating and I had thought he had eaten and come back out to help me. I told him to go eat, I can wait on this last order, but he was concerned and asked, "When will you get to eat, Mother?" I told him pretty soon, although he was finished when I came into the kitchen. He was resting on the sofa and he told me, "I left some lunch for you. It's time you eat, too." He said this with a smile on his face.

During the rest of the afternoon the girls were doing laundry. I went to town to make a few phone calls for Wednesday's berry pick-up. It was a warm day so I got pop for the 'little boys', our way of saying, when we wanted Reuben and Wayne. When I came home they were playing with a neighbor boy on the swing. I told them to share their drinks. With a smile, Reuben nodded his head, and said, "Thanks." Little did I realize that would be his last words to me.

I was ready to enter the fruit cellar for a jar of meat because it was time to start supper, when above the noise of the washing machine motor, one of the girls screamed, "Come quick, Mom. Reuben got hit!"

Amos has written the happenings from here on. In my own humble way, with the help of our Savior, I will try and write a little of how our family coped in the two and a half years now since our dear Reuben's accident.

The first few hours, nights, and days before the funeral I cannot find words for the shock, emptiness, and pain that came over us again and again. In the wink of an eye our lives can be changed and earthly trifles matter so little. Though I had seen his body and knew it was badly bruised, it did not enter my mind that his body could not be viewed till the undertaker asked us if we realized he might not be able to fix him. Another shock and hurt that was hard for me to accept when the casket was brought back and it was sealed.

Neighbors, relatives, friends far or near. They play an important part those first hours, days. Then the weeks and months to follow are spent coping with the loss of a child, especially in those moments when life seems to be crashing down around us.

I was in one of my darkest moments when one night in a dream, I saw Reuben outside our earthly home playing with other children, his face all aglow and shining. His hair all cleaned and so neatly combed. His hair was so dirty and tangled on the accident site; I always had that longing to see his hair clean and neat. I feel thankful to our 'Wonderful Savior' for that dream because I could better accept the casket being closed after that.

For months it seemed I was always tired and exhausted. Tired in the evening and tired in the morning, but life went on and there was work to be done. I am thankful for the kind help of friends, neighbors, and our girls in the weeks and months that followed. Reuben's death and absence were always in my thoughts. My last thoughts before sleep and my first waking thoughts each day were of him as I tried to accept that he was truly gone.

I can now look back and see that our family was in a stage of deep grief. That comes in the "letting go" part. I feel the length of this stage varies from person to person and family to family, and in some ways it never ends. Grief is like a door. The only way to get to the other side is to walk through it. I could always feel when Wayne, our youngest son, was in a stage of grief and was missing his brother.

His way of finding comfort was sitting or standing beside me, whatever I was doing, and in a low voice he would always say one word, "Mom." I always knew he needed to be comforted then.

Two days after our son Aden's wedding, we were helping them move their belongings into one part of our house where they were making their home temporarily. A four year old niece of Aden's wife was playing with our toys when she found a note in a small child's book. She gave it to our daughter Susie. She had no idea what was written on it.

This is what is said:

'Wayne A. Yoder wrote this. Gr. 4, 1994, age nine. I really miss my brother since that terrible day. It was June 13, 1994, Monday. We all miss him, he was so kind. He was about five feet tall. We slept together until that day when he went to heaven. That is the best place to be. God can take better care of Reuben than we could. Reuben is with Jesus now.'

After everyone had left that evening, Susie, Ida, and Miriam were reading the note. When Wayne came into the house and recognized what they had, he said, "Let's throw it in the waste can."

That's when I came on the scene. "Wayne," I said, "that note is precious to me. When did you write it and can I have it?"

He said, "Last winter sometime when I was so lonesome for Reuben I wrote my thoughts on paper."

Some of my most difficult days were when Wayne walked out the door in the morning crying because he was going to school without his brother Reuben. God grant me the serenity to accept the things I cannot change, courage to change the things I can, and wisdom to know the difference.

The first year when we experience those special moments of life without dear Reuben. His birthday, Christmas at school, and family get-togethers and then of course at the end of the year there is the day of his death. Each of these difficult times is another roadmark on our journey toward letting go of our dear child. Through our grief and sorrow we find sharing experiences of the loss of a child can create a special bond among parents who otherwise would never have met. To have friends and stay in touch and speak to other bereaved parents in grief and pain, helps open the way to healing and peace.

This was written with love and tears and a hurt still there. But also with a trust in our Savior to push the question 'Why me?' aside and think of this quote.

'Today I will not imagine what I would do if things were different. They are not different. I will make success with what material I have. May God heal our wounded hearts and grant us the assurance of *His Love*.'   -Lydian

God, how mysterious and strange are Thy ways,
To take Reuben in the best of his days.
Your work and play on this earth are finished,
While we struggle on, many times in a tear.

Beautiful memories woven in gold,
This is a picture we tenderly hold.
Down in our hearts your memory is kept,
To love, to cherish, and never forget.
So while we wait, Dear Lord, we pray,
Grant us strength for each new day.
That we may strive for peace and love,
Until we meet in heaven above.

Alexander Yoder: July 9, 1985 - June 27, 1992

Submitted by: Emery & Esther Yoder, Apple Creek, Ohio

Hello to everyone who might read this book. I want to try and put this on paper with help from above. It is hard for me to write this, but if it can be of help to others I want to do my duty. How fortunate we are that God, the Almighty, does the choosing. What a precious baby and He needed him. Yes, God left Alex in our care for six short years. I will try to write how it happened.

June 27, 1992, was a beautiful day. We were remodeling our house and had dug out our basement. The week before I had left Alex and Emery Jr. at my sister's place because I was afraid I couldn't keep them both watched and something would happen to them. Alex was such a carefree child.

This was Saturday and Grandpa needed pills. Dad, Alex, and I decided go to town, Kidron, in the morning. The reason Alex went along was because he needed a new hat for church the next day. After we came home, I took the hat and wrote Alex's name in it right away, which is a keepsake for us to this day.

Marianna, our oldest daughter, happened to be working that day. The rest were all at the dinner table. Alex always sat between Dad and me. He didn't want to stay at the table until we were all through, but with encouragement he put his head on my lap. That was the last time I talked with him.

After dinner most of the family went to a neighbor's field to make hay. Alex had gone along on the wagon. Daughter Iva and I stayed behind because we were expecting company for supper. I was washing off the walks and Grandpa was sitting on a chair in his front lawn. All at once he said he thinks the pony went into the barn dragging something behind it. Grandpa, 80 years old with breathing and heart problems, started for the barn. I quickly told him I'll see about it, but of course I didn't realize what I'd find.

The pony had gone through the barn, down into the cattle shed and stood there watching me. I started talking to the pony because I was afraid it would take off again. I also talked to Alex, but got no response at all. The pony's rein was so tight that I needed to take off his shoe to get his foot out. I picked him up and walked outside with him.

By then our oldest son, Nelson, had run down from the neighbors from where he had seen it happen. He took Alex from me and laid him on the grass. He gave him mouth to mouth and Alex starting breathing again. Dad was down there, too, by that time. Son Raymond was coming down and we sent him to call the emergency squad right away. Yes, it was a pitiful sight, though all in higher hands. The children brought me a pan of water so I could wash his face. Emery quickly changed clothes. I didn't want to leave him, but everyone encouraged me to change so I could go with the squad. They allowed both of us to go with him.

Son Nelson had been on top of a load of hay when he saw Alex sitting beside the pony. Nelson thought he was playing. I presume he got off the pony with his foot getting tangled in the reins. Alex had come home by himself, got the pony, put the wrong bridle on, and went riding. The bridle had a long rein. Nelson saw the pony take off with Alex dragging behind.

The squad went for the nearest hospital. When we got there I saw Amish people sitting inside. They told us to wait in the waiting room. I couldn't even think and my legs felt like rubber. Soon they came and offered coffee. Next we went to the admitting room, then to the conference room, which I dreaded. By then I just wondered what would be next. The doctor in the emergency room came in and told us he had died. It wasn't long until they came and said that we could see him.

The Amish people, Mrs. Roy Kline, came to me as soon as we left the conference room. What a relief, she lent a shoulder to cry on. Nobody knows what that meant to me. She couldn't have been nicer to us. Emery and I were by ourselves and we just didn't know what to do.

So many things that needed to be talked about with the situation like it was at home. Our house was in no condition to have too many people in it. So finally we decided to use the dowdy house for viewing and the neighbors put up a big tent for the day of the funeral. No words can express what friends and neighbors did for us during that time, and on through the summer.

Yes, we find out from talking with other people that nobody is alike. Some can talk about their grief and some would rather not. We had a long hard summer. At times we thought if only we wouldn't be remodeling, but we think the good Lord had it all planned that way. A year later, on the same day, we lost our Grandpa. It was so hard on him, losing his grandson. He had often said, "Why couldn't it be me?"

Then a month later Grandmother had a stroke. We have been caring for her since. We still have her in her house with family coming in and helping care for her. Since it means a lot to me, I would like to share some comments Alex made to friends and us. I had taught the children the Lord's prayer. The four little boys always slept in one room and they usually said it together. About two weeks before he died, I didn't hear them saying it anymore. I asked them about it and he replied, "Mom, I could never forget Jesus."

His friend told me this since he died. She had taken him for a walk up the mountain. She teasingly asked him what he'd do if a bear came. He replied, "Oh, I wouldn't care if he'd get me. Then I could go and be with Jesus."

Do we have that trust? He cares for you and me.

Manas J. Wingard: June 18, 1973 - Sept. 27, 1974

Submitted by: Martha (Wingard) Yoder, Millersburg, Indiana

Mother started canning vegetable soup in the morning and everything went smoothly and unusually fast. Everything was on the stove to coldpack before it was time to fix lunch so she told the preschoolers she's going to rest a bit.

The milkman came and the children were in the yard waiting for the highlight of the day, pumping their little arms and listening to the air horn go Blah! Blah! as he went up the road again! This day when the milkman looked back to the children he saw someone lying in the driveway. Mom hadn't been resting five minutes when the children came running and said the milkman drove over Manas!

So began the sad journey through shock, grief, days of just wanting to hold him and finally later the joy in knowing he's safe in the arms of Jesus. He was just a wee tot of 15 months. The milkman had talked to him that day and told him to stay on the grass, away from the truck. Knowing no English, Manas wouldn't have understood. After loading the milk he walked around the front of the truck and checked both mirrors to make sure he wasn't in danger. But God had a plan and he never saw him by the right front wheel.

Manas died instantly of a broken neck or skull fractures. He had a tire mark on his arm and the back of his head was like a soft melon, but otherwise he looked like a sleeping baby. The milkman carried him to the house and laid him on the kitchen table and went to get Dad filling silo at the neighbors. Mom carried him outside and waited for Uncle Jay to come up from the back end of the 90 rod field behind the house. It seemed to take him so-o-o-o long!

Very soon neighbors arrived, Lonnie Yoders, Atlee Chupp, Wilma Jean, and many others. Someone fetched the two oldest children from school and everyone sat in the living room and took turns holding him till the coroner came. Precious memories were all we had left, but he had to be in a much more wonderful place!

Mother's first thoughts were that it was all her fault because she wasn't watching him like she should have been. But she later realized God's hands were in this and it was well taken care of. Some are ours for only a while.

The good Lord sent another little boy six months later and that really helped fill the empty arms.

Katie Stoltzfus: Sept. 10, 1975 -Apr. 30, 1984

Submitted by: Jacob & Mary Ann Stoltzfus, Gordonville, Pennsylvania

April 30, 1984, a Monday, was a cloudy day. I washed clothes and hung them out on the side porch. At lunch time, the three girls came home from school by surprise because the teacher was taking the seventh and eighth graders to visit other schools.

Our son Lester went along because he was in the seventh grade. At lunch time we decided to go visit my sister Barbie's schoolroom, Meeting House School. Son Amos, age four, wasn't too willing to go because he wasn't able to walk on account of his accident four weeks earlier. He had been in the hospital over a week having his three large toes taken off his one foot. But we decided to go because it would be something different for him since we had been mostly at home the last month.

Sam, Esther, and Barbie, holding baby Beckie, were in the back seat of the carriage. Dear Katie was standing in the front corner of the carriage. Amos was on my lap with his foot on Jake's lap. At the end of the lane we met someone from Virginia wanting a goat to take along home. We turned around and 15 minutes later we started out again. How well I remember getting ready; pinning Katie's apron for the last time, never realizing. What a great pleasure they had in getting ready.

About a mile from home we were on the right side of the road when a red car came around the corner right toward us. Jake said, "What is that car doing?" To us it never came closer, but it ran right into us. The children in the back seat were seated on the bank of the road. Baby Beckie was still in Barbie's arms. The rest of us were on the road. Katie was thrown away from the rest of us and she was also on the road. The Lord must have taken her soul home to sweet rest right away. Oh, how sweet to think she didn't have to suffer.

Barbie's first thoughts were to go to her uncle Benuel's to care for baby Beckie because she was crying. Then someone stopped with a big dog in his car. He offered to take the girls wherever they wanted. To this day, we still don't know who it was. Surely the Lord's protecting hand was there.

How thankful that the girls could get away because it must have been terrible to see. Everything was dark before Jake's eyes and I can remember hardly anything. The horse had to be killed and the carriage was in pieces. People came because we were so helpless.

Tony Good, driver of the car, had blood on his face. Jake, Sam, Amos, I, and Tony Good were taken to the hospital. Police came into the hospital to talk to Jake and said, "Katie has passed away."

We were still in the emergency room with only a curtain between us when Jake told me. I can still hear those words. At the time I heard it, but it just about didn't mean anything, although I realized brothers and sisters were standing around with black clothes on.

That same evening, Furman brought Katie's body in to the hospital to my room, Jake was also there, so I could view her body in a mirror. I had my neck broken and was lying flat on my back. I felt Katie's soft, silky hair and also her hand, but life was gone. Jake was in the hospital five days. Amos was also in the hospital with a concussion and he was never able to view Katie. He was in for six days.

On Wednesday, Jake was released from 12 to six to go to the

funeral at home. How very much the children needed him. His nose was broken and his face was all black and blue. That same evening, some of the family came to the hospital and had part of the sermon in my room. I was in the hospital for seven weeks. It was a hard time for the children. The first month we had enough going with ourselves trying to get better that we hardly mentioned Katie's absence.

I feel we should have talked more to the children. As time went on I realized some of the children didn't want to talk about Katie which caused some trying times Her sister, with whom she slept and worked with, went through some trying times. It was a year before I could talk to her about Katie. She didn't even want to hear her name.

When school started in the fall I couldn't stand watching the two girls go to school because I had often watched the three girls going before, wondering what the future will bring.

Tony Good, the driver of the car, and his family have become very dear friends. He accidentally fell asleep going around the bend. They are Christian people and they tried to help in every way they could when we weren't able to work.

Katie was eight years old. One daughter older and one younger, how they loved to sing while doing dishes. Things have changed, but as time goes on, time is a healer. How lucky she was to go in her tender years, before sin could harm her.

Katie King: June 13, 1986 - July 17, 1987

Submitted by: Daniel & Elizabeth King, Bird In Hand, Pennsylvania

We were a family like any other living on a farm in Lane County, Pennsylvania. Our oldest was 11 years old and we had five boys and two girls, eight year old Anna and 13 month old Katie.

Friday morning, July 17, 1987, was a very nice summer day and who could have thought what the day would bring. We did our morning chores and milking like usual. We hustled a bit extra so Daniel could be ready when his driver came. We ate breakfast and the driver soon arrived and Daniel was on his way to Lititz, 12 miles away to brother Quillie's to help rebuild a shed that had blown down in a storm several weeks before. He had gotten a load together of the neighborhood men.

I did the laundry then and Anna was taking care of Katie, a very normal thing. She gave her some Cheerios and a bottle of milk and played with her. Ten year old Enos was out tedding hay while 11 year old Stevie was hauling wood with the little wagon. After I was done washing clothes, Anna and six year old Reuben helped too, and soon they were out beside the milk house pulling nails out of boards. We had taken off the milk house roof to replace it.

I nursed Katie for the last time and then after she was done I was playing with her like usual. Soon three year old Abner came in with his doll and wanted my chair, so I let him have it, but for some reason I was not quite done with Katie dear, so I sat on the bed with her. Then I lay back for a little while because she loved so much to be able to crawl all over me.

It was time for me to get to work so I left Katie in the kitchen with five year old Dannie and three year old Abner, and went out to pick string beans in back of the house. I never could recall when the milk truck came, which seems so unreal now. When I was out the boys decided they wanted to go out to the rest of the children and propped the door open so Katie could go out too. She could walk but still crawled, especially on the lawn, etc.

It didn't take me long to pick beans and when I came in I saw the open door so I quickly looked to see where Katie was. I saw her lying in the driveway and the milk truck just at the end of the walks, a few yards away from her. I screamed at him to stop but he did not hear me and had noticed nothing. I ran out and stopped him just before he was at the end of the lane. I quickly ran back to find our dear and precious Katie crushed to death.

The children were there before I was and everyone was crying. They had not seen it happen, but heard my screams. The milkman, Ken Sweigart, was quite shaken but stayed calm. My own feelings could never be explained or put to words. The thought of how well off she is and that she didn't need to suffer made me feel quite calm. It did seem like the angels were hovering over us. But what do we do now?

I wished for Daniel with all my heart and did not know how to get hold of him. Stevie and Ken went down to the neighbor's phone and it seemed like a long time till they came back. Reuben went out to tell Enos. Ken called his company and they notified the police and ambulance. Dave Kauffmans, who are Amish-Mennonites, came along and I was so glad for someone to talk to in Dutch. They called a coroner and the undertaker. All were very good and kind to me.

Meanwhile, after Ken and Stevie came back from the phone, I

went down to the neighbors because they had not told anyone. I heard a neighbor lady talking so I went to her. She was very helpful and tried her best to get hold of Daniel, but didn't succeed. She was able to let our nearest Amish neighbors know. It was an hour before any Amish neighbors came because none of them can see our farm. Around that time the neighbor came home that had taken us to Quillies a week before so he went after Daniel. More people came and then Daniel, two hours after the accident. What a sad meeting, but a load off my shoulders to have him by my side.

The ambulance crew had wrapped up Katie's poor head and carried her to the house which is where she was until Daniel came home. The undertaker was waiting on him. People were so sympathetic and caring. I felt they would have reason to blame me for not taking better care of Katie. Satan tried hard, later on, to get me down with such thoughts, but God is almighty and He led us through those hurtful and sorrowful days, weeks, months, and years.

That morning the milkman couldn't get the truck backed up properly. He tried three times and finally just made do and the hose barely reached. Therefore he was parked in such a way that it blocked his view from the lawn which is why he did not see her. Ken came to the viewing Saturday morning. He and his wife, Anna Mae, were at the funeral.

Three weeks later they visited us on a Saturday evening and he talked and talked. We've been good friends ever since. We barely knew him before because he was only a substitute driver.

Lots of people were in and out those three days. The funeral was Monday. The church people, neighbors, and others were so helpful it just hurt. They baled the hay, did the chores, etc. The women froze corn, cleaned the house, and did many, many things for us. How small and unworthy we were.

We were richly blessed through all the days of sorrow. We had always thought Katie was a precious little girl and found out that some others thought so too. It was a balm to our aching hearts and helped us realize it was all in God's perfect plan. She was not meant to grow up, but was needed in Heaven.

This is now nearly nine years later. In those years we have been blessed with two more little boys and then two little girls, all two years apart. We hope to always be humbly grateful to our loving Father for His loving kindness.

Rosanna Gingerich: Aug. 1, 1973 - Oct. 31, 1974
Daniel Gingerich: Stillborn Apr. 14, 1987

Submitted by: Ivan & Mary Gingerich, Kokomo, Indiana

As new parents, we felt blessed when Rosanna was born the usual way. Her name is a combination of both grandmothers' names and she was their first granddaughter. She grew tall and slender and walked briskly after being a year old.

In 1974, the last days of October were almost like summer. We were busy building portable storage barns at home, so all of us were together in the shop frequently, much to Rosanna's delight. Little did we know about the change ahead of us.

Fall house cleaning and sewing for our daughter had been practically caught up. This included a new suit and head covering which turned out larger than planned, but the Lord must have wanted it so to fit better.

That month the ministers had quoted the verse about the Lord chastening those he loves, so we pondered long on that. Our local chiropractor had inquired about our business and made a remark as though he thought we needed twice as much income, and that bothered us. (We should have set our attention more on things above, rather than those of this earth.)

Halloween of 1974 began almost like any other day that week, but by evening all the common decorations and actions of that celebration seemed more ungodly than ever before. Rosanna's hair was braided that morning and her new suit fitted, so she thought we were planning to go "bye, bye". At noon she ate well of our chicken dinner. Afterward she looked over and said, "Mom, Mom!," tilting her head back and looking at the ceiling as though she wanted to tell us something. Remembering that she did the same a day earlier, we wondered what she meant. Almost immediately she repeated her actions and words. Later as these incidents were recalled, we wondered whether she had seen angels hovering close by.

After her usual short nap, she went along outside to see what the other family members were doing. Her grandpa, our landlord, and uncles were doing some work on the buildings, and they had brought some of their supplies over on an implement trailer. That evening as Grandpa started out with the trailer, none of us realized that Rosanna had left the shop where she had been playing with a nail puller.

As the vehicle began to move, we heard one short, frightened cry and rushed to the scene to discover that somehow her head got in front of a trailer wheel, which went over the skull. Mouth to mouth resuscitation was done without a response, and we could see her short life had ended abruptly.

A kind neighbor took us to the hospital anyway. From there she was transferred to the funeral home where a lot of facial work was done so she could be viewed. The funeral was held on Sunday morning. Even some friends from hundreds of miles away came. Words can't express how unworthy we felt that so many folks sympathized with us at the time.

The bishop who had part of the services pointed out how we need to always dress our children in the rules of the church. Nobody knows when even a young life may end. They had also experienced death in their family circle. Even though others without that experience did their best to comfort us in our grief, a person could almost feel which ones knew how it felt to be in our shoes. It seemed hard to grasp that for months we would have an empty high chair.

Mail time was soon one of the highlights of the day. Often the dishes were pushed back as letters and greetings were read after the noon meal.

Three months later a son appeared to fill our empty arms. Later more children were born until we had three sons and three daughters. The youngest daughter had been taken surgically. Through home birth education, we felt doctors shouldn't discourage us from trying a natural birth for the next one. Complications caused Daniel to be stillborn on April 14, 1987.

Around that time one of the aunts woke up during the night with the song, 'Ich War ein Kleines Kindlein' coming to mind. This was a very trying time. Many sobering thoughts come to mind if a mother is critically low! We thank the Lord that better health was granted. Some of our children have expressed their desire to see the others in Glory.

Naturally there is a temptation to feel that some things should have been done differently, but the Bible tells us to look forward, not backward in our spiritual life. Hopefully we took the opportunity to accept the fact that God wants us to call upon His name at all times, whether all seems to be well or trials weigh us down. It takes His help to understand our companions in this earthly pilgrimage, rather than passing harsh judgments on them. Since our calling involves hard decisions every so often, we ask to be included in others' prayers; returning that favor too.

> *On that precious day of Rosanna's birth,*
> > *How fragile and tiny she seemed to be.*
> *Steadily then as days and weeks went forth,*
> > *Rapid growth in body and mind we'd see.*

> *For all friends she had such a loving heart;*
> > *Eyes would sparkle as she showed her sweet smile.*
> *From parents it was always hard to part,*
> > *Yet God sent separation for a while.*

> *How very busy she kept those small hands;*
> > *Helping her mom and dad was her desire.*
> *Now that she was called Home to better lands,*
> > *A darling Angel she'll be up higher.*

> *The Lord has given, He's taken away;*
> > *An empty place is now left in our home.*
> *No more will our Rosanna pass this way,*
> > *Like David, let's prepare for Baby's Home.*

Vonda Sue Miller: May 16, 1956 - Sept. 10, 1970

Submitted by: Lydia Yoder, Sarasota, Florida

September 10, 1970, is a day that I will never forget. It was a nice summer day, that morning when Vonda, Loretta, and Jane went to school. They usually walked because it wasn't very far from home. For some unknown reason Vonda took Glenn's bicycle that morning.

When they came home, Martha Helmuth rode along sitting on the seat while Vonda did the pedaling. The school was just about a quarter mile north of US 6. Some of the children were walking and some had bikes. As they came to US 6, they didn't stop. A semi was coming from the east and they hit the trailer. Somehow she got underneath the wheels and was thrown beside the road.

I was sewing at the time and was watching the children. All at once I seen that something had happened, so Nora and I ran across the little field. When we got there, Glenn was already there as he had been helping with Jr. and Barbara's new house.

Martha was lying on the road. I said, "Oh, it's Martha."
Then Glenn said, "Vonda is over there. Dead."

Oh no, I thought it couldn't be true. The shock was terrible. Only those that have gone through this know what it is. Death is so final. Somebody had covered her with a jacket. I could not take it anymore, so I went home.

The traffic was lined up to Nappanee. Wayne and Gary were on their way home, and they had got caught up in the traffic when somebody told them about the accident. She had many broken bones, even the back of her head. But only a few scratches on her face. We were so thankful we were able to view her. Martha was laid up a long time because her leg was badly broken.

Sudden deaths are not new for our family. In June 1955, my brother Jerry, 29, was killed in a motorcycle accident. Then in 1978 my mother was in Florida for a few weeks when she lost her life in a car accident. On July 18, 1991, a little grandson Kevin, age 6, son of Calvin and (daughter) Jane Bontrager was killed in a farm accident on our farm. But how lucky to be with Jesus at such a tender age even though it was heartbreaking.

Glenn died on August 13, 1987 from cancer, being sick only two months. I married again on May 17, 1992 to Andrew Yoder from Oklahoma. His wife was my cousin and she also died from cancer on August 14, 1988. I thank the good Lord for being near during these trials and heartaches.

Marilyn Kay Miller: Dec. 7, 1984 - May 16, 1994
Emma Lou Miller: Stillborn Feb. 14, 1996

Submitted by: Dewayne Miller, Ligonier, Indiana

Greetings in Jesus' Holy name. I will try and do our part in this because it is always interesting and touching to hear of other people's experiences.

On December 7, 1984, we had a set of twins, Mervin Jay and Marilyn Kay, born healthy and hearty in every way. We never realized how short-lived our happiness would be with this healthy set of twins, but God had other plans for us.

I can't remember all the dates anymore, but in late February or early March our two oldest boys started coughing, just like they would be starting with a very bad cold. We tried over-the-counter medicines but nothing helped, so we went to the doctor and he gave us sample medicine that was to be real good for bad colds, but still nothing helped. Shortly after that they started to cough harder and then started to pull back when we finally discovered they had whooping cough.

We never knew we had been exposed. I'm very glad we don't know from who or where they got exposed because this would give us a reason to look down on somebody else or give us ill feelings toward them. This was God's way and purpose in our life.

Mom was nursing the twins, and oh, how we hoped this would help keep the twins from getting it. It didn't. God's ways are not our ways. They started coughing, but Mervin coughed a lot harder and finally started coughing until he turned blue around the lips. Marilyn never coughed that hard, so naturally we were a lot more worried about Mervin, but that was not the case as the doctor explained to us later. Marilyn coughed only hard enough to bring the mucus only halfway up then it went back down into her lungs. We didn't realize what was happening until it was too late.

On March 29, 1985, Marilyn started to run a fever so Mom got a driver and went to 'brauch' and get a treatment for her which seemed to help, but a little after midnight her fever started to go up again. We gave her aspirin but that didn't help. We finally washed her off with vinegar which stabilized her for a while, but by morning she started to get worse again.

I called the doctor around eight o'clock and told them we have a sick child, so the secretary made an appointment for us at 11 o'clock. I was disappointed that they didn't tell us to come right away but left it at that and went home and told Mom. She said we'll go right away because Marilyn wouldn't nurse anymore, so I went back to the neighbors and called the doctor again and told them we were coming in now. I asked the neighbor lady to take us, which she did. During this time, our closest Amish neighbor lady came over and took Floyd, three, and Lamar, two, home with her which we were thankful for.

When we got to the doctor's office I went in the front door and told them we have whooping cough and asked if we couldn't come in the back door so we wouldn't expose the other people that were sitting in the office. They didn't believe us, but let us come in the back door anyway. The doctor examined her and told us he doesn't know what it is, but we have a very, very sick child.

His next words put a little fear in us because he said, "I want to see you at the hospital immediately," which was LaGrange Hospital. This was on March 30. At the hospital he examined her more closely and her temperature was 105° by this time, but he still denied it was whooping cough or it being the cause.

They said we have to transfer her to Park View in Fort Wayne which was only part of what we had to accept. My wife had to go to the restroom and when she came up there she met Orva Hostetler Ella. Orva is my wife's uncle. My wife saw there was something seriously wrong. Ella said Orva had a runaway and he has a broken neck.

The doctor said they want to check Marilyn for Spinal Meningitis and if that is negative, they'll send both to Park View in the same ambulance, which they did. Later Orva said he heard a baby cry, but never realized at the time it was a relative.

My wife went with Ella and their son David, with their driver, down to Park View and I went home with my driver and picked up the two boys and took them over to my folks, Mervin M. and Vera Irene Miller, and told them what was going on. I never realized I wouldn't see much of our two boys for the next six weeks, which was a very long time.

I got a different driver to go to Fort Wayne right away and what a sight to behold when I came to the hospital. Our baby was lying in her crib almost naked with four or five tubes in her and hooked up to a ventilator, heart monitor, I.V. and whatever else.

As soon as Marilyn arrived at Park View they gave her a shot to kill the whooping cough germ, which they admitted was the cause. They had to kill that germ before they could start working on the double pneumonia which was the effects of her not coughing hard enough to get the mucus out.

When I asked about her they said they have her stabilized and if nothing else turned up, she'd be getting better. Oh how unprepared we were for what happened next. That night we were both so tired we asked about a bed so they said that we could rent a room on the sixth floor for the night.

If I remember right, it was around ten o'clock when we finally went to bed and about 12 o'clock somebody knocked on the door and asked if this is the Millers. I was out of bed almost in the wink of an eye and they said they wanted to see us downstairs because both of Marilyn's lungs had collapsed. When we came down they had put two tubes in her chest to release the air from her chest cavity and had her stabilized again.

On Monday, April 1, my folks took Mervin to the doctor to get a checkup since Marilyn was so sick. They still denied it was whooping cough even though he had a severe coughing spree right in the doctor's office. They said they'd take tests and they were positive. I can't explain how I felt when the doctor called me at Park View and said Mervin will be going to LaGrange because he is only a few days behind Marilyn as far as his lungs are concerned. He ended up being there for six days but he came out with no side effects for which we were glad.

We can't thank our relatives and parents enough since there was always somebody with Mervin while he was in the hospital. I can't remember if it was Monday night or Tuesday night when I finally went home so I could go to work and my wife stayed at the hospital. Every night I had a way back and forth to the hospital since there was always somebody going down to see Orva Hostetler or Marilyn. Then on Friday night I went down to stay over the weekend and my wife went home. I don't think there was a day that my wife was alone, which the other people can't realize how much easier they made it for us.

Our two oldest boys were at my folks for one week then they took them down to my wife's folks for a week. This is the way it was for almost all six weeks.

After Marilyn was in the hospital for a couple of weeks and not improving like we would have liked to see, we asked the doctor why she wasn't getting better. Finally he admitted they were doing all they could and the rest was up to a Higher Power. They did take a brain scan and said she has brain damage and in time will heal, but we didn't realize she'd be like a vegetable the rest of her life.

Around May third, they said they might as well transfer her back to LaGrange as they could help her just as much now as they could at Park View and it would be a lot closer for us. We were there for seven to nine days when they sent us home with a feeding tube down her nose. About two weeks later she finally started to swallow so they took the feeding tube out. She never got to the point where she could chew her food so we really had to watch what we fed her.

She never smiled, never sat up, and never showed any signs that she understood what we were saying to her. If she got sick we just had to guess what was wrong with her. Around the first part of May 1994, she quit eating but still took some liquids but she didn't run a fever. One night I called the doctor at his home because we were thinking of putting a feeding tube down her nose into her stomach.

The doctor came out after office hours with tubes and checked Marilyn, looked at us and said her blood count is way down, her kidneys have quit working, and her organs are quitting one by one. We asked about taking her to the hospital to put her on I.V.

He said, "If it would be my child I wouldn't because it would only prolong her life a couple days at the most, and as far as putting the tube down, I wouldn't do it, but you can, because it will only make her more miserable." He looked at us again and said, "Why would you want to keep her from going to God?"

How true, but oh how shocking to know one of your children is dying and there is nothing to do but try and keep her comfortable and wait for death to come. It came six days later on May 16, 1994. Only then did we actually realize how much care she really took which we gladly did for her.

How little we realized what other trials we would have to face. Nine months later on February 6, 1995, my sister, the Harley Yoder family, had fire and lost two children. The day of their funeral we buried the two beside our Marilyn. We were one of the last ones to leave, of course, and as I turned to go, a stab of pain shot through my heart and the saying 'zwetta drit sich' came to my mind at the same time. I can't explain in words how I felt. I was so scared. I didn't say anything to my wife because I didn't want her to worry. As I look back now, I feel it was the Lord trying to tell me we have yet another trial to go through.

On February 14, 1996, we had a beautiful little daughter, whom we named Emma Lou, but she was stillborn. I often have to think if this is what it takes to lead me on to Heaven, which I often get a longing for, I want to accept it with the Lord's help.

Elnora Hochstetler: Oct. 9, 1981 - Nov. 18, 1981
Vernon Hochstetler: Oct. 4, 1982 - Nov. 23, 1982
Leona Kay Hochstetler: Feb. 12, 1988

Submitted by: LaVern & Lorna Hochstetler, Tuscola, Illinois

Elnora

We had the joys of a baby daughter, Elnora, born October 9, 1981; not knowing she would have such a short life with us. She was a smaller baby than all our other children. She was born with a red mouth and was very hard to feed. She never went over her birth weight.

We had her to the doctor several times and tried different milk but seemed nothing helped. We took her to the hospital at three weeks old, took lots of tests and still no answer. She had edema so bad her eyes were swollen shut.

She was in Champaign Hospital for one week and no results. They decided to move us to Indianapolis, Ind. That was a hard move so far away from home, with three older children and chores behind, but there was no other choice. So we left at noon for this other hospital and arrived late in the evening.

Once there, they took more tests and x-rays but still no answer to the problems. She got weaker and weaker till she passed away on November 8, 1981. Several weeks after she passed away they sent us a letter saying her bone marrow had been bad. It was a bad B-12 deficiency. They called it Metholmolonicacidemia with homosisteniria.

Vernon

One year later we were blessed with a baby boy, Vernon, born October 4, 1982. He was a little larger and ate better. He'd gain and then he'd lose. So we also took him to the doctor and by the time he was three weeks old, we started out one morning in a clinic in Champaign, then we were sent to a hospital in Champaign . After we told them about our other baby, they wanted us to go on to Chicago to a larger hospital. So by late evening we arrived in Chicago. This felt like a long day with chores not taken care of and the other children behind. But with the Lord's help it all worked out.

Here they soon found out he also had the same disease our other baby had. They gave him large doses of B-12 shots in hopes they could save him. But after three weeks of working with him, we finally saw the good Lord needed another angel in heaven.

He passed away when he was seven weeks old on November 23, 1982. Our thoughts often go to the graveyard and up to Heaven, but we are thankful that they can be angels and have a good home for life.

After these two we had five healthy children whom we are thankful for.

Leona

February 12, 1988, is a day never to forget. It was on a Friday evening around five o'clock. Roads were packed with snow with big snow banks on both sides of the roads. We had decided to go to Tuscola to a chiropractor.

Like always, after the chicken feeders were filled, the children could play. We had an old truck hood turned upside down with a pony shaft attached to it then a twine tied behind the hood with a small sled

Nelson, eight years, was driving the pony and Leona, 12 years, was on the small sled. They were on the road headed toward school. Leona told Nelson there was a van coming down the road so Nelson pulled over as close to the snowbanks as he could, but unfortunately, a classmate of mine, was driving way too fast for the conditions of the road and lost control.

He just hit the edge of Nelson's truck hood and threw him to the left on the edge of the truck hood and broke his left arm and drove over Leona killing her instantly. This all took place when we were on our way home from Tuscola. The closer to home we got, we saw there was a lot of commotion between the school and our house. There were lots of people standing around; plus an ambulance. It never once dawned on us that it could be our own children.

Our neighbor Ida Otto, was the first person I met and she said Leona was killed. Sam Schrock, a minister, was also one of the first ones there. He later told us he applied CPR but there was just nothing there.

Nelson ran to the schoolhouse where some women were there cleaning. He was put on a stretcher and taken to Champaign Hospital. Our neighbor, Nelson Hershberger stayed with Nelson so I could go home to the rest of the family.

They left Leona on the south porch until I came home around nine o'clock P.M. The same evening Nelson came home soon after midnight. The neighbors were all there. The thought of planning another funeral was hard to handle, because before this, we put two little angels in the grave. One of my first thoughts was now she can be with the babies.

God's ways are not our ways, but we want to accept whatever He has in store for us. This makes heaven seem so precious.

Larry Leon Raber: Nov. 20, 1975 - Oct. 15, 1992

Submitted by: Henry Jr. & Ida Mae Raber, Montgomery, Indiana

The morning of Oct. 15, 1992, was just like any typical morning on the farm. This particular morning we loaded out fat hogs, which we do about every two weeks; and we were a little short on time that morning. For our devotions in the morning we usually read or sing two or three songs. This particular morning it was getting late and the girls wanted to go to school and Larry to work so we only sang one song, 'I Need No Mansion Here Below' which was one of Larry's favorite songs. He helped sing so heartily.

He left for work as usual, but was a little late. He worked at my sister and brother-in-law's cabinet shop. Henry Jr., my husband, and Dallas, the next son after Larry, one year younger, went out to pick corn. It was a dreary morning and you could hear thunder rumbling on and off all morning but it didn't seem to get much closer until right around noon. Right at that time a lumber truck arrived at the cabinet shop. They saw there was rain coming up so decided they'd better cover this load of lumber. The driver was going to get on top and cover it, but Larry said, "Here, let me go up there. I can get up there better than you can." The driver was an older man.

Larry got up on the truck and all at once lightning struck and killed him instantly. Larry never knew what happened. The driver was beginning to get up on the truck too, to help Larry and he had one foot on the step and the other on the ground. He was shocked severely and rolled around on the ground for a while. The other workers were running to call the ambulance and asking him if he's all right. Then the man said, "I'm all right, but how's the boy on top?"

That was the first that they saw what happened to Larry. Larry was lying face down on top of the lumber. He turned a dark purple almost immediately. His one shoe was blown off and they found his measuring tape in the field probably around 15 feet away, in several pieces. His skin wasn't burned that we could see but his hair on one side was scorched. His shirt was melted on the right side and his pant leg shredded on the same side. So sudden came the call for him.

We were still at home and they sent a driver over to get us. June and Dallas were still in the cornfield, but when they heard this hard strike, they unhitched and were coming home by the time the driver arrived. We live almost a mile and a half from where it happened.

The driver just told us something has happened to Larry over at the cabinet shop, get ready, he's supposed to take us over. We tried to think what could have happened, but our minds just seemed to be blank. We never once thought about lightning hitting him since there actually was just one hard strike. It started to rain right after it struck.

Dallas told us to go on, he'll put the horses away. We jumped into the truck and on the way over, my brother and his wife, who worked at the Buggy Shop between us and where it happened, were on the road waiting for us when we came back and they also got in to ride over with us. By the looks on their faces we knew something serious had happened. I kept asking, "Fannie, what happened? What happened?"

She couldn't talk so finally I asked, "Fannie, he isn't dead is he?" She just shook her head and said, "Oh, Ida Mae!"

Oh, the feeling of helplessness when we got there. He was lying there so peaceful, face down on top of the truck. Henry Jr. said Larry looked as if he was sleeping and it just had to be that he could wake him up. People were running here and there, the ambulance soon arrived, but all was done human hands could do. So final is death. Oh, to be ready when our Maker calls for us!

I'll never forget the look on Dallas' face when he came over and was told his dear brother was dead. Dallas had put the horses away and then come on over too when he heard the sirens.

Life went on even though we thought at times it couldn't. We tried to think of the things we could be thankful for and never take more than one day at a time. Life hasn't been the same since, but we can say we don't wish him back into this wicked world.

He left many precious memories and many examples to follow. Larry made mistakes, too, but there are some things that really stand out now after he's gone. He was a boy who tried to let his conscience be his guide. If he had said something or did anything that he hurt someone he wouldn't go to bed without saying sorry to that person. Many a night going up the stairs he would softly say, "I'm sorry I said this or sorry I did that."

We found talking about it really helped, especially to those who had somewhat similar experiences. Family and friends mean a lot at a time like this. Here are the words to the song we sang the morning he was called away. We only sang the first and last verses with the chorus. This is certainly one precious memory that we sang this song together that last time when were all still together around our table.

I Need No Mansion

When burdens come so hard to bear,
That no earthly friend can share;
Tears drive away the smiles and leave my heart in pain.
Then my Lord from heaven above,
Speaks to me in tones of love,
Wipes the tears away and makes me smile again.

-chorus-

I need no mansion here below,
For Jesus said that I could go
To a home beyond the skies not made with hands ;
Won't you come and go along?
We will sing the sweetest song
Ever played upon the harps in glory land.

When Jesus comes to claim his own,
I will move to my new home;
I'll walk and talk with Him upon the streets of gold;
A mansion there is waiting for me,
Soon its beauty I will see,
In that city where we never shall grow old.

In loving memory of Larry Leon
born Nov. 20, 1975, died Oct. 15, 1992,
son of Henry Jr. & Ida Mae Raber

On November 20, nineteen seventy-five,
A baby boy all healthy and alive.
We were all excited and happy at the birth of our son,
Our very first baby named Larry Leon.

Oh, how we loved him, he brought us much joy,
  So healthy and happy, our own little boy.
The years passed by swiftly, we watched him grow,
  From infant to boyhood and now he would be twenty years old.
A friendly person, making friends as he went,
  God gave us a treasure when Larry He sent.
His brothers and sisters loved him a lot,
  A special "big brother," why would they not?
Larry and Dallas were almost like twins,
  Always together through thick and thin;
They loved to tease their three sisters dear,
  Marietta, Mandy, and Lela for a few short years.
He grew on to manhood, the size of his Dad,
  Helping where he could, giving all that he had.
Sixteen years old, life was still going strong,
  Our hearts were content as we traveled along.
God had His plans, He showed us so plain,
  When He let lightning hit before a rain.
Oct. 15, 1992, dawned like any other day;
  At around noon the call came to say,
Something has happened very critically,
  You need to come over, oh, what did we see?
He was lying so quiet on a truck load of lumber,
  With no sign of life, he appeared to be in a deep slumber;
So suddenly and final when lightning hit him,
  With a very bright flash, then all seemed dim.
Oh, let this be a reminder for each and every one,
  To be prepared as we know not when our Lord shall come.
We miss him so much when it is time for a meal,
  It is hard to describe the lonesomeness we feel.
Always being a close family and each one so dear,
  We must go on, tho' we've shed many a tear.
Now, three long years have since gone by,
  When thinking of memories sweet we sometimes wonder why.
We want to be patient and trust in God's love,
  Many times we find comfort and help from above;
Let's prepare to meet Him in the sweet by and by,
  In a land of promise where nobody shall die.

Daniel E. Bontrager: Apr. 25, 1925 - Dec. 6, 1996

Submitted by: Glen D. Bontrager, Shipshewana, Indiana (a son)

On October fifth, we children had a surprise dinner party for our folks. This was for their 50th wedding anniversary. Each person gave them a small gift. We enjoyed the day not knowing that Mom or Dad were not well.

Their wedding anniversary was not till November fifth, however that evening my wife and I went over to spend the evening with them. When we came into the house, Dad told me that he wants to tell us something. Then he gave us the shocking news that Mom's cancer was back again and that the doctor wanted to remove the large tumor plus remove her right breast. Mom had had cancer surgery a year earlier and took six chemo treatments. We did not realize that she had signs of it again.

Also that evening Dad said that he was not feeling the best. He has done a lot of painting, and at the time was painting for a factory. Dad said that he did not have an appetite and his feet were kind of swollen up a little. He said most days he only eats half a sandwich. I told him that he needs to drink a lot of water, and he stated that water does not even taste good anymore.

That evening we went home, not realizing what was ahead of our family. The next two days Dad went painting again. He later told me that he had fever those two days and some blackouts during painting. The last two days that he worked were on November sixth and seventh. On Friday, November eighth, Mom and Dad went to a wedding and Dad was to have the opening sermon, but was unable to.

That afternoon they went to the doctor to schedule Mom for her surgery which was to be done on November 29th. That afternoon the doctor also checked Dad and found out that he had blood in his urine. They also gave him water pills for his swollen feet. On November 11, Dad took blood tests and he found out the next day that he had an enlarged liver.

By now it was hard for Dad to be up and around because he had pain and shortness of breath. On Wednesday, November 13th, he took more blood tests to see if he had hepatitis. We would not be able to get the results till Friday, November 15th. During this time Dad was on the couch in pain with shortness of breath as his enlarged liver was pushing against his body organs. Also, his feet were more swollen by then and it was hard for him to walk.

On Friday, November 15th, some of us children and Mom went with Dad to the hospital to do more testing, like an MRI test and chest and pelvic scan. We had to wait three to four hours for the results. This was a long wait as we did not know what to expect. At last Mom was paged and answered the phone. We were all by her side when the doctor said that Dad's liver was full of cancer and that he also had some in his intestines.

We were sent home with Dad with just pain medicine and with no hope of a cure. My brother also talked with the doctor and asked what we could expect. He gave Dad two weeks to live, but Dad gave himself up to the Lord right away and renewed his and our faith in a higher power. Dad kept saying that all the stuff in the world does not mean anything anymore, he just gave himself up right away saying, "God knows best."

The doctor went on a trip and rescheduled Mom's surgery for December second. Mom's tumor seemed to be getting bigger and more uncomfortable as most of the other days I visited Dad. In the PM of Saturday, November 16, I also went over and stayed overnight and was with them on Sunday which was their church Sunday.

Mom and Dad could not attend because Dad was either in bed or on the couch. However, he sat up some on the easy chair. Dad and I shared many things together that day that I will never forget. By this time Dad had his funeral plans made. He personally asked the neighbors to be pallbearers and also told the preachers what scriptures to use at the funeral. I also asked Dad if he could forgive me for all that I had done. He said that he could easily forgive me and holds nothing against anyone.

Mom and Dad were getting a lot of company which we all enjoyed. But we could see that Dad was getting more and more tired. On November 18, Mom and Dad both got anointed. It was so hard on us to see Dad this way, since I never saw him sick or not being at the dinner table or miss chores because of sickness. I guess I took Dad for granted.

His left leg had started to swell some by then, too. Dad was praying for a good and clear mind till his end. He also talked in such a touching way. He said that he was glad that he is able to have his viewing ahead of his death. He enjoyed the company so much, but a lot of talking made him tired.

By November 23rd, his voice started to get weaker, but he

seemed about the same. November 24th we had church at our house and, oh, how we missed Mom and Dad not being here. We always liked to hear him preach. In 1996 he had preached more often than any other year. He said he wishes he could just preach one more time. He always dreaded to see the dark night coming on. Mom said that they talked and talked and cried and cried together at night. Dad even preached some at night.

On November 25th it was more of a struggle for Dad so we got oxygen for him which seemed to help. Dad said that he wishes Jesus was ready for him. We cancelled Mom's surgery since Dad might not be with us much longer and we did not want Mom in the hospital if Dad might pass away.

On Tuesday, November 26th, we got a hospital bed for Dad, because he was getting weaker. He could now rest better in this bed. He was unable to go to the bathroom by himself. On the 28th he had some chest pains and seemed weaker. He had a good night's rest and seemed in good spirits the next day. We were glad that his mind was still so good. His right leg was very swollen and almost purple. On Sunday, December first, the doctor was out and Dad asked him if he had any good news for him; asking him if his end might be here soon.

Mom told the doctor that she wanted surgery as soon as possible since she has a lot of pain from her tumor. Each time we visited Dad, he always said that when he dies, please take care of Mom. On December second, Mom went to the hospital to take tests in case we decided to do surgery. The earliest we could schedule Mom for surgery would be on Friday, December sixth.

The next few days Dad was very weak, but also about the same. His legs were more and more swollen and he seemed to be more swollen farther up in his body. On Thursday, December fifth, we started with Home Care and a nurse came out and checked Dad. She said his lungs, heart, and oxygen in his body seemed good. We wanted to know what she thought if we went ahead with Mom's surgery for the next morning. She said Dad could last two weeks yet, but also said he could pass away tonight. After she left the doctor stopped in and checked Dad. He did not know what to think, but both said that we need to do something with Mom soon. We all prayed like before, God's will be done.

Dad asked the nurse about what would happen if he died and Mom was in the hospital. She said, "Just wait at Heaven's door till

Mom gets there."

On Friday morning, December sixth, at 5:30 A.M. Mom and Dad said their final tearful good byes and Mom left for the hospital for her surgery at eight o'clock A.M. About an hour after Mom left, Dad started having breathing problems and started to get very weak. It just seemed that when Mom left for the hospital, that she released him to go home to the Lord.

I was at work, but kept in touch with my three sisters since they were with Mom in the hospital. They called around eight o'clock A.M. and said that Mom had left for the surgery room. I told my sisters to call me as soon as Mom was out of surgery. During this time, my brother Wilbur called and said that Dad was in a very weak condition and that if I wanted to see him yet, to come over right away.

I told him that in about one hour the girls would call and then I would come over and share with Dad about the surgery. The sisters called and said Mom was back in her room and the doctor said they had taken out a tumor the size of an orange and also some small ones the size of grapes, plus her right breast was removed and her lymph nodes.

When I got to Dad's I could not believe what I saw. He was struggling for the next breath. He had me open the window and we had a fan going as well. The room was cold, but he was hot; even though his legs and arms were very cold. By now he was down to a whisper and like he always said when I left, please take care of Mom. I told him that Mom had surgery and the tumor is removed and that she is resting. He said that he was so glad.

My brother asked Dad, "Can you wait till Mom gets home?"

He said, "No. It's different today and I hope the next breath will be my last."

Oh, surely Dad could not pass away with Mom in the hospital. We three brothers were with Dad and our three sisters were with Mom. I left for home about 1:30 in the afternoon and since regret that I did not stay with him. Two of my sisters stopped in to see Dad on their way home from the hospital, not realizing that the end was so close.

Dad was so concerned to have everything in place for his end, even like having the checkbook balanced. Dad started to slow down his puffing and his breath was weaker. At about four o'clock in the afternoon he opened his eyes and looked towards the door, like Jesus was there at last, and then closed his eyes for the last time. Life had fled without a struggle.

My one sister was still with Mom, not knowing what happened and the other two sisters left for home about 20 minutes before he passed away. We were contacted right away and went to Dad. When I came into the bedroom, it was quiet and calm and Dad looked like he was in a better place without pain. We needed to go to the hospital and tell Mom and our sister LeAnna that Dad was no longer among the living.

Oh Lord, how hard this would be. How would it affect our mom who was recovering from her surgery. We all went out to her room and closed the door. We waited a little bit then I said to Mom that we lost Dad this afternoon. She was on morphine, but she still realized what happened. We all felt so sorry for her that she could not be with Dad. But we were also glad that she did not have to see Dad suffer.

My wife stayed with Mom and the rest of us went home to the body and waited on the undertaker to make the funeral arrangements. Dad died on Friday, December sixth, so plans were made to have the funeral on Tuesday, December tenth. The doctor said he would release Mom to come home on Sunday morning and Sunday would be the first day of the viewing with Dad coming home around ten thirty A.M.

Mom was not allowed to shake hands with the people. On Sunday we had a lot of people for the viewing. Almost used up 1000 cards and the guest book was full the first day of the viewing. Monday we also had a lot of people in to view Dad, but not as many as the day before. On Tuesday we had a very nice day for the funeral, with the main part in the new buggy shed and the rest in brother Wilbur's big house and also in Mom and Dad's house. We had services in three places.

Mom went with the buggy to the graveyard. Preaching in the main part was done by Harley Lambright and his best friend Stevie Esh from Pennsylvania, and by Bishop Daniel Otto. Psalms 90 was read by Deacon Menno Lambright. Preaching in Wilbur's house was done by Marvin Helmuth of Illinois and Dan Stoltzfus of Pennsylvania, and Bishop Vernon Weaver. Preaching in Mom and Dad's house was by Mose Riehl of Penn., and Bishop Henry Miller of Illinois.

We all miss Dad, but we want to accept this as the Lord's will and we are glad that Dad no longer has to suffer. He passed away three weeks to the day after we found out he had cancer. During his illness Dad often said God was not mean to him and that he was glad for this chance. We had a very good Dad. During his illness he said that if he would ever get well again, he would want to visit all the sick people he could.

Good bye, Dad.

Daniel E. Shetler: Jan. 9, 1965 - July 28, 1983

Submitted by: Mrs. Enos Shetler, Fredericksburg, Ohio

It was 13 years ago in July that this happened, but it still stands out in my mind as clearly as if it had been yesterday. Daniel left in the morning as usual and we never gave it a thought how very unusual the day would end. He was working at the carpenter trade. Around 11:30 a kind friend came and told me our son Daniel had an electrical shock and we are to come to the hospital right away and offered to take us. My husband was just ready to leave for the Kidron sale, but we stopped him just in time.

With trembling hands I got ready to go as fast as I could with the help of a dear daughter. We stopped at Fredericksburg to find the shortest route. He was working in Parma, Ohio, which is close to Cleveland, so we had to go all the way to Cleveland to the hospital where they had taken him. That was the longest, most sorrowful, and prayerful ride I ever had. I had in mind he might be gone when we got there, but was hoping and praying that it would not be so.

Our son-in-law, Ervin Petersheim, was working with him at the time and was standing on a ladder. He wanted to saw off something and asked Daniel to hand him the skill saw. Daniel reached for the saw and it shocked him so hard that it pulled it clear up to his shoulder and he couldn't let go. When Ervin saw what was happening, he quickly pulled the cord and Daniel collapsed. He tried CPR and all he knew to do; the squad was called and they did everything they could, but life was gone.

The skill saw was examined later and they found no fault. Some people claimed a skill saw wouldn't have enough watts to kill a person, but it couldn't have been anything else because Ervin saw it all happen. All we could think was his end was here and something had to happen.

He was a very concerned boy of 18 years. He was baptized on his confession of faith the summer before. We are often lonesome for him, but would never wish him back in this world of sin.

My husband also passed away five years ago, so we have many lonely days. There are still three girls and three boys at home which are a great help to me.

David Y. Esh: Oct. 19, 1963 - Aug. 10, 1980
Submitted by: Levi A. Esh, Millersburg, Pennsylvania

The wail of sirens broke the silence of a sultry summer Saturday night. The alarms sounded at four different fire stations, all within a three mile radius. Gordonville responded with their ambulance and Ronks, Bird-in-Hand, and Intercourse responded with rescue squad units.

We knew that something out of the ordinary was going on with all these units responding, but it was not unusual for the local Gordonville Ambulance to go flashing by our house at any hour of day or night. I stepped outside to take in the night sounds for a bit, but then Naomi and I went back to bed, because we had planned to get up early to attend church at brother Dan's over in the Intercourse district the next morning.

As we drifted off to sleep, 18 year old daughter Anna Mary came home from a Saturday evening gathering of dating couples and we could hear her special friend, Jonas Smucker, settle into the spare room upstairs. He lived 13 miles away near Churchtown and plans were to stay over at our house to save his horse some miles for Sunday.

There was one member of the family out yet, 16 year old David. He was our oldest son in the family of three boys and four girls. He was with some friends for a volley ball game at Paul Smuckers near Lancaster. As thoughts turned to him, I resolved that I would try to be a better father to a teenage boy who was growing up so fast. We needed to spend more time with each other to discuss the importance of those precious teenage years. Years that can set a pattern for the rest of a person's life.

It must have been an hour or more later and I was still drifting in and out which was unusual, for I was normally a sound sleeper. I heard a vehicle slow down and turn into our driveway. I slipped out of bed and into some clothes when I heard footsteps come up the walks. As I opened the door, Dick Skethway and Dan Kauffman, both good friends and officers in the Gordonville Fire Company of which I was also on the board and serving as Chairman at the time, came up the steps.

Dick spoke first. "Your son David was killed."

Only five words, but life for us took on a new meaning. Sixteen years later, tears flow freely just to review those first moments of shock. They explained that a drunken driver had smashed into the rear end of an open buggy carrying five boys. Two were dead and three more were hospitalized in serious condition. They offered to take us to the County Hospital Morgue to identify our son, which was hardly necessary, but it gave us something to do and there was nothing which seemed more pressing than to rush to our son's side.

Naomi had not heard me slip out of bed but awoke to the sound of voices at the door. I went back to her and asked her to get dressed, that there had been an accident and we were needed at the hospital. When we were ready to leave, I realized that the news must be broken and that we should not leave the house without rousing the children who remained at home.

I told Naomi that for David life was gone. In stunned silence we traveled with Skethway up Rt. 340 toward Lancaster. We passed the scene of the accident near Weavertown crossroads where firemen were still clearing away the wreckage.

When we arrived at the county morgue, they asked us to wait in the lobby so they could clean up a bit. After a few minutes we were ushered in and found our son with electrodes still attached to his chest and an airway in his mouth. His body was still warm and he appeared to be sleeping. There was a small mark on his forehead and a deeper abrasion on the back of his shoulder. We later found out that the two boys killed were standing on the back of the buggy.

David's right foot was missing and was found wedged in the springs of the wreckage. His left foot hanging by only a few strands. The coroner's report stated that his neck was broken. On a nearby stretcher lay the body of the other fatality. Melvin, a 16 year old son of Naomi's cousins, Henry and Nancy King of Lititz. He showed severe head injuries and a badly bruised body.

There were some telephone calls to make and Al Furman, our funeral director, asked that we request a release of the body. We called Dr. Show, the county coroner, who informed us that there would be some charges and that an autopsy was mandatory. I stated that we had no charges, but was told that this matter was out of my hands. The state would have some charges.

We headed home again and soon had neighbors drop in to comfort us and help in any way possible. Our parents, family members, and ministers arrived. We sat around the kitchen table and made lists of friends and relatives who were to be notified and given funeral invitations. The funeral was planned for Tuesday and we had word through the funeral director that the Kings planned theirs for Wednesday.

As dawn broke on that Sunday morning, we were still around the table when a father and mother arrived with their son, the driver of the vehicle that had crashed into the rear of the buggy. Our hearts went out to this grief-stricken, wayward son who seemed to be carrying an unbearable burden. We could not possibly harbor any ill will toward him. This whole experience had to be looked at as something which had happened as a part of God's plan for us. The unfortunate young man had only been a part of the means of carrying it out.

As friends and relatives came by to comfort us, the chores at the barn were taken care of by neighbors and church people. The diesel engine was heard starting up to do the milking, but we were expected to devote our attention to visitors as others took over our daily duties over the time of the funeral.

Furman brought the body back on Sunday evening and on the surface he appeared unmarked; a young boy fast asleep. Friends came from far and near and as they filed past only a few words were needed. At times there came a heartfelt handshake and no words were spoken. No words were needed. We felt it and knew that here was one who had trod this same pathway at some earlier time.

None of the three survivors of the buggy accident were able to attend the funeral. The driver of the buggy, Benuel King, who also had his horse Bobby killed, lay in guarded condition and hardly moved a muscle until Wednesday and it was weeks until he recovered to the extent that he realized that two of his friends had died. Sylvan Stoltzfus, 17, and John King, 16, were out of the hospital in a week.

Elmer Kuepfers of Linwood, Ontario, and Jake Peacheys of Bellville, Penn., came for the funeral. We were astounded by how many of our friends found out about the accident and promptly made arrangements to come to our side.

Four of David's cousins were pallbearers and over 500 people attended the funeral in neighbor Jake Lapp's barn. By the time of the burial, warm weather was taking its toll and we could see that this earthly body would soon decay. It was time to lay it away and move on.

We attended the funeral of Henry King's son Melvin, the next day. At the graveyard, I was tapped on the shoulder by Melvin's grandfather, Preacher Ephraim Riehl. He made a short statement for which I had to respect him. He said, "Now when you write your weekly Budget letter, do not write about this. You would expose your inner feelings and most people will not understand what you're saying anyway."

I had to respect him for his feelings, for he had trod this pathway some years before when their young son had drowned. The writer's pen has been nearly silent on this subject all these years except an occasional note to someone bereaved in a like experience. To write a few words and express some of the emotions for a book designed to comfort the bereaved, makes it seem fitting to now break the silence. It was a decision not easily made.

Thursday morning came. The funerals were now over and neighbors were not expected to remain on duty for chores. I opened the closet doors to get my work shoes for the first time in nearly a week and was rocked back on my heels. There beside mine, were David's shoes, where he had put them on Saturday evening.

This was only the beginning of a long string of such incidents as we now began the process of healing those deep wounds of sorrow. David had been a young handyman and there were little labor saving gadgets and notes all over the place that were found in the following days and weeks.

He had grown up on the farm, but also spent a lot of hours in the shop and was rapidly becoming a good mechanic. One lady reported that this must have been the young lad who had recently knocked on her door after she had requested service on her refrigerator. She looked past him to speak to an older man who was along, only to find out that he was just a driver while the young lad did the work. She said the service was satisfactory. We found in the following weeks that there were many similar incidents, and for a young boy, he had briefly touched many lives.

The Sunday before the accident, church services were at Ben

Beiler's. David and several others had planned to have an outing with some girls on Saturday evening. We begged that he cancel those plans since it was our church Sunday and we needed to all be together in church. We're forever grateful for those memories as one-armed Preacher Amos Mishler of Indiana delivered a powerful message that day. I can still see David sitting in rapt attention. Amos asked us to appreciate our heritage and the privilege of growing up in a Christian home. He explained that he had come from what we call the outside world, but by God's grace was allowed to enter into our society. His grandfather had been a worldly drunkard.

Would a young lad have a premonition of things to come? I do not know, but have to wonder. That day after church, David drove home and took along Naomi Stoltzfus who lived a mile back Harvest Drive. She offered to walk back, but he insisted on taking her on home. As they drove back the road, he made the statement that he thought that something was bound to happen to slow things down. That the tempo of life among the young folks was going too fast.

In the following weeks and into late October we had visitors nearly every evening. We received over 700 cards by mail and the outpouring of love and sympathy was astounding. With my duties at the shop, I could soon immerse myself in a real busy schedule and the shock of those first days would wear away. That shock that numbed the senses to the point where for several days, the best prepared meal had absolutely no taste.

For Naomi it was a bit harder to get going. She had four year old Ruth to care for and keep her company, but household duties weighed heavily those first weeks and by noon time she was exhausted. The shop workers did a remarkable job of lightening my duties and we set aside time daily for me to spend a long noon hour at the house. We would leave the morning mail for noon time and after lunch spend some precious time together opening and reading letters.

"From the mouths of babes, comes great wisdom!"

One meal time several months later, our family of six remaining children; Anna Mary, 18; Levi Jr., 15; Ada, 13; Lena, 11; Emanuel, eight; and Ruth, four years of age, had a discussion going on about what could be done for drinking problems or the problem of drunken drivers. No one seemed to have a real solution until little Emanuel piped up, "That's easy. Why don't they just quit making strong drink?"

My mother was a soft spoken, unassuming pillar of faith in the following weeks. She wouldn't stay long, but would occasionally drop in and sit for a quiet chat while doing some sewing which she brought along, or better yet, help with some of ours, for button holes were Mom's specialty.

At Christmas time, she confided that she was not feeling well and we knew it was serious when she told us that she had made arrangements for some tests after New Year's. For many years she had a hacking cough but it never really amounted to much. Now when we visited her at the hospital after her day of testing, she stated quite frankly, "The doctor says I have cancer." We swallowed a bit hard and were left speechless. She continued, "And the Lord willing, I can live with that. But if not, I can die."

We had never realized or appreciated my mother's great inner strength and steadfast faith like we did in the months that followed and until her death on June first, at the age of 76. We were often made to wonder if a grandmother's sorrow in the shock of David's death could have triggered a sleeping case of cancer.

We were not alone in our sorrow. Ten days before David's death, Andrew Fishers' teenage daughter, Evelyn, of New Holland was kidnapped. Those last days of his life, we remember David going for the mail or asking Mom if there were any reports concerning Evelyn Fisher. There was a suspect, but he admitted nothing and for weeks huge search parties sought evidence in wooded areas and even dug up garbage heaps at land fills. Finally in October, her remains were found in a wooded area south of New Holland.

A death in the family is traumatic, but ten weeks of agonizing in the unknown would be a terrible experience.

Over this same time, the family of Karen Quinlan of New Jersey, was embroiled in a court case which made national headlines. She was kept "alive" on a breathing machine for several years after an accident while the family fought a court battle to have life support systems disconnected so that their brain dead child could die in peace. They finally won the case and disconnected the system, but the body of the child lay in a vegetable-like state for several more years before passing away. Finally the family could lay the case to rest and begin in the healing of their sorrow.

It is said that deep traumatic experiences bring out the best and the worst in people. We were told this experience could leave us bitter or on the other hand could make us better. The choice to an extent was ours in how we managed to cope with it.

Several weeks after the accident, we were eating lunch one day when a vehicle stopped beside the house and a man stepped out beside the maple tree. I went out to meet him and as I approached him, he turned his back and stepped behind the tree, weeping with his hands over his face. He soon recovered and asked if he could shake my hand. He had come from Dover, Delaware, into this area on business and wished to stop by to express his sympathy, for he had had a similar experience a few years earlier. Several years later we read that this man had taken his own life.

The workings of the Holy Spirit and the power of prayer were keenly felt in the darkest hours. Communion with God was at a higher level than ever before experienced. He had reached into our very midst and plucked a spirit from this world and transported it into the eternal realms. One of our older church members told me that we are in his thoughts daily in prayer as the words "Thy will be done" are uttered in the Lord's prayer.

Scripture passages took on a new and deeper meaning than ever before. The account of the death of King David's son as recorded in the book of II Samuel, chapter 12, encouraged us to brace up and move on with life. By doing so, we were preparing for a better life to come. In Job 1:21 we read, 'The Lord gave, the Lord hath taken away; blessed be the name of the Lord.' In chapter 5:17, Job continues, 'Behold, happy is the man whom God correcteth: therefore despise not the chastening of the Almighty.'

Twice each year we have the scriptures Hebrews 11 and 12 in our churches. Much deeper became the meaning of the passage in 12:6, 'For whom the Lord loveth, He chasteneth, and scourgeth every son whom He receiveth.' If then the measure of his love matched or surpassed the depth of our sorrow, His love for us must be truly great.

One of the humbling thoughts on this issue was the question, "Was our walk in life so far off course, that a correction of this magnitude was needed to draw us back into the fold?" But then we read of the son born blind who was healed by Jesus. The disciples asked who had sinned, the father or the son that he was born blind. Jesus answered that neither had sinned but that it was so that God's works should be made manifest. Likewise, He answered when asked if the 18 Galileans who died when the tower of Siloam fell, had sinned above all others.

We could not help but think of Lazarus who was raised from the dead by Jesus and set before his sisters in full health again. What would be our reaction if Jesus were walking upon this earth and we could call upon Him to restore our son? Then upon further thought, we cannot read any further account of the life of Lazarus. Surely though, at some later date Lazarus had to again pass through death's door. This was all in the hands of God, as was our case, and again we hoped to accept God's will for us and be satisfied with our lot in life.

We are often made to ponder upon the relationship between God and Abraham. It must have taken a steadfast faith to obey the command to offer up a son as a burnt offering by a father's own hand. Abraham's reward was a blessing beyond measure. God gave His only Son to suffer and die for us and our thoughts now spin into an orbit that is far too deep for us mortals to comprehend.

Days stretched into weeks, one day at a time it seemed, and as shock wore off our minds reeled at times. Some days we seemed to have conquered our doubts and fears and to have accepted our lot and were now on track to heal our grief only to have some incident turn up that seemed to take us back to square one and start all over again. After some weeks the "zeitlang", (I know no word in the English language that properly defines this yearning for the presence of a loved one. Homesickness is no substitute) set in and we'd find certain incidents coming to mind that brought us down and we convulsed into tears. We learned to weep and have it out and oftentimes there followed a peaceful feeling as though the very soul had been washed clean. These bouts deepened our faith that God had a plan for all mankind and we could only watch in reverence and awe as His plan unfolded.

We also found that the feeling of "zeitlang" and the feeling of self-pity were first cousins. Both of these grow and multiply by cultivation. Likely we've all met someone who has fallen into the rut of self-pity and feeling sorry for oneself. It's a poison to the soul which all Christian believers are admonished to avoid. The "zeitlang" brought back many precious memories and we learned to avoid brooding over the crushed dreams of our son's future here on earth and to dwell upon those blessed promises of a better land on high.

At a nephew's wedding that fall, the boys filed in by age where both of these fatalities would have been cousins. There was certainly a void in the row and thoughts turned to the boys. However, I tried to place them, not in an earthly grave, but at a Heavenly wedding feast in a mansion on high, where if we could see them we'd have cause to rejoice rather than sorrow.

Weighing heavily upon the mind of any father or mother of a child who has been called away is the sense of responsibility for the well-being of one's children. As I gazed upon the lifeless form of our son in his coffin, I couldn't help but question whether I had done my duty as a father. Had I prepared my son to meet his God? My wish was that if he had in any way fallen short, I would like to bear the blame. Scripture speaks highly of a Father's love and again we could ponder some deep thoughts.

Now comes a time for the hardest part of this narrative. We do not wish to open old wounds nor hurt anyone, but this story would not be complete without an account of the greatest gift, *forgiving hearts*! From the very beginning we could not harbor any ill will and we're grateful to God that it could be so.

On Saturday, August 9th, the day before the accident, we were all invited to a Lapp family reunion on my wife's side. It was the first one ever in our time and there have been none since.

This wayward son, who was the driver of the car which hit the boys, was not just an unknown someone else. He was my wife's cousin. Though he did not attend, the reunion was at his sister's farm and his parents, and all the uncles and aunts and most of the cousins attended. We had a day of visiting of old folks and games for the younger set.

This son, then 29 years of age and still single, had become more interested in sports and travel than the home life of our plain people. After a winter in Florida, he had been put in the ban by the church and up to this time had shown no interest in returning to the fold.

As stated earlier, our grief-stricken cousin carried a heavy burden. He attended the funerals and we spoke with him to tell him that all was freely forgiven. But for some months after the accident, it seemed that he felt life for him held no hope of a redeeming grace.

Finally the decision was made to come back to the old home church and he too could experience the healing of the spirit after a time of deep sorrow. The family came to our house for a Sunday dinner toward spring, but we seldom had personal contact over the next few years.

In 1985, he married a fine young woman and we had a special invitation to the wedding. We occasionally meet over the years at funerals and some other gatherings and at the business place where he works, but our special relationship is never mentioned. Nor need it be. It is certainly a gift of God that we could come from different sides of a deep, traumatic experience and still be friends. Several years ago at a wedding, we shared a book to help with singing in the evening. Each of us certainly had some unspoken thoughts but each of us also knew that this experience had made better men of both of us.

The encouragement and prayers offered in our behalf, place a debt upon us that seems impossible to repay. We shall spend our lifetime trying to pass on these blessings to others in need.

It has been no easy matter to pen such sacred thoughts, but if this narrative can be of any help or encouragement to someone else, it will have been well worth the effort and to God be the glory.

We close with the thought, "What a mighty God we serve!"

Andrew E. Yoder: Sept. 18, 1987 - May 4, 1995

Submitted by: Eli & Annie Marie Yoder, Arcola, Illinois

On Friday, September 18, 1987, Andrew E. Yoder was born at Covenant Hospital in Champaign, Illinois, to the happy parents of Eli and Annie Marie Yoder. Andrew had one brother and two sisters; Joseph, 12; Rachel, ten; and Leah, seven. Andrew was brought home from the hospital Saturday, September 19.

One week later he was taken back for a P.K.U. test, then the doctor said he has Yellow Jaundice. He had to stay in the hospital for Photo Therapy. Which meant he had to sleep under what they call the Bili Lights. Bright blue lights with no covers on him, no clothes, except a diaper. This is against the nature of a baby to lie in a bed like this. We would stand beside his bed trying to comfort him by talking and singing to him, and hold his little hands until he would finally wear out and go to sleep. Maybe 20 minutes later he would wake up and start all over. The nurses would come in about every four to six hours to take a blood sample to see how his jaundice was doing.

After a one-week stay in the hospital, the doctor said to take him home and come back every day to have blood work done. On the following Tuesday, his test was very high again and the doctor said he had to stay in the hospital again.

On Wednesday a social worker came into the room and talked to us about the child. The social worker said, "You could be at home if you had Photo Therapy lights at home."

So checking around was done and a generator lined up to run the lights at least 14 to 16 hours a day. We brought baby Andrew home on Thursday to be under the lights. We took him back to the hospital every two days for blood work for a couple weeks. Then once a week and finally once a month and then every six months.

In the winter he would usually catch the cold very easily. He could not tolerate strong medication on account of his liver problem. He was taken to Children's Hospital in Chicago twice, to Dr. Robert Whitington, a liver specialist. All the doctors said this is something the child will have to live with.

He started school in 1993, but missed lots of school the first winter because he was often sick with the cold and croup. In preparing for his second year in school, we and the teacher agreed to send him to a special school for slow learners. He started his second year at the new school and was very excited about school. He could hardly wait for his ride to go to school.

On Saturday, February 25th, he had a sore throat and was taken to the doctor and got some light medication, but he still felt good enough to play softball that afternoon. On February 26th, Sunday morning, he got up from sleeping under his lights, which were shining down on him in his bed. This was to keep his bilirubin tests down. (The yellowness of his skin.) He didn't feel very good, but he said he was okay to go to church in a neighboring district. People noticed he was very, very yellow that day. He ate dinner at church. Little did we realize this would be the last time to be in church and eat dinner after church for the dear little boy.

We decided to keep him home from school Monday morning and thought maybe he would be well enough by Tuesday. He didn't want to miss any school days because he had perfect attendance so far. He wasn't any better on Tuesday morning and then Wednesday morning around two o'clock he woke up and asked if he could go to school today. I said, "If you have no fever and feel better, you can go to school." I took his temperature and the thermometer read 102. Oh, what a letdown to tell Andrew, "No not today, you have 102° temperature."

He just cried and cried. He had known it was the day for parents to bring hot lunches to school and he did not want to miss that. On Thursday he was taken to the doctor again and changed medicine which made it worse. By Saturday he could hardly walk anymore by himself. He was taken to the doctor again and sent on to the hospital in Champaign, Illinois. By Sunday night he was transferred to Riley Children's Hospital in Indianapolis by ambulance. We checked into Riley Hospital at ten o'clock. They took more tests and changed his I.V.

They took him up to his room at 12 o'clock. At two o'clock two nurses came into his room and said they are going to put a small tube down his nose, through his throat, and into his stomach. They would use this tube to feed him because he needed more than I.V. They tried and tried to put the tube down Andrew's nose but couldn't get it down. They went and got four more nurses. Now the six nurses tried and tried. Of course Andrew lay there gagging, choking, coughing, and crying. Oh so pitiful! Finally, an hour later, they had the tube down to his stomach. We were at his bedside trying to comfort him, but felt very helpless.

Not much improvement from day to day. After an 11 day stay in the hospital in Indianapolis, the doctor said to take him home and maybe things will work out with him at home. We were so thankful to at least have him at home again because they had very little hope for little Andrew.

We expect the doctor's feelings were that he wouldn't last long at home. So at 2:50 P.M. on Thursday, March 16, he got to see home again. He still couldn't walk and didn't feel like playing with any of his toys.

Neighbors, friends, and relatives stopped in every day. We had lots of company which helped us to keep going, but sure felt unworthy of all the concerned visits. Days went by, weeks went by, and not much changed except he couldn't talk at all anymore.

Little children, schoolmates, neighbor children, and children he used to play with in church would come visit Andrew, bringing little gifts and a nice smile and he would smile back. His smile was the last thing that left him.

On Tuesday, April 24, Andrew started to go backwards. On

Thursday, April 26, he could still smile a little, but on Friday, no more smiles and he didn't seem to respond to anything. On Saturday, Andrew cried and cried almost all day. Oh so heartbreaking. We felt ever so helpless.

On Sunday lots of people were here to see how Andrew was doing. He was very low. On Monday around 2:30 P.M. he was out in the kitchen on his little recliner and started shaking all over and rolled his eyes around in his head with jerky movements. He finally settled down and he was so peaceful then. At 4:30 it happened again. By ten o'clock he was in a coma. From 4:30 to ten o'clock we will never forget. Little Andrew was very miserable. We thought his end must be very near. There was no change, no response, and he was running a temperature of 107°. His mouth would not open to be fed anything. We tried to give him water with a little sponge from the hospital, but the water would just run back out.

On Tuesday evening, relatives, neighbors, and friends sat around his bed and sang songs for him for an hour and a half. One of the family members sang Andrew's favorite song and he opened his eyes and looked at her. After the song was sung, he closed his eyes again.

There wasn't much change on Wednesday. In the evening more people came and we sang again. We don't know if Andrew knew people were singing or not, but it was a precious time people spent together with the little precious soul ready to be in heaven with Jesus.

On Thursday morning, May fourth, the sun came up in the east, but at 3:20 in the afternoon we could feel the angels from heaven were there around his bed. They took Andrew's soul to heaven while his parents, brother, sisters, grandparents, and a bishop from church were also at his bedside. Oh what a blessing.

Let us all prepare to meet God in Heaven. May God bless each and everyone who reads these lines and hope God can keep talking to us and remind us humans how serious life really is.

Leroy B. Graber: Oct 27, 1978 - June 14, 1993

Submitted by: Mr. & Mrs. Sam A. Graber, Grabill, Indiana

On October 27, 1978, we were blessed with twin boys; Lewis A. and Leroy B. Lewis was born first and then Leroy. Leroy had a curvature of the spine because of the way he way lying and had to stay in the hospital. Lewis was in the hospital for seven days and

Leroy stayed there for ten days. They came home weighing a couple of ounces different. They weighed five pounds, six ounces and four pounds, 13 ounces. They both lost some, but gained it back soon.

I had help from relatives for three weeks. My mother and sister Susie really helped me out with the sewing. Joseph, our oldest son, helped with the laundry and dishes. He went out to do the chores and when he came back in he said, "Mom, it doesn't even look like I swept."

They were content to play with my stainless steel pots and pans. Saturdays were always hectic, but we enjoyed them. Leroy told Lewis, "We're special."

Grandpa and Grandma got them mixed up once in a while. Sometimes when I would go in to wake them up, I would get them mixed up.

Lewis will never forget when they gave themselves haircuts. I had gone outside to rake leaves and left them inside by themselves for about one half hour. When the children came home from school, they said, "Mom, come quick. Lewis and Leroy gave each other haircuts and they are ashamed of them."

In November of 1987, at the age of nine, we went to the Shrine Hospital in Chicago with Leroy for surgery. Sam was with him the morning of his surgery and he asked Leroy if he was ready and still wanted to go through with it. He said yes. The doctor and nurses all thought he came through the surgery very well. Leroy said, "Mom, I'm good according to all the other people here."

They took a piece off his hip and fused it to his spine so it wouldn't curve anymore. He had to wear a neck brace for a year. He went to school and people used to tease him that he was wearing a football uniform. When he was able, he started helping with chores again.

He always said "Thank you, Mom, thank you", or "Good night, Mom, good night" over and over again. One time he was holding a sparrow and it died in his hands. "Mom, I didn't mean it. Mom, I'm sorry."

He also asked, "Mom, can we get to heaven even if we aren't baptized?"

I told him, "Yes, if we believe in Jesus Christ and live for him."

They used to play basketball a lot. We would call them for supper, but they would keep on playing. Leroy wasn't handicapped in playing and they knew each other's plays. They were the same height until the last year. Then Lewis grew more than Leroy because of where they fused his spine wouldn't grow anymore.

On June 8, 1993, Leroy wanted his pocketbook fixed because his change kept falling out. I taped it, then I put a couple stitches in with a needle and thread. "Mom don't worry about the change. I don't want to make them wait." His driver was there to pick him up for work. His last words were "Bye, Mom, bye." I watched him go and climb into the van never knowing that I wouldn't ever see him doing that again.

I left and went to help my sister-in-law get ready for church. An awful storm struck around three o'clock P.M. and we were just ready to start home, but we waited till it cleared a little. We were ready to go when my nephew, Jonas, and my sister dressed in black, came in and said, "Leroy was hit by lightning."

I asked, "Is he hurt?"

"Yes, he isn't here anymore."

Oh no! We went home and changed clothes. We missed Sam, but met at the hospital. When they called they said he was critical, but breathing. Leroy was a ground boy for his Uncle Ben's construction crew. Ben told Leroy to get in the garage when the storm came up. He picked up a couple more pieces, walked into the garage and turned around. Lightning struck and he fell down and turned black. They did mouth to mouth resuscitation and called the ambulance. Once they arrived they shocked him and got him breathing again and put him on a breathing machine.

Two other boys also got knocked down by the lightning in the same garage. We got to the hospital around 4:30 but they wouldn't let us go back to see him till 5:30. Oh, he looked so peaceful, hooked up to all kinds of machines. To know what he went through, we couldn't believe he looked so good. Then he had one bowel movement after another and it looked like it was cooking. But we still had hope that he would get better. His uncle Ben was surprised and said, "I can't believe he is breathing."

Around eight o'clock that night he opened his eyes and tried to talk, but they had a tube down his throat and he couldn't. I wish we could have taken the tube out to hear what he was trying to say. We told him if he could hear us he should squeeze our hand. He did, but his eyes stayed open and we had to tape them shut. The nurse said.

"I'm sorry, but those signs aren't good."

We still had hope that he would get better. I told the family when they came up Friday evening to talk to him. I knew he could hear by the expressions on his face. They started talking to him and his monitor went up. The nurses came in and gave him a shot and then he passed out. I went up to his bed and told Leroy that I was going home to change clothes since I had been there since Tuesday and this was Friday. He shed some big tears and shook all over. Sam said he had another spell around five o'clock Saturday morning and he couldn't breathe. They took the tubes out but couldn't find anything. I got up there around ten o'clock and twin Lewis, sis Rosalie, and Sam were standing around his bed. I wonder if he heard me come in because he opened his eyes.

Lewis said, "Well Leroy, if you can hear me, squeeze my hand. I love you." Rosalie said, "If you can hear me, squeeze my hand." And I took a hold of his hand and said, "Leroy, if you can hear me, squeeze my hand." He squeezed our hands and that was the last squeeze we got. That was Saturday and then they said they wanted to test his brain Monday. We were there all day before they let us know that his brain was dead and it was up to us to unhook the machine.

We were ready, but we waited till the family was all there before they unhooked him. They didn't want all of us in there until we told them of somebody else that was allowed to have the whole family in the room. They told us he might kick and jerk, but when they pulled the plug he was gone in six minutes. So final. We picked four of his classmates to dig his grave.

He died June 14, around 6:15 and the funeral was June 17, 1993.

-Mother

On October 27, 1978, we were blessed with twin boys named Lewis A. and Leroy B. Lewis was born first and then Leroy, who was born with a curvature of the spine. After many trips to the doctor we finally got in touch with Shriners Hospital in Chicago. It was then decided to do surgery and take a bone from his hip and fuse it to his spine to keep if from getting worse as he gets older.

At age nine, in November of 1987, we went to the Shrine Hospital to do surgery. The Shrine van went back and forth three times a week so we could trade off in staying with him. I was with him the morning of surgery. When it was time to go, I asked him if he was ready and if he still wanted to go through with it. He said yes. We always left it up to him and he wanted to do it. He was aware of his problem, but never complained.

Everything went well, the good Lord was with us, and after 12 days we left the hospital to go home. He was in a neck brace for one year and even went to school with his brace on. Again, he never complained. He was always a very active boy. He was not handicapped in any way and did anything any boy his age could do.

On Tuesday morning, June 8, 1993, the morning started out as usual for us. We woke up and had our morning prayer and then all went out to do chores. After breakfast, we all went to work one by one. Leroy was the last one to leave. He was waiting for his ride, since he worked for his uncle Ben as a ground boy on a construction crew. He was waiting for the driver when he asked his mother to fix his pocketbook because he was losing his coins. While she was sewing his pocketbook the driver came and he said, "Hurry up Mom, I don't want to make him wait." The last words she heard him say were, "Good bye, Mom, good bye."

At three o'clock in the afternoon a severe thunderstorm came up. His uncle Ben and others roofing came down from the roof and went inside the house. Leroy was still outside picking up when his uncle called for him to come inside. He came running into the garage and just turned around when lightning struck and hit him. They gave him CPR right a way and called the EMS. On the way to the hospital they got his heart started again but it had been stopped for 13 minutes.

They called me at work and told me to meet them at home. I didn't know what had happened until I got home. My wife received word at her brother's where she was helping them get ready for church. The first thing I asked was, how bad is he? They said they just called the hospital and he was still breathing, so I had some hope. I went looking for my wife one way and she went looking for me the other way so we missed each other, but met at the hospital. It was 6:30 before we were able to see him. Oh, how peaceful he looked. The first words his twin brother said were, "Oh, Leroy, why is it you? Why not me?"

The first three days he responded to us by the squeeze of the hand or by moving his toes when we asked if he could hear us. He could not talk because of tubes in his throat. We both stayed with him day and night until Thursday night when I went home and came back the next morning. On Friday night my wife went home and when she told Leroy good bye, tears rolled down his cheek.

On Sunday they didn't do anything, but Monday they took more tests and said that his brain was dead. We got all the family together on both sides and the minister to have prayer. They took the machines off around 6:30 P.M. Monday night and he quit breathing in about six minutes.

Oh how sad! The funeral was Thursday, June 17, 1993. Oh, how friends, neighbors, and relatives came to help and be with us. *Death is so final*! I cannot put into words the pain of losing a loved one. I feel it has brought us closer to God. I sometimes think maybe I was living too carefree. I often have to think of the words the minister said that preached the sermon at the funeral. It was hay making time and everyone was busy. Here came Jesus down the road and stopped in for this young boy. How many of us have time for the Lord, or are we too busy?

After the funeral we received lots of cards and visits. I never realized the meaning of cards until then. One person was there to visit and as he left, he turned around and said the good Lord did this. Let's call it good because He makes no mistakes. Oh, how hard to call it good.

After the funeral some of the boys working with him said sometime before this happened they were talking about the number 666. Leroy said he hoped he wouldn't be here when that time comes. Also one man told me he never saw Leroy sit down to eat his lunch without taking his hat off and praying first. Oh, what wonderful memories.

I wrote a song in memory of Leroy to the tune of 'I Was Born to Serve The Lord', and my niece wrote a poem.

- chorus -

It was on the day of June the eighth,
The year was nineteen ninety-three.
A great big limb was taken off,
Away from the family tree.

Leroy went to work that morn,
He went with his Uncle Ben.
But little did he know that day,
That his life on earth would end.

His mother for him fixed his pocketbook,
  She was standing by his side.
The last words he said when he left
  Were, "Good-bye, Mom, Good-bye."

At three o'clock in the afternoon
  The sky got dark in the west;
It rained, it poured, and lightning struck,
  And put Leroy to rest.

Loving Memories of Leroy
"A Light From Heaven"

Jesus looked down from Heaven one day,
  He whispered to Leroy, I can't let you stay.
In this wicked world of worry and sin,
  I'll open my door, won't you please come in?

I know you try very hard to be good,
  Always doing what you think you should.
Never forgetting to bow your head,
  When you're in a hurry, or ready for bed.

I will shine my light brightly, so you can see,
  Which path to choose, to lead to me.
For I am the Way, the Truth, the Light,
  Oh, won't you join my angels tonight?

Your family will suffer... for a time be sad,
  But Leroy, after a while, they will be glad.
They'll realize you're with me, in Heaven so fair,
  And keep trying and praying to meet you up there.

Dear Mom and Dad, don't cry for me,
  Just make me happy, some day to see,
All of you in Heaven above,
  Keep trusting and praying to our "Father of Love."

They rushed him to the Hospital,
  The doctors did all that they could do.
His twin brother Lewis said,
  "Oh, Leroy, why is it you?"

We stood by his bedside day and night,
Through all prayers and tears,
In hopes that he would again see light.
His age was only fifteen years.

And then the day of the funeral came.
Oh my, we thought it could not be.
Leroy is gone, but not forgotten,
He's gone to eternity.

John Miller: Jan. 1963 - June 6, 1992

Submitted by: Eli & Mattie E. Miller, Millersburg, Ohio

Saturday, May 30th, 1992, started out like any other day. It was a pleasant day to be out and we were all busy with our work. Our children, three boys and three girls, were all married except David, the youngest, was still living at home. John, our second youngest, had married Fannie Smucker of Lancaster, Penn., and was living in that area. As the day passed by and we drifted toward the evening hours little did we know what was in store for the rest of the day.

David was invited to a friend's house for supper. My wife and I had supper and got cleaned up for Sunday, as we had church the next day. We talked of things we had planned with friends for the next week. At 9:30 we were ready to go to bed. I got up to turn off the light when there was a knock on the door. I said "What now at this hour?"

I opened the door and was stunned as there stood an English couple, friends of ours that lived about 30 miles from our home. They said, "We are sorry to tell you, but your son John has been in an accident."

They had been the only way to get in contact with us at that hour of day. I asked, "Is he serious?"

They said, "I am afraid so."

After the first shock I asked them what happened. They said he had been in an automobile accident and they were all in the hospital. They had phone numbers we could call for more information. I finally recovered enough to invite them in until we had time to get over the first shock and think about what to do next.

About that time David came home from his friend's house. David and I went to the phone and called the hospital in Lancaster, Penn. I asked how John was and they said very, very critical. I asked if there was any hope, and they said, "Very little."

I asked about the rest of his family. His wife was in critical condition with a broken back, breastbone and collarbone. The youngest, a three year old boy, was in a coma and the oldest boy, 5 years old, had been treated and released.

I asked our neighbors to come and stay with my wife while David and I left to tell the other children what happened. By midnight we were loaded to start for Penn., except for David. He said he would stay home and take care of things and plans at home. We drove all night and arrived at the hospital the next morning around 8:30. John's father-in-law met us at the hospital and tried to tell us what to expect. When we entered the trauma room the nurse told us to take his hand and talk to him, maybe he would respond. He didn't.

The three year old boy regained consciousness Sunday afternoon. The next five days were all about the same, an empty helpless feeling and no response. The children left for home on Tuesday morning and returned again on Saturday morning. We talked with the doctor and nurse every day, but it was always the same, no hope.

On Saturday morning, June sixth, the doctor told us we would have to decide whether to take the breathing machine off or not. He told us John was now brain dead and like a vegetable. He said we should decide this sometime when we could have all day to decide.

Oh, what dark hours were ahead. That afternoon we decided to take the machine off. We hit bottom at about 5:00 in the evening as John passed on about ten minutes after they took the machine off.

His funeral was on Tuesday, June 9, 1992. His age was 29 years, six months and a few days.

THE ACCIDENT

John, his wife Fannie, and their sons, David Lee and John Anthony, were on their way to a friend's house for supper. It had been raining and driving conditions were not too good.

They met an oncoming car which was being followed by a high wheeled pickup driven by a 17 year old boy and his girlfriend. The pickup had to slow down and the driver lost control. The pickup came across the center line broadside, head-on into John's car.

They had to use the 'Jaws of Life' to get John and Fannie out. They took David Lee and John Anthony out the back window of the car.

Losing our oldest child, a daughter, at birth had not been easy, but seeing John go was the low point of our marriage. We have to push on day after day, Lord willing. We will never understand why this had to be so. I cannot write my feelings on paper. People who have not gone through this experience cannot realize how final *death* really is. These feelings that we cannot put on paper are the feelings that the Lord has given us. These we can share with Him and we can say *Thy will be done*, and we can seek comfort in Him for He knows what is best for us.

Fannie has remarried to Sam Beiler. They have added a son to their family. We like to think of him as another grandson.

Ivan B. Weaver: May 18, 1972 - Aug. 23, 1974

Submitted by: Mrs. Henry (Esther) Weaver, Fredericksburg, Ohio

Friday, August 23, 1974, was a beautiful warm summer day. The sun was shining and I was busy fixing food and finishing the weekly cleaning. We had invited some of my husband, Henry's, family for Sunday dinner, and we were also invited to the neighbors for a chicken barbecue that Friday evening, so I tried to finish early.

Our two boys, Ivan, two years old, and Mark, 14 months old, were taking afternoon naps. I had washed Ivan's hair and helped him look at a book. He loved to have somebody read to him in German so he could understand it. This I did before he took a nap, *never* realizing this would be the last time I would wash his brown curly hair.

I was cleaning the garage attached to the house, when Ivan got up from his nap. He helped me sweep the water out. I was then ready to push the buggy out to do the other side. Ivan wanted a ride on the buggy, so I lifted him up. He never got on by himself. He used the tie rope for his horse. I asked him, "Where are you going?"

"To Grandpa's" he said, and I bade him good-bye. He was happily playing. I finished the garage and did a few things in the basement.

When I came back out to get him 15 to 20 minutes later, my heart skipped a beat. It was so quiet on the buggy, and he was not on the front seat anymore. Then I saw he was in the back. I quickly got him out. I called his name, "Ivan, Ivan." He did not respond at all. I was pretty sure he was gone, but I did not want to believe it. His little finger nails were bluish already. His big brown eyes were closed as if he were sleeping.

I laid him on the grass and ran for the neighbors. They were working in the field. I did not have far to go. They called the squad right away. By that time the neighbors were also there.

This happened between 4:00 and 4:30 PM. Henry worked at the Feed Mill about a mile away from home. He heard the sirens, then he was informed there was an accident at his place. When he came home he never expected anything like this. The squad was here and was just about ready to take Ivan to the hospital. Henry got to see him yet before they left.

A kind neighbor took Henry to the hospital to sign some papers and the coroner checked him out to see if he had choked on something. All was clear. The coroner ruled the death an asphyxiation.

I walked around in a daze. I thought maybe there was still something they could do in the hospital. I did not give up until Henry came home. But I knew it was all over when he came home.

There are two little seats in the back part of the buggy for children. Our buggy was small and did not have much room in the back. What we think happened was he wanted to get in the back and somehow fell. When I got him out, his arms were pinned underneath him. His chin was resting on the seat and his throat was tight against the seat which shut the windpipe off.

The coroner told Henry if you hit your chin hard, it can cause a blackout. The next day it was black and blue under his chin. We hope and pray this is the way it was, but we will never know how it happened. I thought if he had suffered, "How can I live with this?" I had put him on the buggy. I felt it was my fault and I was to blame. My husband told me this was God's will and his time was here. But he was *so young*. Often I asked, "*Why? Why?*"

Time went on, and at first it seemed like everything stopped. Yes, for us it did at the time. Soon neighbors, our parents, and brothers and sisters came. They brought Ivan back late that evening yet. We were so glad to have him back close by us. I can still hear the "tick, tick, tick," of the alarm clock all night long that first night. Towards morning I dozed for a few minutes and I dreamed he was in bed with us. *Oh,* how I wished it could be true. Many, many things went through our minds that night.

When Ivan was a baby he was seven weeks premature and the doctor had given him a 50-50 chance of surviving. His lungs were not fully developed. His weight was four pounds, three ounces. He was is the hospital almost three weeks. What a joy it had been to bring him home. He was quite precious. We had been married three and a half years when he was born.

I remember that first night after he was born. I prayed "God, if you will only let us have him for a while, we will give him back." My prayers were answered.

I had never once gave it a thought after that, until this happened. I realized that this was what I asked for. But why at such a young and tender age? I never told anybody how I prayed to have this baby. So why didn't I want to give him back? I was just too selfish.

Funeral arrangements were made to be at my brother's place. Our house was just too small. A lot of people came for the viewing. The sympathy and encouraging words meant a lot at that time. After the funeral we got many visitors and a lot more mail which we appreciated so much.

At the time of the viewing, Mark was starting to get fussy so my cousin and husband took him along home one day. They brought him back in the evening. It helped us, and him too, for he was better again.

We were advised to go in and see Ivan often, for this would be the last time, and it was so final. How true. When we were in by ourselves I used to comb his hair. It seemed his curls were gone, his hair had become wavy.

In 1993 another little Ivan Weaver, also two years old, suddenly passed away in an accident. I was asked to comb his hair. Oh, it sure brought back so many sweet memories.

Very soon after the funeral somebody told Henry he would not want to wish him back. But so soon, we did not find it quite like that. We used to think we would take him back anytime. Yes, it takes a while before you can honestly say that. When you are so heartbroken, it takes time to heal. Now, when little children leave the world, we think, "How lucky." But they are so hard to give up.

Mark was like a completely different child after the funeral. Before they had always slept late in the mornings, now Mark always got up with us. He'd sit on the counter when I packed lunch and fixed breakfast. He just wanted to be wherever we were. He knew things had changed. I often had to wonder what was going through his young mind.

In December we were blessed with another healthy baby boy. We were so thankful. I was in the hospital for a week, then it was time to come home. It was so painful coming home, and Ivan not being there. I just wanted to be by myself and have a good cry, but my helper was there and I didn't want to be a burden for her. So I just tried to keep it all to myself.

The hard parts were like the first time going to church, or family gatherings. When we would be gone all day, I would dread coming home. It always seemed so lonely. For me, I would have been happy just to stay at home, but I did not want to do that to the others. I used to think maybe they could not understand this at all.

I remember after Henry went back to work and it was just Mark and me at home, my brother stopped in and picked us up to spend the day at their place. They never knew how much I appreciated that.

We had a pond in back of the barn and I had always worried Ivan would go back there. But he never went unless we did, or his ten- and eight-year-old uncles came to fish and he went with them. He always enjoyed being with his uncles.

During the summer of 1992 my six year old nephew also died very suddenly in an accident. I grieved for the family, knowing what was to come after the funeral. When the longing and homesickness takes over, when you feel you almost can't go on, you can always pray, which is a great help. This is now 22 years later, but as long as God provides us with a healthy mind, we will never forget him. When his birthday or the day he died comes around another year, those days are special to us.

So many of the greetings we received were, "You have a family started in heaven now." How true. Our wish and prayers are to all hopefully meet in Heaven some glorious day where there will be no more pain, no loved ones leaving us, no more tears, no hearts to be broken anymore, no more longing for our loved ones who have gone on before. Where we may all hopefully angels be... throughout eternity.

Nathan Lee Schmucker: Mar. 7, 1991 - July 1, 1995

Submitted by: Lester E. & Katie M. Schmucker, Albany, Wisconsin

Friday, June 30, 1995, was a warm sunshiny day. Nathan Lee's grandparents were going to spend the night with us since there was a reunion on my side the next day. I had a full day of preparing ahead of me. In the afternoon I mowed lawn and, as I did, Nathan Lee trotted beside me all the time. I think afterwards, this was the last day of his life to share so carefree with Mom. Dad had gone to work at the trailer factory in LaGrange. We had moved to LaGrange County, Indiana, only two months before.

That afternoon Nathan Lee kept looking up to the skies and asking, "Mom, when can I go to Heaven and be with Jesus?"

I would say when God is ready he'll send an angel down and carry you to heaven, but we still want you now. I tried to push aside the thought that maybe he wouldn't be with us too much longer. He would say those words again. I would tell him again that we also wanted him and we'd miss him too much, he couldn't go now. He said cheerfully, "That wouldn't matter, I want to go up, up in the skies."

Grandpa Schmuckers came that night, and we all got ready for the next day. July 1, 1995, dawned. The sun rose with clear skies. I remember saying, "It looks like a nice day for the reunion."

I got my sandwiches and cottage cheese salad ready. After breakfast, everybody got dressed. I had made Nathan Lee and our daughter, Lora Fern, new clothes. Nathan Lee was so thrilled about wearing his new shirt as he loved getting dressed up for occasions like this, especially to go to church. Church was his favorite place, or somewhere where they'd gather to sing. Now he is singing to us with the angels above.

We arrived at the reunion. The men were seated outside on benches and the ladies were all visiting until 11:30 when lunch was ready. I was feeding Lora Fern lunch. When I went to get her a drink of water in the kitchen, a little girl came running in, saying, "Nathan Lee's head is all bloody. Nathan Lee is on the ground with a roof on him."

Oh, those words just throbbed around my head. I tried not to run, but I wanted to see fast. When I got to the scene, some men were standing around Nathan Lee. I ran up quickly and called his name, hoping he'd respond. I knew deep down that he wasn't going to.

Lester was also there. He asked if they checked his pulse. They replied there wasn't any. He didn't move and his eyes were still. Like a lot of people say, we can't put our expressions on paper, it was beyond description.

The six foot by eight foot roof had been detached eight years earlier and set beside the building. It had sank into the ground quite a ways over the years. They had tried moving it before the reunion and decided if it didn't want to budge, they would leave it. It was that solid.

Four children were playing on it that day when the roof started to fall. Nathan Lee was standing on the ground and started to run from it. That is what the other children said. That is how they remember it. It took four to six men to lift the roof and when they did, they found Nathan Lee. He hadn't cried or anything. We think death was so sudden, he didn't have any pain. He had seen the roof falling and had started to run. The soffit part of the roof landed on his head breaking his neck right below the brain.

That day and the day before he had kept wanting to get up on top of something. It had seemed he couldn't get up high enough to suit him.

We think back now and ask, "Why us?," or, "What if we would have done so and so?" But, it is all in God's hands and we shall trust in the Lord for He maketh *no* mistakes. Even so, it was really hard for us to accept and also hard for two-year-old Lora Fern, Nathan Lee's sister. She had always depended on him to help with play or whatever. But life has gone on and we have heard of other experiences. We also feel that we want to help others in a time of need like ours. We believe our experience was to remind us that we are all here to help and love each other. We all want to reach that bright and happy shore, where our loved ones are waiting with outstretched arms.

We can trust that we've started a family and home in Heaven, and it makes us want to not do anything to hinder that. It is all God's will, though. Nathan Lee left to mourn: Dad, Mom, and a sister Lora Fern, grandparents on both sides, and many friends and relatives.

Like many people have told us since, he was just really well-liked. Probably too perfect for this earth. Now he doesn't have to toil anymore in this sinful world. Following is a poem we received.

Life's Clock

The clock of life is wound but once,
And no man has the power,
To tell just where the hands will stop,
At late or early hour.

To lose one's wealth is sad indeed;
To lose one's health is more.
To lose one's soul is such a loss,
As no man can restore.

The present only is our own,
Live, love, toil with a will.
Place no faith in 'Tomorrow,'-
For the clock may then be still.

Gone, But Not Forgotten

In loving memory of my dear son, Nathan Lee,
Who has gone to rest in eternity.
It still seems that it cannot be,
That you left this world so suddenly.

'Twas the first day of July in ninety-five,
You were so happy as at Great-Grandma's you did arrive.
A family reunion there, was held that day,
No one realizing what ahead of them lay.

The older folks were visiting, they all had lots to say,
Little Nathan went playing in his good-natured way.
When all of a sudden a little before twelve,
There you lay stiff, you could no more help yourself.

When the roof you were playing on fell to the ground,
With you pinned underneath, no more to make a sound.
Help was called, there were people all around,

All was done loving hands could do,
But it was to no avail, God needed you!
It seems like your life, it had only begun,
Until the Master called, "Nathan, now your work is done."

Weeks before your death to Mama you'd say,
"I want to go to God and with Him stay."
One day Mom asked him, "Where is God, do you realize?"
"Oh yes," Nathan replied, "He lives in the skies."

Mom then said, "With us no more you could be."
Cheerfully he replied, "Wouldn't matter to me."
Your second cousins Marlin and Samuel were killed shortly before you,
Now you've gone to join them in the heavens so blue.

We miss all three as each day goes by,
It's so hard to understand, we often wonder, "Why?"
Let's all be faithful and do our best,
Hopefully someday we can meet them in the home of the "Blest."

—Sadly missed, loved, and always remembered!

Kathryn D. Yoder: Jan. 6, 1983 - Mar. 13, 1993

Submitted by: Mrs. Emma D. Yoder, Marydel, Delaware

Kathryn was born with Down's Syndrome. She was such a tiny baby compared to our seven other children. She only weighed five pounds, eight ounces at birth and dropped down to five pounds, two ounces.

I had had such problems with high blood pressure before her birth and was so sick to my stomach from the medication after she was born, that we had no idea we had a "special" baby until Dr. Forest told me that evening that he is suspicious of it on account of her floppiness. She also had straight marks across the palms of her hands.

I had visions of having a sickly baby, but other than getting colds easily, she wasn't that way at all. She was very slow in gaining at first and slower than a normal baby in doing other things, too. At first I couldn't see anything that looked like a "Down's" but one day when I had her across my shoulder to burp her I looked at her from the side and all of a sudden saw the look that "Down's" children have on their face. With God's help we accepted her as she was and she became very "special" to us.

In December of 1987 she was sick off and on with what we thought was just a cold, but she was also very pale. We had a new doctor in Marydel who put her on Amoxicillin.

We had our first grandchild on December 3, 1987, in Ohio. We were waiting to go see her until Kathryn felt better. We spent New Year's in Ohio.

After we came home I noticed she wasn't herself again and was very listless and had no appetite. Dr. Kapp put her on Amoxicillin again, but she didn't seem to get better, so on the 18th of January I took her to see her pediatrician in Dover. He said to take her off the

Amoxicillin as it was just causing problems. After that her fever left and she started eating again. But by the 22nd she was having fevers again and her face was puffy.

We took her to Dr. Bierman again who sent us to the lab for a blood test. He said to call him at 4:00, but instead he called our neighbors and said it's important that we call him right away. He told us she was very anemic and her blood count was low.

He wanted our approval to get in touch with the blood specialists in Christiana. When he called back he told us to take her to the Christiana Hospital right away. I'll never forget my feelings as we rode the 50 miles to Christiana. I was almost sure what they would tell us. Her hemoglobin was down to 3.5.

They didn't do a bone marrow test until the next morning and it confirmed that she had leukemia. They also gave her two units of blood. Then they started her on chemotherapy One of us stayed with her all the time until February 15 when we could finally bring her home.

She was only home six days until she had a fever of 102°, so the doctors said to bring her up to the hospital again. She was there for four days with a virus. After she came home she had to go in for a weekly blood test. Once a month we took her to the Wilmington Hospital for a checkup and for some of her chemo which she couldn't get in pill form.

On the 22nd of March she was again admitted with a serious infection of the lungs. She came home the 27th. I have no idea how many bone marrow tests and spinal taps she had, but she was always patient and never complained. Once when she went to the lab, we had a new nurse who wanted to get help to hold her, but I told her she's all right. She'd sit down and hold out her arm!

On August 23, 1988 Kathryn woke up with a severe case of croup at 4:15 in the morning. Her face was turning blue and she lost control of her bowels and kidneys. We rushed her to the hospital by ambulance where she spent one day. After that sometimes I had to get up at night and steam her as she got croup easily.

On October 4, she had a high fever and a rash so the doctors wanted her at Christiana again. They finally decided she had mono. She came home the 10th, but was running a fever off and on for a while. Sometimes her blood count was so low that she had to be taken off her chemo for a week until it went back up. In April of

1990 she came off her two year maintenance program. That meant no more chemo and weekly blood tests, but she would still go in every three months for a checkup.

During the winter of 1991-92 she got a pink eye off and on. The doctor said it was Conjunctivitis and would put her on antibiotics. That would help for a while, but then it would come back again.

Finally the Hematologist said she would have to be seen by an eye doctor. We took her to one in Dover and after checking her he made an appointment with Will's Eye Hospital in Philadelphia, Penn. There they did a biopsy and discovered leukemia had settled in her eye and the chemotherapy hadn't take care of it.

Dr. Delduca said he had heard of this happening, but had never seen it before. She was again admitted to the Christiana Hospital where they did a bone marrow test. It showed she had leukemia cells in her bone marrow. So then we had to start all over again, and with more intensive treatments.

She had side effects that she hadn't had the first time. Her sugar went way high and I had to learn to give her insulin shots. They also put in a central line so she wouldn't have to get pricked so often, but they had trouble with it a lot of the time. I had to learn to flush it and change the dressing. This time she was admitted June ninth and discharged July 17th. She got her first radium treatment to her eye the 17th. Following that I had to take her up every day until she had ten treatments. Sometimes she had to be admitted overnight for some of her chemo. The visiting nurse also came out and gave her some of it.

In the meantime, the doctors had mentioned a bone marrow transplant sometime, but we didn't feel we could make her go through that. After much thinking and praying, we decided not to go on with the treatments since she still had some very intense treatments to go through. It was a hard decision to make. She got her last chemo August 25th and was sick to her stomach from it. She was getting quite a bit of vitamins in hopes that it would help her. She seemed to be feeling good until December 20, 1992, when she complained of a headache and stomachache. She had been going to a "Special School," but after their Christmas vacation, she only went one day.

On the 12th of January I noticed she was yellow. She was sick to her stomach off and on. In February her stomach started getting big and she would just lie around a lot. On the 22nd her doctors said her liver and spleen were enlarged. They advised us to just try to keep her comfortable. They gave her from two to four weeks to live.

What a feeling that gave us and often we had to wonder if we had made the right decision. We called the three boys who lived in Ohio, and Samuels in Kentucky, to let them know. The three from Ohio and their families came in February 27th. She was singing again that night and sang "No Not One". When they left on March first she cried and didn't want them to leave.

The teachers from her school came out regularly to visit her. She often had headaches and I'd give her Tylenol for it. We got a hospital bed for her as she couldn't rest lying flat. She ate very little during that last week, but asked for ice cream. Our neighbors knew it and would bring some up for her.

On the 12th of March she couldn't keep anything down. I called the doctor and he called a prescription to the drug store. Her teacher brought it out. That night we had company who brought ice cream, but she couldn't eat any. That night I stayed up with her and she had a miserable night. She hardly slept at all and wanted a drink constantly.

At 1:00 AM she asked for ice cream and I had to tell her we didn't have any and she said "Well, I'd like to have some." How I wished we had saved some for her. At 2:00 she again asked for some. By that time it was snowing and sleeting, and the windows were all icy. We had seven to eight inches of snow and it was very windy.

At 8:00 the next morning I noticed her moaning was getting weaker and before we could get the boys in she was gone. She just kept looking up as if she saw something.

The weather was hardly fit to be out, but our neighbor with a 4-wheel drive went to let people know. The undertaker said we should call the ambulance to take her to the hospital to be pronounced dead, but they got stuck as soon as they turned off the main road. So she was taken by 4-wheel drive. We were by ourselves until 1:00 PM when Dan's brothers came. They stayed overnight. We postponed the funeral so the boys could make it. A lot of the relatives that wanted to come, couldn't on account of the snow, but we were thankful for the ones that did make it.

She was buried on March 17, 1993. She brought a lot of sunshine to our home and was really missed, but we know she is in Heaven where she doesn't have to suffer anymore.

Bennie Byler: Aug. 16, 1986 - June 3, 1991
Truman Byler: May 18, 1988 - June 3, 1991

Submitted by: Lester & Esther Byler, Dover, Delaware

The day started in bright and clear. Lester went to work, doing carpenter work for David Detweiler. I had some peas to pick in the morning and wanted to can them. So my three children and I enjoyed 'blicking' them in the shade. I had thought, in a year or so we'll have some good help. The children seemed happy.

Bennie asked me, "When will *'da Guta Mann komma'*?"

I told him I didn't know. I didn't realize how soon his time would come to go.

We ate lunch and I put the boys to bed. I told them when they woke up they could all go up to Simons. I wanted to go and help *'risht'* for *'de gma'*. They live just a little farther up the field than we do. Simon's wife, Lena, is my sister.

Bennie slept, but Truman didn't, so I just took him along right away. Lena and I cleaned her china cabinet. About 4:00 Bennie came in and got himself a drink of water. I asked him, "Are you awake now?"

He said, "Yes", and went out the door again. About 20 minutes later Simon's son Robert came in and said there's fire in the barn! ! We ran out right away. Simons had just a small barn with a hayloft. They didn't have a real ladder to go up, so they stood on a small horse wagon, then on a 50 gal. drum barrel and from there pulled themselves up.

Lena crawled up on the drum and said, "Oh, go call the fire trucks!" Wayne, their son was there screaming to come down and our two dear little boys stood back a little. I started for the phone right away; but then thought we have to get the boys out first and went back.

Lena wasn't at the hole anymore and the fire was burning around the hole already. I heard her say, "We have to get a ladder and get the little boys out the window." But we couldn't find a ladder. Smoke was soon coming out so thick we couldn't get close.

Then Lena said, "Oh, Bennie and Truman are still in there." It seemed it just didn't want to sink in to me, but still I knew it. The rest of the children came out of the house. Irene, our oldest and only child now, said "Mom! Bennie and Truman are still in there!" She was jumping up and down and crying.

I felt just like I was in a daze. Help was soon there. I thought I was starting to pass out so I sat down. Smoke and heat got so close I had to sit farther away. Soon two men came and wanted to take me to the neighbors' wash house, Johnny Hershbergers. They lived just beside Simons. They laid me on the cement. Someone went and got my parents right away, John Yoders. They were soon there.

They asked where Lester was working, but I didn't know. He also came before too long. When he came home from work they saw Simons' barn burned down so the driver and the rest of the crew walked up to see what happened.

Lester told me later he thought it seemed like the people just looked at him. One of the neighbors then came and told him what happened. The fire trucks were there and had it under control. Lester came over to the washhouse where I was. A lot of people were there already. It was also raining. They hadn't found the boys yet. I was wondering, what will they find when they do find them? We had decided to go home. What a feeling. They had started forking burned hay.

I really can't remember how we found out what started the fire, but our two dear little boys and Simon's two boys were playing with matches. They said they would light it and put it out, then one time Bennie's got out of control.

About two hours later they came and said they had found them. I can still so plainly remember when they said they found them. Bennie, the oldest had his arms around Truman. When Lena saw them last, they were just standing there. Didn't seem like they had any fear. Truman was sucking his two fingers. He did that when he was relaxed and wanted to sleep. They then took their bodies to the hospital. People came and cried with us. What would we have done without any friends?

A state trooper came and told us if we wanted to go to the hospital and see their bodies yet that night, he would take us. There were a lot of people there and we hated to go, but they told us this would be the only time we would have a chance to see their bodies as it has to be a closed casket funeral.

So we, our daughter, and my parents went. Lester's parents, Mahlon Bylers, had just moved to Clare, Michigan in September, less than a year earlier. We so wished they would still be living here then. We went to the hospital. They put us in a room, then someone came in and told us they won't look natural and asked it we were sure we wanted to see them. We said yes. He went out, then someone else came in and told us the same thing and they wouldn't advise us to see them. They said they're all black, but if we still want to, we may as this will be our only chance. They just wanted to warn us. We all wanted to still go in. They asked our daughter if she wanted to go in and she said yes.

We also had a stillborn last September and she was all black and blue. We tried to tell her that the boys will probably look like our stillborn did, but she still wanted to go in. They then came in again and said things and went back out again. Finally they came and told us we may just look at their faces and we are not to handle them. It was about what we expected, but still we just about couldn't recognize them. Bennie had real curly hair. That looked the same, just dirty and black. But still there was something there that we could see that they were our sons.

What is there to do or say? Death is so final. We came home about 10:30. A lot of people had gone home. They still had supper waiting for us, but who was hungry? We went to bed. There wasn't much sleep there, but we could rest. Time came again to get up. People soon arrived. Dads got a driver and came up early again.

I remember some of us were sitting in the living room talking about how it all happened. Then I said, "If we could just put their Sunday clothes on them."

Dad said, "They are clothed. They are clothed in white."

Yes, I guess, but oh, it was so hard! The undertaker brought their bodies out that afternoon. They put them in plastic and then in the casket. They told us that Dads and we were the only ones that could see them lying in the casket. Once the casket was closed, we were not to open it again.

They put them together in one casket. We said if they found them together, we want them buried that way, too. They tried to put them in the casket the way they found them.

Lester's parents and their children they still had at home and two of his married brothers and their wives came that evening. It didn't suit his other married brother to come. What a sad meeting we had.

Wednesday morning came and time to get up again. People were in and out the whole day. How would it have been if we could have gone in and viewed their bodies? It just meant so much when our friends came and shared our sorrow with us. Lots of food came. A produce dealer Lester had worked for came with cases of things.

Thursday morning, bright and clear. Our first thoughts were today is the funeral. It was the same again; get up and try to face it. Our home Bishop had the main part. We just never realized how hard it would be to sit up there and have loved ones lying in the casket. Oh! How hard it was to have a closed casket, but we want to try and give ourselves up to our Heavenly Father. If this is His will, we want to accept it.

The next weeks and months were very difficult. It was just us two and our only child, our daughter, left. She often cried. It seemed she cried over nothing. There was one night she couldn't sleep until one of us slept with her. We would think she was finally sleeping and we would go back to bed, but she soon cried again. It was such a trying time, but time has a way of going on.

We had lots of mail and company. People brought in meals. They just didn't realize what it meant. We just wished the end of the world would come. The longing to go to Heaven where our dear little children were got so great.

This is now a little over five years later and we are still here on this earth. I just have to wonder how long this earth will yet stand. There did come times when we thought we had given ourselves up, but then it would come back so fresh again. We can always look for a brighter side if we want to. We can think of people who went through more than we did and have it a lot worse. We at least still have each other to talk to. I'm *so* glad for that.

We have now been so greatly blessed with two little girls since the loss of our little boys. The sun does shine again. It is such a good feeling, _They are safe!_ They have a better home than what we could have given them.

Vernon Ray Bontrager: Mar. 30, 1974 - July 26, 1991

Submitted by: Orva S. & Wilma Bontrager, Shipshewana, Indiana

July 26, 1991, was a Friday. We got up in the morning and the day was just like the one before. The men went about their work, and I did my laundry. It was such a clear and beautiful day. Little did we know that God had other plans for us by evening!

The laundry dried so nice and I put everything away. About 3:00

in the afternoon, Dad came in and asked me if I wanted to go with him to Leland's. He is married to our daughter Irene. He had a few things he wanted to discuss with him. We knew our daughter Marie and her husband Josie and their two daughters were coming, but we thought we would be home before too late.

We stayed at Lelands for supper, but left for home right afterwards. When we got home, Josies were there. They were going to leave their two daughters with us for the night and the next day they had plans to go with Josie's family to Sea World. We spent the evening visiting, then at about 8:30 they left for home.

Freeman and Vernon had planned a camp-out for the weekend with some of their friends. Vernon had a moped, so he was going after the tents on Friday evening. He met Freeman Eashs, he is married to our daughter Edna Fern, on the road. He stopped and talked with them for a little while, and teased each of the children a little. He always enjoyed the nieces and nephews so much. Little did they realize that they'd be the last of the family to talk with him. It was a very clear and bright full moon evening.

I got the two granddaughters ready for bed and they were soon asleep. Our children went upstairs and prepared for bed. Dad was in bed already and I had just changed to my nightclothes and was going for the bedroom, when all of a sudden a car came in the lane very fast. I said, "Dad, a car drove in; something must be wrong."

He got up and quickly got dressed. By that time somebody was knocking on the door. Dad went to the door and there was our neighbor's son. He said, "Come quick, somebody hit your son Vernon down by the corner. It was a pickup truck!"

I also quickly got dressed and ran upstairs to tell the kids what was going on. Then we left, not knowing what to expect when we got there. My prayer was "Oh, God, Thy will be done!" We got there, stopped, and jumped out of the car. There he lay beside the road right beside a mulberry tree. Dad went right to him and said his name and took hold of his hand. He then looked up at me and said, "Mom, he's gone!"

"Oh no! I can't believe it."

I do recall hearing the siren coming. It came up our road and it was such a weird sound. I'll never forget it!

Soon there were a lot of people there. The neighbor lady led me behind the pickup truck, and there were our sons, Freeman and Wilbur. Freeman said, "Mom, how bad is he hurt?"

I had to tell him. "Oh, Freeman, he is dead."

"Oh, no!"

We cried and cried. All of a sudden I thought of the kids at home, they would want to know, too. So after a while, the neighbor boy took me, Freeman, and Wilbur home. When we got there, I ran for the house. There was Sue Ella at the door, she also wanted to know how bad the accident was.

There I was again; I had to tell her too! Oh, what a shock! But, God had this all planned for us. He had chosen two people to make His will work out. The timing was just right, nobody else could have made it so perfect. I felt so sorry for the driver of the pickup truck. He also had some very hard moments, I'm sure. He was on his way to pick up his girlfriend, who was at a cousin's house, not very far off. He came to our house the next day, and sat by our sides. Oh, how we loved him, and still do. It was not his fault. God chose him to make the timing so perfect. God works in mysterious ways and we often wonder why so, or why him. Maybe someday we'll all understand.

The next few days were just like a dream. Neighbors and friends far and near, gathered together here to help with meals and show their sympathy. Days, weeks and years have gone by now since Vernon has left us, and so many times we are struck with homesickness and some very depressing times. Only those who have lost loved ones know the feeling. Especially at family gatherings and his brother Wilbur's wedding. "His empty place." But, we do not want to wish him back in this sinful world.

Five years have now gone by, and I think we all had a chance of seeing him in a dream. One daughter dreamed our family had all come home for the evening and we were sitting in our living room, when all of a sudden the door to the upstairs opened up and Jesus came down. He looked at us and said, "I think it's time you can all see Vernon again." He looked upstairs and motioned him to come down. Vernon came down the stairs and stood beside Jesus. She said Vernon was dressed in white and had the sweetest smile and was waving his hand, but he didn't say a word.

Then Jesus said, "Now it is long enough." Vernon turned around and was gone. Then we all started to cry, but Jesus said, "Don't cry." He went around and gave us all a kiss. Then she woke up! Oh, those precious dreams which sometimes mean so much!

We do want to sympathize with other people who have the same experiences. God does not give us more than we can handle, even though we sometimes wonder why things happen like they do. Hopefully someday we will understand.

May the good Lord bless all who read this in future years.

Glen O. Bontrager: June 18, 1979 - Oct. 14, 1986

Submitted by: Orla A. & Sadie Bontrager, Rome City, Indiana

It was October 4, 1986, Glen and Marlin were bathing. My wife went in to check if they were clean, since they were only six and seven years old. She noticed Glen's stomach was very hard. That evening at supper she said something to me about it. I also checked him and it was very firm. We asked him if it hurts and he said it didn't. I don't think he thought anything was unusual, but after we had noticed his firm stomach, we also noticed that his breathing was shorter than usual.

The next day was Sunday, October 5, and communion service was held. We took all the children along and never gave it a thought that this would be the last time we could all go to church together.

The next week he went to school every day except Friday when we had a doctor appointment for him. The teacher hadn't noticed any difference in his health or activity. On Friday we took him to the doctor and he scheduled us to go to LaGrange Hospital that evening yet at six o'clock.

We came home and did the milking and chores first. That evening while I was out in the farrowing house doing the hog chores, Glen came out of the house towards me and was skipping and whistling. I asked him if he wanted to go to the hospital and he really didn't seem to be worried as he didn't feel sick at all. At that time we still didn't notice anything different in his activity or his eating, except that his stomach was so hard and firm.

That evening my wife took him to the hospital and I stayed at home to do the chores the next morning. The doctor had said they wouldn't do surgery till the next day. The next morning, Saturday, October 11, I drove the horse and buggy to the hospital. They had said they wanted to do exploratory surgery to see what was causing his stomach to be so hard. When I came in I talked to the doctor first and he said, "You have a very sick son."

I found his room and asked him how he was feeling. He said he was feeling fine. My wife and I couldn't understand why they told us he was a sick boy when he said he was feeling good. A few minutes later the doctor came and told us that Glen would be transferred to Parkview Hospital in Fort Wayne, Ind.

The doctor said they wanted to take tests and wouldn't do anything else that day anymore as far as surgery. Since I had the horse and buggy there we decided that I would take it home, do the chores Saturday evening and Sunday morning and then go to the hospital. I was not home more than a few hours when our neighbor came and said he had call from my wife saying that Glen would be transferred to Riley Hospital in Indianapolis, and that I should come as soon as possible.

This neighbor, Orland Sprunger, offered to take me, so I made arrangements with the neighbors to do the chores and left for Parkview. When we got there they had already taken Glen and my wife by ambulance to Indianapolis. Here is where I received the shocking news that he had cancer. This is what the doctor had meant when he said that we had a very sick boy. They had suspected this, but didn't tell us until they were sure. From there we went to Indianapolis and arrived shortly after the ambulance. This was Saturday evening.

After a few hours, my wife decided to go home with Orland, the driver. We had children at home and this had all happened so fast and unexpectedly that we hadn't had time to make arrangements. It was a very trying time for me. I was alone with Glen trying to accept the will of God that Glen did have cancer. Being this far away from home made it seem like we were in a world all alone.

On Monday, my wife, Dad, and Mom also came down. I was very glad to see them. Dad went home with the driver, and my wife, Mom, and I stayed.

On Tuesday they took a spinal tap to check his bone marrow. This was very painful. Glen had grown two and a half inches around his waist from Saturday evening until then. It was a very fast growing tumor. In the morning they also took over a quart of fluid off his lungs so he could breathe better. In the afternoon around 4 o'clock, they started him with chemotherapy treatments.

That afternoon they sent his school work down and he sat up with bright eyes and did his school work. Around 9 o'clock he walked to the bathroom alone. When he came back he said, "Mom, hold me until I go to sleep." My wife sat on the edge of the bed and he laid his head on her arm. No more than five minutes later life had fled. He had fallen asleep, an eternal sleep, which God was telling us just minutes before.

I have said it before and I'll just say it again, that the shock to see him die wasn't as hard to grasp as when the doctors had first said that he had cancer. I was so thankful that my wife and I were both at his bedside when he died.

He died just ten days after we first noticed his firm stomach, and just three days after we knew he had cancer. The name of his cancer was Birkitts Lymphoma.

Through all this we realized how kind friends and neighbors were to leave their work behind and to come help prepare for the funeral.

Daniel R. Yoder: Aug. 23, 1973 - July 4, 1993

Submitted by: Roman & Barbara Yoder, Millersburg, Ohio

The day, July 4, 1993, was warm and humid. Daniel had planned his afternoon visiting neighbor Dan M. Yoder, 87. When he was ready to leave he said, "It won't be long." and "Machs Gut." Usually he would leave then stand in the doorway a while. Dan really didn't think about what he had said until after it happened.

Daniel went to our neighbors, Merle D. Millers, to see Marion who had had an appendix operation, but he wasn't home from the hospital yet. Daniel told them he would be back in the evening.

His sister Mary, married to Noah R. Schlabach, had just moved behind the Charm Engine Shop on Thursday evening, July 1. Daniel played for about two hours with his nephew Justin.

Afterwards he went outside and Ben D. Miller was sitting on a double wooden glider. They visited a while. Daniel was leaning on a wooden fence. The fence and glider were about six to eight inches apart. Ben was barefoot and he had his feet up on the other swing. All at once he saw leaves flying and heard a plop. He didn't hear the loud crack, and was shocked to see someone was running back and forth in the yard.

Ben's wife, Anna, looked out the window and couldn't see them. She was running around in the house. She didn't know what to do until Ben called, then she went outside.

Noah had seen it right away and called the squad. Daniel turned purple right away. It was very warm and humid that day. It wasn't raining, but we heard it thunder far off. All at once there was a loud crack. It was raining in Baltic and Rogersville. The sheriff said it can carry eight to ten miles when it is so humid.

Lightning had gone down the tree and out the roots. Where Daniel had been standing there were two slits in the ground. The lightning had gone up over his rubber sole shoes into the leather. One shoe had a hole in the side the size of a pin, the other had a small slit in the back. Daniel had had two quarters in his pocket, and they were melted together. Everything happened so quickly. He didn't have to suffer. The hair on the back of his head was scorched.

God sew it was his time to go, but it was hard to accept. We had never heard of anything like it. With prayers, visits, cards, and encouraging letters, God helped us through our loss. We received a few letters telling about similar happenings with lightning. At the time we just thought it was a dream.

We had bought a team of horses in the spring for Daniel, so we could make our own hay. He had been looking forward to plowing some of our fields in the fall. We have 35 acres. The neighbors had made hay in shares before.

Daniel had been a slow learner. It took a lot of explaining and encouraging to teach him something new.

In the fall of 1992, he had helped his cousin with mason work. They built our porch with brick. It is a keepsake. He hadn't been able to do much heavy lifting. He had helped our neighbor Daniel P. Miller again with farming for the fifth summer. During part of March, April, May, and June he had gone down with the horse and buggy in mornings and, at times, late at night. I often worried about him being on the road with traffic going so fast, but he always said, "Don't worry, Mom."

That was the first thing I thought of when Emery and daughter Elsie came to tell us. They said Daniel got hit, but it was lightning. I heard sirens go, and thought we were going to the hospital until they really explained that he is gone.

In my dreams he is always a little boy. Justin was almost two when it happened. He often asked for Daniel. He can still tell how it happened.

On the day before, Saturday, July 3, we had held a homecoming on my side of the family at our place. He had played unusually good volleyball. Usually he wasn't very alert. We had all enjoyed the day. Daniel and Ervin's Joseph, age nine, had asked each other their age. Daniel had said he would be 20 in August, but wished he wouldn't.

Little did we realize that the Lord would take a loved one away the next day. God's ways are not always our ways, but what He does is right. It is a warning for us all to be ready when he comes.

Ivan Chupp: 1951 - Jan. 1, 1970

Submitted by: Mrs. Sara Mae Chupp, Nappanee, Indiana

The tragedy happened on New Year's morning of 1970. It was a very beautiful clear morning, but very, very cold. It was 10° below zero. We were all snowed in, and the snow plow came to plow us out.

Early in the morning Emanuel had stepped outside. It was so cold as he looked up into the sky, so very clear and full of millions of brilliant, sparkling, twinkling stars. As he had walked to the barn, he had wondered to himself about what this new year would bring.

It was not much later when we got word to come quickly to Elkhart Hospital. There had been an accident. Our thoughts went right to Ivan since he wasn't at home. Before we left, we got word again that there was no life anymore. We had to go identify him.

We had thought, "Oh no!" Such a shock went through us! I cannot put in words how we felt.

We hardly knew what we were doing to get ready to go. Yes, we were praying and crying with numb feelings as we headed for the Elkhart Hospital. As we arrived, we felt like sitting down with our heads hanging low so we wouldn't pass out.

By the time it was all done it was mid-morning. When we got home we had another shock! The house was full of people and commotion getting ready for the funeral.

I just sat down and cried. Many questions were asked, but I could not answer because of the shocked numb feelings we were going through. They had to go on and do the best they could.

That afternoon, toward evening, the body was brought home. Coming in the lane right behind the body of Ivan, was his sister Mary and her boyfriend coming home from Florida. As they were bringing the body into the house, his sister walked in right behind it. Then the shower of crying began again.

That first evening after Ivan's body was brought home and we had gone to bed, I so well remember how Dad and I clung to each other, brokenly. This brought out the love so great for each other. We clung to each other so tight. There and then I thought no two-edged sword could cut us apart. That's what love does!

One evening before the funeral, the young folks came and sang such beautiful, touching songs. It touched my heart so. Just cried and cried. As the evening went on, people coming to the viewing and standing in line for hours, having words of encouragement; one came and asked, "Did you kneel down and thank the Lord for this?"

I thought, "Oh no! How can we do this?"

But often this was done. We felt so different. Another came by asking, "Don't you remember at Moses' time, written in the Bible, how none of the children of Israel could enter the Promised Land? Only those 19 and under could enter in even if Ivan was no church member, as yet."

But Ivan had been so special in many ways. He had always had a grin or a smile on his face. He had been a son of very few words. We cannot remember that he talked back to his parents at any time.

The owner where Ivan was staying at that time, came to us at the time of his death. He said he really admired Ivan. He never heard Ivan say one bad word, was lovable to be around, always had a smile, and didn't drink or smoke.

After the funeral we appreciated people visiting us. They came with suppers, although at the time there was no hunger there. I must think nowadays it's a more common thing. Like many worldly people, some regularly go out to eat at restaurants. I so well remember when our bishop announced in church to abstain from such.

I believe God would be more pleased if parents would stay at home more in the evenings and spend more of their time with the family singing, praying together, admonishing, explaining, and reading together from the word of God. "Only one life twill soon be past. Only what is done for Christ will last!" I can look back now, and see how we as parents failed many times.

Yes, with such swiftness death came by, and took our son Ivan, we had no last good bye. As January comes, it brings sad memories. The day, the month we'll never forget. The depth of sorrow, no words can tell, the loss of one we loved so well; a face that is ever before us; a voice we can never forget; a smile which he always had, will last forever.

Twenty years later his Dad died at 71 years old from cancer. Yes, now I am all alone with no voice in the house except my own. Sometimes I feel forsaken, thinking people have forgotten me. But then I wake up in these times, thinking positive and looking on the bright side of life.

Stay cheerful! Trust God!

Mary Ann Yoder: Oct. 1993 - Feb. 10, 1995

Submitted by: Mr. & Mrs. Melvin R. Yoder, Fredericksburg, Ohio

1995 started off as usual for us, we were happy and healthy and were blessed with two little children. Little did we know what the year held for us.

Aaron was 28 months old and Mary Ann 16 months old. They were 12 months apart and were very fond of each other. They were each other's constant playmates. Often a thought came to us, "What would one of them do without the other?" They were both blonde and blue-eyed, but they had very different natures.

Aaron was more calm. Mary Ann was the youngest and also the leader. She was more spunky and needed more attention, but always had a special sweetness about her. Whenever we'd pick her up she'd give us a hug. Now 16 months after the tragedy that took our dear little girl, those are only precious memories. Something that was very hard for us to accept, that everything about her is now only a sweet memory and nothing for real anymore. We do not know how much Aaron will remember of her. He still talks of how they used to play with each other and laugh.

At the time of the accident, we were living in a house trailer and were building a new house nearby. The children often went with their dad in the evenings to work on the house. One evening, two weeks before the accident, they were in the barn doing chores before going to the house when two white doves kept flying around their dad. He watched them and wondered about them being so tame.

Then they flew to the children and sat around them for a while. The children tried to catch them, but they kept just ahead of them until they finally flew away. It was the only time we saw them around. Later we wondered, "Is that when our little girl was chosen to be an angel in heaven?" It was a bittersweet thought. So sweet to think of her a little angel in heaven! And so bitter is the thought of losing a precious child.

The morning of February 10, 1995, is a morning we'll always remember. Mary Ann had slept with us that last night, something she hadn't done for a few months. She was also up before her dad left for work, which was very uncommon. She had been so happy and just kept waving bye-bye when he went to work. He had held her yet, never dreaming that it would be the last time.

We had planned to go to the neighbor's shop to do some finishing for our house that evening. So, at five o'clock I got the children ready and explained to them that I was going out to hitch up the horse alone since it was too cold to take them along. Mary Ann came running with outstretched arms so I held her yet, little knowing what lay ahead. She just kept saying bye-bye. I finally went outside. On the way out I saw a gas jug sitting outside beside the steps. I thought of putting it away, but then decided I'd better hurry and hitch up so the children wouldn't be alone long. Another "guidance" of God's hands, How little did I realize what a drastic change that gas jug would bring in our lives.

While I was out, we believe Aaron got the door open, and Mary Ann dragged the gas jug inside in front of our natural gas stove, where it exploded. I had been outside about seven minutes when I saw flames in the trailer. I didn't want to believe it. No one was around, so I couldn't scream for help. When I got in the trailer it was full of smoke.

Words cannot describe the feeling I had, knowing our children were in there. I heard Aaron calling Mary Ann farther back in the trailer, then I saw her lying on the floor. When I picked her up I thought life had fled. A numbness came over me and I couldn't really feel until much later.

The next few hours are a blur to me. Later I wondered why I didn't scream or how I ever got to my brother's place, our neighbors, with the children. I had to go with the buggy. My brother called the ambulance. Time seemed to be at a standstill until the ambulance finally came.

We were rushed to Wooster Hospital. My mom was there to go with us since Melvin, my husband, wasn't home from work yet. At Wooster Hospital they worked on her for an hour, but then Life Flighted her to Akron. We could not have any hopes for her since she had third degree burns over 90 percent of her body. All we could pray was, "Please let her die." It was so unbearable to think she was suffering, but we could not yet comprehend how final death is.

At nine o'clock we came to Akron. Then Melvin was there, too, as well as both of our parents. At Akron they worked on her until the next day at four o'clock in the afternoon when she died on the breathing machine. When the doctor came and said, "Mary Ann has died," our worst fears were over. Only someone with a similar experience can realize the feeling of seeing a dear child suffering.

Only after the funeral when we went out to see the trailer did we begin to realize the heartrending separation we'd have to face, knowing we just had to let go, yet wishing to hold on forever.

Now one and a half years have passed since dear Mary Ann was taken from us. The sun seems to be shining brighter once more; though we will always miss her. But if we are living for Jesus, all things are possible.

Sharon Sue Burkholder: Apr. 1, 1953 - Oct. 8, 1981

Submitted by: Mrs. Anna Mae Burkholder, Nappanee, Indiana

The day was a beautiful one, on October 7, 1981. Our two daughters, Sharon and Mary Lou, were leaving for Middlebury, Indiana, to help their sister Fern, Mrs. Perry Yoder, prepare for church services. We talked a bit, then all kissed each other good-bye since I was soon leaving for a two-day visit with friends in Salem, Indiana. I watched them go as far as the eye could see them… never dreaming it was the last time for one of them.

In an hour I also left home with several friends and was blessed with a safe trip south. I had an enjoyable evening at brother Monroe's snitzing apples for lots of apple butter to be made in a large copper kettle the next day. The next morning dawned bright and clear; the cooking was started early and the tangy smell wafted around. Around seven in the morning Mary and I discussed the bright sunshine, it seemed so glorious as we walked around outside enjoying sights, sounds, and smells!

Around nine o'clock the telephone rang and it was for me. As my heart skipped a beat, I ran inside and answered. The voice said, "Anna Mae, this is your neighbor. Sharon has been in an accident. On her way to work this morning, a bread truck hit her."

"What, this just can't be. How bad is…"

"Anna Mae, you don't understand. She is gone!"

"Oh please, it just can't be."

"Yes, it happened at 7:15 this morning. I am coming down to get you, and will be there as soon as possible. Just wait on me there."

Completely numb and at a loss of words, I hung up. However, after I could think rationally, I did call again for more details.

The next couple hours are hard to describe. Neighbors came and helped with the apple butter as Monroe planned to come home with me and the rest would follow later. How I wished I was at home!

Around two in the afternoon the neighbor and son Larry came in the driveway. We left right away for the longest, most memorable ride of my lifetime. On the inside I was crying and praying all the way home. Mercifully, God gave me the strength to walk into our house at 6:30 that evening. Neighbors had gathered and all was ready for the viewing. Oh, what a meeting with family and loved ones!

At that time we pieced together the events of the morning. Sharon, 28 and not married, did housework for the Rod Rogers family. At 6:45 she had said good-bye to her dad and sister, saying "It's such a beautiful morning so I'll leave early and bike in before Rod comes out to get me." Then she left.

Traveling along Highway 6 towards Nappanee there is a slight curve in the road, therefore the bright morning sun can cause an extra glare at certain times. A bread truck coming from behind caught her rear end basket, flipping the bike around against the truck. This caused instant death, due to a broken neck. There was no oncoming traffic, but the truck driver was blinded by the gloriously bright sun. He did not see her at all.

One of the first vehicles to come along was Rod, on his way out to get her! She had worked for them for almost ten years, thus forming a close-knit friendship.

Again, how could I describe the next couple hours? Trying to locate everyone at their work or wherever duties led them. The policeman came out to the house first, so Mary Lou went along to the factory to tell her dad. It was good she did, as the tragedy was too deep to comprehend at first.

Perhaps I could add that this is the part of the grief that was hardest for me to accept. Not being able to share these first trying hours with the family. Why was it planned this way? Being human, I often asked myself. Yet, I realized that an all wise God knows why, and I trust He will reveal it in His own perfect timing

Then followed several days of viewing when friends and loved ones came to show their love and respect. How we appreciated each and every one. One learns how much the home church and neighbors mean to us. Plus the many friends who traveled hundreds of miles to share our sorrow with us.

Sharon had accepted Christ as her Savior in her youth and remained faithful to her end. Yes, she was human and was subject to mistakes, the same as we are, but her desire was to live for Jesus. The funeral was on Monday, October 12.

Giving up a child holds an emotional grief all its own. I can't explain it. My heart bleeds for others who are called to go through this experience. It doesn't matter if we know them or not, they all hurt.

Now there was a big adjustment to make. How can I describe it? First and foremost is the complete dependence one has on the almighty God and His strength and mercy, one day at a time. That empty spot at the table, in her room, and all over are the special reminders. Every time we went to town, we passed by the accident scene which always brought a flood of tears.

A friend who had gone through this experience too, gave us a good bit of advice. She said, "Don't be too hasty in disposing of her things. Time is a healer and in due time the good Lord will help you to think clearly on what decisions should be made." We followed her advice, and it was a gem!

We also felt sorry for the bread truck driver. He was not able to come to the viewing or to continue on the route for a while, being overcome with grief. We took steps to contact him because he was from Niles, Michigan. After the funeral he, his wife, their two daughters, a son-in-law, and a grandchild came to our home, which we appreciated very much. He could hardly express his sorrow enough for our family. We tried to express our forgiveness, and explained that Sharon had an appointment to meet and God was in control of this, even though we may not understand it all now. God makes no mistakes. Thus we became friends and stayed in touch for a number of years.

This is being written thirteen years since we had to part. We often think of her and miss her. By His grace, we hope to meet in the sweet by and by.

Fern (Burkholder) Yoder: Mar. 1, 1955 -Feb. 26, 1988

Submitted by: Mrs. Alvin E. Burkholder, Nappanee, Indiana

"Hey, where is everybody? Let's get started on these chickens!"
These were my words as I walked into the house at daughter Fern
and Perry Yoder's house, armed with various butchering tools. Plans
were for me and some of the Yoder women to help with chicken
butchering.

My first look around told me something was very wrong, as a
sad looking Fern greeted me in her kitchen. That look was etched in
my mind to stay! "Mom, hasn't anybody told you the news yet?
There will be no chicken butchering today and you'd better sit down
to hear the rest."

A very subdued Mom did sit down... and waited. Through tears
she told me of the doctor's diagnosis of a mole that he recently
removed from her back. It was Melanoma Cancer!

Too numb for any words, my mind remembered the doctor's
words for her earlier when he removed that mole. "Now don't worry
about this. It's nothing serious but it will be sent in and tested because that is the law."

This took place soon after Thanksgiving Day in 1986. Upon
discussing the events of the last couple days, our minds were simply
not capable of grasping it all. My husband, Al, had been going
through a number of tests and was diagnosed with cancer of the
larynx the day before Thanksgiving. We were still trying to absorb
this and couldn't think of anything else! I was hardly prepared for
this news as Fern got her diagnosis the day after Thanksgiving. Now
eight years later, I can well remember that day. We just talked and
cried with each other and cared for the children.

That evening it was hard to go to sleep. Is this valley of pain for
real or could I be dreaming?? How totally one must rely on the good
Lord and His love, strength, and mercy. Someone sent us this gem
which we appreciated and often repeated. "Lord, please don't let
anything happen today that You and I *together* can't handle."

The doctor set up an appointment right away for Fern to go to the
hospital and have a larger area removed from her back, explaining
that should take care of all the cancer cells. She did this and got
along quite well. Once again she was able to do most of her work but
seemed to tire easily.

Frequent checkups revealed nothing and the doctor was pleased with her recovery. However, he also explained that this Melanoma is the fastest growing kind of cancer there is and also the most unpredictable. Sometimes these cells hide in the body and no doctor can know it. It could come back in one, five, or even ten years or maybe never. You never know about Melanoma.

As any mother of five children knows, she was busy. This was also their first year on the farm which was an adjustment, but she enjoyed it. The next fall, about December, she began to have pain in her stomach area. She also experienced weight loss and loss of appetite. Our hearts sank. We had thought things looked so hopeful. In January she started taking tests and x-rays. At first the doctor couldn't pinpoint her problem, but by January 25th, she learned there are two small tumors on her liver. They did not stay small very long!

As time went on and January turned into February, I tried to go over and help whenever I had a chance to make the 30 mile trip. Each time she looked paler and had lost 25 pounds by February 9th. That evening I recorded in my diary that there are no words in any language to describe the emotional trauma of a mother seeing a daughter suffer like this. Any Christian mother who of course carried her child close to the heart, will do so as long as the child lives, even after they leave home. God created mothers this way.

On February 11th, she was admitted to Goshen Hospital where they gave her three pints of blood. They took more tests which revealed a large mass in her stomach area. No wonder she couldn't eat! By February 15th, she had surgery because something had to be done. The cancer had grown so fast, it now invaded all the small intestines, part of the colon, and most of the liver. The doctor explained this cancer feeds on a person's blood supply and the growth sometimes goes wild. That's what happened here. A band was inserted under the skin to try and slow it down. This left Fern very weak and miserable.

From then on we, Perry, or his family stayed with her at all times to help with her care. By February 20th, she was filling up with fluid and also had a fever. This was very hard to see! On February 25th, she was very weak and low, but was granted a special privilege. Her cousin Lovina and Richard Mast had a new baby boy, Timothy, who weighed 12 pounds, two ounces at birth. Fern wished to see him, so they were granted permission to bring him in, which they did. I can still hear her words as she smiled and said, "He looks so sweet."

Nurses and all took a peek at this baby! The next day, the 26th, I went over at noon and saw a big change from the day before. She was weaker! Soon after that she went into a coma. Being human, I just can't put into words how one feels when a loved one's life is ebbing away. The nurses were deeply touched to see the five innocent children enter the room that day. We saw several turn their backs to hide their tears. The family and her ministers were all around her bedside and had sung a song when the spirit took its flight at five PM. Tears flowed as one could hardly grasp the depth of the valley we were traveling through. We experienced the love, prayers, and visits of many, many people who visited them at home and at the hospital.

Now funeral arrangements were made. She would be laid to rest on her birthday, March 1st, 1987. She would have turned 33. No birthday gift on this earth can compare with going home to be with Jesus!

Hundreds paid their respects at the viewing and funeral. The many acts of kindness and love by friends far and near were too numerous to mention. It was all appreciated more than we can tell.

Now how can one explain the loss of a mother to school age or younger children? Their ages were from four to 12. Many were the trials, but by God's grace and strength, and with the help of many neighbors and friends, one day at a time, a person can make it. The trauma of emotional pain and suffering can't all be put on paper, but we realize God had a purpose. The fabric of our lives are woven with dark threads among the light ones because God alone knows what it takes to make the tapestry complete and ready for His kingdom. We need to say, "Thank you, Lord, may Thy will be done," even though we hurt.

The healing process does take time and it has its "up" and "down" days. But when one is feeling "down" and clouds hang low, a person spends more time on the knees and depends *completely* on His mighty power.

If there are mountains of trials in your lives, remember that God is right there by your side. He will help you cross the mountains *if* you ask Him.

Perry was a widower for two years, then he married a former school teacher, Eva Mullet. Perhaps one could say these were years of struggles and trials, but also years of growth in the Savior's love;

for all who were involved in the help and care of the family.

In the first year of their marriage together, a paper was found in an old large Bible. This was written by Fern to Eva sometime and was never sent to her! It was a poem entitled "One Day At A Time With Jesus". In conclusion, they think she must have written it during the time Eva was the teacher for their children. She may have stuck it in the Bible and it slipped her mind.

God works in mysterious ways, His wonders to perform. His ways are so much higher than ours!

Erla Weber: Aug. 5, 1987 - Apr, 1, 1988

Submitted by: Elmer & Elsie Webel, Listowel, Ontario, Canada

It was a bright and warm day for April first as we prepared for an 18 mile trip on that Good Friday morning. We wanted to attend North Woolwrich Church and then go to my parents for dinner. It was only about twice a year that we would get to go over to Dowdy (Ibra) Brubachers with two horses and carriage. Little did we know that this would be the first and only time that Erla would visit in their home. She was a happy and energetic little girl, but never liked to be bundled up under the covers for long drives outdoors.

With spring just around the corner we were eager to visit Dowdys after a long winter. Our baby was almost eight months old. A few days earlier we had prepared and fitted some new dresses, and then that Good Friday morning we put on her new little black shoes to go to church. All went well and we had a good visit at my parents. We said our farewells and good byes and little did we know what the evening would still hold.

We had supper at a cousin's place and then started out early on our long drive homeward. They wished us a safe journey home! Was it God's will?

We had problems with our lights, and as we neared Highway 86 we finally got them working. Elmer had an uneasy feeling all evening and wondered which way we should take. The 3 or the 86. We decided to take the highway as usual.

Some of the family members were asleep and I dozed off and on, glad that Erla was sound asleep because it wasn't relaxing if she cried for many miles. About six miles from home she let out a little cry and almost at the wink of an eye, a pickup truck crossed the road and crashed into our two seater carriage that carried us and our five children.

The front seat hit me in the chest throwing baby Erla from my arms and into the ditch. I was found about 20 feet away from the road. The two boys were thrown forward and only had blood on their faces from the one dead horse. Elmer and the oldest girls were unhurt, just stiff and sore from the shock. I was semiconscious for several hours, so it seemed everyone knew more about the accident than I did.

We all got checked at the hospital. We left Verna, three years old, at the hospital with a sprained ankle and also myself, the mother, with chest and leg injuries. There is when they told me that baby Erla had taken her last breath when Elmer picked her up from the ditch. The coroner was soon at the scene.

So suddenly God called her home without much suffering. We were thankful for that and realized *the blessing that remained*, since the carriage looked like a total wreck.

The driver of the truck was taken and checked to see how much he had been drinking. He had been at a friend's home and they warned him to wait there after drinking, but he was in a hurry to get home.

He was so sorry and asked for forgiveness when he and his wife came the next day to visit. His burden was heavy and he has to carry that guilty conscience around that it was his fault that caused the death of an innocent little one.

Through many tears we felt: *A little child shall lead us. Like it is, it will not stay. But like it was, it will never be.*

Many kind friends and neighbors helped along to prepare for the funeral while I spent nearly three days in the hospital. I came home the day before the funeral in a wheelchair. I also used a walker the next few weeks.

I was doped with pain pills and needed a lot of rest and could hardly fully grasp what all had happened. So suddenly it was a reality that we no longer had a baby in the house to love and care for. The playpen and toys, her little bed beside ours were all put away. Our little rosebud was picked by the Master to bloom in His kingdom.

The remembrance of Good Friday, how Christ died and suffered on the cross, it has a new meaning now. His great love for us all and the joy of Easter morning when He was risen.

Tuesday after Easter Sunday was Erla's funeral. It had been a drab and dreary weekend but then as the burial took place and after an inspiring and comforting sermon, we noticed the sun beginning to shine through the clouds. This meant life would continue for the rest of us. We must keep on looking up to where our help comes from and remember our family is now started in Heaven.

The next days and weeks many visitors cared and shared in person or through letters. Their prayers helped carry us through each new day. After the Easter holidays, the children went back to school, and the one teacher who was boarding here at the time. But there was still four year old Verna at home, who keenly missed her baby sister to play with. We tried to explain to them that these little ones go up to Jesus and are well cared for.

It is the *pain* of parting while the heart aches. Oh so many comforting poems to meditate on and also songs or Bible verses and all the letters of similar experiences that meant so much.

A few months later my health returned and I missed my baby and longed to care for her. The Creator had planned that it was spring time and time for planting, so I enjoyed being outdoors more, which helped to heal the wounds.

Memories returned when I would see others her age in church or diapers on a neighbor's wash line. Then that verse would return: Isaiah 49:15 *'Can a woman forget her sucking child and have compassion on the son of the womb?'*

A lot of healing had taken place when 19 months after the accident, another little girl was born to us. We called her Edna and all the children rejoiced to once again have a baby in our home. I realized later that we all spoiled her those first few years. Two and a half years later a boy joined our family. Now we have six children, three boys and three girls.

For months after our accident, the children had fears of driving out on the highways after dark. The horse that was killed in the accident was the same horse that was bought the day of Erla's birth. They were both taken so suddenly.

There were court cases and also visits in jail to see Clare, the driver. It helped to see how sorry he felt and that he wanted to start life anew, never to drink again.

God's ways are so much higher than our ways. All this draws us closer to Him. After eight years, healing has done wonders and many funerals we have attended of little children. It always opens the wound, but sweet memories also return.

Just a few years ago, we were sad to hear that Clare was again tempted to drink, and since then we have not seen him nor heard from him. Oh, that the world's trials and temptations overtook him.

We realize children are only loaned to us and now having teenagers in the family, we pray they can say no to the temptations the world has to offer and be able to follow His footsteps on the narrow road.

We realize now our little Erla is so sweetly resting and safe under His everlasting arms. Some sweet day we'll read the meaning of our tears and then we will understand!

Nine months after our daughter's death, on Christmas morning, it was revealed to me that the little cry from Erla, minutes before the crash was her farewell message, her good-bye to us. So I cherish it in my heart. Hoping some sweet day to meet, to part no more.

O gentle one, we miss thee here,
Sweet form we love so well;
But in our Father's better care,
We know the child is well.

Melvin Kauffman: 1983 - Sept. 26, 1988

Submitted by: Mrs. Ben K. Kauffman, Honey Brook, Pennsylvania

On August 15, 1970, my father, age 42, was killed instantly. I was 11 years old. He was on his way home with a load of horses that he had bought in Shipshewana, Indiana, at the horse sale. My brother David, age 13, was sleeping beside him. The driver dozed off and swerved around another truck to avoid hitting him. The truck Dad was in rolled over on its side, crushing Dad beneath the horses. We were not able to view him. David was left alone with these drivers. He wasn't hurt except a few stitches in his head.

We were awakened by a knock at home when word came that Daddy had an accident and was killed. We thought how can this be. Surely it must be just a dream. Being a child, I couldn't grasp the reality of death. The years went on with more experiences and I could better grasp the feelings of grief, sorrow, and pain.

Ten years after I was married my father-in-law, age 58, died of cancer on July 31, 1987. It was a painful experience to see someone suffer with a lot of pain and it was heartbreaking to see him suffer so. We wish him the peace and rest, but we sorely miss him.

A little over a year later, on September 26, 1988, our son Melvin, age five, was killed instantly in a corn silage cutter. It had been a beautiful morning. Melvin got up earlier than usual that morning and was a happy little lad. He was very excited about the day because the men were filling silo here at our farm. He had in mind to go with the men with their loads of corn.

The corn was extra short that year so the loads didn't get full and there was plenty of room in front of the wagon. He had a few rides a few days earlier. To him this was great, but it wasn't his nature to be with Daddy, to go with him to the fields. He'd much rather be with me, his mother, most of the time.

First thing that morning, I went to get some parts for my husband and little Melvin didn't miss the chance to go with me. Since he was the youngest and the others were away at school, he could almost always go with me wherever I went. Oh, how happy and carefree a little boy he was! It still rings in my ears to hear him sing his songs. He had a habit to sing on the way with our team whenever we went away, but how he put all his effort into singing his songs that morning. I had to think to myself- why is he so extra happy?

I came home and Melvin was excited because the men were filling silo and he quickly took off his coat and hat and ran up to the men, one of his uncles, for a ride. He had one ride, then my husband, Ben (his daddy), told him to go with him now. That way if something would happen, he would be with him. Melvin went with him for one ride and that was the last one, too. Ben had pulled up some distance away from cutter so that it would be safer. Melvin asked if he could throw the corn cobs off the wagon. He did.

Ben was almost done throwing corn bundles onto the corn conveyor or cutter. Before he went for the next bundles he looked to check on Melvin. Then when he went to put the next bundle on the conveyor, he saw Melvin on the conveyor going headfirst toward the rolls that grind the corn bundles. At first thought, Ben went for the lever to reverse it, not knowing he couldn't stop it. But he saw, like the wink of an eye, that life had fled.

There was nobody around so he left him like he was and called for me in the house. I was making dinner at the time but I heard in his voice that something serious had happened.

It went through my mind that it might be little Melvin. With that, I went up to Ben and saw something must have happened. Ben stayed calm and told me Melvin had an accident and that life is over. My first thought was, oh my, he went through the cutter. We then went together to where Melvin was lying on the cutter, headfirst lying on his stomach like he was sleeping.

He had one arm off at the elbow and his head was resting on the other arm. He had two other fingers off and had a few scratches on his face. When I seen him lying there so peacefully, the peace and comfort swept over me to see that he hadn't gone through the cutter.

Ben told me to stay with him while he goes out into the field to tell his brothers of the tragedy. These were some precious moments being there alone with Melvin, but I just couldn't believe what had happened and I kept asking God for help. I knew we couldn't handle this alone. I had asked Ben how did he get on there? He said he didn't have any idea how he got on there and was in a state of shock and he couldn't explain it to me.

Later on Ben kept thinking, 'How could he have gotten on there, or what had happened?' since the wagon was a distance away from the cutter. It was a question we just couldn't figure out, but feel it was a direct leading from God. We tried to think this was supposed to happen although it was a mystery. I was willing to let it go at that.

Soon friends, family, neighbors, and church people arrived with their sympathy. Our hearts ached to see that others cared. They made preparations for the viewing. Many tears were shed and much was accomplished, which we as parents could not have done alone. We had the viewing at home.

Finally around six o'clock in the evening, Melvin's body came. My heart quickened as they placed the casket where they had prepared for it. He did look peaceful and innocent. His face had the same usual looks. Many came who shared similar experiences and needed only to hold our hands.

Melvin was a fine natured boy and small for his age. What struck me most was when children came, especially the same age. I almost just wanted to grab this boy and just hug him. I can well remember how I felt. But I didn't. It was the beginning of a series of feelings of "letting go." I knew it would follow.

Anyone who has come abruptly face to face with the death of his own flesh and blood, knows the incredible feeling it creates. It is a searing pain that seems to cut right through the heart while you struggle to grasp all that happened. You, in reality, need to go on living. This simply can't be true, yet you know it is.

The first night after the tragedy, sleep just didn't come. I didn't sleep at all and my husband only a few winks. Just before it was time to get up to do the milking, I saw a vision. I got a lot of meaning out of that. It made me feel much lighter and I felt like I could go on. I helped Ben with the milking and really, I felt like I had a full night's rest for a while. On the way in after doing the chores, I whispered a prayer, "Lord help me." I felt much refreshed, but I knew a lot of activity would now take place.

Soon after, some of our family came and they were soon making burial clothes. They needed his shirt, vest and pants pattern. It was hard on me to think that this would be the last time I could do anything for our son, our baby. As time went on I felt nauseated and dizzy, and realized it was the results of shock. The day seemed to be a long one with many people in and out. I slept a little better the second night. Before the people arrived, Ben and I and the two other children ages eight and six, gathered around the casket. We wanted to prepare them for the burial of their brother, so that they would realize the peace behind it and not the horror. This was the first time our six year old daughter just wept. We hardly realized what they were going through, but it is amazing what these little minds can handle.

It was a beautiful day for the funeral. The sermon was very touching and fitting. Those ministers cannot realize how much these sermons meant to us. Many words of comfort were shared. After the services everyone filed past the casket for one last view of Melvin. This time his body was carried out of the barn to a waiting team and carriage. The teams of horses and carriages were all numbered and hitched up and lined in order for all who intended to join the close relatives to the cemetery. The casket was opened for the last time for all to have a last look at Melvin. I simply could not comprehend that this would be the last time to see our beloved child on this earth. Surely our loss was his gain. He was laid in a newly dug grave close to where his granddaddy was buried. We were tired and emotionally drained as we drove home.

The next day after the funeral, we knew we had to go on. It was a busy time of the year for the farmers. The corn was drying out so we got helpers to fill our silo. There were three crews to finish up. Oh, I still can't imagine how Ben could even go close to the cutter. He was mostly out in the fields that day, but he knew he had to face it.

As the days went by there were many feelings to deal with. The painful hours grew into painful days and then into months. Our lives and routines changed. It was like facing life again. Oh, that empty lonely feeling I well remembered.

I believe anyone who has experienced heartaches in their life has a love to reach out to others in need. Tears and sympathy come easily while hearing of others who experience pain. It was impossible to continue in life and pretend that our dear child had never existed. He was loved so dearly and was very much a part of our daily life. It is because of the deep love we had for him that we often weep and one does not want to forget.

There is always that feeling of incompleteness. You finally just learn to live with it. When someone asks me how many children we have, I always think of the missing one. I often just say five, or we would have six if all were living. My answer mostly depends on who asks the question. It is nearly eight years now since the parting of our son and I do believe I think of him almost every day. They are gone, but are with you in your heart. They are gone, but not forgotten.

In the year of 1995, on December 21, my mother-in-law died of locust disease at the age of 65. An experience that we will never forget in caring for her. She started with the disease about nine years earlier. Through the years she slowly lost out. For the last two years she was unable to care for herself and was on a wheelchair for four years. She was handled around by a lift because she couldn't do as much as lift her feet or her arms. We had to feed, bathe, and care for her. Her speech got worse, especially during the last year. During the last month we couldn't understand what she was saying, although she tried.

Her children, there are ten of them, were all married except for her youngest son, age 22. We took turns going to her home to care for her and do her household chores. She had been going around the children's homes for two years until she finally wasn't able to do that.

Over the last two months she hadn't been out of bed at all. Though she couldn't talk anymore, we could read her eyes and know what she wanted. Very touching! Her mind was good up to the last day. She was very patient with what she had. Never heard her complain. We have seen a lot of good examples from her. I hope to follow her footsteps as life goes on.

Eight months later, on August 12, 1996, my sister, age 43, died of bone cancer. This is a day I will remember because it was also our son Melvin's birthday. (The one who died.) This was another painful experience as we saw her going through a lot of pain and misery. But we also have some precious memories of her. I tried to go to her home as often as I could and this is precious to me now.

One late afternoon, when I arrived, five days before she died, she was singing with all her effort. She was either singing or talking for 28 hours straight. It was all about heaven. The family helped along till they were played out. It went into the night and she kept on singing till one o'clock the next day, when her voice gave out. From there on she didn't talk anymore. She had a lot of pain. It was so heartbreaking to see her suffer so. We wish her the peace and rest, but the parting of our loved one is so hard.

She was a mother of five and we feel she was much needed yet, but we must leave it all in God's hands and say, "Thy will be done." He does not make any mistakes.

Let us strive to meet our loved ones someday. We are not here to stay.

John E. King: Aug. 1, 1972 - Aug. 9, 1987

Submitted by: Amos & Malinda King, Shippensburg, Pennsylvania

Sunday morning, August 9, 1987, was a bright and sunny morning. We all got up as usual and did the milking, had breakfast, and everybody went about with their chores. I can still see John so plainly letting the cows out and cleaning the cow stable because we were all eager to get ready and leave for church eight miles away. The whole family attended since his oldest brother and sister were in instruction class. A very nice morning drive and we went in three teams because we had three children with the young folks at that time.

Church services began as usual. We had a visiting minister, Elmer Fisher, from across the mountain in Perry County. It was a very interesting morning in church. I could see the boys from where I sat and for some unknown reason I kept looking over at John with very deep thoughts. Too deep to put into words. In a year he would be old enough to go with the young folks.

After services were done dinner was served and some visiting was done. Soon some were leaving to go home or wherever they had planned. Quite a few families were still there when I asked my wife, Malinda, if she was ready to leave because we had planned to stop somewhere else on the way home. Then I asked the two small boys that were with me where John, Amos, and Ike were. They said they were down by the pond in back of the house.

I walked over to the fence and called John. He answered, but I couldn't see him or hear what he said, so I told him to come closer so I could hear him. Then I went through the fence so I could see down over the pond bank and I was amazed to see him in the water right after dinner and especially out in the middle of the pond. He was in water up to his chin.

There were two other boys with him and the rest of the nine boys were over on the far side in shallow water. When I called him, his two friends said they would go with him over to the other side since they were good swimmers and they could see what I wanted. They said the pond was not very deep since it was very dry that summer and they were irrigating out of the pond all summer.

I told John that we had planned to make a stop and that he and his two younger brothers should get their team and start for home soon and that we would be there in time to help with the milking. He said, "Okay, we will go right away. See you later."

When I had first seen John in the deep water I tried to stay calm and not let him know that I was alarmed, so that he wouldn't get excited. Then I turned around to leave and I heard something, so I looked back over my shoulder and he was coughing and pushing his hair out of his eyes. I was really concerned, but kept on going to the barn for my horse which was not far from the pond.

The question that later bothered me was, 'Why didn't I stay till he was out of the water?' I got my horse and came right back out of the barn when I saw Daniel, his friend, come running and heard him say, "Amos' John is in the water."

I knew right away what was going on. There were about eight or ten men standing by the barn door so I hollered for help. When I ran past the house, one of the women was coming out, so I told her to go to the phone for help because there was a boy in the water.

I figured when we get there we would still see him going up and down, so I was throwing things out of my pockets on the way down to the pond. But no John was in sight. Oh no, then my mind went to God, please help. We were soon in the water trying to find him but it was about ten minutes before we got him out.

I saw right away that it looked pretty hopeless. About that time my mind went blank and I could not think what should be done next, but there was soon lots of help there. Oh God, please help us. I was not prepared for something like this.

The ambulance arrived and they called for the air flight helicopter which was there in about 12 minutes. They worked on him for awhile but it did not look good to me. It looked so hopeless to me. I wished they would just let him rest, and as they were getting ready to air lift him I asked the doctor if he thought it was worthwhile.

He said, "Yes, we have a good heartbeat."

But he was not breathing on his own. My heart just wanted to cry out to God to save him from death, but at the same time I did not want to wish him here on earth if it was not God's will. Our bishop was there. He told me it is now in God's hands and we did all we could for him. Yes, it was beyond our control, and who are we to protest against the divine will of God. We profess to believe and trust in Him, which we were trying to do, but I knew that I would first have to give up myself and my will.

My wife, Malinda, and I left for the hospital. When we arrived we were told he was in the emergency room with a good heartbeat and on a breathing machine. His brain scan on the left side did not look good. The hospital chaplain soon found us and took us to a room and he said to just make ourselves at home. He would be back as soon as John gets to his room. We waited a short time and he came and said John was now in his room and we were to come over and talk to him. It was very hard to see him with all those tubes and needles in him. Oh, my heart just broke down again and again. My wife and I just could not get much of a conversation going because there wasn't much to say.

When we left for the hospital, different people asked to go along, but I said it would be more necessary to go home with the children and help with the chores. We would stay in contact by phone, but now I wished that somebody was with us.

My brother John and his wife came down and brought the

children along around 6:30 PM. They had taken John down for another brain scan. When they brought him back we were all allowed back into his room. The doctor told us his brain on the other side was losing out and his heart was getting harder to control. Around 9:15 the doctor told us that they could not do any more for him. I told him we do not want to prolong his life if it is not God's will since he was brain dead.

I thought I had given myself up in case this would happen, but I soon found out I had hardly started. Oh, what a blow. How could we go on? I knew as the father of a family, I had to make the start. I just wanted to stay there and cry my heart out and go with John. But then I thought of my wife and the rest of the family. Why can't we just all go with him? I cannot find the words to express myself.

We got home around 11 o'clock and there were friends, Nab's brother and sister, church friends there. Sometime later our parents arrived and then is when it really hit me. We started to make plans for the funeral but it was getting late. Around 2:30 we went to bed, but there was no sleep. The next few days my mind was just kind of blank at times. I just could not grasp what was going on.

The day of the funeral came and my heart just felt like it would break at any time. Then as we got up from prayer, there was a big hand right in front of me reaching for me. I very much felt the presence of God and it was then that it seemed like he was telling me, go get up and keep on going because you are still needed here on earth. That was a great help to me, but then after the funeral and burial, we came home and ate dinner and visited. Then soon everybody left for home. What a lost feeling.

Steven S. King: May 18, 1977 - June 21, 1994

Submitted by: David & Lena King, Gap, Pennsylvania

A beautiful Sunday morning as the sun gradually inched higher in the cloudless sky, giving promise of yet another sweltering day in our early summer heat wave.

Our 17 year old son, Steven, had risen early that morning to help with a neighbor's chores. Now being his bouncing, full-of-energy self, he was preparing to leave to attend church at a friend's home 18 miles away. Taking his team and a friend along, whom had just come, we were saying those last good byes. He had his swimming trunks in his hand, planning on taking a dip in the nearby meadow pond after church.

"Be careful, Steven," I said, "don't forget, you're not a real good swimmer."

To this he replied, "Yeah Dad, I know," and then he was on his way, never to again return to his earthly home. My eyes followed his team as they headed south to their destination. I watched until they passed beyond our view. Unknown to me, someone else would bring Steven's team home. An experience, before unknown, awaited us that day. Death was no stranger to us, parents, friends, relatives, but never such as this - our responsibility and our future, *our child*!

While spending Sunday evening at home with our children, except the three oldest attending youth gatherings, two men from the church area where Steven was, brought us the shocking news of a near drowning. "Yes it was Steven. We can't say, but we didn't see any response. They were working on him. We don't know how long he was under water."

Such were the answers we received from someone who saw Steven and had little hope of recovery. Our first thoughts were, "Why?" Our dependence on him, our dream shattered! We also had immediate and strong thankful thoughts of Steven's spiritual life being in order, and of him having attended instruction class for baptism. Although in a displaced situation, a calmness unexplainable, yet an urgency pressed us.

A State Police Trooper now entered our drive with the report, "Your son has been revived and is being transported to Lancaster General Hospital."

Making arrangements to leave, we first spent time together with those of our family at home, asking God for strength and that His will be done.

Steven had been swimming in what he thought to be a safe depth, but unknowingly, had stopped to rest in water where he couldn't quite wade. Being tired, he panicked and went under. The four boys swimming with him couldn't get him out. They all had ahold of him at some time. Several men, seeing the commotion and hearing yelling, came to help. One of these, a six-footer, could wade to the spot where he found Steven. Together they got him out and CPR was started. But he was under water too long for those conditions. The damage was done. It was only a matter of time.

When we first saw Steven in the emergency room, the quote "Where there is life, there is hope," fitted us perfectly. Although on full life support, they told us he could breathe on his own. Memory pictures of our son in the hospital stay with us. He looked, at first, very much his usual self. Deeply tanned, muscular body, clear eyes, although not focusing on us, were opening and closing.

As Sunday and the night wore on, we battled with the turmoil that Steven's life must continue. We couldn't find that assurance from the medical staff, or from his statistics, or from what we could see.

Monday was a day of resignation. We needed to abide under the shadow of the Almighty. Psalm 91 was of great comfort. "The Lord is my refuge and my fortress, My God, in Him will I trust." Our greatest comfort was the safety of abiding in God's presence.

My Bible opened that morning to that Psalm and on that we built. We could plainly see Steven's declining condition, a difference every couple hours. We didn't know how long, it was only a matter of time.

In an interview with Dr. Eshleman, Steven's presiding doctor, on Monday evening, he confirmed what we knew. Steven was going. He told us if we choose to, life support could now legally be disconnected, according to that day's EEG test. However, just having evaluated him, Steven could still breathe on his own. Considering Steven's age and prime physical condition, he recommended waiting until noon the next day, doing another evaluation, and if his vitality declines as he expects it to, then if we consent, Steven's life support would be disconnected.

Our family was given a private consultation room and our group gathered around the table, asking God to show us His will. We each expressed ourselves as willing to support and consent to the doctor's recommendation. We felt better after this. Steven had a private intensive care room, the staff supporting us in a professional and caring way.

Tuesday morning was traumatic. Steven's vital signs plummeted. It was only a matter of time and we felt that time slipping through our fingers as we spent the last precious hours at his bedside. At 12:30 we left the room as Dr. Eshleman did the evaluation, then gathered us together, saying "Steven's life is fast approaching an end."

I asked, "How much more time do you want?"

To this he reverently replied, "It is not my time, it's your time.

Whenever you and the family decide. We'll be waiting outside the room."

He then extended a handshake as a sign of commitment. Softly they closed the large glass roll doors to unit seven and pulled the curtains. Our family, alone with Steven, felt the depth of God's spirit upon us. We again prayed for God's will and leading, and sang one of Steven's favorite German songs, 'We'll rise and go to a better land, our home is not below', and also part of 'Will The Circle Be Unbroken?' We strongly felt the time was here to release Steven from life support. Who are we to stand in the way of fulfillment and the Lord's will? The staff had told us, "It takes more love to release than to keep," and out of our hearts depths we wished to him that 'Better Land" he so often sang about.

As the doctor and staff, outside, waited for our decision, we expressed ourselves each in turn, agreeing to release Steven. We then each gave him a good-bye kiss and said "Good night, Steven."

I then walked outside our unit to the central station where Dr. Eshleman and the head nurse stood waiting. As I approached, he extended his hand, and as we clasped in solemn handshake, I gave the consent of our family to release life support. His eyes over-flowed with tears as he accepted this.

After I reentered the room, Dr. Eshleman sent a technician who quietly and reverently walked in, shut off the equipment and closed the door and curtain as she left us alone to witness the awesomeness of a soul slipping into Eternity. Our responsibility, our son of 17 years in his prime and joy of youth!

We watched in awestruck silence as he took a breath, then several small, shallow attempts and Steven's life peacefully flowed away. His entire body changed, eyelids slit open, hands slowly closed to midway, head tilted back slightly as his color changed. Steven had gone, only the shell remained.

After making the announcement to our support group in the waiting room, plans were made to return home. Home without Steven!

Death, an unfathomable event. The viewing, the funeral and burial, the closeness and support. God had reached into our midst and into our depths. Words that fully express cannot be written. Unreality plays its role and yet our innermost being is touched with the finality of death. We cannot avoid death, but with God's grace we can bear it.

We struggled to submit and strain to accept that which we'd so much long to deny. At this same time we feel and know God's love for us, a purpose in Steven's life and death.

Grief, an unfathomable experience. Time continues as we grieve. The deepness of inner yearning and waves of homesickness engulf us. Grieving is hard and tiring work, but through time we become a "better instead of bitter" person when we allow ourself to grieve properly without self-pity. It is when we realize that the depth of grief and homesickness has worth, no long fight against or bypass, that values of great worth appear. Our lives are remolded beyond the temporalness of our existence, searching, reaching, and ever longing to be absent of this body, and to be present with the Lord, which, as Paul writes, is far better.

Unhurried grief is our new normal. We now need to readjust, restructure, and to live around this vast gap in our midst. One of us has gone. We need to move on in life with willingness, ever keeping our eyes on the goal of reuniting and being with Jesus. Becoming stronger in faith, more compassionate in ministering, and ever increasing in love and duty.

We cherish memories of a life well lived, then cut off as the youthful bloom began to unfold. This remembrance becomes ever sweeter and more precious than gold. By submitting to God's high and perfect will, and facing life in "betterness instead of bitterness", then surely our son's life was not in vain.

Lester Weber: Nov. 15, 1978 - Dec. 19, 1994

Submitted by: Henry & Sarah Weber, Mount Forest, Ontario, Canada

We just want to share a little of our son Lester's fatal accident, since I, myself, have a hunger to hear of others' experiences. We can learn from these and not feel so alone with one's feelings and emotions.

On December 19, 1994, a mild Monday, tragedy came into our lives and home. As we were finishing the noon meal the phone rang. Dad went to answer it and Lester and I, seated across the table from each other, tried guessing who the caller was from listening to Dad's conversation. After the call he explained a neighbor had bought a farm in a new area, between 20 and 25 miles from there and Dad planned to help plow tomorrow. It was planned that their son Cleon and our son Lester, 16, would each take a tractor and plow Monday evening and head for the new farm.

We had asked a driver to take Lester to his uncle's place who lived in the same area to help for the week. The driver could not make it until in the afternoon and he had not shown up yet so he was cancelled. My mother's heart sank when I heard of the plans and had to fight back tears because it seemed too big an undertaking since Lester had just turned 16 on November 15. The law in Ontario is that they need to be 16 before operating a motor vehicle on the road, so that was no problem. There are times when it hurts to "let the children let go of your apron strings", as the saying is, and this time I found it almost unbearable.

Lester wasn't eager either because he said, "But we just cleaned the plow and put it in storage on Saturday." Since the plans had been made they were followed. Before leaving, Lester came in to get more clothes and his heavy coat. It was mild, but chilly for the long drive. As he headed out the door I said, "Machs gute."

With a nod of his head, he left.

It was around two o'clock. What do I do now? I was still fighting tears and the sinking feeling. I went for the seed catalog. Around 2:30 PM I glanced at the clock and was relieved to feel the pressure gone. Maybe all will be well after all. At 2:40 PM the phone rang and it was the neighbor again. He asked if Henry was there.

I replied, "Yes, he is out in the barn."

Then he said, "The boys have had an accident and we'll be over to pick up both of you."

He did not say what happened, how, or anything else, so I had a lot of questions.

I did ask him, "It is our turn to provide transportation for the scholars. Shall we ask someone else?"

"Yes, do."

"Shall we also let Laverne know?"

"Yes."

Then we hung up.

Laverne, 18, was helping at his cousin's place for the year and wasn't home yet, but we were expecting him home that week. Several times during the past month I had mentioned to Lester that I could hardly wait till the whole family will be together again. It never materialized, but God knows it all. Here in our area and church group, it is the practice to let teenagers, 16 and older, to help families who do not have grown children to help with their work. That is why Laverne was away from home.

With the neighbor's lack of information, my heart was sinking. He knew something we did not and that was that it was our son not theirs, because Cleon had called and asked them to come. With that I went to find Dad in the barn. He came down from the silo saying, "Oh no, what now?"

Back in the house I called a neighbor to see about the scholars. She said they could and that our two girls, Verna, 13, and Elsie, seven, could stay at their house as well. How I appreciated that caring offer to my reeling mind. Next I called Laverne. His cousin answered. Next I called Lester's uncle where he was headed for. By then it was time to change clothes. I reached for my black dress. Dad asked, "Black?"

"Yes, that is what I feel I should wear."

Shortly the taxi arrived with the neighbor and another of his sons along. The young lad was fighting back tears when he came to the house to see if we were ready. We still did not know any more details. We got into the car and at the end of the lane, a right turn was made which was away from the local hospital. Once the neighbor man talked Dutch to the English driver. Why wasn't his wife along and I was to go? Questions, questions.

Across Highway 6 the taxi driver wondered if his son would be at the scene, so we gathered we were heading for the accident. At the top of a rise we noticed the flashing red lights. Ahead was one tractor and plow with a dented fender and over there - a tractor and plow completely upside down in the ditch. No truck, car, or anything else was involved. The dented fender had come from farm use and had nothing to do with the accident.

What had taken place was that as Lester made a right-hand turn, the front wheel of the tractor dropped into the ditch, which wasn't all that deep, but with the weight of the plow behind it, it flipped completely upside down. He had just passed a driveway and also missed a guy wire of a hydro pole which was between the tractor and plow.

There was no commotion. People were just quietly waiting. We got out of the car somehow and a sergeant officer met us and said to the neighbor, "Come aside, will you?" He asked, "Isn't there a small lad around? He is my son," then motioning to us he said, "These..."

The officer swallowed and with tears in his eyes he said, "Unfortunately, there is no hope."

To this I replied, "This must be the hard part of your job. Fourteen years ago it was my parents, three years ago my sister."

Another officer standing close by said, "This was an appointment."

Often we have been thankful for those words to help keep our thoughts more positive. We were deeply thankful that no one else was involved if Lester's time was up. Later a lady from church who does cleaning for the sergeant also shared how the sergeant said, "That was Lester's time, place, and way to leave this world, because there was no reason for it to happen."

It comforts us to think people who are more involved in that kind of work, can perceive a difference.

At the scene I strongly felt, "God called and Lester answered." I just stood there and felt something drain out of me and something else fill me. An officer reminded me to go over to my husband who had gone off to cry a little. When the crane arrived to lift the tractor to remove Lester, we were offered rides home. First we headed for Laverne, to break the news to him. He came along home with us. We might have been gone around an hour. We called the neighbor to say the girls may come home. When we saw the girls coming, we called again and told them what had happened. When the girls came in we also told them. There is no easy way to break harsh news, is there?

An officer had promised that we could see Lester at the hospital, so we were waiting on that move. In the meantime, I brought in the fluffy wash which included Lester's yet, too. I had Laverne clear out the sunporch which Elsie used as a playhouse during the summer. Neighbors came. One brought soup for supper, for those who could eat. So many caring deeds. Would I have something on hand to share if things were turned around?

At 5:30 PM, an officer came and said that Lester has been moved to Stratford Hospital for an autopsy, which was required by law for accident victims. What now? Stratford was one hour away from here. Laverne and Verna desired to see him, so a driver was gotten and the bishop and his wife went with us at 7:30 PM. More friends were coming, but we left anyway with our family, but not complete anymore. How it hurt!

We arrived and a chaplain met us. One is on call 24 hours a day at that hospital. He took us to the small room where Lester was on a stretcher. So real, yet so unreal. Then the tears flowed. That was very precious to us to again see him in his everyday clothes. His pleasant twinkling eyes closed forever, but we hope and trust, "*Safe in the arms of Jesus.*"

We would encourage anyone in similar circumstances of again viewing a loved one in his natural form if possible. To feel him, to see that it is an earthly body left behind. Experiences will vary, yet God is real and close to help each one to carry on one step at a time.

Many memories, mixed feelings, and emotions. He was 16. Was he ready to meet his Maker? Several weeks earlier, Verna had remarked that Lester was so nice the last while. He had been blessed with a quiet, pleasant personality which people appreciated. That fall, one evening, he had been burning garbage while we went to a parent-teacher meeting; he also collected the empty spray containers that were to be returned to the feed store and burned them. The smoke made him drowsy, so he went to the tractor and fell asleep till Dad came over to check on him when we returned home. After that he matured still more.

Just the last Monday morning we were discussing how each breath is a gift of God. As long as we are young and healthy, we do not realize it so much. I still have a picture of him lounging in the easy chair as I glanced past his Dad's legs and between his sister, I was wondering what I would see, but the sweetness I saw on his face made me feel at peace.

Quite a few people remembered his face the last Sunday he was at church. I noticed a light that rested on the empty bench in front of him and reflected up onto his face. It went till the next summer before I realized the sun does not shine in a west window in the morning. I feel it is another of God's ways to help ease our hurt which the Lord knew this happening would create.

On Tuesday morning at the breakfast table, Dad said to the children, "You are not to feel we love Lester more than you, because we are grieving. During the summer when the thought came if one of the children should go, it caused as many tears for one as the other."

On awakening from a sleep the verses, 'My grace is sufficient for thee', II Corinthians 12:9; and 'Trust in the Lord with all thine heart and lean not unto thine own understanding', Proverbs 3:5, were there to comfort us. This was after the accident, but before the funeral.

When we "Trust in the Lord", feelings and emotions fall into place better, but when our "own understanding" is used, I find the hills and gullies are steeper and deeper.

Lester has been laid to rest in the same cemetery where his stillborn brother and sisters were laid to rest. The Bible says we are to gather our treasures where rust and moth doth not corrupt. The Lord is helping us in that, so with our hurts we remember we are also richly blest, with a larger family in heaven than on earth. God makes no mistakes.

Steven B. Sensenig: Feb. 8, 1984 - Aug. 10, 1994

Submitted by: Marvin & Lydia Sensenig, Shippensburg, Pennsylvania

There was nothing to tell us on the morning of August 10, 1994, that this day would be different than any other one. Before the day would be over, our lives would change in the twinkling of an eye. Never to be the same again. We were the typical family, living ordinary lives on a dairy farm, raising a family of five boys and three girls ranging in age from three years to 18. We had the usual ups and downs that go with raising a family, minor illnesses and injuries, but nothing major. Life seemed good; maybe too good. Maybe we were taking for granted that it would continue so.

This day would be different. Our two oldest boys left for their jobs and we ate breakfast rather hurriedly because our plans were to help at our school for its pre-opening cleaning and repairing. With some instructions to the ones at home, we left, never knowing we would not be seeing Steven alive again on this earth. He was our fifth child and always very active; hyperactive really. He was ten years old and his younger brother seven. They were always together. Steven, the leader, Marvin, the follower, and sometimes getting into things as boys will.

As our work at school progressed, the women finished with the cleaning and the men were still working at making a new fence around the schoolyard. We women sat relaxing and visiting in the schoolhouse. It was 11 o'clock AM. Suddenly a young girl from the farmhouse adjoining the school property appeared and said our oldest daughter, then 13, was on the phone wanting to talk to one of us. Steven had been hit by a truck. No other details.

I found out that my mind could not absorb the full impact of such shocking news. My first thoughts were, oh my, what was he doing now? I imagined some bumps, etc., but not what it really was. As I ran out to tell Marvin, his shocked face seemed to jolt the seriousness in my own mind. At that moment, as I was facing the road a short distance away, a medic unit went flashing past. We had not heard the sirens because the tractor and post pounder made a lot of noise. Only then did my mind forcefully realize the seriousness. An ambulance was needed! He must be badly hurt! Oh, I wanted to get home. As Marvin ran to the phone because our daughter was still waiting on the phone, I couldn't think what to do. Everything was a blur.

A pickup truck drove in just then and someone suggested I get him to take me home, which he did. Later I wished I would have waited on Marvin coming back from the phone. He then took the team and with school only a little over a mile away, I still felt it must have been a long time coming home. In such a time you just don't think, doing only what is given to do.

I so hoped he would still be there when we came home, and he was. As we rounded the curve a short distance from our farm, there were two medics there and a few other stopped vehicles. Medical people were bending over a still body on the road. As we approached the scene, I caught sight of a tangled bike in a heap in the middle of the road and knew instantly what had happened.

I was out of the truck almost before it stopped and ran to our son lying there so still. Too still. Oh, is he hurt badly? I could see he was unconscious. His eyes were open, the pupils dilated even with the bright sun overhead. I knew it was serious as they worked on him doing CPR. There was little sign of injury. A few bruises on his forehead and chest. My mother instinct wanted to snatch him to myself, to help somehow. Between the people working, I found a little space.

Kneeling beside him I took his hand, calling his name. There was not one flicker of response as they worked on him, one giving CPR, one suctioning him, and occasionally forcing air into his lungs. As they hooked him to some wires, I was told to stand back and he was given an electric shock. That was the only movement he ever made.

Marvin had arrived by then and as we stood watching, our minds were numbed to disbelief. This was one of our precious children. I remarked that it looks like he is gone. I found out it was even hard to pray. It seemed I could only ask to please let him live. I always like to think God reached down and gave us the needed strength even before we asked, as he has promised. He sees our every need.

An ambulance arrived and he was loaded up and we decided I would ride along and Marvin would follow with a neighbor. The twenty miles to the hospital seemed a long way. Many thoughts passed through my mind, all in a jumbled mess. At the hospital I was escorted to a small room after answering some questions. A social worker sat with me as we waited for a report. After what seemed like a long time, but before Marvin arrived, a doctor came in and quietly and gently told me they could not save our son.

Although not unexpected, the words were stunning. As Marvin arrived a short time later, this same doctor followed him inside and broke the news to him. Our close neighbors, who are also the bishop and his wife of our district, had come with Marvin and how glad we were to have them for support at this, the hardest time in our lives. We were asked if we wanted to see him before we went home. We said yes and were taken to him.

I find no words to describe that emotional time. Our son, so full of life, now so still and gone from us forever in this life. Oh, can it be true? As I stroked his tousled hair and still warm face it seemed he would wake up with his flashing smile and merry blue eyes. But he had gone to meet his Lord.

Later we rode home, dreading to break the news to the rest of the our family. Our two oldest sons were still at their jobs. One was five hours away. The message came to him that one of his brothers was killed, but he didn't know which one. It was a long ride home.

We then found out how it had happened. Steven's younger brother, Marvin, had just learned to ride bike and they spent lots of time in this way. They were not allowed to ride on the road and had plenty of room in our barnyard and field lane. On this morning they were racing toward the road to see who could reach it first. Steven had too much speed and although he braked, he didn't stop before reaching the middle of the road.

The police pointed out the skid mark of the wheel on the loose gravel and a short black mark on the road. Our barn stands very close to the road so the driver of the stake bed truck did not see him until he popped out from beside the barn in front of him. He tried, but could not avoid hitting him.

The following days are a blur in my memory. It seemed it could not be. Friends, relatives, and neighbors arrived. Necessary work was done and funeral arrangements made. The funeral was a large one with the meeting house overflowing, and some standing outside the windows. We felt unworthy of all the kindness shown to us during this time and weeks after. But we needed it. God gives comfort and strength in many ways and through others is one way.

Steven was ten years, six months, and two days old. Ten short years. Time goes on and brings healing, but the ache, the emptiness, and memories linger on. In life we loved him dearly. In death we love him still. In our hearts he holds a place, no one can ever fill. Since then we have been blessed with another daughter.

The Lord giveth, the Lord taketh. Blessed be the name of the Lord.

Audrey B. Sensenig: Aug. 22, 1972 - May 29, 1974
Andrew B. Sensenig: May 30, 1981 - Oct. 16, 1994
Submitted by: Eleanor Sensenig, Leonardtown, Maryland

Audrey

Twenty-four years ago we were blessed with our first baby. A girl named Audrey. When Audrey was a year and a half, our little boy, Gregory, was born. Before he was quite four months old, Audrey was killed.

We had a roadside stand selling produce for ourselves and others. My husband, Paul, worked as a carpenter, but during the busy strawberry season he was at home. At this memorable moment he was out at the stand waiting on customers and I was in the house tending the baby. Suddenly I became aware of extra commotion outside. A horn blowing and someone shouting. I looked out the window and saw Audrey lying on the ground in the parking lot.

She had slipped out of the house, having just learned to open the storm door by herself when pulling something over to stand on. I quickly put the baby down on the couch with pillows like I often did, but soon heard him screaming. I ran back inside and found him on the floor so I took him along.

It appeared that a car had backed over Audrey and then left the scene. I felt like I just wanted to hold her, but knew I shouldn't move her. The wait for the ambulance seemed so long. Finally they took Audrey to the hospital. A cop took Paul along and I stayed at home with the baby.

I closed the stand and walked to my sister Kathryn's house. That is where Paul came for me after the cop brought him home again. He had to tell me that Audrey was pronounced dead on arrival. This happened on a Wednesday afternoon. The funeral was on Saturday. Family and friends came and willingly helped all they could.

Audrey was saying everything already at 21 months old and was a pleasant little sunshine in our lives. So she was sadly missed for a long time. Our home seemed so quiet and empty. Even four month old Gregory seemed to miss his older sister. When friends came to visit, Gregory got all excited when he saw little children.

Time goes on and eases the hurt, and the memories become more precious instead of painful.

A year later we moved onto our own farm, in a new house. The widening process of the highway where we had lived, took the little house and lot.

Andrew

It happened on a beautiful Sunday in the fall. My husband Paul and I with Amy, 16; Warren, 11; Jean, eight; Elaine, six; and Clifton, four; went to church in the carriage. Andrew, 13, followed on the bicycle. Gregory, 20, and Robert, 17, went in the buggy. We were planning to have relatives as dinner guests because Paul's mother, Elizabeth Sensenig, and his brother and wife, Sam and Arvilla Sensenig were in the area from Missouri.

Andrew had instructions to come home right after church to turn on the oven and put the casseroles in that I had prepared. We also left for home as soon as possible, after a few words here and there. On our homeward way we saw commotion up ahead with cars braking and someone trying to flag down traffic so we pulled into a driveway. We could see there had been an accident. The woman who lived there had just come out of her house because she heard unusual commotion. She talked a bit, we knew her well, but she didn't know what had happened.

Paul thought we should go on home so we would not add to the confusion and traffic. We could continue right through these people's lanes and fields, coming out close to home. But I said, "No wait. Let me go see who it is." We could see a few of our group's young folks standing nearby, so I ran over to where someone was lying on the road. When I got close, I thought I recognized the shirt, which gave me a jolt. I asked anyway, "Who is it?"

John Wenger, a cousin who was coming for dinner and was biking with Andrew, answered, "Andrew."

I grabbed John's arm and said, "No!"

With shock-filled eyes he nodded.

Stunned, I stood there for a moment with one of the girls who had happened upon the scene, laying a hand on my arm. I realized I had to return to Paul and the children to tell them. Paul got out of the carriage after driving up to a tree, and let Amy watch the horse. We walked back to Andrew where quite a crowd was gathering. We found out a passing car had run into Andrew's bike from behind, throwing him up on the car and breaking the windshield. He then was thrown up higher, coming down on the road. The driver came to a stop after running into a sign post. He was an older man on medication which made him unfit for driving.

This happened near a curve, on a very busy road, and it took a lot of traffic directing. The road had wide, black-topped shoulders, making it very nice for horse and buggies and bicycles.

When we returned to the scene, a rescue worker was already working on Andrew. She happened to be the driver of one of the first cars to come to the scene and had emergency equipment along. Only then did someone call for an ambulance. It seemed like a long time until the first sirens were heard. Soon there were cops and sheriffs and an ambulance. Also a fire truck. The medic called for a helicopter because there were obvious head injuries. They worked over Andrew a long time, even after the helicopter was there and waiting.

Since we had been in a hurry to start home, we were the first horse and carriage to arrive. Some boys of our group who were soon there, went back to direct all the church people the other way, using a lane as a detour.

When they finally had Andrew on the stretcher and in the helicopter to start to the Children's Hospital in Washington D.C., a sheriff took Paul and me home. The sheriff said he would be back in 30 minutes to take us to the hospital. This was at 12:30. I would much rather have gone right away but I didn't say anything.

One of the boys had brought our horse on home. At home we had all this company, going ahead with the meal. Outside our door I felt as if I needed a push to make me enter. I was carrying Andrew's shoes, hat, and pants that someone had put in my arms.

We got a few things ready expecting to be picked up soon. Instead, we waited and waited. Finally two hours later, a sheriff came, but not the same one. He had never been in Washington and lost his way. Paul could have directed him, but he didn't know the sheriff wasn't merely taking a different route until it was too late and the area was unfamiliar. The sheriff asked directions, first at another hospital and then at a fire house, where luckily, a D.C. cop was available to escort us in. The trip took two hours when it should have only taken one.

By then it was 4:30 already and first a chaplain took us into an office to get information, then he took us to a Family Consultation room, where he prayed and encouraged us. Also he brought in a few doctors to talk about Andrew's case. Then, finally, they led us to Andrew's bedside.

It was hard to accept that this was our son, amid all those bandages and machines. They had a heat lamp above him so he wouldn't feel so cold to our touch. We could hold his hands and touch his arms. We stood there for a while, watching his chest rise and fall, due to the breathing machine, and medication in his veins was keeping his heart beating. We realized that there would never be anything more. No hope of returning consciousness because the brain was so severely damaged. We had to say the word for them to remove the life support.

I felt numb and couldn't comprehend it all, even when the alarm went off to indicate that the heart had stopped. They took us back to the consultation room while they prepared Andrew's body so that we could see him without all the tubes and noises. We talked about calling our neighbors to let family and friends know, but decided it would be better to just let them wait until we got home.

This time the sheriff had no trouble getting us there. It was around eight o'clock. We sat up late, just not feeling like going to bed. When we did go, we were able to rest and sleep a little bit. It was a Washington D.C. law that all those dying in the District are sent to the morgue where they wait for an autopsy.

We could do nothing about it and our local undertaker tried to hurry them up. We couldn't go ahead and set the funeral date until the undertaker knew when he could get the body. The funeral wasn't until Friday, five days after the accident. Later autopsy reports showed a transection of the brain stem and cerebral edema.

It seemed like an awfully long week. Neighbors and friends came as well as all the church people, bringing food and helping with the preparations. My sister Sally helped out a lot, just staying and seeing to everything.

On Thursday afternoon the coffin was brought, then lots of people came for the viewing. We were thankful that the body could be prepared for viewing. Andrew's face was still swollen. More relatives came from Missouri, Kentucky, and Pennsylvania, to attend the funeral. A few of Paul's family stayed after the funeral, helping us over the first difficult days. There were lots of adjustments to be made. Now, instead of four scholars, we only had three.

Esther Smucker describes it all so well in her book, 'Goodnight, My Son'.

A year and a half later when Gregory got married, someone asked how many children we have. I felt slightly confused, not having been asked this question in a long time. I said we still have seven and she of course thought I meant seven when Gregory leaves. I said I meant seven living. Why didn't I just say seven with Gregory, or six after Gregory leaves?

We can feel confident that we now have two children in heaven. May we all meet them there.

Norman Bontrager: June 19, 1971 - Mar. 23, 1985
Lydia Mae Bontrager: Feb. 6, 1931 - July 5, 1991

Submitted by: Mahlon M. Bontrager; Shipshewana, Indiana

Norman

It happened March 23, 1985. I went to Vernon Lambrights to do some remodeling on the house. It was a nice spring morning. Our three sons were at home cleaning the trany shed. The two older boys would load and Norman would unload.

Then it happened. For some unknown reason the horses became spooked coming toward the barnyard. The older boys told Norman to jump off, but we still don't know if he fell or jumped and never will. The other boys helped him walk to the house. Mom came out and was concerned. He sat down and Mom asked him, "Are you all right?"

"Yes," Norman said, "I'm all right."

Then they helped him lie down and he passed out. They helped him sit up again and he came back right away. The older boys said they were going to take him to the hospital. Things were starting to change so they took him to the First Aid in Shipshewana and they then took him to LaGrange Hospital. I was still at Vernon's.

Yes, it was God's will to take Norman home. He passed on, on the way to the hospital. This all happened and I didn't know. One of the boys came and told me Norman was hurt. His brother was very shook up. I asked if it was serious and all he said was, "Yes, somebody will come to take you to the hospital."

Our neighbor was there in a short time. By that time my mind was going around trying to cope with what had happened. The doctor met me at the door. In my heart I knew that he had passed on. The doctor said he was sorry, but what could he do? It was all in God's hands.

I asked where Mom was and was told she would be there soon.

Then they told me what happened. The next day is like a dream. Authorities pronounced a broken neck. Norman always loved his mother and father. Two weeks before the accident, he had done the chores, got ready to milk, and then came to the house and asked, "Mom, what would you do without me?"

Mom said we would try next best.

How little did we know what was ahead. Teachers, friends, neighbors came to the viewing and funeral. It had to be God's will. Norman had told friends in his class that he wouldn't be in school Monday. Well why? He didn't give an answer. After it happened it seemed like God was working in Norman.

Three months later I was so homesick I didn't know what else to do. We would talk about what had happened. Find some private place and pray to God for help. It always came back that it was God's plan. We wouldn't wish Norman back in this world. I feel he is with Jesus in a wonderful place. Praise God for everything.

Lydia Mae

This was not as sudden in some ways, but it was very sudden for me. A lonesome husband and family. In March Mom had blood clots in her lungs. We went to the doctors in Goshen. In May she was in the hospital for ten days. We came home and we thought things were better. Doctors had said the clots were gone. Mom did the household duties and gave her love to the family like she always did.

On July 5th, 1991, we had an appointment with the doctor. Everything looked good. We went home happy. Then it happened. Mom came to the front porch and had a stroke. She passed out, then came to a few minutes later and passed out again when we got to the hospital with the First Aid. She was in the intensive care unit from Friday evening till the following Friday noon when God called her home.

Now what will this husband do? I always have to come and pray to God for help and He is willing to help.

David M. King: Sept. 27, 1970 - Aug. 17, 1990

Submitted by: David & Annie S. King, Gordonville, Pennsylvania

In January of 1990, Dave had a small lump on his leg, but didn't complain to us till February. He went to the family doctor and he gave him some pills because he thought he had an infection from his leg, where he had hurt it in July of 1989. He had it sewn at the hospital, but thought it was healed. He went to the doctor a week later and he took blood samples and gave him a shot. We aren't sure what kind it was, but spots came out on the other leg. He told us to go to a specialist, and we also gave him some natural medicine.

Until then we thought Dave was a healthy boy. Always willing to help around home on the farm, he worked at Vintage Sales Stables one day a week for five years, at the tagging chute. He was always a happy boy.

We took him to a specialist on the Thursday before Good Friday and he sent him to the hospital for tests. He had a fever then and didn't feel the best, but he said if he went to the hospital he might be able to go with the young folks over Easter, which he always enjoyed. He didn't have a girlfriend yet, but was about ready to ask one as we found out later.

On Easter Monday, we were in the hospital with him when the doctor came in and said we were to come with him to another room. When we were in the room the doctor gave us the shocking news and said Dave has Lymphoma cancer, which is in the lymph glands and a a bad case.

We went back to Dave's room again and he asked, "What's wrong?" So we had to break the news to him. Oh, what a hard thing to give ourselves up. We cried with him for a while, then he said, "My future is ruined. I'm so young and who will ever want me even if I get well?" We had to brace ourselves up to try and comfort him.

He was in the General Hospital three weeks for tests and they didn't give him anything but Tylenol 24 hours a day and IV. He got phone calls and visitors. Some said to try different things rather than chemotherapy, which they wanted to start the fourth week. The doctor gave him a 45 percent chance. The people meant well to try and help, but we didn't know what to do. Some told Dave to try Mexico, so we went to talk with some people who had been there.

The doctor sent Dave home for five days before the chemo treatments were to start. We made plans to go to Mexico. We talked to the bishop and friends and made plans to fly because he wasn't fit to make the trip that took three days and three nights. On Thursday I called the doctor in Mexico and he said to come as soon as possible. We tried to get a direct flight from Philadelphia, Penn., to San Diego, Calif., for Monday but they had one for Friday morning so we took that flight.

What a hard decision to make. We were farming and Dave was working at home. It was corn planting time, but the other children said they could manage if this would help him. We had one son and two daughters married and one daughter, 15, and two sons ten and 13, still at home. The children all went along to the airport to meet the plane. What a hard day to leave the children and Dads as we went on the plane. They all watched as we went up into the clouds out of sight. We were on the plane six and one half hours. It was a nice ride, but not a pleasure trip. Dave said how nice heaven must be, as nice as it is above the clouds, which was a wonderful sight.

We landed at San Diego and a driver was there to take us to the hospital in Mexico. What an experience. They drive so fast in Mexico and whoever gets to the stop sign first can go. Our driver had some lumber along so he had his back window open and smoke came in. Then he stopped somewhere to unload the lumber first before we went to the hospital. We finally got to the hospital and all the strange people with a different language. The doctor and one of the nurses could talk English. No other Amish were there, but one couple from Indiana, the whole time we were down there. We were there for almost five weeks.

The people that were patients could talk English. We got there on Friday and didn't see the doctor until Saturday. They took blood tests and X-rays and started with laetrile and vitamins and some infection medicine. He used to get a high fever so we would wash him off with cold washcloths. Then they gave him IV and two units of blood and the next day they started with chemotherapy treatments.

The first treatment he got made him short of breath and he shook all over so the nurses came with more covers. They thought we meant he was cold, but what he needed was something else so they gave him a shot to relieve him. The Mexican nurses just didn't understand what we meant at first.

A couple days after his first treatments, his lumps went down and he felt better. We thought he was getting good results. He had his hopes up pretty good, but before it was time for another treatment it seemed his lumps started to come back.

We learned to know a lot of people down there and we sure got acquainted with each other. It seemed like we all had about the same thing in common. About five weeks later the doctor said he thinks we can go home and go on with the treatments then come back in three months. We went home on the plane again and all the children were at the airport to meet us. What a family reunion to meet them all again.

Soon we had to get a doctor to give the medication or treatments. They gave him blood first and the next morning when we came to the hospital we were shocked. Dave was yellow! The doctor said he must have gotten hepatitis from the blood transfusion, so he had to fight that off, too. He was in the hospital for about a week again. Then he was at home for a couple days till his counts went down again. The doctor said he has the fast growing cancer and it seemed they couldn't keep ahead of it.

After that he was in the hospital again from June 29, till August 6. They were giving him chemo every so often, but finally they didn't know what to do, so we brought him home. He was only 19 and he had his whole life ahead of him. The grandchildren used to come in to visit him and he just loved it when they came along. He got a lot of mail and company which meant so much. He used to say how will I ever pay the people back for what they did for me. It really brought a closeness to our family.

After he was at home, we had a precious week, but also a hard week. We tried some more natural medicine and on Saturday evening he said he wished to be baptized. They took a vote at church on Sunday and Wednesday evening they baptized him. What an experience. We had our children, Grandparents, Grandmother, and ministers here. Dave was very weak so they baptized him in bed, but he had a good mind. Very touching. We sang a couple hymns after the service.

He seemed better on Thursday, but Friday morning he died. The night before he wanted to hold our hands and he told us nice dreams and also visions, too deep to write on paper. We want to be thankful for all, but the zeitlang comes over and over.

We had the funeral on Monday and over Sunday a lot of young folks were in and out to view Dave. Monday was a large funeral, then going out the lane behind his body and to the graveyard was very touching. Those who have experienced it know all about it.

We learned to know a lot of people through this experience and we want to be thankful for all good health and so on. Life isn't the same, but we still have to go on. The weddings at home and Christmas dinner etc., bring a lot of tears, but we want to take God's ways as they come and hope to meet again some sweet day.

Joel Yoder: July 9, 1986 - Aug. 2, 1995

Submitted by: Amos & Rachel Yoder, LaGrange, Indiana

It is with love and precious memories that I write of our dear son Joel. After having two daughters, Ruth and Hannah, and one son, Freeman, we were so happy to have another son. And he came right on his Daddy's birthday! It was on July 9, 1986. How little we knew that a little over nine years later we would need to put him in his little grave.

In the short years he was with us, he was such a lively, active, and ambitious young lad; so full of life and energy and around home he was just "everywhere". Either he was helping with the work, playing with his smaller brother Jacob, or riding our little pony.

Wednesday, August 2, 1995, the morning was clear and sunny, promising another warm day. Everyone was refreshed from the night's rest. The day before had been a busy one, with Daddy gone carpentering again and the boys, now 13 and 9, also hauled out hog manure again. My day's work had included cutting school shirts for Joel and one for going away Sunday evenings, etc. How pleased he was!

In the evening after supper, the children all went out to play knockout. After the game, Ruth, now 16, made popcorn and Joel made Kool-Aid. We all had a nice evening.

The day before that, which was Monday, my husband didn't go to work and he and Joel worked together most of the day. One thing they did was clean out the tool shed. Then in the evening Grandpa and Grandma and one of Amos' brothers and their family came for their birthdays! Joel was so happy and gave Grandma such a pleased "Thank-You," when she gave him a little gift. "Precious Memory!"

Coming back to that memorable day. Daddy left for work and we proceeded with duties of the morning. Joel was up earlier, which was rather strange. He went back to bed for a while yet. Did the Lord put it on his little heart that "it wasn't time yet??"

Later he got up and worked to get dressed, but couldn't find a pair of pants that were comfortable. He was growing more chubby and they were getting tight. So I helped him and found a pair, clear at the bottom of the drawer. They were a faded grey cotton and were rather stiff. He protested a little, but I reassured him rather jokingly that "I think they'll "go" with your legs." Everything was fine then and he went down the stairs. Our last conversation was over...

He went outside to help Freeman haul manure again. They hoped to be done by noon. I decided to go to the spare room and get out bigger pants for Joel and brought down a stack. I hoped to sew shirts that day, but God had other more important plans.

I soon heard Freeman calling me faintly, "Mom! Mom!" I hurried out and found him red-faced, panting, and half crying. "The horses ran away and went over Joel!"

I asked him, "Is it bad?"

And he said, "I don't know!"

I quickly told him to go call the ambulance! "Dial 911."

And I started running back to the field! Oh my, Daddy's not at home and I just kept saying, "No! No!" until I thought of submitting to however God wills.

I knew which field they were working in, our farthest field, about a half mile away, so I made myself walk. But, oh the dread and apprehension that gripped my heart! I knew he was lying somewhere, alone and hurt and I didn't know what I'd find! Part of me wanted to find him and part of me didn't, which made me feel bad!

But when I got to the field, which is beside our woods, I couldn't see the team or anything! Where are they?! I soon heard the siren and knew help was on the way! But where was our dear Sonny?! Did the horses perhaps run into the woods and it happened there? I called his name a few times, but it sounded so feeble. I certainly feel the Lord was with me while I waited, but I almost can't put into words the feelings that I had! Of course, it seemed a lot longer than it really was until the ambulance came. But then they hadn't brought Freeman along back! But he was there shortly and then we all drove back to where it happened at the edge of the woods. The lady that was along got out very quickly and checked Joel. "He's gone." Oh, heart wrenching words!

I had thought it could be this way, but Freeman hadn't. And now he blamed himself and said, "It's my fault!" and wept. I put my arm around him and we just cried together. I told him he shouldn't feel that way, he was part of God's plan.

They had made a sharp turn in the field and one of the horses' buckles on the reins got caught in the ring on the hames. They had gone running for a distance, but they got them stopped. Joel tried to loosen it just standing on the ground. The team was big and he couldn't reach it. Freeman felt responsible to hold onto the reins, so he told Joel to go up on the tongue to loosen it. Joel did, and then the horses started running again! He held onto the harness for a while, but finally let loose! He was run over by the machinery cart, to Freeman's utter dismay!

Freeman and the team went on for around a hundred feet; a little ways into the woods until they got caught between two trees. He then hurried back to Joel and asked him if he should get the ambulance, he answered, "Yes." Freeman then ran all the way up to the house. For some reason God wanted Joel to be by himself when He came for him, though we don't feel he was alone. We think he soon saw the angels and Jesus and they took care of him so tenderly.

We knew we had to contact Daddy right away, but he was 20 miles away! Very thankfully, Freeman knew their driver's phone number. He is our neighbor. So Kim, the EMS lady, called him to go after him. "There's been an accident; come home right away!"

Oh, the pain that struck his heart upon getting such a message! He didn't know who or how, but felt there surely must be a death! It was such a long way home and he thought it's probably one of the boys. In his anguished heart he couldn't decide with which one he'd soonest part...

Ruth had gone over to the neighbors to mow their lawn, so Kim went over and told her the shocking news and brought her home. She brought her, Hannah, and Jacob back to where we were. A few of the neighbor men had also come back. And finally Amos arrived, too! We needed him so much!! Then we were all together, only Joel lay so still and pale and peaceful, as if asleep! Already his body felt cool.

More neighbors and his grandmother and an uncle came back. And then they took him away. Needless to say, we were numb in our shock and grief and somehow the Lord helped us through the rest of that day and the days following. We could hardly pray and the prayers and comfort from family and friends meant so much! We needed to make funeral arrangements and decided to have it at home. It stuck us deeply when we realized Joel had helped clean the shed only days before!

We got guilty feelings of "if onlys" and almost felt like we should have another chance, but we soon felt and knew that we couldn't harbor such feelings; we are all human and make mistakes. God forgave us for things we could have made better for Joel and didn't!

That first day was a hard one for Freeman! It was almost more than his young heart could take. That night we were alone, for which we are still thankful, and we took time to talk about things and tried to soothe his feelings of guilt. After that it was a little easier for him and he talked fairly freely about it to his uncles and cousins.

When we were plagued with thoughts and questions if this really was God's will, we thought of several events. Hannah, age 15, had a dream the night before it happened that Joel got killed. How it struck her heart as scenes unfolded!

The day before it happened Joel had said to Freeman, "Everybody has to die." And that day when asked what time it happened, I didn't exactly know, sometime after 8:00. Around noon when Amos checked the time on his watch, it had stopped at 8:15! God's hand. When we thought of these things it brought peace, but nothing calmed us more than when we thought of his evening prayers. More than once we had stood to the bottom of the stairs and listened. Most of the time the two boys said it together. Almost always Joel added, "Let thy will be done, not mine, Amen."

I often found relief in writing poetry and think it was a blessing of God. It also helped others. Others were hurting, too. Especially the widows! Mail time was a special time and we know the prayers of others and the power of the Lord was upholding us. Still, the time came when we needed to get a hold and work on our spiritual life ourselves and not just depend on the prayers of others.

We must say, this traumatic experience was a real test of our faith. After some time was around I developed feelings that Jesus has had him for a while now and we'd like to have him back! No, we couldn't and wouldn't take him out of his bliss and peace! But our heart had such deep longings and yearnings! It took some time till God's love and comfort could really penetrate.

How is this love, with such a deep hurt? But we recognize our rebellion and it didn't feel good until we replaced it again with, "Thy will be done." It helped when we realized that this was God's pattern and plan for our lives. There were times when we felt almost helpless and then we needed to just let go and let God.

And now after almost two years, we can say, God is so good! He can and does comfort! And how precious is the plan of salvation! A way had been made that Joel can have peace and rest and Life Eternal, as well as all those who love the Lord and do according to His will! To God be all glory and praise! Someday, someday we hope to see him again in Heaven!

Jacob was four when this happened and he missed his brother and playmate so much. One day he asked me, "Could Jesus come down and bring Joel and take me up, too?"

At another time he was playing church and was preaching. Of course, I was listening for any feelings he might express. He was talking to Jesus, and asked, "Why did you take Joel? We wanted him yet."

How it touched our hearts! Sometime later he told me, "Perhaps something should go over me, too." I almost didn't know what to say at first. But we are thankful that he doesn't seem to have a fear of death. He has adjusted well.

About three months after his death it was discovered that Joel had sometime written his name very faintly on the corner of page number 185 in the Church and Sunday School Hymnal.

The title of the song is: We shall Sleep But Not Forever. None of us knew the song and how it touched us to read it! It was almost like he came back to comfort us! How special!!

   -1-

We shall sleep, but not forever, there will be a glorious dawn;
We shall meet to part, no, never, on the resurrection morn.
From the deepest caves of ocean, from the desert and the plain,
From the valley and the mountain, countless throngs shall rise again.

-Chorus-
We shall sleep, but not forever, there will be a glorious dawn;
We shall meet to part, no, never, on the resurrection morn.

-2-
When we see a precious blossom, that we tended with such care,
Rudely taken from our bosom, how our aching hearts despair!
'Round its little grave we linger till the setting sun is low,
Feeling all our hopes have perished with the flow'r we cherished so.

-3-
We shall sleep, but not forever, in the lone and silent grave;
Blessed be the Lord that taketh, Blessed be the Lord that gave.
In the bright Eternal City, death can never, never come!
In His own good time He'll call us, from our rest, to Home Sweet Home.

'Twas a boy so bright and lively,
Healthy cheeked and eyes alight.
Joel, little ray of sunshine,
Precious in the Savior's sight.

Precious son he was to Daddy,
Little choreboy, helper dear,
Precious to his loving Mother,
How she loved to have him near.

Also loved by Ruth and Hannah,
Freeman, Jacob they had fun,
As they played a game of softball,
One night after chores were done.

Little did we know the future
Plan of God, the Father's will,
That dear Joel, bright and lively
Would so soon be cold and still.

For one morning things were different,
Suddenly the Lord said, "Come,
Now your life on earth is over
And I want to take you home."

Shocking grief o'ertook the family,
  Loved ones who are left behind,
Why so sudden? Why so cruel?
  Questions racing thru' the mind.

Hard to grasp the truth so final,
  Grief severe it seems unbound.
And sometimes thru' out the day
  It seems he has to be around.

But he's gone to live with Jesus,
  To a land more fair than day.
There forever to be happy,
  So it seems that he would say.

"Be of comfort, my dear parents,
  Do not grieve about the way,
That the Saviour chose to take me,
  On my final earthly day.

"Jesus had His arms around me,
  And I never was alone,
Then I was in Heavenly splendor,
  And saw God upon the throne.

"I'm enjoying precious moments,
  Singing with the angels fair,
Blissful in the arms of Jesus,
  Warmth and love beyond compare!

"When you're lonely, when you miss me,
  Shed a tear when you are blue,
When you're happy don't feel guilty,
  I, in Heaven, am happy too.

"I still love you, lonely family,
  I still love you, yes I do.
Here I am in wait to meet you,
  In the morn beyond the blue."

  — Written by his Aunt, Mrs. Daniel (Lovina) Byler

Joel died of head injuries. The EMS lady said at first the wheel went over his head. We almost didn't think that was very probable as the only injuries we could see were some scratches on his one cheek. Otherwise he looked unmarred. His one shoulder was broken and the opposite leg pretty bad, indicating the wheel maybe crossing him. He didn't have internal bleeding. She said as his abdomen didn't get hard. Upon her acceptance of the possibility, we feel he may have received his head injuries when falling down, between the horses.

It almost came as a jolt to me, when I later remembered I never once thought about which hospital we'll go to once the ambulance arrives or going without my husband! Why? I don't know except that it was the Lord's choice that day.

Though we sorrow because our loved one's no longer here, we also rejoice because Christ conquered death and fear. The sting of separation has been taken away by the joy we have in awaiting our reunion day. But thanks be to God, who gives us the victory through our Lord Jesus Christ. I Cor. 15:57.

— Written by Joel's Mother

Delbert Wayne Miller: Sept. 2, 1975 - Sept. 11, 1979

Submitted by: Mr. & Mrs. Harley Jay Miller, Goshen, Indiana

September 10, 1979 was a nice Monday, we had a busy day. The men baled hay. We had some help. Our grandchild Harlan had come along. He and Delbert had an enjoyable day together, both being four years old. We had a litter of puppies and they had them on our little wagon, and drove up and down our walks laughing and enjoying themselves. I can still picture them, not realizing what lay before us.

We had dressed a beef and put it in the cooler at the butcher house on State Road 4. It has since burned down. Our intentions were to bring it home Tuesday morning to cut it up. Monday eve. Harley decided to do feed grinding yet. This was after supper at 7:15. He had the tractor and grinder and had been in the calf patch getting oats. As he came back to the gate, Delbert and his younger brother Marvin, two years old, were following him. Harley opened the gate, Delbert went through the gate, and Harley went on the tractor. Some of the other children were playing in the yard, so he thought he ran on to the other children, and not seeing him, he started forward.

The front end of the tractor came up and he knew there was no bump there. He stopped and found Delbert there. He didn't respond. One of the boys went to the neighbors, Ellis Masts, and they called First Aid. Our Rosa had learned in school to give CPR and so she worked on him till Ellis Mast's Ann came. Ann is a nurse. She worked on him, pounding his chest, etc. till First Aid came.

I feel she kept his heart going. He was bleeding out of his mouth some. They suctioned him and forced oxygen into him. They took him to Goshen Hospital. We followed him out. Finally we could see him, all wired up, on breathing machines, IV, and getting blood. Before midnight he was taken to Parkview Hospital in Fort Wayne.

Harley went with the ambulance. Ellis Masts took me and Mervin down. Mervin went along home then with Ellis's. Around 2:00 they came and said he has a skull fracture over his head from ear to ear, and is losing spinal fluid. He also had a broken left foot. His kidneys were working and he gagged over his tubes in his throat which gave us some hope.

At 9:00 A.M. they took a brain scan to see how his brain was and while they were doing that, he died at 9:15A.M. They said there was very little activity there and if he had pulled through, he would have been like a vegetable, very helpless. So we thank God that He took him. It was hard giving up a precious child, they are so much a part of us! But again we know where they are and how lucky on their part. They could enter those Golden Gates without a question. The days following were hard! People from far and near came, neighbors did our work for us. It made us feel very unworthy, but we appreciated it all. He was four years and nine days old.

Marie E. Yoder: Oct. 11, 1968 - May 15, 1988

Submitted by: Emanuel H. & Fannie (Miller) Yoder, Baltic, Ohio

Daughter of Emanuel H. and Fannie (Miller) Yoder. Sister of Mabel, Katie Mae, Saloma, Eli, Lizzie, Elsie, and Roy.

Services were held May 18th at the residence by Bishop Neal C. Miller (the home Bishop), Ervin Miller, and Lester Hochstetler of LaGrange IN.

At the Roy Barkman residence, by neighbor Bishop Abe L. Miller, Minister Andy J.A. Yoder, and Wm. Schrock of LaGrange IN.

Also at the Atlee J. Miller residence by Bishop Noah N.L. Yoder of our west district and Minister Abe J. Yoder of Middlebury, IN.

Marie was working part-time at the local grocery store plus helping her dad in his axle shop. She started running a lathe in the shop at the age of 15.

In March of 1988, Marie was asked to do the household duties at her sister Saloma's after the birth of their firstborn, a daughter. Although she was not one to complain, she did remark that she feels so tired, plus she started bruising very easily, too. Her left hip was about the worst. Just from leaning against the checkout counter at the grocery store. She kind of shrugged it off thinking she might be low in iron. And maybe since she's doing different work, that's why she's more tired. A few more weeks passed with more and more bruises, now on her arms and legs. But by April she started with sore throat and headache, also she got so dizzy.

On Tuesday, April 26, 1988, she finally decided to go in for a blood test. She started spitting up blood. Then we knew something serious was happening as she had dark bruise spots in her mouth. By Thursday the doctor wanted her on IV. So she was admitted to Union Hospital in Dover, Ohio, and was immediately given two units of blood.

At home, feelings of fear showed on all our faces and many questions went through our minds. But no answers other than she's very anemic. So far it had always been happening to other families, why us? On Friday they took more tests, plus the bone marrow test. They also gave her four units of platelets to clot her blood.

On Saturday the tests came back showing Mylogeous Acute Leukemia. We were told there was a 50-60% chance for recovery. What awful words! She wrote in her diary, "It was an unhappy day for me! I was really shocked and unprepared for such an answer!"

What a shock for such a young girl with many dreams for the future! Only to have her dreams shattered! Doctors thought the only chance is the bone marrow transplant, as this is a very fast growing type. That was the hardest decision we ever made. At this time this was quite new and a lot to go through.

But she then read an article in Reader's Digest of a bone marrow transplant patient and she didn't think she wanted to go through all that.

She was on IV all the time while at the hospital, but felt pretty good, and was up and around taking along her IV. She had many visitors at the hospital, also phone calls.

On Wednesday, May 11th, we took her home. The doctor said there was only a ten percent chance for recovery. But we wanted to try some herbs and prayed for a miracle. "Lord let it be Thy will, not mine."

On Thursday, Ascension Day, she seemed to become more restless and tired. She had pain in her side and stomach area. Many visitors came and went. She ate a little, but by Sunday she went downhill fast. She said, "The things in my room aren't mine anymore." She showed no interest in the gifts people brought her.

We tried to draw some pain for her. The most she complained about was, "If only I could rest." How our hearts ached for her. Then Sunday evening she asked for something to eat. She ate more than she had at any time since she had come home. Many visitors were here again, but she didn't visit anymore.

Dark clouds started coming in from the west. Thunder rolled, lightning flashed. God seemed closer than ever. By bedtime she seemed less restless, somewhat different. She had a very fast heartbeat the last few days, but then Sunday evening it suddenly slowed down. We sensed that her time had come to leave us. We all gathered around her bed when she took her last breath at 11:30 P.M.

Finally, her last request was fulfilled. "Now she can rest in peace." The neighbors were told and were here soon. Arrangements were made with them and the undertaker.

The next morning friends and neighbors came from every direction. How comforting and helpful! Just having them here to help us bear the pain and sorrow has meant a great deal.

Many friends, known and unknown, came during the viewing. She had many friends. She was the type of person to remember someone after meeting him or her only once. The funeral was Wednesday, May 18, 1988. The air was chilly, but the sun shone.

And then life had to go on without Marie, how unbearable it sounded! With God's help and our many friends life seems easier to bear. We wouldn't wish her back on earth to suffer. We have our many happy memories to remember her, but we still miss her. It is now almost nine years ago when we parted with her. We pray our loss was her gain. God heals the pain but a deep scar remains forever.

Good-Bye Marie

Every time we think of you,
* It makes us want to cry.*
The memories that stir our hearts,
* Seem to ask the question, "Why?"*
But we don't have the answer,
* Yet of one thing we are sure.*
While man is weak and helpless,
* God does have a cure.*
His promises are so comforting,
* They're for all of us to share.*
So even if we don't know why,
* He indeed has told us where.*
Now don't worry about us, Marie.
* Our God will see us through.*
Even now He is consoling us,
* And maybe you have asked Him, too.*

-Gone, but not forgotten-

Father tries to save sons and perishes-Nov. 2, 1955

Simon J. Slabaugh: 47 years old
Glenn Slabaugh: 10 years old
Simon Slabaugh Jr.: 9 years old
Larry Slabaugh: 5 years old

Submitted by: Two daughters and one son

I was a nineteen year old teenager when we had the tragedy of the fire where my three brothers and my father perished. There were thirteen living children at the time of the fire. The two oldest were married, Omer and Mary. The names of the children at home were as follows, from the oldest to the youngest: Verna, Martha (me), Barbara, John, Edward, Glenn, Simon Jr., Howard, Larry, and Sue.

This is what I recall of that fateful day. Mom and Dad had gone to Mannas Hochstetlers in the morning and had a load of apples made into applebutter. It was just another day in their lives of the responsibility of raising a large family. They had taken the baby of the family to Mary's place, the married daughter, for the day and it got late, so she was left there for the night. Howard, age six, went home with a cousin from school so he wasn't at home. Barbara, age seventeen, was at Omers house in Plain City, Ohio. Verna, age twenty-one was working in Breman, Ind., staying in the home and baby sitting. The rest of us were at home.

After I had come home from work I helped with the chores and helped with supper and decided to catch up on sewing. The sewing room was built on from a small house Dad had moved from an adjoining farm, so it was an old building. Just before I quit for the evening I built a fire. It was chilly and after it got warmer I closed the damper and went to bed. I was in bed at least an hour when I heard Dad yell loudly for us to get up, the house was on fire. I remember smelling smoke then already.

He told me to wake up the boys, Edward and John, to go to the neighbors to call the fire dept. I don't recall who got the horse and put the bridle on, but I do know Edward rode the horse over to the neighbors, Stanley Pippengers. I remember Mom and Dad fighting the fire, and Dad getting the hose which I believe was frozen. He was also getting water out of the faucet and pouring it on a fire that was possibly already burning in the attic. I recall seeing Mom standing at the outside door throwing stuff in and possibly slowing the fire down.

By that time Dad possibly decided it was getting too bad and ran upstairs to get Glenn and Junior. The house was full of smoke. We soon realized Dad was not coming down and John and I went in the front door and tried to get upstairs. There was fire on the ceiling and I heard my brother crying in the bedroom downstairs. I tried to get in the back way, but there was furniture in front of the double doors, which we hardly ever used and I could not open them. I took John by the hand and took him outdoors.

I told Mom I couldn't find Dad. She said go and get a ladder and maybe I could get in through the front porch window upstairs. John and I ran to get the ladder and tried and tried to put it up against the porch, but the roof slanted downward and it just kept sliding off. Neither could we get it up to the window on the side of the house. After the fire was out the ladder stood against the side of the house not quite reaching the upstairs window.

We lived on the home place so there was a grandpa house right next door and that was where Esther had spent the night so we ran over to Grandma's house. That was where the neighbor found us when he came over after Edward had woke them up to call the fire dept. I have never written down my feelings and what we went through that night. I still have to weep. There was so much weeping and moaning going on. I almost can't stand to this day hearing sirens and smelling smoke and going to bed if I am not very sleepy, and this has been over forty years ago.

That evening the neighbor took us all over to their house, and even as it got towards daylight we still had not comprehended that Dad was gone, and that he and the three boys, Glenn, Junior, and Larry, had met their Maker.

Then there were comforting things that happened. The kind friends and neighbors that were there to give us comfort and food and clothing. We didn't even have any shoes on our feet. They had a house started within a very short time.

I cannot imagine what Mother went through, but God is so faithful. I especially remember one evening we would take turns to find a prayer in the prayer book to say, and I have a feeling Mom was wondering if perhaps she had done something to deserve this, or the enemy of our soul was telling her that God isn't near.

These are my thoughts now. I did not think these thoughts then, but after putting four of our own children in the cold grave I know how the accuser of the brethren acts.

Anyway it was my turn to find a prayer and say it. I have always been a very practical person and do not like to take too much time to do anything, so I found a nice short poemlike prayer. I had my eyes open to say the prayer and after I got done my little sister, age three, asked what that bright light was she had seen when we prayed. I'm sure Mom needed a confirmation that God was a very present help in time of trouble.

God's blessings as you write these stories.

—Submitted by a daughter, Martha (Slabaugh) Schmucker

November 2, 1955, It was cold with the first light snow of the season. My sister Martha built the fire in a wood stove for the night and went to bed. No one is quite sure if the stove puffed and got more draft or if she didn't shut it down far enough.

The stove overheated and I'm not sure if the fire started by the stove or at the chimney. When I saw it the whole west wing was in flames. I don't remember coming out of the house. The first I do remember Martha woke all of us out of our first sleep.

There were only six children home that evening, Martha, Edward, Glenn, Junior, Larry, and myself. I was sixteen when this happened. Martha and I tried to set up a ladder to get to the upstairs, but it was so windy, we couldn't get it set up. The heat and smoke were too thick, we couldn't get in on the east side. Later, looking back, it took a long time to get over things that we should have done. I came out in only underwear and a pair of pants.

The house had burned completely down. The next morning I remember seeing where Dad had lain, you could see his rib bones and also some of his other bones. They then started to haul the ashes and stuff out in order to look for more remains of the three boys. Glenn, ten years; Junior, nine years; and Larry, five years. They never made it out along with Dad. The bones of the boys and dad would not have filled a boot box. I remember the funeral, but couldn't recall it being the largest some had ever attended. We had two hearses and we put two coffins in each one.

I never heard my mother complain about her lot in life. She taught us to always do our best and always give our best. She was a great believer of the Lord. It meant a lot when we kept the same faith. She always was glad to see us when we came home. Her children, and then the grandchildren, were very special to her.

She liked to fix food that she knew we liked and that were our favorites when we were there at meal time. Our own children still talk about her and the food she fixed when we were there.

The first three years I did the farming with the help of neighbors and family. Then a brother-in-law Menno Yoder took it over. We children learned a lot about giving in those times.

—Submitted by a son: John H. Slabaugh

November 2, 1955 brings to mind a tragedy that can not be put in words. I vividly remember the phone call. The weather conditions were very cold, blowing snow and an ice storm. I was 17 and staying with my brother Omer in Ohio as they were expecting a new baby, when we received the call. We immediately packed up and started for Indiana. All the way I prayed and hoped I could come home and surely this could not be true. We were all so much in shock, we must have appeared to be very cold at heart. Not so.

Why? God, why? Did you really have to take our loved ones, our house, all our clothes, plus all our other precious childhood things we had stored away?

Here was a family of eight children with no clothes to go to the viewing or to the funeral. Within a day's time this was all supplied. We had many kind friends and neighbors that worked many hours, days, and months to help us put things together and get started again.

We thought the news reporters were very cruel to put a picture in the paper of a box with bones as to what they found in the fire.

It was about a month later that I finally realized that my mother was a widow. I can not put in words the steps we had to work through to try to pick up and go on in life. We had Mom's mother living in a house right beside our house and that is where we lived, cooked, slept, everything until a new house could be built. We received many useful and beautiful things to use.

—Submitted by a daughter: Mrs. Eli A. (Barbara) Hochstetler

A TRIBUTE TO MOTHER

God had a special plan for my mother,
A different life than most, she had to face.
My Mother was faithful and trusted God,
And she was victorious in God's grace.

I was three years old, and don't really remember,
When my Dad and three brothers burned in a fire and passed away.
Now Mother was by herself with ten of us children,
And I know she had many a lonely day.

I never heard her complain about her way of life
And the responsibility of ten children to raise.
Often I would find her reading her Bible and praying;
For the life that she lived, I want to give her praise.

My brothers and sisters all got married and left home;
Soon it was just me and mother,
We would work, and go everywhere together.
She had special time for me, and others.

When I would come home from school...
How I loved for Mother to be there,
Usually we would sit down and have a snack,
And just talk and together share.

She enjoyed crocheting in the evenings,
And we would play games, or I would read.
I remember how she enjoyed her grandchildren and
When they came to see her, it made her happy indeed.

I remember her concern when I became a teenager
And Glen and I started to date.
Often she would lovingly remind me.
Please don't stay out too late.

She met a man from Ohio,
And was married to him a year,
Before Glen and I were married.
A new life for us; and God was very near.

Then came our first son Brian;
I enjoyed taking Brian to Mother's, and spending the day,
She would hold him and watch him smile.
He is such a good baby she would often say.

To see us move away
From Indiana to Illinois.
It was very hard for her,
She missed us and Brian and Troy.

Then one day my phone rang,
My mother called to let me know,
That in her stomach was a hard lump
And to surgery she had to go.

One week later another phone call,
They said my mother had cancer.
It was a shock and we were rather sad,
God had another special plan for her.

In the next five months that she lived,
She would often say to me,
"What a privilege to prepare myself to die,
And get ready for the Glory world to see."

I know it was difficult for her...
To break those earthly ties,
To not see the grandchildren grow up
Would often bring tears to her eyes.

Those five months that mother had cancer,
Never did I hear her complain
About this earthly life she had,
Through all the suffering and her pain.

At the time that Glenda was born,
Mom was quite sick and needed in bed to be.
Glenda was only three weeks old
When we took her to Mother to see.
I gave her to Mother to hold awhile;
Mom said, "Oh, she's beautiful."
And Glenda gave Mother a big smile.

God took Mother home
To be with Him in heaven above.
God gave me a little daughter,
To hold and to love.

Mother passed away on a cold Dec. day;
I had the privilege of being there,
And I will never forget the sadness..
Yet rejoicing in her parting that I could share.

My mother wasn't perfect,
But she did her very best.
I loved her just the way she was,
I really miss her, but now she has eternal rest.

This is my challenge to all of you;
If your mother is still living,
Tell her you love and appreciate her,
Show it to her with thanksgiving.

Wendall Kauffman: Aug. 12, 1977 - July 18, 1995

Wendall Dale Kauffman, 17, of Arthur died at 5 a.m. Tuesday, July 18, 1995, at his residence.

The funeral will be at 10 a.m. Friday at the Sunnyside Mennonite Church with the Rev. Jacob Graber officiating. Burial will be in Sunnyside Church Cemetery. Visitation will be from 2 to 4 p.m. and 6 to 8 p.m. today and Thursday at the Church. Edwards Funeral Home is in charge of arrangements.

He was born Aug. 12, 1977, in Decatur, the son of Dale L. and Louise Plank Kauffman.

Surviving are his parents; three sisters, Angie, Lisa, and Tanya, all at home; paternal grandparents, Levi and Mary Kauffman of Arthur; and maternal grandparents, Jonas and Gertie Plank of Arthur.

He was preceded in death by four Great-grandparents.

Kauffman was a member of the Sunnyside Mennonite Church and an honorary member of the Arthur Volunteer Fire Department and the University of Illinois Fire Department.

Memorials may be made to the Wendall Kauffman Memorial Fund.

"Learning to Trust"

by Wendall Kauffman, Aurthur, Illinois

On August 3, 1994, my world came crashing down. I was diagnosed with cancer. This was one of the rarest kinds of cancers and the doctors don't know much about it. I was shocked and terribly upset. I thought, "Why me? What did I do to deserve this?" God answered me. He said, "My son, I didn't give you cancer to punish you. Just trust me and I'll take care of you." That made me realize God had a very special purpose for me.

In the short time I've had cancer, I've learned to trust God. Psalm 25:2 states, "Oh my God, I trust in Thee: let me not be ashamed, let not mine enemies triumph over me." Cancer is my enemy and it will not triumph over me. God brings trials and temptations into our lives to help us learn how to trust. Isaiah 26:4 states. "Trust ye in the Lord forever: for in the Lord JEHOVAH is everlasting strength."

One of the most familiar passages that demonstrated trust is I Samuel 17:33-50 (34 or 35-50). David trusted that God would keep him safe from Goliath's hand. The Lord guided and protected David as he fought Goliath. The Bible is full of stories about people who trusted God. We can learn from each and every one of them.

My point is that no matter how large or how small your problem is, trust the Lord to help you through it. Proverbs 3:5 states, "Trust in the Lord with all thine heart; and lean not unto thine own understanding." (I interpret this as saying,) "Trust God with everything; don't trust yourself."

I've worked through this difficult situation by praying to God for understanding. I also listen to what people have to tell me, because some have been through the same experience. God has put many comforting words in the Bible for everything we as humans might face. The most important thing that has helped me to get through this, is the love of family, friends, and most importantly God. As I said earlier, prayer has helped me, but to feel prayer is part of trust. For example when I was in the hospital, I started thinking about the fact… (How come… why do I have cancer) and I started getting mad. Well, I didn't want to get mad so I started praying and soon God soothed the anger and pain; and He really comforted me.

God has always been there for me and I never realized it. When my eyes were opened I started praying and trusting more. By the way people talk to me and by the way they write letters, I can tell it made an impact on them. That makes me feel good, but God gets all the glory.

I hope I never forget to honor and praise God for what He has done for me.

If it wasn't for God I'd be lost and you would be lost. "So think about this; you can trust God with all your problems or you can be lost in darkness because you trust in yourself and others; and 'refuse' to trust in God. It's your choice; either trust God or be lost, think about it."

Index

Z